UN-SMITING THE SHEPHERD

Answering the Critics, The Fight Against the Character Assassination of the Hon. Min. Louis Farrakhan & Strong Black Leadership

"Un-Smiting The Shepherd": Answering The Critics, The Fight Against The Character Assassination of The Honorable Minister Louis Farrakhan & Strong Black Leadership

Copyright 2022 Demetric Muhammad

All rights reserved. No part of this publication may be reproduced, distributed, or transmitted in any form or by any means, including photocopying, recording, or other electronic or mechanical methods, without the prior written permission of the publisher, except in the case of brief quotations embodied in critical reviews and certain other noncommercial uses permitted by copyright law. For permission requests, write to the publisher, addressed "Attention: Permissions Coordinator," at the address below.

www.ResearchMinister.Com

Ordering Information:

Quantity sales. Special discounts are available on quantity purchases by corporations, associations, and others. For details, contact the publisher at the address above.

Cover Art: Hannibal Muhammad

Printed in the Nation of Islam

ISBN- 978-1-7375613-2-3

"Un-Smiting The Shepherd"

Answering The Critics, The Fight Against The Character Assassination of The Honorable Minister Louis Farrakhan & Strong Black Leadership

Demetric Muhammad

Introduction

"Un-Smiting The Shepherd & Uniting The Flock"

All my life I have watched Minister Farrakhan defend Black people.

Theology Professor Andre C. Willis said this about Minister Farrakhan's defense of Black people:

> There is simply no Black person in the world that has — over so many years — been as consistent, as unrestricted, and as forthright in defending the humanity of Black people throughout the world against its attackers.

Not only has the Minister defended us against unjust criticisms, insults, character assassinations and age-old stereotypes, he has also courageously and forthrightly defended our leaders. Minister Farrakhan has defended the common man and woman and he has also defended the talented high-profile members of the Black community. His defense of Black leadership is extraordinarily significant. Because even though the Minister has defended us, we as a people have not reciprocated that defense.

One Jewish critic of Minister Farrakhan, Daniel Pipes has noted:

> ...a well-established pattern of African-Americans who, finding their reputation in tatters, turn to the Nation of Islam, which then provides them with solace and help.

In fact, Black leaders who are not approved of by the white ruling class in America are the frequent victims of well-funded and highly coordinated character assassinations. And most of the time when Black leaders are attacked and vilified within the mainstream media, there is hardly any outcry from the very folk who are the beneficiaries of the work of our courageous leaders.

Keep in mind that it is now common knowledge that the United States Government through the Federal Bureau of Investigations (FBI) has targeted for destruction, Black leaders and the movements that they lead. Through reviewing the government's hand in the destruction of Black movements and Black leaders we see that character assassination has always paved the way for physical assassinations. Once a leader is sufficiently smeared through the media, once their name and reputation has been effectively scandalized, they are a ripe target for assassination, wherein there will be no public sympathy or outcry.

Smite The Shepherd, Scatter The Flock
The assassination of Black leaders leads to the assassination of Black movements. The targeting of Black leaders for smear campaigns is purposed to destroy the cause the leader represents. In his book The 48 Laws of Power, author Robert Greene lists as the 42nd law of power, **Strike the Shepherd, Scatter the Flock**. Greene defines this law by stating:

> One resolute person, one disobedient spirit, can turn a flock of sheep into a den of lions...Do not waste your time lashing out in all directions at what seems to be a many-headed enemy. Find the one head that matters-the person with the willpower, or smarts, or, most important of all, charisma.... Finally, the reason you strike at the shepherd is because such an action will dishearten the sheep beyond any rational measure.

Long before the popular writings of Robert Greene, we read of this strategy in the pages of the Bible. In the Bible the old English word "smite" is used to articulate this strategy as "smite the shepherd." Consider this phrase in the following Biblical scriptures:

> "You will all fall away," Jesus told them, "for it is written: "'I will smite the shepherd, and the sheep will be scattered.'-Mark 14:27

> "Awake, O sword, against My Shepherd, against the man who is My Companion, declares the LORD of Hosts. Smite the Shepherd, and the sheep will be scattered, and I will turn My hand against the little ones."-Zechariah 13:7

> "Then Jesus said to them, 'This very night you will all fall away on account of Me. For it is written: 'I will smite the Shepherd, and the sheep of the flock will be scattered."
> -Matthew 26:31

According to the Collins dictionary of the English language the word smite has the following meanings:

1. to strike or hit hard, with or as with the hand, a stick, or other weapon; 2. to deliver or deal (a blow, hit, etc.) by striking hard; 3. to strike down, injure, or slay; 4. to afflict or attack with deadly or disastrous effect; 5. to affect mentally or morally with a sudden pang; 6. to affect suddenly and strongly with a specified feeling; 7. to impress favorably; charm; enamor

Character Assassination & the Crucifixion of Black Leadership

The life of Jesus according to Minister Farrakhan is a great guide to understanding the assault on Black leadership and how the strategy of "smiting the shepherd" has applied within our history as a people. The Minister stated in an article written by him entitled **The Aim of The Enemy** the following:

> As a revolutionary, the life of Jesus, as recorded in the Gospels is a wonderful example to study. Every Black leader of consequence has been crucified and has knowingly or unknowingly followed in the footsteps of Jesus.

Character assassination is a prime component part in the destruction of Black leaders and the movement of Black people for liberation. The Minister has boldly declared that Black leadership has walked in the path paved by Jesus, in the Bible. We therefore see the character assassination of Black leadership as part and parcel to the crucifixion of Black leadership.

At the death of Michael Jackson, the Honorable Minister Louis Farrakhan delivered a lecture wherein he expounded upon this reality in the following words:

> Crucifixion in the Modern Roman Empire—America—is just like the crucifixions of Ancient Rome. Ancient Rome is gone; Modern Rome is going. In Modern Rome, the Counter Intelligence Program of the United States government, under J. Edgar Hoover, has always feared that somebody would rise from among us and unify Black people, and should they go to war with a foreign government, we might join on to that foreign government, and come against them. This also happened in the time of Jesus, the prophet, and Herod, the king, who wanted to kill all boy babies to prevent the Messiah from coming into the world. So today, there is a plot against the Black male. It's real, brothers and sisters.... Do you notice how every one that got crucified got first crucified in the Media? The Media is used to de-magnetize the person who

has attracted large crowds. So, "to de-magnetize" you means to make you, now, unattractive to the people that once were attracted to you.

The Minister's powerful lecture entitled **The Crucifixion of Michael Jackson and all Responsible Black Leaders** is an example of his long history of defending Black leadership. Consider the following list; this is only a representative sampling of many persons and groups that the Minister has defended against the unjust smear campaigns from the media.

> Qubilah Shabazz -Malcolm Shabazz - Charles Rangel - Congressman Mel Reynolds - Mayor Willie Herenton - Congressional Black Caucus - Mayor Kwame Kilpatrick - Benjamin Chavis - James Luther Bevel- Father Michael Pfleger - Rev. T.L. Barrett - Alderman Dorothy Tillman - Harold Washington Cultural Center - Imam Jamil Al-Amin (H.Rap Brown) - Bloods and Crips - Hip-Hop Community - Stan Tookie Williams - Sistah Souljah - Bishop George A. Stallings - Rep. Bobby Rush - Arsenio Hall - Oprah Winfrey - Mike Tyson Rev. Jesse Jackson - Michael Jackson - O.J. Simpson - Rep. Alcee Hastings - Julian Bond - Rep. Cynthia McKinney Rep. Earl Hilliard - Tawana Brawley - David Dinkins - President Barak Obama - Rev. Charles Coen - Rev. Eddie Carthan

Moreover, the Minister exposed that the crucifixion of Black leaders also includes the assassination of their revolutionary ideas. He stated:

> In a crucifixion, they nail your hands. They nail your feet. They strip you of your followers by propaganda. They break your legs, so that after you are dead, there is no support for your ideas. It's not the man as much as it is the ideas of that man. So, they must not only kill the man—they have to kill his idea, so that a generation won't come up after him, fueled by his ideas!

The crucifixion of revolutionary leaders and their ideas is a component part of the smite the shepherd strategy. Russian leader Vladimir Lenin acknowledged this phenomenon wherein after revolutionary leaders are assassinated, their ideas are re-interpreted and watered down, by the same government and media that participated in their assassination. Lenin notes:

> what in the course of history, has happened repeatedly to the

theories of revolutionary thinkers and leaders of oppressed classes fighting for emancipation? During the lifetime of great revolutionaries, the oppressing classes constantly hounded them, received their theories with the most savage malice, the most furious hatred and the most unscrupulous campaigns of lies and slander. After their death, attempts are made to convert them into harmless icons, to canonize them, so to say, and to hallow their names to a certain extent for the consolation of the oppressed classes and with the object of duping the latter, while at the same time robbing the revolutionary theory of its substance, blunting its revolutionary edge and vulgarizing it.

Republican strategist and author of the book **The Death of the West**, Pat Buchanan has also weighed in to provide insight into our understanding of the "smite the shepherd" strategy. Dubbing it as a part of the politics of personal destruction, Buchanan notes how certain causes are defeated by assassinating the character of those who champion those causes. He writes:

> Dishonor or disgrace a nation's heroes, and you can demoralize its people.

The Character Assassination of Black People En Masse
This kind of campaign to demoralize us as a people has been executed over and over again by the white power structure in America against Black leaders and the movement for Black liberation. Author Jerome Davis, who wrote the book **Character Assassination**, highlights how character assassination has not been limited to Black leaders but has been a key element within the overall oppression of Black people in America. He notes:

> The moving picture industry has in the by and large libeled the Negro. Dr. Lawrence Reddick in The Journal of Negro Education says this: "The treatment of the Negro by the movie is inaccurate and unfair. Directly and indirectly it establishes associations and drives deeper into the public mind the stereotype conception of the Negro. **By building up this unfavorable conception, the movies operate to thwart the advancement of the Negro, to humiliate him, to weaken his drive for equality and to spread indifference, contempt and hatred for him and his cause.**

The media and the entertainment industry are no doubt united in the "smite the shepherd" agenda against Black America.

Novelist and screenwriter Dalton Trumbo observed:

> "[Hollywood made] tarts of the Negro's daughters, crap shooters of his sons, obsequious Uncle Toms of his fathers, superstitious and grotesque crones of his mothers, strutting peacocks of his successful men, psalm-singing mountebanks of his priests, and Barnum and Bailey side-shows of his religion."

In examining the role of the entertainment industry and the mainstream media as co-conspirators in the "smite the shepherd" campaign against Black people and our leadership, we are also exposed to the role of certain Jewish groups. Minister Farrakhan stated in his message **The Crucifixion of Michael Jackson and all Responsible Black Leaders** the following:

> There are certain members of the Zionist faction of Jews that have always wanted to control the means by which your crucifixion could take place.

As explained by Trumbo and Dr. Reddick, the entertainment industry's assassination of the basic character of Black people has been counter-productive to Black progress within America. But according to the Anti-Defamation League of B'nai B'rith, negative portrayals of an entire people within media and movies is not only counter-productive to progress, it constitutes a real and present danger to the survival of the people who are the subject of such negative portrayals. From the ADL's founding charter, we read:

> For a number of years, a tendency has manifested itself in American life toward the caricaturing and defaming of Jews on the stage, in moving pictures. The effect of this on the unthinking public has been to create an untrue and injurious impression of an entire people and to expose the Jew to undeserved contempt, and ridicule. The caricatures center around some idiosyncrasy of the few which, by the thoughtless public, is often taken as a pivotal characteristic of the entire people.

The ADL has been the lead group from the Jewish community that has condemned and criticized Minister Farrakhan. They have been the lead group behind the character assassination of Minister Farrakhan, which has as of this date and time resulted in his censorship throughout the mainstream media and social media.

Considering how the ADL has been the principal architect of the "smite the shepherd" campaign against the Honorable Minister Louis Farrakhan, the words of their founding charter are amazing. It proves that they know the danger of character assassination, yet they use it with great skill against Minister Farrakhan. And they have never protested nor used their considerable influence to hold Hollywood accountable for their negative and dangerous portrayals of Black people. And this is all the more troubling when we reflect that America's entertainment industry has been largely the result of Hollywood's Jewish founding fathers. As Neal Gabler wrote in **An Empire of Their Own**:

> What is amazing is the extent to which they succeeded in promulgating this fiction throughout the world. By making a 'shadow' America, one which idealized every old glorifying bromide about the country, the Hollywood Jews created a powerful cluster of images and ideas—so powerful that, in a sense, they colonized the American imagination.... Ultimately, American values came to be defined largely by the movies the Jews made.

Writing for the Jewish Forward online edition, author Batya Ungar Sargon addresses the Jewish character assassination of Black leaders in her article entitled, **Why Do Jews Keep Tearing Down Black Leaders?** Within her article she writes:

> Tamika Mallory. Marc Lamont Hill. Alice Walker. Angela Davis.
>
> Every week seems to bring with it another black leader running afoul of the Jewish community — and an angry, effective response.... It all lends to a spectacle of an insensate mob out to attack any and every black leader.
>
> And I feel sickened by it. When did Jews become the face of attacks against the black community? When did we abandon the sacred legacy of Rabbi Avraham Yehoshua Heschel marching across the Edmund Pettus Bridge, Torah scroll in hand? How must this look to the Black community, to say nothing of Black Jewish members of our own community?... It's not just an outraged mob, either, that's been coming for black leaders; it's an effective one. Hill lost his job at CNN. Davis lost an award. The Women's March is

> teetering, with local marches defecting every week.
>
> There's a lot of talk about anti-Semitism on the left, but when push comes to shove, when the Jewish community is angry, we get our way... this tearing down of black leaders is a horrifying spectacle to behold.

Un-Smiting the Shepherd

In an interview with Chicago radio legend Cliff Kelley in 2009 on WVON-Chicago, the Honorable Minister Louis Farrakhan made the following appeal:

> I wish that my Black brothers and sisters would help Brother Farrakhan to get out of prison. I am not in a prison of "steel bars"— I am in a prison of public opinion manipulated by the media and their hatred of the truth that is in my mouth that would set our people free. Help me to get out of prison. Stop looking at the Nation of Islam as though we are some enemy to Black people. Open the door of the schools, and let us go in and teach! We don't have to teach religion. Just teach truth, and these young people will rise up! They will be disciplined. They will see their future, and then the condition in our community will change.

This book contains more than 80 articles purposed to "help Brother Farrakhan to get out of prison"; to defend the Honorable Minister Louis Farrakhan against his critics and enemies. This book is purposed to be a weapon in the movement to free the Honorable Minister Louis Farrakhan from the prison of public opinion that has been weaponized against him.

If "smiting the shepherd", scatters the flock; then un-smiting the shepherd can unite the flock. Smiting the shepherd involves character assassination. Un-smiting the shepherd involves character protection. And so many of our great leaders have died and had their movements destroyed; most never received the defense from their people that they deserved. I am proclaiming that this phenomenon ends in the leadership of the Honorable Minister Louis Farrakhan. Minister Farrakhan exists today as the embodiment of the great Black leaders of the past. He is like an emblematic seal of those who suffered before him. And I bear witness that Allah (God) has made him to stand on the foundation laid by the great leaders of the past and to go farther and stand stronger and move wiser because they paved the way for him. In honoring Minister Farrakhan, in defending Minister Farrakhan, we honor and defend the great leaders of the past.

He is the culmination and fulfillment of those who came before him. Think about it. From the Most Honorable Elijah Muhammad he has the anointing of Allah (God) and is the possessor of divine wisdom. And like Dr. Martin Luther King Jr, the Minister has beautiful, powerful eloquence that makes him peerless among all who speak on behalf of Black people. Like Marcus Garvey, Minister Farrakhan has the magnetic appeal to attract the masses of the people to the ideas of Black liberation. Like Paul Robeson, the Minister has an artistic and athletic background that adds dimension and nuance to his leadership profile. When former congressman Gus Savage traveled on one of Minister Farrakhan's World Friendship Tours he exclaimed:

> I always believed that you could unite Black people in America. I did not know your power in Africa, and, if you have this same power in the Arab and Muslim world you are the most dangerous man on the planet to these forces that rule by divide and conquer. So, when you get back to the United States, they are going to jump on you with both feet.

The Minister's international strength, which is an element of his leadership that is greatly feared by his/our enemies is another example of him fulfilling the desires and hopes of some of the great Black leaders of the past who desired a unification of Blacks in America with Blacks abroad.

The cover of this book shows Minister Farrakhan emerging from a background of some of the great men and women from our people's struggle for liberation. It was inspired by a banner that he commissioned for the Nation of Islam's 2014 Saviours' Day. The Minister has always honored and defended the great leaders of the past, and we pray that this volume honors and defends him so that all who have been victimized by the propaganda against Minister Farrakhan may learn the truth about the Minister and be benefitted by the wisdom of Allah (God) that he uniquely possesses. Thank you for supporting our effort to "Un-Smite the Shepherd"

Demetric Muhammad, October 2022

Contents

MAIN SECTION: Articles & Essays Written by Demetric Muhammad In Defense of the Person and Preaching of the Honorable Minister Louis Farrakhan

Against All Odds: Allah (God) Empowers Minister Farrakhan & the Million Man March 23

    Impact 23

    Opposition 23

    Success 25

    No Platform Strategy 26

"Is America in the crosshairs of God's wrath?" 28

    Scholars Bear Witness of America's Divine Peril 28

    Scholars Bear Witness Jewish People Not Real Children of Israel 29

    Biblical Scripture Rightly Interpreted Exposes Black Man's Plight 30

American Jewish Committee Makes Veiled Threats Against Farrakhan Followers 33

An Open Letter to Neal Steinberg: "Our Love For The Minister Shall Not Be Mocked!" 37

Imam Michael Saahir Wrong On Minister Farrakhan...again! 41

    Commendations 41

"Hey, Didn't Y'all Kill Malcolm?" 48

Be Careful, You Might Be an Anti-Semite If… 52

    You might be an anti-Semite if you've got the "Wrong Preacher" 54

    You might be an anti-Semite if you're "Well Educated" 54

    You might be an anti-Semite if you're "Young" 54

    You might be an anti-Semite if you're "Militant (Disciplined)" 55

"Warrior Sperm": The Mischievous Subtext To the Farrakhan Women's March Controversy 56

Courage to Speak What God Has Written: Farrakhan reminds us of the other side of God 60

DIVINE PESTILENCE: Did The Censorship of Minister Farrakhan Produce The Rise of COVID-19 ? 68

  CENSORSHIP OF TRUTH: NOI & SOCIAL MEDIA 69

  The COVID-19 Pestilence as Allah's Response to Suppression of Truth 71

  Scientific Evidence Supports the Minister 73

  Censorship As Hiding The Light From the Enslaved 74

  Censorship As The Ultimate Aim: "To Kill A Preacher" 79

  Epilogue: Scriptures Related To Censorship 80

    The Crude Censorship of the Wicked Who Used Their Fingers To Prevent the Prophet's Message From Entering Their Ears 80

    Allah's (God's) Promise To Raise Up A People Who Won't Fear The "Censurership" of the Wicked 80

    The Wicked Desire To Censor The Divine Wisdom (Light) of Allah 80

    Nature Will React To The Censorship Of The Disciples 81

    Allah's (God's) Wrath Results From The Censorship of The Truth 81

    Satan As The God Of This World Who Uses Censorship To Hide The Light of Allah 81

    The Motivation Of Satan's Censorship; Fear of Being Exposed 81

    Allah's (God's) Prophets Censored Because The Wicked Don't Want To Be Disturbed By Truth 81

  The Case of Prophet Jeremiah: His Enemies' Conspiracy to Silence/Censor Him 82

RESPONSE TO FORWARD MAGAZINE: DEAR JANE EISNER, WE ARE LOUIS FARRKHAN & WE DON'T FEAR THE CENSURE OF ANY CENSURER 84

NOI Prison Reform Ministry Under Attack! Facts Rebut False Narrative of Propaganda 93

How Minister Farrakhan's Jewish Controversy Marks Him as The "Jesus" of Our Times 98

The Honorable Minister Louis Farrakhan: Black America's Head of State 103

Did Farrakhan Praise Hitler?:Fact Sheet of Truth Destroys Popular Slander. 107

- Context & Brief Timeline 107
- ADL Exposed for Lying On the Minister 109

"You Are All Gods": 111

"The Earth Swallows The Flood": Minister Farrakhan, Hip-Hop Controversy & End-Times Prophecy 115
- Spiritual Intersection 117

Empathy: Minister Farrakhan, Conflict Resolution & The Restoration of Brotherhood 120

Facebook Punishes Minister Farrakhan With Slave Code Laws 124

The Year 1974 and Why Farrakhan Is Good For Morgan State 128

Farrakhan is Innocent, FBI is Guilty 133

Farrakhan Vindicated!: Charges of anti-Semitism exposed as anti-Black racism, fear mongering and money scheme 137

Who Is The Original Woman?: The Mis-Education of Trump Rally Chanters . 141
- Original People 141
- Congresswomen Signs of God's Presence 144

GOD'S PROPHETS CRITICIZE, REBUKE & WARN ISRAEL: VINDICATION FOR REP. OMAR 146

"Guilty by Association"? Defending the Nation of Islam in the Fresno Shooting Case; Exposing the Plan to Equate Black Nationalism with Extremism, Terrorism. 151
- Not our teaching; Not our practice 152
- Mental illness not religion lies at the root 153
- Catholicism isn't blamed for pedophilia; Islam shouldn't be blamed for terroristic acts 154
- The Nation of Islam's hidden history of courageous crime fighting 154
- Minister Farrakhan's message and ministry is totally opposite the crimes alleged to Kori Ali Muhammad 156
- White devil teaching nothing compared to Black devil teaching 158

Conclusion: Minister Farrakhan, Black Nationalism Set-Up For Take-Down 162

Happy September 17th! :Theology, Ufology and Black Liberation in Minister Farrakhan's Vision-Like Experience... 168

Part 1 168

   A Special Day in the Nation of Islam 168

Happy September 17th!! :Theology, Ufology and Black Liberation in Minister Farrakhan's Vision-Like Experience... 173

Part 2 173

   Ufology 173

   God Rides Upon A Cloud 174

   The Mother Plane 175

Hidden History: NAACP's Black Face & White Mind 179

   Minister Farrakhan & Muslim – Christian Unity 179

   NAACP Infamous President Joel Spingarn 180

Hidden History: 200 Black Leaders Unite Against Jewish Pressure, Threats . 184

   Black Leaders Unite Summon Courage 184

   Scholars Bust Myth of Black Jewish Relationship 185

   Jews Silent On Trayvon et. Al. 186

   Minister Farrakhan deserves Black leadership to close ranks around him 187

"In Good Company": Hon. Min. Louis Farrakhan Among Great Black Leaders Opposed By Jewish Groups 189

   The Oppressor Can't Love The Liberator 189

   Jesus 190

   Prophet Muhammad 190

   Marcus Garvey 191

   Malcolm X 191

   Hon. Elijah Muhammad 192

   Minister Farrakhan 192

Jesus Is the Name of The Messiah(s) 193
    Jesus: Basis for Muslim – Christian Unity 193
    The Historical Jesus Was A Sign of The Messiah 194
    Modern Black Messiah to End Satan's World 195
4 Murdered Black Girls and a Christmas Boycott 197
    Christmas Boycott Theologically Justified 198
    King, Muhammad, and Christian Scholars Agree 201
Master W. Fard Muhammad Revealed Supreme Wisdom, Evidence Now Comes Forth 205
    A Teachable Moment 205
    Master W. Fard Muhammad and What He Revealed 206
    Evidence For The Truth of Revelation 206
Master W. Fard Muhammad: An Introduction To The Theology of The Nation of Islam 209
    Theology 101 209
    OUR SAVIOUR 211
Minister Farrakhan as The Defender of Black People 213
    Quotes 213
    Jewish Acknowledgement 213
Minister Farrakhan Visits Monroe, a city of Lynching 217
Like Farrakhan Dr. Martin Luther King Jr. Attracted Jewish Opposition 222
    Joel Spingarn Spy Master 223
    Rabbi Grafman Charges Anti-Semitism 223
    Dr. King Confronted Jewish Slum Lords 224
    Stanley Levinson Dr. King's Jewish Advisor 225
    ADL Espionage Against Dr. King 225
Muhammad Ali's Beloved Teacher, The Most Honorable Elijah Muhammad 226
Heeding Muhammad's Warning Is America's Only Way Out! 233

- Muhammad & Farrakhan Have Divine Authority 233
- What Should Black People Do? 235
- Muhammad's Wisdom & Warning Diagnose America's Time of Confusion . 238
  - Review of Muhammad's Wisdom & Warning 239
- My Disappointment with Imam Michael Saahir 242
- "Of Termites & Vipers": Minister Farrakhan and the Hard Sayings of Jesus . 248
  - A Sample of Some of the Hard Sayings of Jesus include the following verses found in the New Testament 249
- Open Letter to Congressman Todd Rokita, R-IN 252
- Pharaoh's Fears Alive in Jamaica: 255
- The Magnificent & Brilliant Professor Toni Morrison: An Oracle For Her People and Their God 260
- Rabbi Bertram Korn:Considering the Sources of Minister Farrakhan's Research 266
- The Roots of Injustice: The American Slave Codes, Laws that Criminalized Black Life in America 270
- Stop the Mischief Making!:Setting the Record Straight on the Nation of Islam & the Police 275
  - Divine Wisdom For Policing 276
  - Nation of Islam Lauded By Law Enforcement 278
  - Minister Farrakhan's "Dopebusters" 279
- The Censorship of God's Ideas and Perspective 282
- The Criterion (Standard) of Love & Leadership 286
  - Leadership 288
  - Love 289
- "The Crucifixion of Lazarus": 291
- "The Godfather of Harlem" And The Corruption of Black History 295
- The Messiah Is A Black Woman's Son 300
  - The End Times Messiah 300

- Women's March Farrakhan Controversy 300
- Black People's Suffering & Expectation For A Deliverer 301
- The Divine Rise of Women 303
- Fear of A Black Messiah With An Iron Rule 304

The Mis-Education of Yvette Carnell et.al. 309

The Strategy of Ritual Defamation: Chicago Sun-Times & Chicago Tribune Unite Against Minister Farrakhan 317
- Elements of Ritual Defamation 318

The Unconquerable Nation of Islam: 90 Years of Service & Survival 322

The Word of God is Dangerous: The Real Reason Facebook Banned Our Beloved Minister Farrakhan 326

Rabbi's Words Connect Jewish Talmud to Anti-Black Violence, Police Killings 331

The Fear of Black Manhood: Jude Wanniski Explains the Farrakhan Ban 337

The Mysterious Death of a Muslim Minister 342
- Holes in the Official Account 343
- A History of Murder and Attempted Murder of Muslim Ministers 344
- The Importance and Significance of Brother Robert's Work 348
- Black Muslim Leadership through the Eyes of the Oppressor 351
- Revolutionary Muslim Leadership in Haiti 354
- Conclusion: 357

Why Farrakhan Is Loved By Black America, and Is Always Welcomed Among Us! 360
- The Minister's Message Literally Gives Life 361
- Minister Farrakhan's Impact in Black America is Vast and Overwhelmingly Positive 362
- Minister Farrakhan's Generosity 364

The Wicked Use of Science & Chemistry to Stop Black Liberation 367
- The Prophet Daniel & Min. Farrakhan 367

Yacub's Needles 367

The Slavemaster's Alcohol 368

The CIA's Crack Cocaine 369

Drapetomania 370

Woe Unto Charleston!: An Open Letter To The Clergy of Charleston, South Carolina 372

FEATURES SECTION: Articles Written by Some of the Students of the Honorable Minister Louis Farrakhan In His Defense

Abdul Arif Muhammad

The Mis-Education of Henry Louis Gates, Jr. 380

Glenn Beck: A Minion of the Synagogue of Satan 385

Unmasking Mr. Dershowitz 390

Abdul Hafeez Muhammad

"YOU DON'T HAVE MINISTER FARRAKHAN'S ASSIGNMENT" 397

Abdul Haleem Muhammad

MINISTER VANQUISHES NAP-TOWN CRITIC FOR "FARRAKHANSPLAINING". 403

DR. MUHAMMAD REMINDS WALL ST. OF SINS AGAINST BLACK PEOPLE, DEFENDS MIN. FARRAKHAN 407

Abdul Rashidullah Muhammad

SAN FRANCISCO MINISTER: MINISTER FARRAKHAN'S DETRACTORS, THE REAL ENEMIES OF OPPRESSED MASSES 410

Abdul Sabur Muhammad

"IF THIS IS A REPRESENTATIVE DEMOCRACY; WHO DO YOU REPRESENT? A MESSAGE FOR BLACKS IN POLITICS" 412

Abdul Shahid Muhammad

WOE TO THE SLANDERERS: A MESSAGE TO THOSE WHO CONTINUE TO ANSWER THE CALL TO SLANDER MINISTER FARRAKHAN 417

Cedric Muhammad

The Economic Blueprint: The Unity Of Booker T. Washington, Prophet Muhammad and Minister Farrakhan 424

Dawud Muhammad
SUN-TIMES OPINION FAILS AS FACTS VINDICATE FARRAKHAN & PFLEGER ... 427

Dennis Muhammad
THE MIS-EDUCATION OF CLARENCE PAGE ... 429

Dezarae Muhammad
MINISTER FARRAKHAN'S STERLING RECORD DESTROYS CLAIMS OF HOMOPHOBIA ... 434

Ilia Rashad Muhammad
September 17— A Divine Sign of Min. Farrakhan's position ... 437

Jackie Muhammad
Re: Your Attack on The Honorable Minister Louis Farrakhan ... 441
The 2 Messiahs ... 446
- Definition of Messiah ... 446
- Aaron: The First Messiah ... 449
- The Concept of the Messiah and the Growth of Zionism ... 450
- The Dual Personalities of Melchizedek ... 450
- God Empowers the Messiahs ... 451
- Prophet Muhammad on the Messiah ... 451
- Job Description of The Messiahs ... 454

Michael Muhammad
SAN DIEGO TRIBUNE STORY STINKS, REHASHES ANTI-FARRAKHAN PROPAGANDA ... 456

Nzinga Muhammad
RABBI BOTEACH, SENATOR BOOKER & THE FARRAKHAN LITMUS TEST ... 462
DEFENDING FARRAKHAN MYTH BUSTING: "OUR MINISTER IS NO MISOGYNIST!" ... 466

Rahman A. Muhammad
YOUTH DEFEND MINISTER FARRAKHAN: A DEMAND TO DENOUNCE THE ADVERSARIES OF THE BLACK COMMUNITY ... 469

Tracee Muhammad

ANGELA RYE, NAYSAYERS SLANDER OF FARRAKHAN SHALL NOT STAND 472

Willie Muhammad

"YOU CANNOT MAKE REAL LEADERS DENOUNCE THE HON. MIN. LOUIS FARRAKHAN!" 476

Against All Odds: Allah (God) Empowers Minister Farrakhan & the Million Man March

Impact

According to Gary Fields and Maria Puente of USA Today, the Million Man March called for by the Honorable Minister Louis Farrakhan was an extraordinary and historic success. They noted that some of the March's signature quantifiable achievements include:

> "Increased interest among black men in serving their communities; increased child support payments by black fathers; a decrease in black-on-black crime; and up to 15,000 new applicants wanting to adopt black children"

The Million Man March brought together nearly 2 million Black men from all walks of life, various religious orientations, diverse and disparate parts of America and the world. And these men, 80% of whom self-identified as believers in Christianity, came at the call of Minister Farrakhan, the Muslim leader and National Representative of the Most Honorable Elijah Muhammad and the Nation of Islam. This was a historic and improbable achievement to say the least.

It is all the more improbable when we reflect upon the strong and formidable opposition faced by our beloved Minister. The success of the Million Man March powerfully proved that in spite of tremendous opposition, Allah (God)-the Lord of Creation and Author of Life itself-empowered Minister Farrakhan, protected Minister Farrakhan and guided Minister Farrakhan to navigate a rough and tumultuous political, religious and economic landscape to arrive at the National Mall on October 16, 1995 victorious.

Opposition

Let us not forget that the Honorable Minister Louis Farrakhan had been censured in a 95-0 vote by the U.S. Senate in 1984. This period of time coincided with the beginning of a vicious campaign of anti-Farrakhan propaganda lead by the Anti-Defamation League of B'nai B'rith, the Simon Wiesenthal Center and the Southern Poverty Law Center.

Jewish opposition to Minister Farrakhan dogged the Minister's trail since the time of the presidential campaign of the Rev. Jesse L. Jackson Sr. And in 1993 Rabbi David Saperstein wrote a letter to Coretta Scott King and Rev. Joseph Lowery chastising these Civil Rights icons because they invited Minister Farrakhan to the 30th anniversary of the March on Washington without getting permission from the Jewish community to do so.

Attempts to derail Minister Farrakhan also included the 1994 controversy involving the daughter of Malcolm X, Qubilah Shabazz, who had been arrested in an FBI sting operation. She had been lured into a "murder plot" against Minister Farrakhan by former childhood companion, FBI informant Michael Fitzpatrick. Minister Farrakhan was guided by Allah (God) to see through the federal government's machinations and refused to view the daughter of Malcolm X as an enemy. Instead Minister Farrakhan came to her aid and hosted a demonstration of reconciliation with the wife of Malcolm X, Dr. Betty Shabazz. This event had been called for by Minister Farrakhan to serve as a fundraiser for Qubilah Shabazz, because the Minister maintained that she had been tricked and manipulated into going along with a plot to assassinate him, and that it was not of her own doing.

This controversy taking place in 1994, just a year prior to the Million Man March, was no doubt orchestrated by Minister Farrakhan's enemies to sabotage his efforts.

Through the build-up to the Million Man March, the mainstream media sought to separate the message of the Million Man March from the Messenger of the Million Man March-Minister Farrakhan. Some examples of the media's opposition to the Minister include the following

Charles Krauthammer in the Washington Post who wrote:

> "In an ironic and tragic turn of the civil rights revolution, there is today a powerful movement within the black community away from Martin Luther King Jr.'s vision of integration toward a new kind of separatism, self-imposed and adversarial. Its most extreme advocate is, of course, Louis Farrakhan, who portrays African Americans as an occupied people in an alien land."

The Washington Post also carried the negative piece about the Million Man March written by Richard Cohen called "Marching Behind a Bigot." The New York Times columnist Bob Herbert's column called "Harmony or Discord" wrote:

> "Today there will be another gathering in Washington... It will not be an attempt to bring seemingly disparate elements together... unlike the effort by Dr. King and his colleagues in 1963, it will not be an attempt "to transform the jangling discord of our nation" by celebrating, in blatant and brave defiance of all the odds, the ideal of brotherhood.
> Today's gathering is the opposite of that. It is the theme of inclusiveness turned upside down. ...Instead of unity, it has promoted divisiveness on many fronts. As of white versus blacks were not conflict enough, Louis Farrakhan has succeeded in pitting black against blacks."

Success

The media's negative prelude to the March was rendered essentially ineffective in persuading Black men, and some women also, from responding in strong numbers to the Minister's call to atonement, reconciliation and responsibility.

In fact, news agencies were made to eat their words as reports of a peaceful and tranquil event flowed from all observers. Executives from CNN noted:

> "2.2 million households tuned in to Mr. Farrakhan's... speech - meaning that more people watched the two-hour-long address on CNN than any other special this year, including Mr. Clinton's State of the Union Message and the Popes address to the United Nations. "We got the kind of numbers that basic cable only sees from first-run movies," said Howard Polskin, a vice-president of CNN."

Michael Marriott of the New York Times wrote:

> "From dawn to dusk, there was no evidence of drug deals and the drive-by shootings or crack pipes and gang colors. The throng was as good natured as a church meeting.... What much of America witnessed on the evening news was the site of hundreds of thousands of black men, respectable and responsible, in search of solace and solutions."

Jewish Rabbi Bruce Kahn exclaimed:

> "I am White. I am a rabbi. I attended the Million Man March where I stood hour after hour in the midst of a sea of excited, highly principled, welcoming Black men. I listened to the speeches and shared in the grandeur of an extraordinary moment in history. Mostly, it was my privilege to bear witness to how important this gathering was to the African Americans who were present.
> On that Monday, I was enveloped in an overwhelming sense of joy, pride, responsibility, thoughtfulness, hope and love. Yet, no one

seemed to dodge one bit an awareness of what is wrong and what needs repair in Black neighborhoods across America. Speaker after speaker, especially Minister Louis Farrakhan, confronted self-destructive behavior by too many Black males in a hard-hitting, no nonsense, clearly defined and agonizingly descriptive fashion. The people around me did the same. But there was so much more that made this day unique. It was a day of atonement and affirmation. This was a day for recognizing that most Black men in America care about their families, work hard, have a love of God and country, and possess a strong and positive moral code which embraces confession and atonement. That is not a message that is perceived by the media or transmitted by it."

No Platform Strategy

Allah (God) indeed blessed the Minister with success. He proved that He is with Minister Farrakhan to bring about the mental and spiritual resurrection of the Black man and woman of American and the world.

The Minister's success and the media's failure to thwart him produced a shift in their strategy of opposition. They had previously avowed to give nothing but negative coverage of any and all news items surrounding Minister Farrakhan. After the Million Man March proved that Minister Farrakhan would still be successful in attracting large crowds of Black people to hear his message in spite of negative media coverage, mainstream news outlets decided that they would go from negative coverage to no coverage at all.

So, from 1996 until 2007, Minister Farrakhan was virtually ignored in the mainstream media. He only was able to escape this media embargo, or "no platform" strategy with the advent of social media. And since social media has become ubiquitous as a means of communications and news content sharing the Minister has become a household name again. And this, in spite of the efforts of his enemies.

Social media has spawned and given rise to the "citizen journalist"; it has given the common man and woman the ability to create their own broadcast stations via their social media accounts. Everyday people are now empowered, to share with their friends and family ideas and information that they like and agree with, even when these ideas and information are hidden by the mainstream media.

Currently, however, Minister Farrakhan's Jewish opponents are working hard to cause the social media companies to adopt "no platform" strategies against Minister Farrakhan's message. This article is being written one week after social media giant YouTube summarily decided to terminate the Nation of Islam's main YouTube channels.

It will be interesting to see how this current episode in the fight to establish the truth turns out. With history as our guide, it should be clear to see that Minister Farrakhan is not a man who is alone in his fight against the forces of falsehood and evil in this world. He is supported by men and women who believe in truth, all over the world, who have committed to support him, defend him and to proliferate his message to the ends of the earth. And most importantly, he is supported, anointed and authorized by Allah (God)!

Long Live the Spirit of the Million Man March!

"Is America in the crosshairs of God's wrath?"

Christian Scholars, Biblical Scripture, Jewish Historians & Natural Disasters Cited in Support for Farrakhan's Divine Warnings!

In an excellent interview with Final Call Editor in In Chief, Richard Muhammad, the Honorable Minister Louis Farrakhan said ... *"America now is in the crosshairs of God Himself..."* The Minister has often pointed to the violent or extreme weather patterns in America as evidence that the country is being divinely chastised. And according to a 2013 article in USA Today America has the most extreme weather on the planet! Writer Doyle Rice wrote in the aforementioned article that,

> "North America — and the USA in particular — has the world's wildest weather extremes: No other part of the planet can boast its ferocious weather stew of hurricanes, tornadoes, droughts, floods, wildfires, blizzards, heat waves and cold snaps."

What follows in this article is a brief factsheet prepared to shed light on the Minister's serious warning to the American people, and to refute the ADL's renewed propaganda against our beloved Minister.

Scholars Bear Witness of America's Divine Peril

Edward Tracy: "On what comfortable and convenient grounds can the U.S.A. claim immunity from divine judgement? The nation that forgets God goes backward-backward to defeat, backward to destruction. That we (U.S.A.) are going backward cannot be denied? We are regressing spiritually, morally, legally, financially, governmentally, and that with alarming acceleration."

Herbert Armstrong:" Just as God has bestowed on us such material blessings as never before came to any nations, now to correct us so we may enjoy such blessings, He is going to bring upon our peoples such national disaster as has never before struck any nation! Many prophecies describe this!"

Ruth Graham (wife of famous evangelist Billy Graham): "If God doesn't punish America, He'll have to apologize to Sodom and Gomorrah."

Dr. Martin Luther King Jr: "We have fought long and hard for the goals we've achieved, but therein lies my deepest concern, that in this struggle for integration, which we are achieving, I do genuinely believe that we will be integrating into a burning house,"

Thomas Jefferson: "Indeed, I tremble for my country when I reflect that God is just: that his justice cannot sleep for ever…"

The ADL, under its new leadership, has recently renewed its anti-Farrakhan campaign. They have listed Minister Farrakhan as an extremist "anti-Semite." They call the Minister this, not for any real anti-Semitism, but because he says it is the Blacks of America and their Native American brothers and sisters who are the real Children of Israel. Thusly the Minister has pointed to America's mistreatment of Blacks, Mexicans and Indians as being the root cause of her being in the "cross hairs of the wrath of God."

But as angry as the ADL is at Minister Farrakhan for delivering this gospel to sold-out arenas around the country, there are well – respected Israeli and Jewish scholars who have proven that their own people are **not** the real Children of Israel who are described in the Bible/ Torah. Consider the following sample of their voluminous research.

Scholars Bear Witness Jewish People Not Real Children of Israel

Professor Schlomo Sand: "Moses could not have led the Hebrews out of Egypt into the Promised Land, for the good reason that the latter was Egyptian territory at the time. And there is no trace of either a slave revolt against the Pharaonic Empire or of a sudden conquest of Canaan by outsiders.

"I was not raised as a Zionist, but like all other Israelis I took it for granted that the Jews were a people living in Judea and that they were exiled by the Romans in 70 AD. "But once I started looking at the evidence, I discovered that the kingdoms of David and Solomon were legends. "Similarly, with the exile. In fact, you can't explain Jewishness without exile. But when I started to look for history books describing the events of this exile, I couldn't find any. Not one." *(Professor of History, Tel Aviv University, Israel. Author of the Invention of the Jewish People).*

Professor Ze'ev Herzog: "The many Egyptian documents that we have make no mention of the Israelites' presence in Egypt and are also silent about the events of the exodus…. Generations of researchers tried to locate Mount Sinai and the stations of the tribes in the desert. Despite these intensive efforts, not even one site has been found that can match the biblical account." *(Professor of Archaeology, Tel Aviv University, Israel.)*

Rabbi David Wolpe: "The truth is that virtually every modern archeologist who has investigated the story of the Exodus, with very few exceptions, agrees that the way the Bible describes the Exodus is not the way it happened, if it happened at all." *(Senior Rabbi, Sinai Temple, Los Angeles, CA. Named the "#1 Pulpit Rabbi in America" by Newsweek magazine).*

Professor Israel Finkelstein: "The conclusion—that the Exodus did not happen at the time and in the manner described in the Bible—seems irrefutable when we examine the evidence at specific sites where the children of Israel were said to have camped for extended periods during their wandering in the desert and where some archaeological indication—if present—would almost certainly be found." *(Jacob M. Alkow Professor of the Archaeology of Israel in the Bronze Age and Iron Ages at Tel Aviv University.)*

Again, the ADL and the Southern Poverty Law Center hate the narrative espoused by the Honorable Minister Louis Farrakhan, specifically the part where the Minister boldly declares that it is the Black man and woman of America who fit the Biblical description better than any other possible contender.

A sample of the Biblical scriptures that point to the Black man and woman of America include the following prophecies

Biblical Scripture Rightly Interpreted Exposes Black Man's Plight

Children of Israel in Bondage for 400 years (Acts 7:6-7; Genesis 15:13-15): The Hon. Elijah Muhammad teaches that the most popular English slaver John Hawkins began bringing Africans as slaves to the Americas also in the year 1555. To date we are 461 years in bondage.

> "The transatlantic slave trade was, in many ways, still in its infancy during the 16th century, but thousands of captive Africans were already being loaded onto European ships and transported across the sea to Spanish America and Brazil every, year, especially after 1560. In this vein, an expedition under the command of John Lok reportedly returned to England with "certayne blacke slaves" in 1555." (Slaves and

Englishmen: Human Bondage in the Early Modern Atlantic World by Michael Guasco p. 67)

Children of Israel names were changed while in bondage (Daniel 1:7): We came to America with African and Islamic names, but our slave masters changed our names and gave us their names to identify us as their chattel property.

> "The slaves had been stripped of their status, their names, their families and friends, and their customs and culture. They were surrounded by fear, distrust, and sometimes hatred. No wonder it was commonplace for newly arrived slaves to try to run away or sink into a deep, sometimes suicidal depression. They stood naked to misery, not knowing what would happen to them." (Slavery in America by Dorothy and Carl Schneider p. 78)

Children of Israel oppressed through special laws and statutes (Psalms 94:20; James 5:6): Special laws known as the Slave Codes were written and executed to deprive Blacks in America of the right to read, marry, own property, testify in court, vote in elections, practice our native religion and constitute families.

> "Surely never before has mischief been framed by law with more diabolical ingenuity than in this infernal code. Your analysis of the slave laws is very able, and your exhibition of their practical application by the Southern Courts, evinces great and careful research." (Judge William Jay to Author William Goodell of the American Slave Code p.9)

Children of Israel corrupted and "robbed and spoiled" (Exodus 1:10; Isaiah 42:22; Daniel 5:2): Because of our strong birth rate, that far exceeds our slave masters and their children, Blacks have been poisoned, sterilized, aborted in the wombs of our mothers, infected with diseases, miseducated and blocked from all paths to freedom and independence.

> "Employers in the South had made a practice of supplying their black workers with cocaine (Grinspoon and Bakalar 1985:39). According to Ashley (1976:81), plantation owners had "discovered things went better with coke." Thus, they kept a steady supply on hand to increase productivity and keep workers content. Cocaine was also a cheap incentive to maintain control of workers. "A shrewd boss doling out one-quarter gram a day per man could keep sixteen workers happy and

more productive for a full seven days on a single ounce" ("Coca and Cocaine in the United States" by Richard Harvey Brown, pg.1)

American Jewish Committee Makes Veiled Threats Against Farrakhan Followers

In 1972, the FBI's chief liaison to the Anti-Defamation League and the American Jewish Committee wrote a report that was published by the American Jewish Committee. Milton Ellerin's report published by Philip Hoffman of the American Jewish Committee identified the Nation of Islam as follows:

> "Only one movement (The Black Muslims), though looked upon by disfavor by the major Black civil rights groups remains consequential, strong, cohesive and influential..."

On August 24, 2020, this same American Jewish Committee trotted out writers Dov Wilker and Holly Huffnagle to encourage the Black community to "unfollow Farrakhan" or suffer the consequences. The article is written to point out the persecution of high-profile Blacks who have been the victims of Jewish campaigns to injure them professionally because of their love and support for the Honorable Minister Louis Farrakhan. Wilker and Huffnagle wax "godfather-esque" in their "make them an offer they can't refuse" type piece that is purposed to stoke fear and to intimidate the followers and supporters of Minister Farrakhan.

According to Wilker and Huffnagle:

> "Efforts to combat anti-Semitism online seem to fire up Farrakhan's base. Some celebrities and community leaders heap praise upon Farrakhan…. But it's their careers, reputations and pursuits of justice that suffer when they defend Farrakhan."

What Wilker and Huffnagle make clear is that Blacks who support strong Black leaders that the Jewish community does not approve of, namely Minister Farrakhan, will continue to be punished with career sabotage and industry black-balling. And this punishment of Black celebrities and entertainers must be understood as a public robbing of their constitutional right to the freedom of speech, expression and religious belief. It is clear that when it comes to the Black community the AJC's professed liberal ideals and virtues don't apply.

For those of us in the Nation of Islam, there is no way for us to read the Wilker and Huffnagle piece and not view it as a veiled threat.

The history of the Nation of Islam and its conflict with Jewish organizations documents that organizations like the American Jewish Committee and the Anti-Defamation League stop at nothing to destroy our ability to earn a living and promote our religion. Moreover, while Wilker and Huffnagle attempt to describe what has happened to Nick Cannon, Tamika Mallory, Min. Rodney Muhammad and others as a naturally occurring result of defending Minister Farrakhan, the truth is that it is the result of a well-orchestrated campaign to crucify strong Black leadership; leadership that teaches Black people to do for ourselves what Jews have done for themselves through intra-group unity and cooperative economics.

In The Secret Relationship Between Blacks and Jews volume 2 we learned of the efforts of the Anti-Defamation League of B'nai B'rith and the American Jewish Committee to destroy the Nation of Islam. An illuminating passage states:

> "In 1942: A secret Anti-Defamation League of B'nai B'rith file entitled "Temple of Islam Infiltration" states that a "Negro employed by us" proved "quite instrumental" in an FBI raid on the Chicago mosque resulting in 82 arrests."

We also learned in this monumental and epic work published by Minister Farrakhan that:

> "In 1959 The American Jewish Committee sent Black spies from the Urban League to Mr. Muhammad's Newark, New Jersey, appearance."

The ADL and The AJC spied on and collaborated with law enforcement to sabotage the Nation of Islam. They did this despite the fact that they privately admitted that the Nation of Islam is NOT ANTI-SEMITIC. The Secret Relationship continues by making this eye-opening revelation:

> "Arnold Forster of the ADL admitted that we have no documentable evidence of anti-Semitism on the part of the Temple of Islam movement or Elijah Muhammad. Nathan Edelstein of the AJC wrote that 'We doubt whether the bulk of its followers are presently committed to anti-Semitism.'"

And despite internally admitting the Nation of Islam is not anti-Semitic, these Jewish organizations continued to publicly persecute the Nation of Islam by working in collaboration with the mainstream media, and the federal government to falsely label the Nation of Islam as anti-Semitic.

The July 19, 1963 edition of the Detroit Jewish News discusses how certain Jewish groups were notified by the federal government that it was getting rid of Nation of Islam federal employees. The firing of Nation of Islam federal employees, it is clear, resulted from the AJC and ADL's campaign to falsely paint the "Black Muslims" as anti-Semitic. Its article states:

> "The United States Government Tuesday began moving against the anti-Semitic Negro extremist group known as the "Black Muslims," firing a dozen from Federal jobs. The Justice Department recently revealed to the Jewish War Veterans that an active investigation of the fanatic activities of both the Black Muslims and the American Nazi Party."

In the early 1990s the ADL used it influence in the United States federal government once again to injure the Nation of Islam financially. It worked to eliminate the Nation of Islam as a security presence in federal apartment houses. Prior to the arrival of the Nation of Islam Security force, these apartment communities had been the inspiration for movies like New Jack City due to their reputation for being home to open air illegal drug markets and the criminal activity that resulted from them. Once the Nation of Islam established a presence in these communities; they became veritable oases of peace and safety for the poor and struggling people who lived there. The Nation of Islam's heroic work in crime ridden areas is well-documented. Former Housing and Urban Development chairman Henry Cisneros told the Congress:

> "we have conducted over 1,000 interviews of residents and management, and they illustrate that these security guards have been effective in transforming many drug-ridden properties into places which are now safe and peaceful…. Almost all the residents interviewed lauded the jobs that the reviewed firms have done and asked that the contracts not be terminated."

The persecution of the Nation of Islam by Jewish groups throughout our history is what Wilker and Huffnagle seek to remind us of. Wilker and Huffnagle are of the same playbook as Steven Freeman of the ADL who promised in 1994 punish any and all celebrities, organizations and universities who give a platform to Minister Farrakhan and the Nation of Islam.

And despite the carefully worded threat that if we continue to follow Farrakhan, we will "take the fall for echoing Farrakhan's message," the Black community is beginning to close ranks around the Honorable Minister Louis Farrakhan. In their article they note that Nick Cannon has not repudiated Minister Farrakhan, though he has apologized for words he spoke that offended these Jewish organizations. And recently Black Twitter has sided with the Honorable Minister Louis Farrakhan, by calling out the Wiesenthal Center and ADL for being silent on the killing of Breonna Taylor, but conspiring to get Nick Cannon fired from Viacom for merely speaking words. In a "wisdom of the crowd" moment their lament is 'how could a man suffer more from the words that he spoke than killers suffer from the actions that they took that resulted in the taking of the life of an innocent woman?'

Wilker and Huffnagle should go back and study the scriptures, especially the Torah. For Minister Farrakhan could not have withstood the powerful opposition of the Jewish community all these years if he was not a man that Allah (God) is protecting. And the same protection that Allah (God) has given to Minister Farrakhan, he extends to all who defend and help him in his messianic work.

For most surely Wilker and Huffnagle's article sounds like the sentiments expressed by Pharaoh, whom the Holy Qur'an records as threatening to punish his "enchanters" for believing in the God of Moses and Aaron. Surah 7:123-124 states:

> "Pharaoh said: You believe in Him before I give you permission! ...I shall certainly cut off your hands and your feet on opposites sides, then I shall crucify you all together!"

And it is the Nation of Islam and its supporters who are resolved today in the modern era like the "enchanters" were resolved in the Holy Qur'an, to be unafraid of Pharaoh's threats and said

> "There is no hurt (in what you threaten us with). For surely to our (true and everlasting) Lord we are bound to return."-Holy Qur'an 26:50

An Open Letter to Neal Steinberg: "Our Love for The Minister Shall Not Be Mocked!"

Once again Neal Steinberg appears in the Chicago Sun Times to push his false narrative of anti-Black vitriol. He is angry with Black America because we love Minister Farrakhan.

I am not surprised. The members of the oppressor's class within a society never approve of the liberator of those whom they oppress. In other words, why would the slave master approve of the liberator of his slaves? In the history of American society, there were enormous fortunes made as a result of the enslavement and oppression of Black people. Wealth and a rapid rise to global prominence, on the world stage of nation-states, accrued to the ruling class of whites in America as a direct result of her maintaining the dubious "peculiar institution" of chattel slavery.

Mr. Steinberg reveals just how ensconced he is in the oppressor's worldview, within his recent rant against the Honorable Minister Louis Farrakhan. And at no time has he ever cited or documented where Minister Farrakhan's statements have been proven to be false. Instead, he toes the line of what is becoming a popular cottage industry of "anti-Farrakhanism," by applying a pejorative label and false characterization to the Minister's statements without ever pointing out to his readers just where Minister Farrakhan is false. He instead makes an emotional appeal and resorts to ad hominem attacks to prove his worthiness as a bona fide "Farrakhan Hater."

But I want Mr. Steinberg to know that his opinions of Minister Farrakhan are worthless. To refer to our beloved Minister as "a toothless old lizard" is to offend millions of us who live in Black America. To reduce our sincere love of Minister Farrakhan to what you describe as a "low rent naughty pleasure" is to insult the entire Black community, not just in Chicago, but throughout all of America. Your insulting and offensive language against Minister Farrakhan and the Black community rises to the level of that which offends Allah (God). Because the Minister is the anointed servant of Allah (God) and the Black people of America are a people Allah (God) has targeted for salvation and restoration. You cannot stand in opposition to either today and enjoy the favor of Allah (God).

Mr. Steinberg, we love Minister Farrakhan because is the strongest leader we have in Black America. Consider what even Minister Farrakhan's critics have concluded as to his peerless role in the Black community over the past 40 years:

National Review Magazine:

> "To a great extent, in other words, Farrakhan now is the black leadership—the cutting edge, the storm center, the presence against which others are measured."

Abraham Foxman:

> "**The only leadership** that now exists in that community"—the "African American community"— "is Louis Farrakhan. Farrakhan can assemble 20,000 people several times a year…"

Professor Michael Eric Dyson:

> "For the first time in African American history; a non-Christian leader is a significant, if not **the significant leader** within Black America."

Author Julius Lester:

> "The appearance of Louis Farrakhan at Madison Square Garden on October 7 demonstrated, without doubt, that **he is now America's preeminent black leader**."

Professor Mattias Gardell:

> "**Farrakhan is able to attract larger audiences than any other black spokesperson**: 35,000 people showed up at Madison Square Garden, New York; 17,000 in Los Angeles; 26,000 in Detroit; 19,000 and then 15,000 in Atlanta; 15,000 in Chicago; 21,000 at Jacob Javits Center in New York, and 10,000 in Baltimore."

We love the Minister because he has been the leading defender of the character and innate goodness of Black people in America and around the world. Professor Andre C. Willis said it best when he said:

> "There is simply no Black person in the world that has — over so many years — been as consistent, as unrestricted, and as forthright in defending the humanity of Black people throughout the world against its attackers."

We love the Minister because he has been kind and loving towards us. Consider the words of Henry Louis Gates as he described what legendary scholar C. Eric Lincoln said of our beloved Minister:

> "Certainly, the Farrakhan I met was a model of civility and courtesy. I was reminded of C. Eric Lincoln's account of the last couple of visits he paid to Farrakhan at his home: "Louis insisted on getting down on his hands and knees on the floor to take my shoes off. You know, I'm overweight, and it's a difficult task to get shoes and socks off. And so, Louis said, 'I will do that.' And I said, "No, no.' And Louis said, 'No, I want to do it.' He took my shoes off and rubbed my feet to get the blood circulating."

We love the Minister because he has dared to teach us the hidden truths; the uncomfortable truths. He has been a guide to us, and when we followed his divine guidance, it has saved our lives and the lives of our children. West coast journalist Fahiza Alim wrote of the Minister:

> "Moreover, marijuana, "drop out," and "free love" were the buzzwords of my generation. The Beatles, Jimi Hendrix, Sly and the Family Stone, our Pied Pipers of modernity, lured us into a dark and swirling hole of hedonism. And Farrakhan, espousing the teachings of Elijah Muhammad, brought me out of the tailspin. Until that point, I had been taking birth control pills to keep from getting pregnant. But after listening to Louis Farrakhan speak about how potent a drug must be to be capable of shutting down one of nature's powerful biological functions-that of reproducing itself-I stopped.
> It took me another 2 years to ovulate or produce eggs again. And some years later, the pharmaceutical companies revealed that we had been guinea pigs and the pills prescribed to some young women were about 10 times more potent than they should have been.
> "You are poisoning yourself," Farrakhan has said. "Why kill the fruit of your womb and prevent maybe another great Black Leader from being born? Hasn't Pharaoh killed enough of our children?" I am glad I heard him, I stopped taking the pill. And now I am the proud mother of 4 children: a daughter and 3 sons."

We love the Minister because he has been a hero to us; he is our champion. Famed Law Professor Derrick Bell said of the Minister:

> "I see Louis Farrakhan as a great hero for the people. I don't agree with everything he says, and some of his tactics, but hell, I don't agree with everything anybody says."

We love the Minister because he is bold enough to speak out loud and on the mountain top, what we all think and feel within our private thoughts. Pulitzer Prize Winner William Raspberry put it this way:

> "Farrakhan says what so many black people believe but have learned not to say in public: for instance, that Jews wield tremendous influence in the news and entertainment media... Nor do blacks doubt the disproportionate influence of Jews on American foreign policy, particularly with regard to political and economic support of Israel. But we also know that to say these things is to be accused of anti-Semitism. That's why blacks can cheer when Farrakhan says them, even in gross overstatement."

Mr. Steinberg, I could go on and on. But I want to publicly educate you and to condemn your vile characterization of the Black community's love for a man whom we should love. For us not to love Minister Farrakhan would anger the God that blessed the womb of his cherished mother to serve as the portal of his entry into the world. To not love Minister Farrakhan would constitute a grave sin on our part. Our love of the Minister is not only justified, it is sanctified! And though you condemn us for loving a man whom you hate, I am happy to report that we have found that not only do we love Minister Farrakhan, he has demonstrated over and over again, he loves us to. Scholar, Professor and Chicago journalist Don Wycliff noted:

> "All his hatreds aside, one thing is clear about Farrakhan: He loves black people. He loves them so much that he has made himself hated by virtually every other group in this nation to prove his love for blacks. He loves them so much that he will criticize them as no white person and dam few black people could. Indeed, he boasted about that in his overlong (but far more coherent than most critics gave it credit for being) speech at the Million Man March. "I point out the evils of black people like no other leader does," Farrakhan declared, "but my people don't call me anti-black, because they know I must love them in order to point out what's wrong so we can get it right to come back into the favor of God."

Imam Michael Saahir Wrong on Minister Farrakhan...again!

"And those who believe say: Why is not a chapter revealed? But when a decisive chapter is revealed, and fighting is mentioned therein, thou seest those in whose hearts is a disease look to thee with the look of one fainting at death. So, woe to them!"

-Holy Qur'an Surah 47 Ayat 20

An Indianapolis Imam has written an open letter to the Honorable Minister Louis Farrakhan. His letter was penned to express an unnecessary concern that the Minister's bold and inspired message, delivered in Miami, Florida recently, was a call for a race war. I would like to address him, his concerns and some general misconceptions regarding the history of the Most Honorable Elijah Muhammad and the Honorable Minister Farrakhan.

The imam's concerns are unnecessary for several reasons.

It should first of all be established that the Imam is wrong for claiming that the Most Honorable Elijah Muhammad never took a theme of "Justice or Else". The theme "Justice or Else" was boldly emblazoned atop the inaugural issue of the Nation of Islam's revolutionary news organ the Muhammad Speaks newspaper in October 1961.

Secondly, all the history of the Nation of Islam both prior to and post 1975 is indicative of the Nation of Islam's role within American society as a self-respecting, law-abiding peaceful people. Prior to the departure of the Most Honorable Elijah Muhammad in 1975 various law enforcement agencies went on record to document how much of a valued resource the Nation of Islam was in their respective cities.

Commendations

"One thing I can say-where ever Muslims go, crime goes down. We policemen are always happy to have them in a community; it makes our job that much easier." **-Chicago Deputy Police Superintendent Sam Nolan (January 1974)**

"As a large group of people, the Muslims tend to be law abiding and seem to have a rehabilitating influence in the community." - **Thomas W. Chochee, Police Chief Compton California**

"Un-Smiting The Shepherd" -41

(February 1974)

"Addicts must be treated as persons and not statistics, and to the Harlem State Senator that means therapy, rehabilitation and employment. He said that the State chief executive could learn a lesson from what the Nation of Islam has done to remold ex-drug addicts by giving them a sense of pride in self and kind."-**NY State Senator from Harlem Sidney Von Luther (March 9, 1973)**

"The Muslims have done more to rehabilitate narcotics addicts than any corrective agency in the country."-**NY State Senator Basil Patterson from Harlem at the National Society of Afro-American Society of Policemen's tribute to the Nation of Islam (July 5, 1969)**

Post 1975 Minister Farrakhan's message has been bold and challenging to the white elite power structure. All in that hierarchy of power, wealth and influence have deemed him to be a threat. Yet the record is clear. Just like his spiritual father, the Most Honorable Elijah Muhammad, Minister Farrakhan has been a rebuilder, a restorer and a peacemaker.

Most notable in this area of establishing and maintaining peace in the society, is the formation of an unarmed protection and security apparatus that was affectionately dubbed "The Dopebusters." The Dopebusters or as they were officially known – NOI Security Agency, began in 1988 in Mayfair Mansion public housing apartments in Washington, D.C. Because of their success in eliminating drug crime in the areas they patrolled, their legend spread causing them to eventually broaden their operations into many major cities throughout America.

When Jewish pressure intervened to remove Minister Farrakhan's peace forces, it became necessary for congressional hearings to take place. During those hearings Housing and Urban Development (HUD) director Henry Cisneros made the following commentary about the "Dopebusters."

*"since the security firms first began their work in 1988 and throughout the review we have undertaken in this instance, there have been no complaints filed against these firms regarding any inappropriate religious activities. In fact, we have conducted **over 1,000 interviews of residents and management, and they illustrate that these security guards have been effective in***

transforming many drug-ridden properties into places which are now safe and peaceful."

Cisneros' weighty testimony as the leader of a division of the United States federal government mitigates against any concerns over Minister Farrakhan and his followers being associated with acts of violence. Director Cisneros went on to push back against the notion being promoted by U.S. Representative Peter T. King of New York that for the federal government to do business with Minister Farrakhan's followers was equivalent to doing business with a hate group. According to Cisneros:

"The FBI Domestic Terrorism Unit does maintain an internal list of groups known to have committed terrorist acts, which is at times used as an indicator of hate groups or hate crimes. Organizations such as the Aryan Nation are on that list. **The Nation of Islam is not**. *In addition, in the last 5 years, the United States prosecuted more than 50 criminal actions against members of so-called hate groups, alleging violations of civil rights. Although these hate crimes prosecutions have involved members of the Ku Klux Klan, the Aryan Nation, and skinheads,* **none of the actions have involved members of the Nation of Islam. This is a point of law, a definable, observable point of fact.***"*

Moreover, were we to believe that Minister Farrakhan would be even capable of calling for a race war; it would need to be based on the Minister having a history of violence against other races. And this is quite frankly laughable. Even with the controversial relationship that Minister Farrakhan has with members of the Jewish community there has never ever been so much as a bloody nose produced as a result. Jewish rabbi Bruce Khan noted that any fear of physical violence coming as a result of Minister Farrakhan is an unnecessary concern. Rabbi Khan attended the Million Man March. He wrote afterwards that, **"the people who listen to him [Minister Farrakhan] do not go chasing down Jews, or gays or Whites or Koreans to beat them and murder them... They are sufferers who know how tough it is to get a fair shake as Black people. They want that to change. They hear in Minister Farrakhan's words inspiration and instructions to begin to bring about that change. That is the message on which he focuses and on which they focus. That is not the message on which the media focuses."**

I would ask Imam Saahir, who is a brother that I have great

respect for, to review in totality the Minister's message in Miami as well as a more thorough study of the Minister's history. For I believe that this would help him to have a greater appreciation for the harmony and closeness of Minister Farrakhan's work to that of the Most Honorable Elijah Muhammad. It is wrong for Imam Saahir to lift the history of the Most Honorable Elijah Muhammad in a way that opposes Minister Farrakhan. For years various members of the Sunni community have condemned Minister Farrakhan for his promotion of the teachings of the Most Honorable Elijah Muhammad. They have essentially said "get rid of Elijah and get with the Qur'an." Now when the Minister invokes the Holy Qur'an to guide and pastor to the suffering mass of Black victims of injustice, Imam Saahir inserts a distorted view of the Hon. Elijah Muhammad to "correct" the Minister.

This is wrong and offensive!

The world knows that there has been no one more committed to the teachings of the Most Honorable Elijah Muhammad since his departure in 1975 than Minister Farrakhan. He is THE source for any who sincerely want to learn just what Elijah Muhammad and the Nation of Islam are all about. For when you look at Minister Farrakhan, you are looking at not just a theoretician but one whose theoretical understanding of his teacher's message has been refined through his courageous practice and implementation of that message. Being both theoretician and practitioner, Minister Farrakhan is guided by more than what may be written down in books or articles. For ever since he stood to rebuild the Nation of Islam in 1977, he has traveled the path blazed for him by the Most Honorable Elijah Muhammad. And this has furnished the Minister with an unmatched insight into his teacher's words, actions and programs. If you want to know Elijah Muhammad you must inquire of Minister Louis Farrakhan. To do otherwise is to accrue a sterile, academic and incomplete portrait of a man that in over 80 years, the academy has failed to understand.

Being the best student of the Most Honorable Elijah Muhammad, Minister Farrakhan is often misunderstood just as his teacher was many years ago. Imam Saahir's concern over the Minister calling for a race based indiscriminate retaliation against white people is unnecessary. His misunderstanding and misinterpretation of the Minister is similar to those who may have misinterpreted the Most Honorable Elijah Muhammad in some of his bold prophetic utterances during his historic Uline Arena address in 1959.

No one in their right mind would ever say that Elijah Muhammad was suicidal. Yet his words in the Uline arena address might be misinterpreted in a way that makes one think he was urging his audience towards a mass suicide. His comments appear in his book *The Fall of America* and in *Message to the Blackman in America*.

On page 36 of Message to The Blackman in America he writes:

"If a million of us throw ourselves in the fire for the benefit of the 20 million, the loss would be small compared to the great gain our people will make as a result of that sacrifice. Hundreds of thousands of Muslims gave their lives in Pakistan to get their nation's independence. They were successful. The black men in Africa are fighting and dying today in unity for their independence. We sit here like pampered babies. We cannot even stand on the floor, not to mention taking a chance of crawling out of the door. We are too careful of shedding blood for ourselves. We are willing to shed all of it for the benefit of others."

This sounds like Mr. Muhammad is suggesting that a million Black people sacrifice themselves for the whole of the 20 million Blacks living in America. In his book the Fall of America he mentions that 10 million of us might just as well sacrifice ourselves to leave 10 million behind to enjoy the fruit of our sacrifice. In an elucidation of the aforementioned he goes on to say on page 8-9 of The Fall of America:

> "If you and I are deprived of justice, if the federal government will not punish our murderers and our rapers. I say to you. we must get together and find some way to punish them ourselves!"

I strongly encourage my brother Imam to read these words of the Most Honorable Elijah Muhammad and reconsider his position in the light of what I am sharing with him that proves the complete falsity of his missive to the Honorable Minister Louis Farrakhan.

The words of the Most Honorable Elijah Muhammad as documented here perfectly harmonize with that of his best student – the Honorable Minister Louis Farrakhan recently in Miami, wherein he said: *"The Qur'an teaches persecution is worse than slaughter then it says, retaliation is prescribed in matters of the* slain. Retaliation is a prescription from God to calm the breasts of those whose children have been slain. **If the federal government will not intercede in our affairs, then we must rise up and kill those who kill us,** stalk them and let them feel the pain of death that we are feeling,"

I would encourage my brother Imam to bring his views into harmony with his teacher Imam Warithudeen Mohammed who delivered a beautiful khutbah on February 25, 2000 for our annual Saviours' Day convention. In that Khutbah he said of Minister Farrakhan that, **"When the brother Muslim stands upon the Qur'an, the last of the revealed books and the complete book for all times and all societies, and when he stands upon faith in Muhammad as God's last prophet and Messenger to all the worlds, mercy to all the worlds, we are to support him in that."** Surely Minister Farrakhan's words on retaliation are on the firm foundation of the Holy Qur'an.

Imam Mohammed's words point us to some of the great Islamic principles of brotherhood. Prophet Muhammad (saw/pbuh) is reported by Abu Hurairah to have said **"Do not help Shaitan against your brother."** This open letter to Minister Farrakhan goes against this principle because Imam Saahir could have requested to meet with the Minister in private to discuss his points of disagreements with his words in Miami. This calls to mind the words of the great Imam Siraj Wahajj about the importance of Muslim unity and the value of Minister Farrakhan. On September 21, 2008 Imam Siraj told the Final Call Newspaper that, **"Minister Farrakhan holds the key to the development of (Islam) in this country**—so we're going to talk about where we go from here, let us now continue the process so that we can move even further on toward the development of Islam in America **because the attack is against Islam and they don't ask you the question (are you) Sunni or Shiite, (are) you with the Nation (of Islam) or what? No. We have to recognize that the enemies of Islam are united against us,"**

Despite my respect for Imam Saahir's, book titled *The Honorable Elijah Muhammad: The Man Behind the Men*, I acknowledge that he is developing a bad track record of openly criticizing the leadership of the Honorable Minister Louis Farrakhan.

On December 13, 2008 he penned a very mean-spirited open letter to Minister Farrakhan titled *Thanks, but No Thanks*. In that letter

Imam Saahir wrongly attributed a motive to Minister Farrakhan of trying to interfere with Imam Mohammed's community after his passing. You reacted quite negatively to the Muslim Journal's interview with the Minister. Imam Saahir took time to condemn core Nation of Islam belief's and in an arrogant self-aggrandizing stroke wrote:

> "...don't be surprised if you, Minister Farrakhan may have to sit under the feet of some of Imam Mohammed's students before you may qualify to approach us in the manner that you are trying to pursue in this interview. Imam Mohammed has taught his students well, very well."

Such words on the part of Imam Saahir are unbecoming of a man in his position. The humility of Minister Farrakhan is such that he will accept truth regardless of the person sharing it. He has said that every man or woman that he meets can teach him something that he doesn't know. But to arrogantly suggest that he is the Minister's superior is unintelligent and is a claim that easily evaporates before the facts of history.

No. Imam Saahir was wrong on Minister Farrakhan in 2008 and he is wrong in 2015. His history and pattern of public condemnation of Minister Farrakhan undermines the work of Imam Warithudeen Mohammed in reconciling and unifying with Minister Farrakhan. Why would he want to help the Shaitan in furthering the divide among the Muslim ummah? One wonders that he should find a better use of his time in responding to issues such as the New York Times article condemning Islam as a "religion of rape." That is a more worthwhile cause to occupy Imam Saahir's attention. Uniting with Minister Farrakhan to combat the rising tide of Islamophobia in America would be wiser since such propaganda negatively impacts all of the diverse communities of Muslims in America.

But instead Imam Saahir has rushed to be at the forefront joining in with the propagandists in criticizing a man whom he refers to as his Muslim brother. This is unnecessary, unwise and antithetical to the noble principles of brotherhood as espoused by the religion of Islam.

"Hey, Didn't Y'all Kill Malcolm?"

May 19th is a very significant date in Black History, for it is the birth anniversary of Minister Malcolm X (el-hajj Malik Shabazz). Brother Minister Malcolm became a strong leader of within the Black community and a strong student and helper of the Most Honorable Elijah Muhammad.

His tragic assassination has created an emotional and psychological wound that has existed within the Black community for many years. And the most striking characteristic of this wound involves the propaganda that has been circulated far and wide that blames the Nation of Islam for the assassination of Malcolm X. It is striking because Malcolm X is a fruit from the tree of the Honorable Elijah Muhammad and the Nation of Islam. So, to make millions of folks within the Black community to feel the Nation of Islam killed Malcolm X is to cause those millions to stay away from the Nation of Islam. And as a result, the benefit that Malcolm gained from the Nation-which is that of personal transformation and real-world exaltation- is denied all who the propaganda deceives into refusing to drink from the well of wisdom and truth that Malcolm X drank from; the well of the Hon. Elijah Muhammad.

In the early days, of this 55-year-old controversy, the Most Honorable Elijah Muhammad was blamed. But since Allah (God) caused the Honorable Minister Louis Farrakhan to arise and rebuild the Nation of Islam, Minister Farrakhan's name has been thrown into the mud. And nowadays many who are uninformed and have been misinformed, blame Minister Farrakhan for the assassination of Malcolm X.

As a student of Minister Farrakhan's ministry class and a member of his research team my work and study has taken me to many places. And often I am invited as a guest speaker and lecturer at mosques, churches, schools, community centers, and media. And it has been my experience that no matter what the subject or topic we have prepared to address, I am invariably asked some variation of the question "Hey but, didn't yall kill Malcolm?"

This question especially comes up when I am blessed to speak to audiences of young people.

So, in order to respond properly and truthfully, we spent several years researching the subject of the assassination of Malcolm X. And we are now happy to publish our findings. And within the information that we have found are powerful and profound hidden truths that serve as definitive vindication of the Honorable Elijah Muhammad, the Honorable Minister Louis Farrakhan and the Nation of Islam.

Some of the many fascinating facts and hidden truths we found included the lessons that all within the Black community should learn about how propaganda and misinformation have become weapons used by high powered governmental agencies like the FBI, CIA and Homeland Security. These divisions of the federal government use media sources to target strong Black leaders and organization for the purpose of neutralizing the positive effects of said leaders and organizations among the suffering masses of Black America.

Malcolm stated profoundly and accurately the following:

> "When I am dead... He [the white man] will make use of me dead, as he has made use of me alive, as a convenient symbol..."

In my research, I learned that Malcolm X was loathed and despised by the media, the American government and Jewish groups like the Anti-Defamation League of B'nai B'rith. And nearly all public obituaries found in major mainstream newspapers condemned Brother Minister Malcolm referring to him, as did the Los Angeles Times did on February 22, 1965 when it published that:

> "For a dozen years the name Malcolm X had been almost synonymous with hatred of the white race...After the break [from Elijah Muhammad], he made it clear he still hated whites, whom he called "white devils."

Yet the image of Malcolm X, some 30 years after his assassination, was used to decorate a U.S. postage stamp. This is difficult to understand unless we consider that a sanitized version of Malcolm X was reintroduced into the public sphere at a strategic time to coincide with the rise of the rebuilt Nation of Islam and the Honorable Minister Louis Farrakhan.

It is clear that the ideas that Malcolm X remained wedded to throughout his life, those being primarily Black Nationalism and Islam, remain issues that the federal government consider subversive and anti-American. Yet a government sponsored, media driven romantic portrait of Minister Malcolm X has been widely circulated. However, the fact that Malcolm's ideas are still hated and opposed by the powerful forces that rule America makes us to know that the professed mainstream love of Malcolm is part of a propaganda strategy. The propaganda strategy has been aimed at de-magnetizing the most popular Black leader of the past 40 years-Minister Louis Farrakhan.

In this new book, the first published book in 55 years to vindicate the Nation of Islam in the case of the assassination of Malcolm X, we discuss in detail the plot to "resurrect Malcolm X to bury Minister Farrakhan." And this was primarily done through weak, yet widespread, efforts to blame Minister Farrakhan for Malcolm's assassination.

We learned so much in our research. Our findings document the innocence not only of the Honorable Minister Louis Farrakhan, but also the initial target of the propaganda campaign, his teacher, the eternal leader of the Nation of Islam, the Most Honorable Elijah Muhammad.

An important section is devoted to unraveling and exposing the slander against the Most Honorable Elijah Muhammad and his domestic life. This slander, that evaporates when closely examined and weighed against facts, is thoroughly discussed and debunked within the presentation of our research.

The weight of more than 400 sources is brought to bear upon the important task of myth-busting the propaganda aimed at destroying Black America's most tangible and salvific hope, which is the Nation of Islam.

The reader will get an opportunity for the first time, to review the testimonies of Minister Malcolm's inner-circle. These courageous brothers and sisters, his helpers in establishing the OAAU and Muslim Mosque Inc., go on the record in their insistence that the Nation of Islam is innocent of Minister Malcolm's assassination. In my personal interview with Malcolm's secretary Sister Sarah Mitchell, she reiterated much of what she wrote many years ago in her manuscript that discusses her work with Malcolm X called "Shepherd of the Black Sheep." In this book we present her words that revealed that the day of Malcolm's assassination he had planned to take back the accusations made against the Nation of Islam that they were seeking to take his life. According to Ms. Mitchell:

"During his final hours, Malcolm spoke of plans for explaining to the general public how hasty and mistaken he had been in accusing Black Muslims of bombing his home. He said, "You won't find a single instance where Muslim men ever moved to attack women and children. I know their tactics and their limitations. And I' m telling you things happening to me these past weeks go beyond the realm of the Muslims." Malcolm was convinced that a conspired maneuver was already in motion whereby, if anything happened to him, Elijah and his organization would be blamed or vice-versa."

Of an important note from the perspective of historical and contemporary issues, is our presentation of the role of anti-Semitism in the assassination of Malcolm X. Today Minister Farrakhan is pejoratively dubbed as the leading Black anti-Semite. In the 1960s, the Anti-Defamation League of B'Nai B'rith placed that label on Malcolm X. In this book, I discus the role this dubious distinction played in Brother Minister Malcolm's assassination; and in so doing some previously hidden hands are exposed.

I strongly encourage those who have an interest in the assassination of Brother Minister Malcolm X to consider what we have been blessed by Allah to research and present to the world. An article is not space enough to overview the entire 326-page book. But perhaps this thumbnail sketch of its contents may inspire the reader to add this important work to your personal home library.

This book is available on our website www.researchminister.com.

Be Careful, You Might Be an Anti-Semite If...
The Plot to Link Minister Farrakhan with Recent Violent Attacks & The Absurd Markers of Black Anti-Semitism

I recently read the ignominious[1] article published by the Jewish Press.Com. It republished blogger Vic Rosenthal's astonishingly outrageous piece that attempted to associate the Honorable Minister Louis Farrakhan and other Black activists with a recent series of violent attacks on members of New York's Jewish community. What Mr. Rosenthal has written is nothing more than a propaganda piece aimed at continuing to malign Minister Farrakhan and the cadre of young leaders who are awakening to commit their courage and energy in the struggle for liberation.

Rosenthal is a part of the absurdity that has become associated with the irrational charge of anti-Semitism. Let's examine briefly why Rosenthal is wrong about Minister Farrakhan.

First of all, there have been various groups among the Orthodox Jewish community-the same community that has been attacked-that have come to the defense of Minister Farrakhan over the years. They admire him and have studied him through the lens of scripture; some have studied the Minister's life and have drawn relevant parallels between the Jewish expectations of the Messiah and the life of Minister Louis Farrakhan. Orthodox Jewish Group Neturei Karta came to the defense of Minister Farrakhan. They responded to the character assassination campaign against the Minister Farrakhan, wherein it was falsely claimed that he called Judaism a "gutter religion." Reacting to this calumny Neturei Karta wrote in defense of Minister Farrakhan the following:

> "The media widely reported that the Minister had referred to Judaism as a 'gutter religion.' This error (or distortion) was deeply troubling to the Nation of Islam. The reason was that in Minister Farrakhan's vocabulary the phrase 'dirty religion' has a particular meaning. It referred to adherents of a faith who sinned against the tenets of that faith. The 'dirty religion' is the distorted faith which emerges from its

---

[1] "characterized by or bringing on ignominy; shameful; dishonorable; disgraceful; contemptible; despicable; degrading; humiliating ""Definition of Ignominious," Collinsdictionary.com (HarperCollins Publishers Ltd, January 12, 2020), https://www.collinsdictionary.com/us/dictionary/english/ignominious.

52-STUDENTS OF FARRAKHAN

manipulation by hypocrites or sinners.... The use of 'dirty religion' in the Minister's lexicon could have been discovered by any researcher interested in generating light instead of heat," the statement reads.[2]

Moreover, Rabbi Bruce Kahn has adeptly noted the complete absence of violence resulting from the ministry of the Honorable Minister Louis Farrakhan. According to Rabbi Kahn:

> "It seems clear to me that despite what I consider to be the horrifying insults that have issued from the Minister, the people who listen to him do not go chasing down Jews, or gays or Whites or Koreans to beat them and murder them. They do not do that for two reasons:
> First, he warns them against such violent behavior. Second, these verbal onslaughts do not constitute the main thrust of his message. As unacceptable as they are, they are also tangential. His listeners know that. They are sufferers who know how tough it is to get a fair shake as Black people. They want that to change. They hear in Minister Farrakhan's words inspiration and instructions to begin to bring about that change. That is the message on which he focuses and on which they focus. That is not the message on which the media focuses."[3]

Rosenthal is guilty of an old trick and stratagem. What his piece attempts to do, is what was done to Malcolm X in 1964. Malcolm, had been dubbed an anti-Semite by the ADL (Ant-Defamation League of B'nai B'rith) and his preaching against the economic exploitation of Black people in Harlem was being blamed for violence. The May 9, 1964 edition of the Amsterdam News published the following:

> "The District Attorney of Queens County attempted this week to link the speeches of Muslim leader Malcolm X with the knife slaying of a white woman merchant in Harlem. The woman's husband who was also knifed at the same time, is in critical condition, at Physicians Hospital in Jackson Heights, Queens. District Attorney Frank D. O'Connor in whose county both Malcolm X and the two stabbing victims live was asked to comment on reports published in the daily press that Negro youth have been roaming Harlem streets trained by

---

[2] "Exile and Redemption," Nkusa.org, 2020, https://www.nkusa.org/Books/Publications/exileandredemption.cfm.
[3] Rabbi Bruce Kahn and Chaplain William E. Alberts, "Mainstream Media as Guardian of Racial Hierarchy: A Study of the Threat Posed by Minister Louis Farrakhan and the Million Man March," 1996.

Muslims to attack white people."[4]

Malcolm X, Minister Farrakhan and the membership of the Nation of Isla have no record of committing violence against Jewish people or Jewish property. To do so would be against our religion. We are a community of believers in Allah (God) and are only permitted to fight when we are attacked. At the close of all of our mosque meetings, we adjourn those in attendance with a reminder to never be the aggressor. And the Holy Quran teaches us that Allah (God) does not love the aggressor.

As time passes, it becomes clear that a Black man or woman can be labeled an anti-Semite for the most absurd reasons. Consider some of the following quotes wherein the markers and predictors for anti-Semitism among Black people have been identified.

You might be an anti-Semite if you've got the "Wrong Preacher"
"An Orthodox rabbinical leader charged today that Negro clergymen have a "highly significant" role in the inception and spread of black anti-Semitism, either by failing to discourage it or by originating it and serving as a " core of racial antagonism." The charge was made by Rabbi Jacob J. Hecht, executive vice-president of the National Committee for the Furtherance of Jewish Education."[5]

You might be an anti-Semite if you're "Well Educated"
"Surprisingly, educated Blacks are among the most anti-Semitic of all groups in American society.... certain educated Blacks seem to have adopted Malcolm X's view that Jews are among the most substantial barriers to Black economic and political progress."[6]

You might be an anti-Semite if you're "Young"
"Dr. Charles Y. Glock, director of the University of California Survey Research Center, pointed to Negro youth as a problem facing those concerned with anti-Semitism. What is going on in the young Negro community, he noted, is a paradox that his survey team must study further. For, Contrary to the white community where anti-Semitism increases with age levels, the young Negro is more anti-Semitic than his

---

[4] "Seek To Link Malcolm X To Slayings In Harlem," New York Amsterdam News, May 9, 1964.
[5] "Rabbi Says Negro Clergy Have Significant Role In," Jewish Telegraph Agency Daily Bulletin Black Anti-Semitism, March 17, 1969.
[6] Reed D. Rubenstein, "Democrats Are Not Facing Up To Divisive Jackson Candidacy," Detroit Jewish News, October 7, 1987.

father and mother."[7]

You might be an anti-Semite if you're "Militant (Disciplined)"

"James Farmer, executive director of the Congress of Racial Equality, asserted this week that anti-Semitism among Negroes was increasing as one aspect of the militance of the Negro fight for civil rights."[8]

These extraordinary qualifications for anti-Semitism highlight the absurdity of the charge of anti-Semitism leveled against many in the Black community. For when we aspire to be "young, gifted and Black" it has nothing to do with anti-Semitism. When we pursue the goal of being "well-educated" it has nothing at all to do with anti-Semitism. When we visit our favorite church or mosque to hear our pastors and imams, the Jewish people are the furthest thing from our minds. And when we send our sons and daughters to military academies or instruct them to live a clean, sober disciplined life, it has nothing to do with wanting to harm Jews. We are simply aspiring to be our best selves and to maximize our God-given potential.

These published statements, when taken altogether might cause one to believe that anti-Semites are spiritual, well-educated, youthful and disciplined. If this is the case, then every Black household in America is a potentially anti-Semitic household. Because we all aspire to be spiritual, well-educated, youthful and disciplined; and we teach our children to be the same.

I say to Mr. Rosenthal, leave Minister Farrakhan alone and stop interfering with the widespread proliferation of his salvific ministry. We in the Black community love Him and we won't allow you to separate us from this man whom Allah (God) has given to us as a most magnificent gift.

---

[7] "Young Negro Anti-Semitism Pose Problem and Paradox," B'nai B'rith Messenger, November 5, 1965.
[8] "Negro Anti-Semitism Is Result of Growing Militancy," The Sentinel, June 20, 1963.

"Warrior Sperm": The Mischievous Subtext to the Farrakhan Women's March Controversy

> "For unto us a child is born, unto us a son is given: and the government shall be upon his shoulder: and his name shall be called Wonderful, Counsellor, The mighty God, The everlasting Father, The Prince of Peace. Of the increase of his government and peace there shall be no end, upon the throne of David, and upon his kingdom, to order it, and to establish it with judgment and with justice from henceforth even forever."
> -Isaiah 9:6-7

> "And he who overcomes and keeps My works until the end, to him I will give power over the nations – 'He shall rule them with a rod of iron; They shall be dashed to pieces like the potter's vessels' – as I also have received from my Father; and I will give him the morning star." -Revelation 2:26-28

Throughout the previous year of 2018, and with a continuing move into the year 2019, there has been a barrage of attacks against the noble name and reputation of the Honorable Minister Louis Farrakhan. The Final Call Newspaper, The Nation of Islam Research Group, The Executive Council of the Nation of Islam and The Student Ministry Class of the Nation of Islam have all found ourselves in a campaign to defend the truth. Specifically, we are engaged in a campaign to defend our beloved Minister; The Honorable Minister Louis Farrakhan. And we will not cease in our campaign! We sincerely love and appreciate our beloved Minister Farrakhan; we thank Allah (God) for him and all that he means to us; all that he has done for us. We also have a duty and owe a debt of gratitude to Allah (God) for bringing our beloved Minister Farrakhan to birth through the blessed womb of his mother and as the seed of his beloved father.

The duty of the believers to defend the truth is clear. Allah (God) states in the Holy Qur'an in Surah 21:18 the following command to fight falsehood with truth. This ayat is cited here from 2 English translations of the Holy Qur'an published by Muslim women:

"Nay! We hurl The Truth against falsehood so it prevails over it. That is when falsehood is that which vanishes away. And woe to you for what you allege." (Dr. Laleh Baktihar Translation)

Rather We hurl the truth against falsehood and it cuts right through it and it vanishes clean away! Woe without end for you for what you portray! (Aisha Abdurrahman Bewley Translation)

In fact, the Honorable Minister Louis Farrakhan has made a very public demand for a showdown between the Nation of Islam and our nefarious adversaries. He has challenged them to prove their charge that he is an anti-Semite! The Minister, and those of us as his students and disciples earnestly desire an opportunity for a public showdown and airing of the facts of the situation that we might "Hurl truth at falsehood" and prove the lies against our beloved Minister to be nothing more than propaganda designed to further harm the Black community through assassinating the character of its strongest leader and warrior.

I recently read where inside of Israel various sperm banks are placing a high priority on the sperm donations of Israeli soldiers. According to Haaretz magazine article written by Tsafi Saar on October 6, 2015 entitled **Demand for Israeli Combat Soldiers' Sperm Is on the Rise An increasing number of women are requesting that their sperm donor be an archetypal Israeli male. It has to be asked: How come?**

"But why on earth would a woman want the sperm to come from a donor who's a combat soldier? The demand for this type of sperm has grown recently, as reported on the Israeli Mako website. It's unlikely the reason is that these males have a healthy profile, so what's happening here? Since I fail to understand why, I turned to those who might be able to explain the phenomenon. Prof. Orna Sasson-Levy, head of the sociology department at Bar-Ilan University and a researcher of military and gender issues, believes that **"the combat soldier embodies a set of qualities that are perceived as befitting Israeli men: physical strength; determination; courage; dedication; commitment; discipline; and mental health. He's not just tall or successful, but encompasses many qualities combined. It's hyper-masculinity."**

In the Journal of Gender Studies, I read an article entitled **Falling in love with a [sperm] warrior: conscripting women's wombs to the dissemination of a religiopolitical ideology** by Ya'arit Bokek-Cohen. In it the author states:

"I was particularly interested in magazine articles that focused on sperm bank managers reporting a **higher-than-usual demand for sperm donated by men who are either presently, or were in the past, combat soldiers in the Israeli Defense Forces (IDF)**. Coincidently I talked with two young women who attend a course I teach on 'The Family in the Era of Change'. Both of them are registered at online dating websites, and they shared with me their impression, that since the beginning of the war on 8 July 2014, **more and more young men who sent them messages tended to highlight their combat status, either during their compulsory service or at present, as reserve soldiers**. In accordance with research findings that reveal sperm recipients' fantasies about marrying the donor, I propose that in the Israeli context, a modified version of the same phenomenon may, and heterosexual recipients' fantasies of marrying a strong and brave combat soldier can be fulfilled. It is a prevalent notion that **warriors possess personality traits such as assertiveness, decisiveness, consistency, and a willingness to sacrifice for others in general and for one's people in particular."**

This is fascinating research. And in my judgment, it cuts right to the heart of why vehement opposition was leveled against Tamika Mallory, Linda Sarsour, Carmen Perez and the Women's March, as they were pressured to repudiate Minister Farrakhan. This research suggests that Jewish women want to give birth to sons who will fight their adversaries and enemies. Consequently, Jewish groups don't want their enemies to be able to do the same. So, they have made Minister Farrakhan, a man who embodies all of the characteristics of a soldier and warrior, and his relationship to women's activists, a target for negative media and propaganda. Consider the following bombshell revelations!

According to RT.com's article from September 2, 2018 titled **Israel targeted Black Lives Matter in bid to counter support for BDS – censored documentary leak:**

"Exclusive footage from Al Jazeera's censored 'The Lobby-USA' documentary released by the Grayzone Project exposes some of these tactics. The long-awaited documentary's release has been stalled for almost a year due to political pressure. *"The major problem with Israel is with the young generation of the black community,"* Judith Varnai Shorer, Israeli consul general in Atlanta, explains in the footage, before going on to boast of a dinner she held with *"very important"* black community leaders whom she said can be part of Israel's *"activities.""*

That a foreign government has targeted a "minority" population inside of America as their main enemy is outrageous!

Minister Farrakhan's strong influence, coupled with the fact that he is so thoroughly interwoven within Black youth culture, is therefore seen as a major problem for the adversaries of the Black community, namely Jewish groups. They see in him the very characteristics that they want to see in their own sons. And so, they oppose the Minister out of fear that the women of the Black, Muslim, Hispanic and poor White communities will give birth to sons who have the Farrakhan heart and mind. They are hoping that when Allah (God) puts a period to the end of Minister Farrakhan's testament-which we pray will be many many many years into the future-that they won't have to worry about strong Black leadership, the kind that is unafraid to hold them accountable for the harm they have done to the Black community.

That Jewish women want to reproduce warriors and soldiers is also tied to their religious beliefs. The promised Messiah will be a warrior king who rules with a rod of iron. They do not believe in Jesus as the Messiah. They are awaiting the Messiah to come into the world to be their King. But unlike many who see the Messiah's return to be on a cloud, the Jewish belief is that the Messiah will enter the world through the womb of a Jewish mother. Rabbi Efraim Goldstein in **The Promised Child** stated that:

"It was the hope of every Jewish mother that her child might be the key to Israel's future. **"With the pain of labor came the comforting thought, "Maybe my child will fulfill God's promises to the nation. Maybe my boy will be Messiah."**

This Messianic hope of Jewish mothers reminds us of former FBI Director J. Edgar Hoover's campaign to identify the Messiah among Black Americans. Hoover put in his cross hairs, Malcolm X, Elijah Muhammad, Martin L. King Jr. and Stokely Carmichael. All of these men had in common that they were influenced by and "in league with" Elijah Muhammad.

Today, the Elijah Muhammad inspired Messiah among Black people is the Honorable Minister Louis Farrakhan; and Black America has been impregnated with the "warrior sperm" of his revolutionary ideas.

Courage to Speak What God Has Written: Farrakhan reminds us of the other side of God

The Final Call Newspaper has done a magnificent job in covering the epic and historic national tour of the Honorable Minister Louis Farrakhan as he crisscrosses the country preparing the Black community for the 20th Anniversary of the Million Man March. This 20th anniversary theme is "Justice or Else."

The Final Call has been an indispensable source for accurate coverage of the Minister's tour. Their work documents his victories over the propagandists who work to distort his message and keep the masses of the public from hearing the Minister's analysis and God-given guidance. The Final Call along with Minister Farrakhan's Twitter Army gives us visibility into how profoundly the Minister is impacting the masses. The John and Jane Q. Public of the Black community have taken to social media to express their approval of the Minister's message.

In fact, the popularity of Minister Farrakhan in social media offsets the mainstream media's policy of refusing to cover the Minister. This has been their strategy regarding the Minister ever since the overwhelming success of the original Million Man March in 1995. It was there that the media giants learned that even though they hated Minister Farrakhan, Black people loved him. They learned that to vilify Minister Farrakhan was to greater magnetize him among his own people. They concluded that both positive and negative coverage of the Minister only served to help his cause. They concluded to adopt a new policy which is to act as if Minister Farrakhan doesn't exist at all. It is the media's attempt to essentially bury the Minister while he is still alive. And this has indeed caused various persons who were used to following the Minister's work in the media to wonder if he is still alive.

Unfortunately for those whose desire it is to keep the Black community oppressed, deceived and corrupted, the Honorable Minister Louis Farrakhan is alive, strong and bolder than ever in his speaking truth to power.

I am writing this piece to address what I have witnessed in social media and the blogosphere concerning the Minister's recent message in the city of Miami Florida. There the Minister in his own powerful and inimitable way, drew from critical passages of scripture to minister and really offer pastoral care to the Black community during our time of suffering.

As a Minister, one must be skilled in accessing the relevant contents of the sacred books of God and religion for the purpose of the healing mental, spiritual, emotional and behavioral conditions of their congregations. It is a skill that often makes the work of the minister or pastor similar to that of a physician or pharmacist.

We study the word of God as it is found in the Bible and the Holy Qur'an. We study the condition of the people. And we pray and ask God for guidance in the applying of His word in an effective and meaningful way in the lives those we are called to serve. And often times we are amazed and surprised at how He guides us. Many times, He leads us to lift passages of scripture that are not popular. Yet as the Bible says in 1Timothy 3:16-17: "*All Scripture is God-breathed and is useful for teaching, rebuking, correcting and training in righteousness, so that the servant of God may be thoroughly equipped for every good work.*" And whereas professional ministers and pastors excel at this function of their calling, the Honorable Minister Louis Farrakhan has mastered this skill and ability.

At issue are the words spoken by the Minister in the passion of message in Miami wherein he stated:

> "Death is sweeter than to continue to live and bury our children while White folks give the killers hamburgers. Death is sweeter than watching us slaughter each other to the joy of a 400-year-old enemy. Death is sweeter. The Qur'an teaches persecution is worse than slaughter then it says, retaliation is prescribed in matters of the slain. Retaliation is a prescription from God to calm the breasts of those whose children have been slain. If the federal government will not intercede in our affairs, then we must rise up and kill those who kill us, stalk them and let them feel the pain of death that we are feeling,"

I have noticed that many white Twitter users and bloggers have sought to mislabel this as Farrakhan's call for a race war. Popular internet personalities Glenn Beck and Alex Jones have also propagandized the Minister's words in this way. Some bloggers are openly calling for the Minister to be arrested for inciting violence. Yet it is crystal clear that the Minister is not encouraging the Black community towards the posture of the aggressor. He is rightfully instructing us to be willing to defend our life to the fullest. He is really in this quote articulating the hidden message in the slogan "Black Lives Matter." He is saying that "Black Lives Matter" so much that we must be willing to defend "Black Life" even if it means killing those who are seeking to kill us.

He is saying what every gun owner and believer in the U.S. Constitution's Second Amendment believes in and practices. Numerous articles were written when President Barack Obama first came into office about how gun sales and ammunition sales were on the rise in the period just before he took office. The conservative community, which is largely white and rural, are the largest demographic of gun owners. Many have pledged to both kill and die to preserve their right to bear arms. The right to bear arms in America is considered by most to be a fundamental right that they are unwilling to even discuss doing away with despite the rise of gun related crimes.

The blog writers and Twitter users who have seized upon the Minister's words are both seeking to make mischief and simultaneously expressing what might be considered the "mind of Cain." I recall Minister Farrakhan teaching us once that our former slave masters and their offspring feared that one day they would have to answer for their role in the destruction of the American Black man and woman. They fear as Cain did when he slew Abel in the Bible. Cain's fear caused him to say in the Bible's Genesis 4:14, *"that every one that findeth me shall slay me."*

So, when Minister Farrakhan, a man who has proven that he has the magnetic appeal to cause millions of Black people to follow his directives, stands and says that "if you kill us, we will kill you," that age old fear is triggered. And the result is their move to demonized the Minister and call for his arrest and murder.

The Islamaphobes throughout the country have sought to highlight and make mischief with the Minister's invoking the passage of scripture from the Holy Qur'an on the subject of retaliation. The passage in its entirety comes from the longest Surah (Chapter) of the Holy Qur'an, Surah 2 wherein we read in verse 178-179:

> "O you who believe, retaliation is prescribed for you in the matter of the slain: the free for the free, and the slave for the slave, and the

female for the female. But if remission is made to one by his (aggrieved) brother, prosecution (for blood-wit) should be according to usage, and payment to him in a good manner. This is alleviation from your Lord and a mercy. Whoever exceeds the limit after this, will have a painful chastisement. And there is life for you in retaliation, O men of understanding, that you may guard yourselves."

The translator Maulana Muhammad Ali asks us to compare this to the Christian Bible in Leviticus 24:19-21 wherein it reads:

"Anyone who injures their neighbor is to be injured in the same manner: fracture for fracture, eye for eye, tooth for tooth. The one who has inflicted the injury must suffer the same injury. Whoever kills an animal must make restitution, but whoever kills a human being is to be put to death."

The translator makes note that the

"The Jewish law [found in the Bible] of retaliation is greatly modified in Islam, being limited only to cases of murder, while among the Jews it extended to all cases of grievous hurt. The words retaliation is prescribed for you in the matter of the slain, mean that the murderer should be put to death. After promulgating that law in general terms, the Qur'an proceeds to describe a particular case, for example, that if a free man is the murderer, he himself is to be slain; if a slave is the murderer, that slave is to be executed; if a woman murdered a man, it was she that was to be put to death. The pre-Islamic Arabs used in certain cases to insist, when the person killed was of noble descent, upon the execution of others besides the murderer; they were not content with the execution of the slave or the woman, if one of them happened to be the murderer. The Holy Qur'an abolished this custom. There may be circumstances which alleviate the guilt. In such cases the murderer may be made to pay a fine to the relatives of the murdered person. Such money is called diyat or blood-money. The reference to the alleviation of the guilt is plainly contained in the concluding words of the verse: This is an alleviation from your Lord."

The translator makes an important distinction between the Jewish law found in the Torah (Old Testament) and the Holy Qur'an. His note that the harsher law is to be found in the Jewish text reminds me of a similar observation made by University of Pennsylvania Professor Philip Jenkins.

Professor Jenkins article entitled *Dark Passages: Does the harsh language in the Koran explain Islamic violence? Don't answer till you've taken a look inside the Bible* was written for the Boston Globe in March of 2009. According to Professor Jenkins,

> "in terms of ordering violence and bloodshed, any simplistic claim about the superiority of the Bible to the Koran would be wildly wrong. In fact, the Bible overflows with "texts of terror," to borrow a phrase coined by the American theologian Phyllis Trible. The Bible contains far more verses praising or urging bloodshed than does the Koran, and biblical violence is often far more extreme, and marked by more indiscriminate savagery. The Koran often urges believers to fight, yet it also commands that enemies be shown mercy when they surrender. Some frightful portions of the Bible, by contrast, go much further in ordering the total extermination of enemies, of whole families and races - of men, women, and children, and even their livestock, with no quarter granted. One cherished Psalms 137 begins with the lovely line, "By the rivers of Babylon we sat and wept"; it ends by blessing anyone who would seize Babylon's infants and smash their skulls against the rocks."

The mischief involving the distortion of Minister Farrakhan's words in a part of the campaign to brand all Muslims as violent extremists and it is also a part of the campaign to demonize Black leaders that have not been approved of by the white powerful elite. Their out of context excerpting of the Minister's message is actually the way they have historically handled our beloved Minister. For there is not one of the blogs or Twitter users who point to the Minister's words in Miami offered to place his words within the context of his multi-themed 2 hours long speech. Had they done so, they would have allowed the reader or viewer to bounce the Minister's words on retaliation off of his comments regarding Black on Black crime and violence.

Thanks to The Final Call Newspaper, we have other salient and powerful component passages of the Minister's Miami message to consider. The Final Call's coverage of the Minister's Miami message included the following quote *"How can we charge others with the crime of killing us without due process and lying about it when we are killing each other? And we won't march on ourselves, nor will we even rise up to condemn ourselves for what we are doing to ourselves. And in the gangs when we kill we don't talk, so nobody is arrested and charged with murder and brought to what is called justice."*

If one were to compare and contrast both quotes, it would be clear that the Minister is not exempting Blacks who murder other Black people from the scripture's prescription of retaliation. And statistically since more Black people are murdered by other Black people it would seem as though the white community would laud the Minister's words on retaliation. Because if we are going to "kill those who kill us," we will end up killing quite an array of different killers, where the greater percentage would be the Black victimizers of other Black people.

Distortions, out of context quotes, omissions and out-right lies comprise the schedule of offenses in the long legacy of abuse that the Honorable Minister Louis Farrakhan has suffered from the media. In 1997 Unitarian Universalist the Rev. Dr. William E. Alberts of Boston Massachusetts authored a trailblazing critique of the media's handling of Minister Farrakhan that documents the mischief of some of America's major news organs in the coverage of Minister Farrakhan.

On page 29 of Rev. Alberts's report entitled **Mainstream media as guardian of racial hierarchy: A Study of the Threat Posed by Minister Louis Farrakhan and the Million Man March** we learn the collusion between the major newspapers and the Anti-Defamation League of B'Nai B'rith. This section of the report addresses the Jewish community's charges that Minister Farrakhan praised Adolph Hitler by calling him a "very great man."

The report cites a March 11, 1984 radio broadcast made by Minister Farrakhan that included the following commentary:

> "Here comes the Jews don't like Farrakhan, so they call me Hitler. Well, that's a good name. Hitler was a very great man. He wasn't great for me as a Black person, but he was a great German. Now I'm not proud of Hitler's evil against the Jewish people, but that's a matter of record. He rose Germany up from nothing. Well, in a sense you could say there's similarity in that we are rising our people up from nothing, but don't compare me with your wicked killers."

According to Rev. Alberts's report, the Minister's statement of Hitler being a "great" man is no different than when author William L. Shirer wrote in his book **The Rise and Fall of the Third Reich** "Adolph Hitler is probably the last of the great adventurer-conquerors in the tradition of Alexander, Caesar and Napoleon..."

Shirer was honored by Israel before his death in 1993.

Rev. Alberts also discusses the intentional editing of the Ministers' quote on Hitler by ADL 's Alan Schwartz who was at the time the ADL's assistant director or research. Schwartz's was challenged by Boston Globe writer David Nyhan when he found that their allegations against the Minister omitted 2 important sentences that the Minister stated that greatly help contextualize his comments regarding Hitler. In the ADL's re-publishing of the Minister's words they intentionally omitted the sentence

> "Now I'm not proud of Hitler's evil against the Jewish people," and "Don't compare me with your wicked killers."

This was done intentionally so that the ADL could label the Minister as an anti-Semite which, because of Jewish power and influence, would dog the Minister's trail for decades into the future.

This current episode of seeking to sensationalize an out of context quote from Minister Farrakhan is competing to be the new deceptive reporting that gives birth to the contemporary false characterization of the Honorable Minister Louis Farrakhan. As the millennial generation awakens to view Minister Farrakhan as a leader that they can follow, forces are at work to confine the Minister again in a prison of public opinion. These forces are working to undo the gains being made by the Minister's message among the young that have been greatly facilitated by seminal events over the last few months. Events such as The Breakfast Club interview, the Sway in The Morning Interview, The Big Boy Interview and the social media publishing of scores of photographs displaying young Hip Hop artists and Reality TV stars embracing the Minister have broadened his ever-increasing appeal.

As a closing thought on the Minister's words during this current controversy, I include the words of Jewish Rabbi Bruce E. Khan of Baltimore's Temple Shalom. He attended the Million Man March in 1995. And despite his obvious disagreements with the Minister's criticism of the Jewish community's relationship with the Black community, his introduction to Rev. Alberts's report offers a relevant defense of Minister Farrakhan in this current controversy. Rabbi Khan wrote:

> "There is only one Black American who could have pulled off the Million

Man March. Give him the credit he deserves for doing so. It was one of the single most positive events in the social history of our country. The people who were there attended for several reasons, not all of which had to do with Minister Farrakhan. But without him the March would not have been envisioned nor would it have succeeded. It did succeed. If it did nothing more than give a huge boost to the trampled upon ego of the Black American male, it succeeded. **It seems clear to me that despite what I consider to be the horrifying insults that have issued from the Minister, the people who listen to him do not go chasing down Jews, or gays or Whites or Koreans to beat them and murder them. They do not do that for two reasons: First, he warns them against such violent behavior. Second, these verbal onslaughts do not constitute the main thrust of his message. As unacceptable as they are, they are also tangential. His listeners know that. They are sufferers who know how tough it is to get a fair shake as Black people. They want that to change. They hear in Minister Farrakhan's words inspiration and instructions to begin to bring about that change. That is the message on which he focuses and on which they focus. That is not the message on which the media focuses."**

DIVINE PESTILENCE:
Did The Censorship of Minister Farrakhan Produce The Rise of COVID-19?

On July 4, 2020 the Honorable Minister Louis Farrakhan described the COVID-19 pandemic as a pestilence from heaven. The Minister stated:

> "Our iniquitous behavior is a pestilence on the earth so God answers with a pestilence. His anger is at a point where He has to punish the inhabitants of the earth for their iniquity. So, punishment from God's pestilence is to turn against you the things that you depend upon for your sustenance."

In studying the Minister's words, I have become acquainted with powerful Biblical scriptures that provide strong support for the Ministers' bold pronouncement. It is within the Bible's New Testament where I found the book of Romans, authored by the Apostle Paul. Paul's writings in Romans includes the following relevant verse of scripture:

> "For the wrath of God is revealed from heaven against all ungodliness and unrighteousness of men, who by their unrighteousness **suppress the truth**."-Romans 1:18 ESV

The Amplified Bible translates this verse with more detail when it presents it as:

> "For God's [holy] wrath and indignation are revealed from heaven against all ungodliness and unrighteousness of men, who **in their wickedness repress and hinder the truth and make it inoperative**." - Romans 1:18 AMPC

This is a verse of scripture that should be taken under serious consideration, especially by the leaders of the American government. Many in political leadership, whose positions in leadership are permitted as a result of the "consent of the governed" are now engaged in truth suppression. They are at this time engaged in extraordinary acts of censorship in order to manufacture the "consent of the governed", by denying the American public access to experts and scientists who disagree with the widespread use of COVID-19 vaccines.

This verse helps us to see that censorship, when it is an act of the suppression of the truth, is a sin that evokes the wrath of God!

Censorship in the form of the "no platform" strategy is currently being used against persons such as Dr. Joseph Mercola, Robert F. Kennedy Jr. and many others. In a report published by the newly formed CCDH (Center for Countering Digital Hate) a group that has been pejoratively dubbed as **The Disinformation Dozen**, has been targeted for censorship. This list is comprised of some of the top social media influencers who share valuable information and represent the millions of Americans that disagree with the vaccine and its related mandates.

CENSORSHIP OF TRUTH: NOI & SOCIAL MEDIA

Included within this list is a student of the Honorable Minister Louis Farrakhan, Brother Rizza Islam. The inclusion of a Nation of Islam member in the current campaign to censor those who are informing the public about the dangers of the COVID-19 vaccines raises larger issues related to both history and prophecy.

Brother Rizza has been a consistent and effective communicator of facts and evidence that is being omitted from mainstream media outlets. And even prior to the COVID-19 pandemic, he used his social media platforms to awaken the Black community to the dangers associated with the MMR vaccine, helping to publicize the CDC's own scientific evidence that the MMR vaccine lies at the root of the devastating rise of autism in Black boys.

As a fellow student of the Honorable Minister Louis Farrakhan, I can, in this instance, speak for all of the Minister's students by saying that that whatever good works that we have done is a credit to our teacher. Whatever we achieve is a result and a reflection of our teacher the Honorable Minister Louis Farrakhan. For we are unashamed to let the world know that Minister Farrakhan is our teacher. We understand what is recorded of Jesus in John 15:17-19 wherein it reads:

> "This is My command to you: Love one another. **If the world hates you, understand that it hated Me first**. If you were of the world, it would love you as its own. Instead, the world hates you, because you are not of the world, but I have chosen you out of the world."

We understand that Minister Farrakhan's critics and adversaries are ours also. We are honored by this fact.

For a number of years now there has existed the idea that Minister Farrakhan's influence within social media is problematic. This idea has been promoted by groups like the Anti-Defamation

League and those whom they influence. Brother Abdul Qiyam Muhammad, who serves as Minister Farrakhan's social media representative shared with me that since October of 2018, the Minister's social media accounts have been targeted for censorship. A snapshot of the sabotaging of Minister Farrakhan's social media presence includes the following:

- Netflix reneges on agreement to show Minister Farrakhan Music documentary
- May 2019 Minister Farrakhan's official Facebook Account banned
- May 2019 Minister Farrakhan's official Instagram Account banned
- July 2019 Twitter freezes Minister Farrakhan's official Twitter account
- January 2020 Twitter suspended Minister Farrakhan's account
- June 2020 Twitter reinstated Minister Farrakhan's account

In addition to Minister Farrakhan's account being the target of censorship, some of his most prominent students on social media have also been targeted:

- December 2018 Brother Ben X YouTube channel was terminated
- March 2021 Brother Abdul Qiyam YouTube channel was terminated
- March 2021 Brother Rizza Islam YouTube channel was terminated

During the 2021 Saviours' Day address Student Minister Ishmael Muhammad enumerated how the Nation of Islam has been censored and denied access to major platforms that others freely use to proliferate their ideas and messages.

- Nation of Islam official account is banned from Livestream
- Nation of Islam official account is banned from Vimeo
- Nation of Islam official account is banned from YouTube
- The Final Call official account is banned from YouTube
- The Final Call Store is banned from Shopify
- The Nation of Islam App is banned from Google Play store
- The Final Call Digital App is banned from Google Play store

In addition to these censorship tactics; there is also the "shadow-banning" of Minister Farrakhan's research team and various of his student ministers who are active in promoting his message within social media.

That the Nation of Islam is being censored in this modern digital age is no small thing. The Nation of Islam means a lot to Black America, and by extension, to all sincere truth-loving men and women of all races and ethnic backgrounds. Consider how the Nation of Islam's salvific effect on the Black community has been lauded for many years. Legendary Black writer James Baldwin said this:

> "Elijah Muhammad has been able to do what generations of welfare workers and committees and resolutions and reports and housing projects and playgrounds have failed to do: to heal and redeem drunkards and junkies, to convert people who have come out of prison and to keep them out, to make men chaste and women virtuous, and to invest both the male and the female with a pride and a serenity that hang about them like an unfailing light. He has done all these things, which our Christian church has spectacularly failed to do."

Professor Mattias Gardell noted:

> "Minister Farrakhan has a unique capability; he is able to reach deeply into the souls of black youths…is able to talk to them in a way that really makes them listen…this rapport enables Farrakhan to criticize and redirect destructive behavioral patterns."

The COVID-19 Pestilence as Allah's Response to Suppression of Truth

In thinking about what Paul wrote in Romans 1:18 on how God's wrath is revealed from heaven resulting from the wicked suppression of the truth, I see parallels between the COVID-19 pandemic and America's long history of the censorship of the truth. Paul's writing helps me to understand just why the Hon. Min. Louis Farrakhan was guided by Allah (God) to proclaim to the world that this pandemic is a result of Allah's (God's) wrath.

In thinking through this series of current events, I thought about a particular episode in the New Testament's record of the life of Jesus. According to the book of Luke, the following exchange took place between Jesus and the Pharisees, who wanted to silence the disciples of Jesus. The Pharisees had become annoyed by the widespread appeal of Jesus that was characterized by his disciples and followers' expressions of gratitude to God and their celebration of Jesus's teachings and miracles. In Luke 19:39-40 we read:

> "And some of the Pharisees called to Him from the crowd, "Teacher, rebuke Your disciples. But He answered and said to them, "I tell you that **if these should keep silent, the stones would immediately cry out.**"

The Pharisees desire to silence the disciples of Jesus in the book of Luke is analogous to the modern-day censorship of Minister Farrakhan and his students.

Jesus's answer however offers a rich insight into how Allah (God) might use nature to respond to the censorship of the truth and come to the defense of Jesus and the disciples. He said if the disciples are censored, the very rocks or stones that are found in nature will cry out in praise of Jesus!

In other words, Jesus was making it known to the Pharisees that if they were successful in their attempt to silence, censor and mute the praise and proliferation of Jesus and what he teaches, nature and the earth itself will react on his behalf.

Jesus in this profound expression is alluding to how Allah (God) uses the elements of the earth and the forces of nature as His weaponry and the chief implements of the execution of His wrath. This is similarly communicated within another episode of the New Testament when it was said of Jesus that "the winds and the seas obey Him." (Mark 4:41)

In **The Review of Religions**, January 1994 edition, author Hazrat Mirza Tahir Ahmad discusses 13 types of divine punishment identified within the sacred text of the Holy Qur'an. In point number 12 of his itemized listing he includes pestilence with the following notes:

> "Pestilence: **Climatic changes, of aridness or humidity, leading to a teeming of life forms which subsequently become a source of pestilence, causing disease and epidemics** – locusts, frogs, head-lice, scorpions, mosquitoes, vermin, bacteria and germs that cause blood disease such as cholera or others affecting the circulation of blood.
> 'Then We sent upon them the storm and the locusts, and the lice and the frogs, and the blood (these were separate) clear signs. -Surah 7:134"

The scriptures are filled with descriptions of the forces of nature being weaponized by Allah (God) whenever He determines that He will punish the wicked. In the Bible, in Psalms 29:10 we read:

> "The Lord sat as King at the flood"

We know that he sends rain, hail, snow and earthquakes. Yet most of us had not been so acquainted with His use of disease. COVID-19 is educating us as to the power of Allah (God) to use disease as a divine pestilence. As the Honorable Minister Louis Farrakhan said in his extraordinarily significant July 4, 2020 message entitled **The Criterion:**

> "I want to tell you right up front you will not conquer this virus because it didn't come from Wuhan. It did not come from Fort Detrick in Maryland because if you had made it, you would know how to handle what you made. But you don't know this virus, it's new it's different.... This virus is a pestilence from heaven so scholarship from hell can't deal with a pestilence that came from heaven."

Scientific Evidence Supports the Minister

In studying the Minister's Criterion message, I came across a study on the emergence of viruses from the frozen perma-frost regions of the earth. Consider the following proposed series of events that a group of scientists have prepared to explain the presence and global transmission of the COVID-19 virus:

> "The following sequence is proposed: (1) virus emergence after hot Arctic summers, predominantly near solar irradiance maxima or involving wildfires, indicates release of large amounts of ancient viruses during extensive permafrost melting, which are then incorporated in autumn polar air circulation, where cold storage and little sunlight permit survival. (2) Pandemics onset in winter to spring at rather few locations: from climate data on Wuhan, emergence occurs where the North Polar Jet stream hovers while intersecting warmer, moist air, producing rain which deposits particulates with the viral harvest on a vulnerable human population. (3) Spring and summer increases in COVID-19 cases link to high solar irradiance, implicating ultraviolet immune suppression as one means of amplification. (4) Viruses multiplied by infected humans at close range being incorporated in atmospheric circulation explains rapid global spread, periodic case surges (waves), and multi-year durations. Pollution and wind geography affect uptake and re-distribution."- **Possible Roles of Permafrost Melting, Atmospheric Transport, and Solar Irradiance in the Development of Major Coronavirus and Influenza Pandemics**

What makes this research so insightful is that it appears to harmonize with a passage of scripture found within the Bible's book of Job, wherein it reads:

> "Have you entered the **storehouses of snow or observed the storehouses of hail, which I hold in reserve for times of trouble, for the day of war and battle**?"-Job 38:22-23

The study's authors which include, Anne M. Hofmeister, James M. Secklerand Genevieve M. Criss conclude by stating:

> "Release of stored viruses from melting permafrost has great potential to contribute a large variety of related and unrelated infectious agents. The present paper constructs a model of how environmental processes could assist release from PF (permafrost) and promote global spreading via atmospheric transport in the earliest stages of a MRVP (major respiratory virus pandemic), focusing on the plethora of data on COVID-19 during its developmental stages and its shared features with major influenza pandemics."

Censorship As Hiding The Light From the Enslaved

Long before there was a COVID-19 pandemic, censorship has been a strategy of those in the positions of power in America, their goal being to deny the masses of the people the right to hear the truth. In his monumental book entitled **A Torchlight for America**, my teacher-the Hon. Min. Louis Farrakhan included a chapter called "Hiding the Light". The Minister wrote:

> "God has chosen from among the former slaves, the blacks. He has put in the head of the Honorable Elijah Muhammad and in the heads of us who follow him, a light; a torchlight that shows the way out of America's worsening conditions, for blacks and for all of America. But America's treatment of us and America's treatment of the Honorable Elijah Muhammad is like the treatment of Daniel by the proud kings of Babylon. It's terrible that some of those with power and influence label me a Hitler, a racist or a hater, so that they can justify their own people, or agents among our people, in attempts to defame and otherwise harm me. This is hiding the light."

The Nation of Islam is a culmination and a manifestation of the historical efforts of Black people in America to achieve freedom, justice and equality; total and complete liberation. What is being done to censor the Nation of Islam ill effects all Black people in America and injures America's status with Allah (God). It is the wrong course of action.

In many ways what is being done to the Nation of Islam is what has always been done to the Black community. As an enslaved mass of people, our oppressors have always understood that if we ever become educated, enlightened and morally strong they will no longer be able to oppress us. And they have targeted for the most severe opposition, those who have arisen within the Black community with an idea or message that they feared would inspire Black people to retaliate against our oppressors. They have even feared certain ideas in the minds of Black people more than they feared guns in the hands of Black people.

This was made known in the reactions to Nat Turner's rebellion. It was in the immediate aftermath of Nat Turner's rebellion that Virginia state legislator Henry Berry stated the following:

> "Pass as severe laws as you will to keep these unfortunate creatures in ignorance. It is in vain unless you can extinguish that spark of intellect which God has given them. ...Sir, we have as far as possible closed every avenue by which light may enter their minds. We only have to go one step further to extinguish their capacity to see the light and our work will be completed. And they would then be reduced to the level of the beasts of the field and we should be safe."

Several important ideas are expressed in this quote that place the censorship of the Nation of Islam and all who seek to enlighten the Black community within the proper context. Mr. Berry is advocating the notion that in order for whites in power to have safety and security, the Blacks they oppress must be destroyed mentally such that they are in the severest form of ignorance possible; a condition in which there would be no appreciable difference between the slaves on the plantation and the livestock on the plantation-both to be used as beasts of burden.

He also makes it quite clear that he is afraid of the enslaved having access to what he calls "light" (divine knowledge); much more than he fears the enslaved having access to guns and other kinds of weapons. This is extraordinary because it suggests that Mr. Berry interpreted Nat Turner's rebellion as the result of an "enlightened" mind. He sees Nat Turner's rebellion as the end result of educating and enlightening the enslaved. Nat Turner had both the ability to read the English language and the ability to read the Bible. These were 2 capabilities that most among the enslaved did not possess. And Mr. Berry and his ilk desperately wanted to keep it that way.

Mr. Berry also proposes attacks against those who enlighten Black people and he also proposes mentally incapacitating Black people in a way that would make us incapable of becoming enlightened. These are extraordinary expressions of a diabolical nature. Yet even though they are words coming from the mouth of Virginia legislator Henry Berry. They are the same ideas as expressed by Pharaoh within the Holy Qur'an wherein it reads:

> "**Come, we must deal shrewdly with them** or they will become even more numerous and, if war breaks out, will join our enemies, fight against us and leave the country."-Exodus 1:10

And Mr. Berry's infamous words similarly remind me of the Psalms wherein it states:

> "With cunning they scheme against Your people and conspire against those You cherish"-Psalms 83:3

Mr. Berry's appeal stated as "We only have to go one step further to extinguish their capacity to see the light and our work will be completed," is Pharaoh's appeal "Come let us deal wisely/shrewdly with them." The various Bible commentaries elucidate the underlying motive here. Gill's Exposition on the Entire Bible annotates this verse with the following note:

> "**Come on,**.... Which is a word of exhortation, stirring up to a quick dispatch of business, without delay, the case requiring haste, and some speedy and a matter of indifference: **let us deal wisely** with them; form some wise schemes, take some crafty methods to weaken and diminish them gradually; not with open force of arms, but in a more private and secret manner, and less observed": - Gill's Exposition of the Entire Bible

Censorship of the truth is never a good thing; but it is especially harmful when the truth that is being censored is a divine truth that is meant as a mercy to an errant nation, a nation who has been judged by Allah (God) to receive punishment. Yet as the Holy Qur'an makes us to know something of the methodology of Allah (God), we know that:

> "**And thy Lord never destroyed the towns, until He has raised in their metropolis a messenger,** reciting to them Our messages, and We never destroyed the towns except when their people were iniquitous."

Elijah Muhammad and Louis Farrakhan are divine Messengers of Allah (God). Their ministry represents Allah's (God's) Mercy to America. The censorship of Allah's Mercy is the requisitioning of

Allah's Wrath!

Instead of censoring the Minister and opposing his message, we all should take heed to what Allah (God) causes him to speak. He gave to us this prescription in his global message entitled The Criterion:

> "But if you want to stop it, you have to go to heaven. ...So, if you really want to end the virus... Go in your chamber and look at your record. Have you sinned? Is there anyone here who has not sinned? Raise your hand. I don't see nobody. I can't say that I have not sinned. ...The Scripture says, pray to me, and I will forgive you. The God will forgive you. He says He will not punish you while I'm among you. But He won't punish you if you're in the middle of repentance."

That scientists have identified the process by which ancient viruses stored in frozen perma-frost are unleashed and facilitate major respiratory virus pandemics bears witness to Minister Farrakhan's statements that this pandemic is from Allah. Within the Nation of Islam, we were given a lesson to memorize way back in the 1930s. It states in part:

> "What makes rain, hail, snow and earthquakes? ... In fact, that all the above is caused by the Son of man."

This lesson teaches us that while many in today's time are intrigued by what has been called "climate change," we know that the climate is not just changing on its own. The change in the climate is related to the judgment of this world. We know that the climate is being changed by Allah (God) who appeared in the person of Master W. Fard Muhammad. And that all that is being done on a global level are component parts of Allah's (God's) judgement of this world and his plan to bring in a new world using the Black man and woman of America as its foundation.

Lastly, I emphasize that the methodology of Allah (God) relative to His documented reaction to errant nations who qualify to be visited by His divine wrath always involves His anointing a man from among their poor class of people. This man's job is to serve as a Prophet or Messenger of Allah (God). This man's function is to provide a means by which wicked societies can escape the wrath of Allah and come back into the favor of Allah (God). He provides this means of escape through his preaching ministry. As long as the Prophet or Messenger is allowed to freely preach "thus sayeth the Lord" the wicked are allowed time to hear the preaching and teaching of the Prophet/Messenger and to obey Allah's (God's) words coming through him. The time given to wicked and errant societies by Allah (God) to hear and obey the Messenger; the time given to the wicked to repent is called Mercy and Grace.

The Honorable Minister Louis Farrakhan has described the American right to the freedom of speech as America's saving grace. He stated in his brilliant Million Man March address the following:

> "America, America, the beautiful. There's no country like this on the earth, and certainly if I lived in another country, I might never have had the opportunity to speak as I speak today. I probably would have been shot outright and so would my Brother Jesse; and so, would Maulana Karenga and so would Dr. Ben Chavis and Rev. Al Sampson, and all the wonderful people that are here. But because this is America, you allow me to speak, even though you don't like what I may say. **Because this is America, that provision in the Constitution for freedom of speech and freedom of assembly and freedom of religion—that is your saving grace.** Because what you're under right now is grace, and grace is the expression of Divine love and protection which God bestows freely on people. God is angry, America. He's angry, but His mercy is still present. Brothers and Sisters, look at the afflictions that have come upon us in the Black community. Do you know why we're being afflicted? God wants us to humble ourselves to the message that will make us atone and come back to Him and make ourselves whole again. Well, why is God afflicting America? Why is God afflicting the world? Why did Jesus say there would be wars and rumors of wars and earthquakes in diverse places and pestilence and famine, and why did he say that these were just the beginning of sorrows?
> In the last 10 years, America has experienced more calamities than at any other time period in American history? Why America? God is angry. He's not angry because you're right; **He's angry because you're wrong, and you want to stone and kill the people who want to make you see your wrong."**

Moreover, Minister Farrakhan applies this principle to the process of human self-development and moral awareness when he published The Self Improvement Study Guides, wherein we read the following:

> "If you will notice, this inner voice (self-accusing spirit) does the work of a Messenger of Allah (God). **Would you knowingly kill one of Allah (God)'s prophets or messengers? What would be the punishment if you did?** Every time we act to still the voice of correction, coming

from within ourselves, we are in fact murdering the Messenger of Allah (God). The result is spiritual blindness, leading to spiritual death, leading ultimately to an untimely physical death.

If we desire to stay alive spiritually, we must never still the voice of Allah (God) within. We must protect it, for in our moral awakening, it is the best friend that we have; for it is Allah (God) working on the inside of us. The more we feed on truth and right guidance from Allah (God) the stronger the voice becomes. That inner voice is like a seed which can ultimately grow into its perfected state, to be the Mind of God Himself in you."

Censorship As The Ultimate Aim: "To Kill A Preacher"

The Most Honorable Elijah Muhammad wrote about the ultimate aim of this world. It is helpful to look at his profound exposure of the rulers of this world, whom the scriptures call Satan, through the lens of their current efforts to censor the truth. He writes:

> "The ultimate aim is to do as their people have always done-try to destroy the preacher of truth and those who believe and follow him."

Notice, here that it is to destroy or **'to kill a preacher'**, that is this world's ultimate aim! To kill one whose preaching challenges the status quo by exposing the sins of the world's leading superpower nation is an act of censorship on a grand scale.

Minister Farrakhan has furthermore stated that when it comes to the history of White America's crimes against Black America, it is best likened to Cain and Abel in the sense that when Cain killed Abel he desperately feared retaliation. According to the Bible in Genesis 4:14, after Cain killed Abel he exclaimed:

> "I will be a fugitive and a wanderer on the earth, and **whoever finds me will kill me.**"

The fear of retaliation motivates the government's censorship activities. The fear of retaliation is the underlying reason for the current campaign against teaching Critical Race Theory within America's schools and educational system. As discussed earlier in this writing, Henry Berry attributed Nat Turner's rebellion to Nat Turner having been educated in a manner that gave him access to "light" that fed his intellect. The result was an enslaved man drawing the very rational conclusion that slavery is wrong and that slave owners were worthy of the punishment of death at the hands of those whom they had enslaved.

In addition to this fear of retaliation (i.e. the mind of Cain), the wickedly wise rulers of America are aware of the Biblical prophecy that foretells this modern day in which we live as the time for the exposure of Satan as the ruler of this world. The book of Thessalonians discusses how the "man of sin" will be revealed and will be consumed with the spirit of the mouth of Christ. In other words, Christ will come back to reveal and expose Satan, leading to the people under Satan's influence awakening from his deceptive powers and "falling away" from him and choosing instead to join Christ in His work of destroying Satan and building an entirely new world, the long awaited and yearned for Kingdom of God on earth. Elijah Muhammad and Louis Farrakhan are fulfilling this prophecy now, and it is because of their work of exposing Satan, that the Nation of Islam is the target of government sponsored censorship. However, the censorship of the Nation of Islam's message only serves to hasten the fall of America. I believe that it is the censorship of the Honorable Minister Louis Farrakhan and the Nation of Islam that is the main causal factor in Allah's (God's) decision to issue forth His indignation and wrath through the disease form pestilence known as COVID-19.

Epilogue: Scriptures Related To Censorship

The Crude Censorship of the Wicked Who Used Their Fingers To Prevent the Prophet's Message From Entering Their Ears
Surah 71:7-And whenever I call to them Thou mayest forgive them, they thrust their fingers in their ears and cover themselves with their garments, and persist and are big with pride.

Allah's (God's) Promise To Raise Up A People Who Won't Fear The "Censurership" of the Wicked
Surah 5:54-O you who believe, should any one of you turn back from his religion, then Allah will bring a people, whom He loves and who love Him, humble towards believers, mighty against the disbelievers, striving hard in Allah's way and not fearing the censure of any censurer. This is Allah's grace — He gives it to whom He pleases. And Allah is Ample-giving, Knowing.

The Wicked Desire To Censor The Divine Wisdom (Light) of Allah
Surah 61:8-They desire to put out the light of Allah with their

mouths, but Allah will perfect His light, though the disbelievers may be averse.

Surah 9:32-They desire to put out the light of Allah with their mouths, and Allah will allow nothing save the perfection of His light, though the disbelievers are averse.

Nature Will React To The Censorship Of The Disciples
Luke 19:39-40-And some of the Pharisees in the crowd said to him, "Teacher, rebuke your disciples." He answered, "I tell you, if these were silent, the very stones would cry out."

Allah's (God's) Wrath Results From The Censorship of The Truth
Romans 1:18-For the wrath of God is revealed from heaven against all ungodliness and unrighteousness of men, who by their unrighteousness suppress the truth.

Satan As The God Of This World Who Uses Censorship To Hide The Light of Allah
2 Corinthians 4:4-In their case the god of this world has blinded the minds of the unbelievers, to keep them from seeing the light of the gospel of the glory of Christ, who is the image of God.

The Motivation Of Satan's Censorship; Fear of Being Exposed
John 3:20-For everyone who does wicked things hates the light and does not come to the light, lest his works should be exposed.

Allah's (God's) Prophets Censored Because The Wicked Don't Want To Be Disturbed By Truth
Isaiah 30:10-21 - "10 They tell the prophets to keep quiet. They say, "Don't talk to us about what's right. Tell us what we want to hear. Let us keep our illusions. 11 Get out of our way and stop blocking our path. We don't want to hear about your holy God of Israel." 12 But this is what the holy God of Israel says: "You ignore what I tell you and rely on violence and deceit. 13 You are guilty. You are like a high wall with a crack running down it; suddenly you will collapse. 14 You will be shattered like a clay pot, so badly broken that there is no piece big enough to pick up hot coals with or to dip water from a cistern." 15 The Sovereign Lord, the Holy One of Israel, says to the people, "Come back and quietly trust in me. Then you will be strong and secure." But you refuse to do it. 16 Instead, you plan to escape from your enemies by riding fast horses. And you are right - escape is what you will have to do! You think your horses are fast enough, but those who pursue you will be faster! 17 A thousand of you will run away when you see one

enemy soldier, and five soldiers will be enough to make you all run away. Nothing will be left of your army except a lonely flagpole on the top of a hill. 18 And yet the Lord is waiting to be merciful to you. He is ready to take pity on you because he always does what is right. Happy are those who put their trust in the Lord. 19 You people who live in Jerusalem will not weep any more. The Lord is compassionate, and when you cry to him for help, he will answer you. 20 The Lord will make you go through hard times, but he himself will be there to teach you, and you will not have to search for him anymore. 21 If you wander off the road to the right or the left, you will hear his voice behind you saying, "Here is the road. Follow it."

The Case of Prophet Jeremiah: His Enemies' Conspiracy to Silence/Censor Him

"Then said they, Come, and let us devise devices against Jeremiah; for the law shall not perish from the priest, nor counsel from the wise, nor the word from the prophet. Come, and let us smite him with the tongue, and let us not give heed to any of his words."-Jeremiah 18:18

Commentaries:

Keil and Delitzsch Biblical Commentary on the Old Testament- "Even the solemn words (Jeremiah 18:15-17) of the prophet were in vain. Instead of examining themselves and reforming their lives, the blinded sinners resolve to put the troublesome preacher of repentance out of the way by means of false charges."

Geneva Study Bible- "Then said they, Come, and let us devise plots against Jeremiah; for the law {g} shall not perish from the priest, nor counsel from the wise, nor the word from the prophet. Come, and let us smite him with the {h} tongue, and let us not give heed to any of his words.... (h) Let us slander him and accuse him: for we will be believed."

Gill's Exposition of the Entire Bible- "Then said they, come, and let us devise devices against Jeremiah.... Being enraged at the judgments threatened them, they propose to enter into a confederacy and consultation together, to think of ways and means to stop the mouth of the prophet, and even to take away his life; since he had told them that God had devised a device against them, they were for devising devices against him; that so they might walk after their own devices, without being teased and tormented with this prophet: come, and let us smite him with the tongue; by saying all the evil we can of him: by threatening him with pains and penalties; by loading him with reproaches and calumnies; by taking away his good name, and lessening his character and reputation among the people; and so the Targum, "let us bear false witness against him;"

Matthew Poole's Commentary - "This faithful dealing of the prophet with them did only enrage them (as is usual) against the prophet; they plot against the prophet, how to be revenged on him, because he would cross their humours, and would not prophesy as they would have had him.... Let us smite him with the tongue, expose him by railing on him, telling lies about concerning him, representing him to be what we know the people hate, abusing him to his face, informing against him; or, in the tongue, let us silence him, command him to speak no more; or, for his tongue, for prophesying at this rate; and for his."

Barnes Notes On The Bible- The Jews were only hardened by the foregoing prophecy, and determined to compass Jeremiah's death. Let us devise devices - i. e., "deliberately frame a plot" for his ruin (see Jeremiah 18:11 note) .... Let us smite him with the tongue - Their purpose was to carry a malicious report of what he had said to king Jehoiakim, and so stir up his anger against him.

Matthew Henry's Concise Commentary - "When the prophet called to repentance, instead of obeying the call, the people devised devices against him. Thus, do sinners deal with the great Intercessor, crucifying him afresh, and speaking against him on earth, while his blood is speaking for them in heaven. But the prophet had done his duty to them; and the same will be our rejoicing in a day of evil."

RESPONSE TO FORWARD MAGAZINE: DEAR JANE EISNER, WE ARE LOUIS FARRKHAN & WE DON'T FEAR THE CENSURE OF ANY CENSURER

Dear Jane Eisner,

I have read your column that you published yesterday on Forward.com.

Your article calling for the public censure of the Honorable Minister Louis Farrakhan is offensive to Black people in America. After 60 years of tried and true leadership and service to the Black community, we stand with Minister Farrakhan and will not give up our love of, support for and solidarity with our beloved Minister. You may see him as your enemy, but I want you to know that he is **"our beloved Minister."** He belongs to us. And we belong to Him. I am speaking for the 40 to 50 million Black people in America. Allah (God) gave him to us, because of what America and its all-encompassing society of oppression and subjugation of Black people did to render us a people bound inside a veritable furnace of affliction. So please understand from this day forward, that when you condemn Minister Farrakhan, you are condemning all of us. When you call for his public exile, you are calling to exile all of us. When you call for his removal from the public sphere, you are calling for our removal from the public sphere. **Because We are Louis Farrakhan.**

Louis Farrakhan is more than just an individual person or man. He is a people. He is the spirit and animating force for liberation inside of Black America. He is our heart and our soul. He is the personification and embodiment of the huddled masses of our Black enslaved ancestors who yearned to breathe free of the lash of the overseers' whip and to be free of the chains of chattel bondage. Through the scientific exploration of the human genome, it has been discovered that there is such a phenomenon in human biology known as **epigenetics.** Simply put, epigenetics is the study within the field of genetic research that has documented that when people suffer trauma, the trauma and suffering leaves markers and imprints on the cellular structures of that people. These markers are transferable from one generation to the next. These markers carry the effects of environmental dangers, pain, agony and abuse on down in to the subsequent generations of the suffering people's offspring. When applied to Black history in America, this area of bio-science helps one to understand where Louis Farrakhan comes from. His mouth is the mouth that our muted and traumatized ancestors could not have. It is loud, bold and stinging in its condemnation of our enemies. His courage is the fearlessness that our enslaved ancestors possessed but had to tamp down as they were forced to choose between standing up for themselves or being murdered by their slave masters. His rebuke of the enemies of Black people is the rebuke that the slaves had no power to openly express outside of their shanty slave quarters. He speaks from the mountain top what they could only murmur in hush harbors and private settings. Our ancestors' suffering produced Louis Farrakhan; their spirits inhabit Him. They approve of Him. **Again, We are Louis Farrakhan.**

If you don't agree with him, you ought to just leave him alone. Because we are tired of the Jewish leaders and organizations making his job difficult. No Black group or Black leaders are ever found haranguing or dogging the trail of the leaders of the Jewish people. You should really give up your paternalistic feelings towards us. We don't belong to you. We are no longer your slaves. Allah (God) has come for us, to rescue us from your evil. The spirit of Allah (God) visited Black people in America in an embodied form; in a corporeal form; in human form. His spirit came to us; His wisdom came to us; His power came to us; and His love came to us in the person of Master Wali Fard Muhammad. As an intelligent woman, I am sure you know the Torah. You know the greatest of the signs and manifestations of God is when he performs what the religious scholars refer to as a theophany. Abraham was visited by God in human form in Genesis' 18th chapter. Moses was visited by God in human form in Numbers, chapter 12. And Jesus proclaimed that 'God – the Father' was a man that would come and provide testimony affirming his authority to rebuke the Jewish leaders of his day and time in the Book of John, the 8th chapter. You should know, that Louis Farrakhan is backed by Allah (God) in human form today in the person of Master W. Fard Muhammad. And He also has the backing and protection of His teacher -the Most Honorable Elijah Muhammad.

But your article suggests that while you should be considering Farrakhan's place within the scriptures, you are instead obviously upset that the Black community appears to be closing ranks around Minister Farrakhan. You appear to be frustrated over the growing appeal and continued relevance of our beloved Minister. I think you have at least a private appreciation, even though you won't say it publicly, that all of Black America at this point have been positively impacted by our beloved Minister. This is why white America and Jewish leaders utilize what has been called the Farrakhan Litmus Test. You want to know if any rising and prominent Black person, whether or not they are possessed of the mind, heart and spirit of our beloved Minister. Because you want a continued Master/Slave relationship with the Black community, you naturally deem Minister Farrakhan's message as being like an acid that is corrosive to your old antiquated ideas of White supremacy and Black inferiority.

And really its true. You are upset because when you reflect on, what is more than likely a limited amount of Black people in your daily life-most of whom you engage with while they function for you in some service capacity-you don't know whom of them privately have a heart filled with love and admiration for the man you have written of as needing to be shunned and publicly silenced. But I am here to let you know, we all love Farrakhan whether we say it out loud or not. Our souls leap up for joy when we hear Him speak. Your Black shoe shine man loves Farrakhan. Your Black newspaper boy loves Farrakhan. Your Black waiter and waitress at your favorite restaurant loves Louis Farrakhan. Your Black dental hygienist loves Farrakhan. Your Black postal carrier loves Farrakhan. **We are Louis Farrakhan.**

Ms. Eisner, you wrote: *"Louis Farrakhan, leader of the Nation of Islam, is an unrepentant bigot. His hatred of, and disdain for, Jews, gay men and lesbians, trans people and white people in general is consistent and unwavering. It forms the basis of his prophecy and his politics"*

What you have written is false. The definition of a bigot is **"a person who is intolerant toward those holding different opinions."** That definition doesn't fit Minister Farrakhan at all and you know it. The Minister called for a Million Man March. He never set pre-conditions on what opinions or beliefs that those men needed to possess in order to answer the divine call to come to Washington on October 16, 1995 for that glorious Day of Atonement. In fact, 80% of the million plus men in attendance were of the various Christian denominations that predominate the Black communities of America. And since you want to say the Minister is a bigot and can't tolerate folks who have different opinions, you should know that in a report entitled **"How African-American Men View Various African-American Leadership Types: Findings from the Million Man March"** by Joseph P. McCormick, II; Associate Professor at Penn State's York campus we find that **"among those in attendance on the day of the Million Man March, Louis Farrakhan, who initiated this event, not surprisingly, had a higher proportion of respondents who saw him as "very important" than any of the individuals about whom a question on leadership importance was asked. About 83 percent of the respondents when asked about the leadership importance of Farrakhan and others rated the head of the Nation of Islam as being "very important." Reverend Jesse Jackson (73.2%) and Secretary of State Colin Powell (70.8%) ranked second and third respectively in this rating on leadership importance. Associate Justice Clarence Thomas trailed at a very distant fourth with almost 20 percent of the respondents deeming him as "very important" in terms of leadership importance."**

By your logic, you're suggesting that this large representative sampling of Black America, that came at the call of the Honorable Minister Louis Farrakhan, came to follow and proclaim the importance of a bigot. Wow, I guess you feel that Black America is by and large full of bigotry. That is astonishing. Nothing could be further from the truth.

Also, the Minister is not intolerant to gays and lesbians. This is a direct quote from the Minister regarding the gay and lesbian brothers and sisters as a part of his message in Jackson, Mississippi March 25, 2011. **"I love my people who are lesbian, homosexual, transgender. Don't make no difference, I love you. But I have to teach you that which will make us more pleasing in the sight of God because his wrath now is coming down on America and on the world. And if you're not on the right side, you will receive a terrible chastisement."** Please identify Ms. Eisner where the bigotry is in what the Minister has said. If you are a Jew, then you recognize what the Minister is saying as being consistent with the contents and sentiments of the Torah-the Jewish book of scriptures. I would think you would agree with the Minister's position of what practices are approved of and disapproved of by Yahweh/Jehovah-the God of Israel.

Ms. Eisner you wrote: *"Farrakhan is also the aging, fading leader of a black nationalist sect that reached its peak of power two* decades ago and has steadily diminished ever since. The Nation of Islam, credited with doing good work in blighted neighborhoods no one else would touch, is now largely irrelevant. Farrakhan is a figment of the past, more the crazy beloved uncle than a force for much of anything."

What you have written here is not only false, but also disingenuous. If Minister Farrakhan was fading, you wouldn't be spending time and energy trying to smear his noble name and reputation. And to be very candid with you, the Nation of Islam has yet to reach its peak. We are poised to predominate in the Black community. Allah (God) is creating the circumstances and conditions for the full blossoming of the Black Nation. I really pray that you live a long time to see the Nation of Islam in its full beauty and splendor. Allah (God) is with us to save and reform all Black people and human beings of other races who want righteousness and renewal away from the wickedness of Satan.

Minister Farrakhan frequently trends in Twitter and throughout social media. This is an objective indicator that he is certainly not a figment of the past. His visit to our dear sister Aretha Franklin's funeral proved to you that our beloved Minister has deep roots among Black people and is still strong and mighty in terms of magnetism and appeal. So much so, that in 2013 Abraham Foxman told Haaretz magazine that **"The only leadership that now exists in that community"—the 'African American community'— is Louis Farrakhan. Farrakhan can assemble 20,000 people several times a year..."**

Also, routinely when surveys are conducted, Minister Farrakhan's approval rating and ranking of importance is great in the Black community. Just a year ago the Rasmussen Reports conducted a survey that showed that among the Black electorate, more than 50% approve of Minister Farrakhan.

Ms. Eisner you wrote: *"This 85-year-old throwback, who has been on his deathbed more than once, is like a Phoenix of our racial politics, rising up again and again, making mischief, never really going away but never causing real harm, either.... Farrakhan must be exiled from the public stage, stripped of honor and attention. Twitter should suspend him. Members of Congress, as well as other public leaders, should stop defending him. His free speech is his right, but that doesn't mean we have to listen to him, legitimate him or excuse him."*

What you have written here is mischievous and sinister. The Minister has never ever been known for mischief. He is now, and has always been a peace-maker. Ms. Elma Lewis told BET in 2003 that she was one of his neighbors from his childhood Roxbury neighborhood, where he grew up. She said of the young Louis Walcott, who became known as Louis Farrakhan that: **"He was the jewel of the neighborhood really, in the church and school, wherever he went; he had a real talent for lighting up the world."**

Professor Mattias Gardell said of Minister Farrakhan that **"Farrakhan has a unique capability ...able to reach deeply into the souls of black youths...is able to talk to them in a way that really makes them listen...this rapport enables Farrakhan to criticize and redirect destructive behavioral patterns... Minister Farrakhan and the NOI clearly have been instrumental in bringing the gangs together and redirecting their activities toward community improvement and political empowerment... In May of 1993, a 3-day National Summit for Urban Peace and Justice was held in Kansas City, gathering 150 members from gangs in 2 dozen cities."**

Now Ms. Eisner, I don't know if you have ever read the Holy Qur'an. I am going to, here, share a verse of it with you that is relevant to what you wrote calling for the Minister to be "exiled from the public stage, stripped of honor and attention..." This is Surah 5, Ayat(verse) 54: **"O you who believe, should any one of you turn back from his religion, then Allah will bring a people, whom He loves and who love Him, humble towards believers, mighty against the disbelievers, striving hard in Allah's way and not fearing the censure of any censurer. This is Allah's grace — He gives it to whom He pleases. And Allah is Ample-giving, Knowing."**

You don't have any power to censure the Minister. He is Allah's (God's) servant. He does not fear you, nor do we who are His students fear you. We are living in the beginning years of the reign and rule of Allah (God) as His enemy Satan/Shaitan is being set-down. The time we live in is known to scriptural scholars as the Days of Allah or the Days of Judgment. You have no power to censure or silence a man whom Allah (God) is with his mouth, backs up and supports what he teaches. And really, how can you truly censure a man who is now bigger than flesh and blood. **Again, we are Louis Farrakhan.** For his ideas and His mind have permeated the atmosphere and it has touched nearly all of us and many of us have breathed it in, so that He is a part of us. You would have to censure 40 to 50 million Black people; you would have to censure the millions of Hispanics, Native Americans and even poor white people who believe in and agree with Minister Farrakhan. This, you are unable to do, even though you wish it.

Ms. Eisner you wrote: Locals in Chicago told me that his footprint has shrunk dramatically ...So, I can understand why African Americans and Muslims are resentful for feeling that they have to be held accountable for every publicity-seeking statement Farrakhan makes.... Farrakhan may be aligned with some on the political left, but his actual political behavior puts him far closer to Donald Trump, whom he just about endorsed for president. Farrakhan favors undemocratic strongmen (the late Libyan leader Moammar Gadhafi was his financier); rogue nations (Iran), and numerous conspiracy theories (the 9/11 attacks were an inside job; homosexuality was unleashed as a form of castration, etc., etc.) Even radical feminist figures like Angela Davis have denounced Farrakhan for his exclusion of women.

Again, what you have written is worthy of condemnation and rebuke. The Minister's footprint has not shrunken. Not long ago, conservative pundit Armstrong Williams wrote an article on how the Nation of Islam could be Chicago's Savior. He was urging city officials to partner with us so that we could have the resources and support to ramp up our anti-violence initiative in Chicago. Mr. Williams wrote: **"The fact is, the Nation of Islam brings to the table things that other private security firms and the police don't: Credibility within the community. It is one of the few community-based organizations that actually recruit in the prisons and also offer transitional services to ex-offenders. One of the problems cited by HUD with regard to the group's Baltimore contracts was that it had hired ex-offenders as guards. But this was actually a strength. The Nation of Islam had in fact cleaned up ex-offenders, taking them off the streets, getting them off drugs and instilling them with discipline before redeploying them in neighborhoods where they were known and now respected."**

Also, you have a lot of nerve to write a piece that is essentially calling for Minister Farrakhan to be denied a platform to express his transformative message, and then you proceed to write that

Minister Farrakhan favors **"undemocratic strongmen."** Tell me Ms. Eisner, by what democratic process have you concluded that the Minister should be "exiled and stripped of honor and attention" when it is his own good works and long struggle that has naturally brought honor to his name and person? You promote pure wickedness by suggesting this. You also write that the Minister believes in "conspiracy theories". This is completely false. When the Minister points out how various groups act in concert to do evil and harm to the Black community, he brings an abundance of documentation. His messages, when transcribed are able to be footnoted using the highest of academic standards. Publications like yours and others are just too interested in distributing propaganda and smear type pieces, that you don't even want to examine what Minister Farrakhan uses to justify the powerful points he makes. Why don't you apply the rules of the academy to Minister Farrakhan's speeches? Go and check his sources. Don't argue with the Minister, just interrogate and analyze his sources. If you can impeach his sources, then his arguments are automatically done away with. Are you afraid to expose the documentation that substantiates the Minister's positions?

Angela Davis is entitled to her opinion. And I challenge you to prove she denounced her brother Minister Farrakhan. You really need to stop trying to sow dissension among Black leaders and groups who may disagree with one another. Just because she disagrees with Minister Farrakhan over certain issues, doesn't equate her denouncing the Minister. You now are guilty of what you charge the Minister with of making mischief.

Ms. Eisner you finish your article by writing: "The double standard here is mystifying, approaching hypocritical. But if good people everywhere are willing to call out hate speech and hurtful behavior in politicians and pundits, comedians and corporate titans, then Farrakhan cannot be exempt. If Democrats and many Republicans find President Trump's bigoted speech unacceptable, then Louis Farrakhan cannot be excused. The answer is not to give bigotry a pass. The answer is to denounce it wherever it is."

Let me take a moment to show you the double standard of hypocrisy. I agree that it is mystifying. But not in the way you suggest. You have prominent white leaders like Pat Buchanan, Henry Kissinger, Fred Malek and others who say all kinds of things, that if said by the Minister would be condemned as anti-

Semitic. Yet, the ADL and other Jewish groups give them a pass. Pat Buchanan is still on the McLaughlin Group and has had other high paying commentator gigs even after saying the following: **"Hitler was also an individual of great courage, a soldier's soldier in the Great War, a leader steeped in the history of Europe, who possessed oratorical powers that could awe even those who despised him. But Hitler's success was not based on his extraordinary gifts alone. His genius was an intuitive sense of the mushiness, the character flaws, the weakness masquerading as morality that was in the hearts of the statesmen who stood in his path." – St. Louis Globe – Democrat, Aug 25, 1977**

I close by saying this, Minister Farrakhan is not a politician. President Trump is. Don't compare the Minister with Mr. Trump, that is a false equivalency, logical fallacy. The Minister speaks the word of God, which is necessarily controversial because the word of God, from the mouth of the Messenger of God, enters into societies after they have deviated from the path of moral correctness that God expects of nations. When a man or woman is sent to correct errant behavior, those who are guilty of errant behavior aren't happy to receive him. The history of the Prophets of God in the Torah and the Holy Qur'an show that that the wicked sought to kill the prophets and messengers of God, because they preached the truth.

And truth be told, many of the critics of Minister Farrakhan have so much hatred in their hearts for the truth he speaks that they want to end his life; as the Holy Qur'an says: **"Vehement hatred has already appeared from out of their mouths, and that which their hearts conceal is greater still."-Holy Qur'an 3:118**

But the God of Louis Farrakhan is "maliki -yaum-ideen" (Master of This Day of Judgment) and He protects Him and encourages Him to deliver His divine message: **"O Messenger, deliver that which has been revealed to thee from thy Lord; and if thou do (it) not, thou hast not delivered His message. And Allah will protect thee from men."-Holy Qur'an 5:67**

By Allah's (God's) Grace, Mercy and Divine Providence, The Minister will be successful, but those who oppose Him will not.

NOI Prison Reform Ministry Under Attack! Facts Rebut False Narrative of Propaganda

In a vicious flourish of lies, the Washington Examiner has published a full-frontal assault on one of Black America's most cherished institutions-the Nation of Islam; to be more specific, the Nation of Islam's legendary Prison Reform Ministry. Yes, the same Prison Reform Ministry that was started by the Most Honorable Elijah Muhammad with over 80 of his male followers who were imprisoned in 1942 because of their religious beliefs; the same prison ministry that produced Minister Malcolm X as well as thousands of other men and women who emerged from their time of confinement in prison, to serve as luminaries in their various fields of endeavor.

Consider the actual lived experience of Bro. Charles X:

"In prison they had DVDs of the Minister at that time and they had DVDs playing in the chapel called "Obedience Is the Highest Form of Sacrifice." My attraction was to the brothers who were in the Nation; they were so clean and lean and in prison we all had the same uniform, but they were different and I was attracted to the discipline of these men. My mother came to visit me in the prison and she said my whole demeanor and attitude was different. She looked at me and she said, "Baby, I don't know what you're doing but keep doing it." I read Message to the Blackman and I felt so strong and powerful and it made me really want to be somebody...I stopped all sport and play and it was serious business for me from that point on...I went to prison a drug dealer and with no love for anybody and when I got into the teachings I fell in love with Black people."- **Charles X in The Nation of Islam, Louis Farrakhan and the Men Who Follow Him by Dawn Marie Gibson**

The experience of Brother Charles X, is a common one. And this article will rebut the propaganda piece written by Ms. Goodman and condemn it.

It was the Nation of Islam's Prison Reform Ministry that Tupac rapped about in his legendary anthem **"I ain't mad at ya"** a song where he narrates that which has become a common cultural norm in the Black communities when a family member is convicted of a crime, goes to prison and experiences a life transformation resulting from their encounter with the teachings of the Honorable Elijah Muhammad. The legendary rapper spoke:

> Now we was once two niggas of the same kind
> Quick to holla at a hoochie with the same line
> You was just a little smaller, but you still rolled
> Got stretched to Y.A. and hit the hood swoll
> 'Member when you had a Jheri Curl, didn't quite learn
> On the block, wit'cha Glock, trippin' off sherm
> Collect calls to the crib, sayin' how you've changed
> **Oh, you a Muslim now? No more dope game**
> **Heard you might be comin' home, just got bail**
> **Wanna go to the mosque, don't wanna chase tail**
> **It seems I lost my little homie, he's a changed man**
> **Hit the pen' and now no sinnin' is the game plan**
> **When I talk about money, all you see is the struggle**
> **When I tell you I'm livin' large, you tell me it's trouble**

Consider these important facts that the Washington Examiner omitted:

FACT: The Nation of Islam's Prison Ministry has been recognized by Prison Officials for its Positive Impact On the Prison Environment

Throughout our history of bettering the lives of the incarcerated, testimonies like the following articles and letters published in the Muhammad Speaks Newspaper, have been characteristic of the NOI Prison Ministry Reform.

FACT: The Nation of Islam's Prison Ministry has been recognized by scholars for its beneficial role with correctional settings

"The success of the Nation of Islam, as we shall explore in this book, is due to two interconnected factors. First, the Nation of Islam has provided an effective prison-bound mechanism of protection to those who convert to its brand of Islam. Second, the literature of the Nation of Islam claims that not only has it converted a large number of inmates to Islam, but has also successfully reintegrated them into its social and economic infrastructures thus preventing them from recidivating and being re-incarcerated. Accordingly, this transformation from a convicted-felon to a rehabilitated Muslim convert takes place through several stages as prospective convert-inmates are taken under the Nation of Islam's prison-bound protective networks to be gradually assimilated into the Nation's version of Islam based on the teachings of the Honorable Elijah Muhammad, the founder and the spiritual leader." **-Hamid Reza Kusha, Islam in America's Prisons, Black Muslims' Challenge to American Penology**

FACT: The Nation of Islam's Prison Ministry and the inmates it developed did the pioneering litigation that expanded and secured the Constitutional Rights for all incarcerated persons

"During the 1960s and 1970s, Black Muslim prisoners were primary actors in the process of filing legal actions to obtain judicial recognition and enforcement of a limited range of constitutional rights for incarcerated offenders (King, 1969). **The Muslim prisoners are widely recognized for their important role, as evidenced by commentators' characterizations of them as "the major catalyst" ("Constitutional Rights," 1962, p. 999), those "who carried the torch of [B]lack protest" (Jacobs, 1983, p. 36), and "the fuse to this legal explosion" (Cripe, 1977, p. 31).** Despite this recognition of their importance, further analysis of the details of their role has been called a "high priority for building a body of research on prisoners' rights" (Jacobs, 1983, p. 36). **The Muslim prisoners' cases have had a profound impact upon the entire correctional system, both because they helped to change the existing relationships between "keeper" and "kept" during the 1960s and because they provided the legal vehicles for all incarcerated persons to attempt to vindicate their constitutional rights.** The development of the Black Muslims and their assertive doctrines coincided with the federal courts' increased receptivity to demands for recognition and protection by various political minorities throughout American society. The simultaneous development of these phenomena, influenced by common factors in the changing political and social environment of the 1950s and 1960s, resulted in the significant expansion of constitutional protections for prisoners and transformed the previously deferential relationship between the judiciary and state correctional agencies." - **Black Muslims and the Development of Prisoners' Rights Author(s): Christopher E. Smith Source: Journal of Black Studies, Vol. 24, No. 2 (Dec., 1993), pp. 131-146 Published by: Sage Publications, Inc.**

FACT: The Nation of Islam's Prison Ministry has as its primary emphasis "self-improvement" and uses as its primary text Self-Improvement: The Basis for Community Development

written by the Hon. Min. Louis Farrakhan

FACT: The use of contract service providers is a standard practice within the correctional industry to help ensure that inmates of all faiths are allowed to practice their faith while incarcerated

"There are a variety of possible scenarios in which a chaplain may be required to use outside contractors. In some situations, a contractor may be hired to conduct religious worship services that fall outside of the chaplain's own denomination. For example, a Protestant chaplain may hire a contract imam to perform worship services for the Islamic inmates if there is no Muslim chaplain on staff to meet this need. Outside contractors of the same faith background as the chaplain may also be recruited in the following instances: the prison chaplain is a lay person who is not allowed to perform certain, liturgical duties; there is an inordinately large number of inmates of that faith background who require multiple worship services a week; or the prison's physical layout is such that separate worship services are needed such as in a high-rise building.

A signification portion of most U.S. prison chaplaincy budgets are earmarked for the hiring of contractor services. -Jeneve Brooks-Klinger, Encyclopedia of Prisons and Correctional Facilities

FACT: During the infamous Attica uprising, it was Nation of Islam inmates who helped protect the innocent hostages from being harmed.

Author Mark S. Hamm discusses the hidden history of how Nation of Islam Muslims protected hostages during the Attica uprising:

"**Beginning on September 9, 1971, Muslim prisoners swiftly organized themselves in order to protect forty-three guards taken hostage during the legendary Attica prison rebellion in upstate New York**. Five grueling days later, during which time three prisoners were stabbed to death after being marked as snitches, twenty-nine prisoners and ten guards were killed by the crossfire of two hundred attacking New York State troopers in a bungled attempt to retake the facility. At this perilous moment, an agreement to end the siege was mediated by two Moorish Science prisoners, Carl Jones-El and Donald Noble, and a loquacious Nation of Islam prisoner from the Virgin Islands named

Herbert Blyden X.40 On September 15, the brother of a slain guard appeared on the CBS Evening News to tell Walter Cronkite that he "no longer considered inmates animals" after hearing that Black Muslims had helped save the hostages. Nevertheless, afterward, the riot police roamed the Attica yard, beating and torturing scores of naked inmates, many of whom were seriously wounded."- **Mark S. Hamm, The Spectacular Few**

The work of the Nation of Islam, is a great benefit and blessing to the American Penal System. The history, as we have shown, is overwhelming what we have been blessed to achieve.

Instead of U. S. Representative Peter T. King and the Southern Poverty Law Center's Mark Potock condemning the Nation of Islam, they should leave us alone. The Nation of Islam, which is comprised of tax paying citizens, has a right to do business with the American government. As effective as Minister Farrakhan's message is and has been, it should be supported with the resources it needs to remain a strong presence within the prison system.

How Minister Farrakhan's Jewish Controversy Marks Him as The "Jesus" of Our Times

All throughout the history of the Black experience in America, various Black leaders have been dubbed or identified as "Black Moses." Harriett Tubman and Marcus Garvey are just 2 who were considered to be "Black Moses".

That a Black leader be designated as Black Moses is significant. And it powerfully suggests that if the suffering of Black people in America gave birth to leaders who fit the description of Moses; one day our suffering would give birth to leaders who fit the description of Jesus.

From my study both the Most Honorable Elijah Muhammad and the Honorable Minister Louis Farrakhan fit the description of Jesus. One only need examine their teachings, their beneficial impact on Black people and their suffering as a result of the truth that they have taught to understand why I have drawn this conclusion.

Jesus' love of God and righteousness made him bold and courageous. In Jesus' life and work we see how **"love removes fear."** And the New Testament records that his ministry became a problem for Jewish leaders whose corrupt practices enslaved the poor; Jesus challenged them and they opposed him.

So, the **Jesus Model of Leadership**, among Black people in America, is recognized when we see Black leaders facing the powerful opposition of America's Jewish leaders. The Jesus model is characterized in loving and kind leadership; the Jesus styled leader is gentle and merciful in his interactions with the poor; yet he is simultaneously a man known for a bold and courageous ministry that speaks truth to power. And these are characteristics of the life and work of the Hon. Min. Louis Farrakhan.

For instance, as the beautiful photo of Minister Farrakhan and Sen. Barack Obama was made public for the first time in over 12 years, Jewish leaders like Alan Dershowitz and Jonathon Greenblatt have reacted negatively. Greenblatt, the current leader of the ADL (anti-defamation league of b'nai b'rith) has called for former President Obama to repudiate Minister Farrakhan. In a twitter post he wrote:

"In Israel catching up on news about 2005 photo of Obama &

Farrakhan. Over his career, @barackobama has denounced the bigotry of Farrakhan. Time to do so again. Leaders always should make sure that there's no doubt: America is no place for those who advocate #antisemitism or hate."

Similarly, an ADL memo from 1994 entitled the **Legitimation of Louis Farrakhan** wrote that:

"Minister Louis Farrakhan, leader of the Nation of Islam (NOI)… has recently attained a new level of acceptance among certain mainstream Black organizations and leaders. His "legitimation" has been reflected most notably by his participation last summer in the Parliament of the World's Religions, his obtaining federal funds for NOI's anti-AIDS efforts and the security services it has been providing at several federal housing projects, and his warm reception at the annual legislative meeting of the Congressional Black Caucus (CBC) last fall."

The memo's author Steven Freeman recommended that:

"ADL is not going to make Farrakhan go away. What we can and should do is impose an obligation on those who deal with him, or, as in the case of universities, give him a platform."

Freeman's recommendation that the ADL **"impose and obligation"** on all who accept the Minister is like the coded language seen in movies like the Godfather when the Godfather portrayed by Marlon Brando says **"make him an offer he can't refuse."**

Freeman's coded language of retaliation for those who refuse repudiation of the Minister is the modern equivalent of what we read of in the New Testament book of John. The book of John reveals to us that not only had the Jewish leaders planned to crucify Jesus; they had also planned to **crucify Lazarus**.

"When all the people heard of Jesus' arrival, they flocked to see him and also to see Lazarus, the man Jesus had raised from the dead. Then the chief priests decided to kill Lazarus, too, for it was because of him that many of the people had deserted them and believed in Jesus." – John 12: 9-11

From the perspective of the Jewish leaders who opposed Jesus, Lazarus had produced the **"legitimation" of Jesus** and was causing many others to believe in Jesus. In the modern era persons such as Rev. Jesse L. Jackson Sr.; Actor Bruce Willis;

Mayor Ed Rendell; Congressman Keith Ellison; Congressman John Conyers; and Presidential candidate Barack H. Obama are just a few famous individuals who Jewish leaders have demanded that they repudiate the Honorable Minister Louis Farrakhan.

Another parallel from Jesus' Jewish controversy to Minister Farrakhan's Jewish controversy is to compare the scripture found in John 7:13 to the comments of journalist William Raspberry. From the Book of John, we read:

> "But no one had the courage to speak favorably about him in public, for they were afraid of getting in trouble with the Jewish leaders."

From Journalist William Raspberry we read:

> "Farrakhan says what so many black people believe but have learned not to say in public: for instance, that Jews wield tremendous influence in the news and entertainment media. That doesn't mean that most blacks accept Farrakhan's notion of a small Jewish cabal that meets in Hollywood or in a Park Avenue apartment to decide which ideas and trends are to be foisted off on the public. But few of us doubt the disproportionate influence of Jews-for good or ill- on what we see on television or in the movies. Nor do blacks doubt the disproportionate influence of Jews on American foreign policy, particularly with regard to political and economic support of Israel. But we also know that to say these things is to be accused of antisemitism. That's why blacks can cheer when Farrakhan says them, even in gross overstatement."- Raspberry, William, The Washington Post, March 2, 1990

Another parallel is found in John 7:1 wherein we find the following:

> "After this, Jesus traveled throughout Galilee. He did not want to travel in Judea, because the Jews there were trying to kill Him."

Compare this to Professor Mattias Gardell's report on Jewish efforts to kill Minister Farrakhan:

> "Pickets with Jews shouting "Who do we want? -Farrakhan! How do we want him-Dead!" are far from unusual and the Jewish Defense Organization had Farrakhan on top of the death list found by police investigating a bombing of Arab-American facilities. The Jewish Defense League has staged at least one "Death to Farrakhan" march, on Saviours' Day, October 7, 1985." –In The Name of Elijah Muhammad

In another place in the book of John we read:

> "Nevertheless, many of the leaders believed in Him; but because of the Pharisees they did not confess Him, for fear that they would be put out of the synagogue." –John 12:42

Compare this to the history of Minister Farrakhan being loved and lauded by many leaders in various fields; yet many of these leaders become quiet when the Minister is condemned by Jewish leaders. Rapper Nas spoke on this phenomenon when he said:

> "It's like everybody's scared to speak out about what's in their heart, just because they're scared of who is going to come down on them. They're scared they're going to get "blacklisted." They're going to get all their endorsements taken away from them. They're scared that they can't feed their families." -Nas, interview with the Final Call Newspaper

And yet despite all of this opposition and harassment of his supporters and admirers the Minister continues to be strong, courageous and mighty! As outgoing ADL director Abraham Foxman said of the Minister, he really is the last man standing. Foxman noted:

> "The only leadership that now exists in that community—the African American community— is Louis Farrakhan. Farrakhan can assemble 20,000 people several times a year..." -Abraham Foxman in April 2013 issue of Ha'aertz Magazine

The Minister's strength and widespread appeal is the result of his anointing. So just as the Jewish leaders in the New Testament falsely attributed Jesus' fame to Lazarus; the modern Jewish leaders falsely attribute Minister Farrakhan's "legitimation" to Black celebrities and politicians. Truth be told, it is not Minister Farrakhan who is the net beneficiary of his interaction with famous folk. It is quite the opposite.

Yes, we have had "Black Moses", but we now in the life, work and ministry of the Honorable Minister Louis Farrakhan we can behold "Black Jesus." The dilemma now before Black America is a question of whether or not we are going to stand by and allow the modern Jewish leaders to crucify a man who has always defended the Black community, even when it has been unpopular? Theology Professor Andre C. Willis is spot on when he says of the Minister:

> "There is simply no Black person in the world that has — over so many years — been as consistent, as unrestricted, and as forthright in defending the humanity of Black people throughout the world against its attackers." -Andre C. Willis

Who then among us will defend Minister Farrakhan? Or will we once again allow a good man to be crucified?

The Honorable Minister Louis Farrakhan: Black America's Head of State

Professor Ernest J. Allen wrote of the Honorable Minister Louis Farrakhan the following:

> "Minister Farrakhan is the first African American since El-Hajj Malik el-Shabazz to be received by African and Middle East governments as a defacto head of state."

Professor Allen's words came back to my mind recently, and I have thought about them since learning of the Minister Farrakhan's visit to the Holy Cities of Mecca and Medina, Saudi Arabia. The Minister and a delegation of extraordinary men and women from the Nation of Islam's leadership traveled recently to experience the last 10 days of Ramadan as guests of the King and his government.

It is no secret, that as Black people in America we have routinely had an ambivalent relationship with the office of the president of the United States of America. Our ambivalence began long before the Donald J. Trump administration. In fact, what President Trump displays of crudeness, insensitivity and racist rhetoric is miniscule when weighed against some of his predecessor presidents, 12 of whom actually owned Black people as slaves. There is enough to write an entire book or series of books detailing the infamous record of how the office of the U. S. President has functioned as an evil Pharaoh in the history of Black people in America.

So, while the international travels and relationships of the U.S. President are of little interest to "John and Jane Q. Public" of Black America; when we see our entertainers, athletes and leaders travel abroad we are eager to learn all about it.

Minister Farrakhan has a long record of important and significant international activity. His travels and global moves have not been that of a mere tourist. Certainly, the Minister has enjoyed visiting the historic sites, but his travels have been in the spirit of and pursuant to the cause of global unity that is powerfully expressed within the teachings of the Most Honorable Elijah Muhammad. The Minister has traveled performing the work of an ambassador, diplomat, conflict resolver and head of state on behalf of Black America. The Minister, as the most keen and astute student of his master teacher-the Most Hon. Elijah Muhammad, has always drawn inspiration from the seed-like ideas planted in the fertile soil of his mind by his teacher. The Most Honorable Elijah Muhammad loves the human family. And his basic teachings to his beloved Black community in America, is that we should see ourselves as a global people. He has taught us that we are first the brothers and sisters of the black, brown, red and yellow peoples of the world. And he has taught us that we are even brothers and sisters in faith with whites who accept and practice Islam. He published a newspaper called Muhammad Speaks and its masthead artwork consisted of the outstretched hands of a Blackman in the western hemisphere clasping the outstretched hands of a Blackman in the eastern hemisphere. This powerful artistic symbol of the mission of the Nation of Islam colors the work and global travels of our beloved Minister-the Blackman's president and head of state-the Honorable Minister Louis Farrakhan!

In a very significant meeting between Minister Farrakhan and former South African hero and president Nelson Mandela, President Mandela reported:

> "Our meeting was able to cover those things that we considered to be fundamental. And there was no issue that arose on which there was disagreement. He has explained his position. His views are identical with the principles that I put forward."

Minister Farrakhan's global importance and head of state status is at the heart of what Jude Wanniski concluded about our beloved Minister. Mr. Wanniski was an economist, political strategist and advisor to President Ronald Reagan. He said of the Minister:

> "I believe Minister Farrakhan is the most important Muslim leader in the world, who can best represent the concerns of the Islamic world to our government."

Such an admission from a member of the ruling class of whites in America is extraordinarily significant. Especially when we consider that it is among the white ruling class that Minister Farrakhan's most powerful enemies exist. It is also important in light of the fact that currently America is deeply entangled within the conflicts, disputes and destiny of various important Muslim dominated countries. The daily news cycle routinely covers news about developments in Iran, Saudi Arabia, Russia and

Israel/Palestine. Minister Farrakhan enjoys strong relationships with various leaders in all these countries. These are all countries that Minister Farrakhan has visited and engaged with their religious, business and political leaders.

In the Fall of last year, the Minister traveled to Iran for high-level talks with the Iranian government and its Supreme Leader. His visit to the "mother town", which is the term of endearment used within the Holy Qur'an for the city of Mecca, occurred during this year's Ramadan observance. Both these Islamic countries have been at odds with one another regarding sectarian religious issues. But recently the Saudi government has become a political ally of Israel, which is a political foe of Iran. The potential for war between these 3 countries and America is brewing.

From America, the Minister has issued various warnings to the Islamic leaders of Iran and Saudi Arabia. He has warned them against shedding each other's blood in a time of war that may be instigated by the American and Israeli governments. The Minister has pointed to the community of Imam Warithuddeen Mohammed and the Nation of Islam as an object lesson and example for the Saudi's and the Iranians. He has highlighted the fact these 2 American Muslim groups, despite serious religious disagreements-disagreements that parallel that of the Shias and Sunnis- have refused to physically fight one another nor shed each other's precious blood.

I am reminded also of a quote from distinguished Islamic scholar Dr. Aminah McCloud when she stated of the Minister's relationships with countries that are frequently identified as adversaries to America.

> "Now, in the last decade of the twentieth century, while the overall number of traditional black Muslims living in America continues to swell, the realities of the Muslim condition in the world community and the tensions between the ummah and the domestic realm remain constant. Minister Farrakhan is trying to bridge these two worlds-and link his at-home concerns with the greater ummah. When Farrakhan visits leaders in Iran or Libya, an uniformed observer might see only that the Minister is willfully consorting with America's enemies, rather than recognizing the visit as an expression of his commitment to ummah..."

Minister Farrakhan's abilities to work amidst hostilities in Muslim countries were on display in Syria in 1983. It was in 1983 that the Reverend Jesse L. Jackson invited Minister Farrakhan to accompany him on a mission to secure the release of a Black American Naval pilot, Lt. Robert Goodman. After his plane was downed flying over Syria, Lt. Goodman was held by Syrian authorities. At that time the Syrians had no intention to release him, and it appeared that President Ronald Reagan had no intention of seeking his release. About this peace mission, Chicago Attorney Thomas N. Todd said Minister Farrakhan:

> "was a 'substantial part of the success' of Mr. Jackson's Syria mission to free Lt. Goodman, although he got little publicity at the time."

Minister Farrakhan's significance on the world stage was also evidenced in him being selected as the Deputy Commander of the World Islamic People's Leadership by the late Libyan leader and advocate for A United States of Africa-Muammar Ghadaffy. In 1997 this group co-sponsored the International Islamic Conference in Chicago where Sheikh Mohammed Sobhi Bello of Cyprus declared of Minister Farrakhan, in a historic ceremony:

> "In the symbol of the leadership and the knowledge of the Qur'an, we signify that by putting this cap (turban) on the head of our leader, Brother Louis Farrakhan in order to show our appreciation and to show that he is knowledgeable and will lead the Islamic Nation, inshallah, with his inspiration."

There are numerous examples of the Minister's international strength of influence. But one of the most culturally relevant was his completing the building of a mosque that was initiated by the late author Alex Haley. Alex Haley, who was a Christian, desired to build a mosque in honor of his Islamic heritage in the village of Juffre in the Gambia, West Africa. But Alex Haley was not able to complete the construction project before he passed away. So, when Minister Farrakhan learned of Mr. Haley's noble efforts, he committed to and subsequently completed the building project and he named it the Alex Haley Mosque and School.

The Minister's Mecca trip brings all of this and so much more to mind. He is truly the representative of the Black people of America on the world stage. And we thank Allah for gifting us with such a beautiful and noble servant to represent us to the broad and vast international community. Allahu-Akbar!

Did Farrakhan Praise Hitler?
Fact Sheet of Truth Destroys Popular Slander

The vitriolic slander against the person and ministry of the Honorable Minister Louis Farrakhan continues to spew forth from a host of Jewish periodicals. These periodicals are currently carrying out a campaign of slander that aims to further the "no platform" policy against the message of the Honorable Minister Louis Farrakhan. These publications and their false allegations against our beloved Minister have repeated certain lies about Minister Farrakhan over and over again during the past 36 years; so much so that their lies are now widely believed to be the truth by many who have fallen victim to the anti-Farrakhan propaganda. The anti-dote to lies and falsehood is the truth. Let us take a look at some critical facts which comprise a strong dose of truth that once and for all buries the popular lie that Minister Farrakhan praised Adolph Hitler.

Context & Brief Timeline

Rev. Jesse Jackson Sr. of the Rainbow Push Coalition launched a major campaign to become the first Black president of the United States in 1984. Rev. Jackson agreed that justice and fair treatment of the Palestinian people be a governing principle of America's foreign policy towards Israel. Many in the Jewish community were angry with Rev. Jackson because of his 1979 meeting and photo-op with Palestinian leader Yasser Arafat. An example of Rev. Jackson's posture toward the Palestinian / Israeli foreign policy includes the following:

> "Many pay lip service to self-determination but refuse to apply it consistently. Some support self-determination for all but the Palestinians, because they confront our closest ally in the Middle East. But to ignore self-determination is only to exacerbate the problem. In the Middle East, Israeli security/Palestinian self- determination are two sides of the same coin. We must do for them what they cannot do for each other: break the cycle of violence, provide guarantees for mutual security in exchange for mutual recognition, land in exchange for peace."

As a result of Rev. Jackson's position Jewish groups sought to ruin his campaign. The March 12, 1984 *Time Magazine* article reported on Jewish harassment of Rev. Jackson:

"Jackson's defenders noted that he has been the target of harassment throughout the campaign. A group called Jews Against Jackson, an offshoot of the radical Jewish Defense League that has been disavowed by leaders of most Jewish organizations, pledged publicly to disrupt his candidacy. Two of its members were arrested for interrupting his announcement speech on Nov. 3 in Washington, D.C. A window in Jackson's New Hampshire campaign headquarters in Manchester was smashed, and his campaign offices in Garden Grove, Calif., were fire bombed. Jackson's life has been threatened."

Threats against the life and candidacy of Rev. Jackson and his family moved Minister Farrakhan to come to his defense. On February 25, 1984 Minister Farrakhan made the following statement:

"I'm saying to the Jewish people who may not like our brother, it is not Jesse Jackson that you are attacking. Remember this now. You're not attacking an individual. Jesse's gone past that now. When you attack him, you attack the millions that are lining up with him. You're attacking all of us. That's not intelligent. That's not an intelligent thing to do. That's not wise. We know that Blacks and Jews have had a good relationship in the past. We've gotten along well, because you're a suffering people and so are we. But my dear Jewish friends, you must understand that everything comes of age. We cannot define our self interest in terms of your self-interest. And because our self-interests differ because we've come of age, why dislike us? Why attack our champion? Why hurl stones at him? Why feed the Press so that they can create a climate into which hatred and bitterness and strife can be poured, creating the same kind of climate that led to the assassination of John Kennedy, the assassination of Martin Luther King, Jr., Malcolm X and Bobby Kennedy. Why create that kind of climate when you have the power to turn it around and show the world that you have sense? Don't you realize what you're doing?... This is a foolish thing that you are doing. I say to you as intelligent people, sit down and talk with Rev. Jackson. Sit down Jewish leaders and talk with us. We are ready to talk with you. Sit down and talk like intelligent people who have future at stake. But if you harm this brother, I warn you in the name of Allah, this will be the last one you harm. We are not making any idle threats, we have no weapons, we [don't] carry so much as a pen knife. But I do tell the world that Almighty God Allah is Backing us up in what we say and what we do, and we warn you in His name --leave this servant of Almighty God alone. Leave him alone. If you want to defeat him, defeat him at the polls. We can stand to lose an election, but we cannot stand to lose our brother..."

February 27, 1984-This powerful defense was the precipitant of Nathan Perlmutter of the ADL and Nat Hentoff of the Village Voice labeling Minister Farrakhan as a "Black Hitler."

March 11, 1984-The pejorative designation of Minister Farrakhan as a "Black Hitler" caused the Minister to defend himself against an attempt at character assassination by making the following statement:

> "Here the Jews don't like Farrakhan and so they call me 'Hitler.' Well that's a good name. Hitler was a very great man. He wasn't great for me as a Black man but he was a great German and he rose Germany up from the ashes of her defeat by the united force of all of Europe and America after the first world war. Yet Hitler took Germany from the ashes and rose her up and made her the greatest fighting machine of the twentieth century, brothers and sisters, and even though Europe and America had deciphered the code that Hitler was using to speak to his chiefs of staff, they still had trouble defeating Hitler even after knowing his plans in advance. Now I'm not proud of Hitler's evil toward Jewish people, but that's a matter of record. He rose Germany up from nothing. Well, in a sense you could say there is a similarity in that we are rising our people up from nothing, but don't compare me with your wicked killers."

ADL Exposed for Lying On the Minister

William E. Alberts of the Monroe Trotter Institute authored a report entitled, *Mainstream Media as Guardian of Racial Hierarchy: A Study of the Threat Posed by Minister Louis Farrakhan and the Million Man March.* He documents the ADL's manipulation of Minister Farrakhan's words so that they could make him appear to be an admirer of Adolph Hitler. Alberts writes:

> "In 1984, Boston Globe columnist David Nyhan reported that the Anti-Defamation League (ADL) of B'nai B'rith deleted Farrakhan's words, *"Now I'm not proud of Hitler's evil against Jewish people, but that's a matter of record... But don't compare me with your wicked killers."* Nyhan wrote that the ADL defended the deletions: "Alan Schwartz, assistant director of research for the ADL, in New York, said in a phone interview... that he omitted the two sentences for reasons of brevity and that he in no way twisted Farrakhan's remarks to make the black

Muslim leader seem more pro-Hitler than he is."

Nyhan then articulated the ADL's obvious distortion of Farrakhan's words: "But the fact remains: Farrakhan originally said, 'I'm not proud of Hitler's evil against Jewish people,' and he added, 'Don't compare me with your wicked killers.'" To delete these phrases changes Farrakhan's meaning. However, neither readers in 1984 nor during the March were made aware of Farrakhan's rejection of the comparison with and condemnation of Hitler as one of "your wicked killers." The deletion of such a critical context and the reported explaining away of its significance could indicate a tendency (on the part of those who constantly condemn Farrakhan as anti-Semitic) to only report and print the news that fits the agenda or bias of the racial status quo. The omission of such an important context makes suspect other charges against Farrakhan. It also indicates the need of an in-depth study of the "secret relationship" between Jews and Blacks committed to uncovering the whole truth rather than only those facts that fit preconceived views."

This brief overview of facts makes it crystal clear that it was the ADL who first invoked the name Hitler to smear Min. Farrakhan for courageously defending his brother, Rev. Jackson. Minister Farrakhan examined their reference to Hitler to defend himself against the scandalous association of him -a man of peace- with Hitler-one of the most wicked killers in world history. The facts are clear. The facts vindicate Minister Farrakhan so that he might receive the help, support and honor he so richly deserves.

"You Are All Gods":
Why Divine Embodiment Is The Most Important Religion To Heal The Hood

"I have said, You are gods; and all of you are children of the most High."

—Psalms 82:6 (KJV)

"For you are the temple of the living God; as God has said, I will dwell in them, and walk in them; and I will be their God, and they shall be my people."

—2 Corinthians 6:16 (KJB)

"And when thy Lord said to the angels: I am going to create a mortal of sounding clay, of black mud fashioned into shape. So, when I have made him complete and breathed into him of My spirit, fall down making obeisance to him. So, the angels made obeisance, all of them together"

—Holy Qur'an 15:28-30 (M. M. Ali Translation)

"My servant continues to draw near to Me with supererogatory works so that I shall love him. When I love him, I am his hearing with which he hears, his seeing with which he sees, his hand with which he strikes and his foot with which he walks."

—Prophet Muhammad (pbuh/saw) (Hadith Qudsi No.25)

"What do you want to be when you grow up?"

Once upon a time this was a question asked of children and the response was "policeman, fireman, doctor or lawyer." What is interesting about the traditional responses to this question is that each profession involves helping other people. Each of those professions is service oriented. And each of those professions is an honorable vocation for any young child to aspire to. During the days prior to racial integration in America, most Black children grew up in neighborhoods where their neighbors were actually policemen, firemen, doctors, lawyers, architects and business persons. This was one of the many benefits of living in a Black ethnic enclave in America. And while most intellectuals at that time, and some today, decried the segregationist laws that produced separate Black communities, there were many benefits to that separateness, which the Black community desperately needs today. Those times—pertaining to Black children and what they aspired to be when they grew up—were ripe times of noble aspirations.

Today many Black youth aspire to be athletes and entertainers, and many possess an admiration for prison life that borders on actual aspiration. Their aspirations reflect the poverty, blight and crime present in the communities in which they live. These are post-integration communities. The Black community today in America's inner-cities have over time witnessed the Black professional class migrate to suburban areas that are racially more diverse and often predominantly white in racial make-up. So even though *"the mind can achieve whatever it can conceive,"* it is nearly impossible for the mind to conceive what it has never seen an example of.

In that sense there needs to be a new aspiration in the "hood." Young Black men and women must no longer look to Hollywood for the images that will shape and mold their self-concept. The men and women, boys and girls who live in the impoverished inner-cities must have a new model to emulate and embody. The "hood" needs a mental make-over. This mental make-over involves a new and radical change to our understanding of the origins of life and a reappraisal of human potential. The religious teachings of the Nation of Islam can be of great benefit in this regard.

The Honorable Elijah Muhammad once said, "Every time you look at a Black man, you are looking at God." He suffered great criticism for such a bold pronouncement. Even those who credit his ability to reform the downtrodden have disagreed with his revolutionary theology. But the Honorable Elijah Muhammad's teaching and insight into the reality of God is a reaffirmation of the Bible that describes God in human form, visiting and liberating the Hebrew slaves. The Nation of Islam's theology is also an acknowledgement of God's ability to do today what he did during the time of the prophets and peoples of yesterday.

Scholars and theologians recognize the Honorable Elijah Muhammad's teaching as a major theme in religious studies known as Divine Embodiment. The subject of Divine Embodiment covers the Bible's human manifestations of God known as theophanies as well as the Holy Qur'an's personification of God known as anthropomorphism. Basically, Divine Embodiment means that the ultimate goal for human life is to unite with the source of that life, which is God Himself. Man and woman are potentially gods. This is borne witness to by the above quotes from Christian and Islamic sacred texts. Moreover, the Bible teaches that man and woman are created in the image and likeness of God (Genesis 1:26); David confirms and clarifies this by saying that "you are all gods, children of the most High God. (Psalms 82:6)" The Holy Qur'an teaches that Allah (God) made man out of Black mud and caused the angels to submit to him (H.Q. 15:28-30).

If Black clergy would begin to teach and promote the idea of Divine Embodiment as the goal of human life, it could revitalize their shrinking congregations. The *Economist* magazine reports on the rise of atheism in America:

> "...the past seven years have seen a fivefold increase in people who call themselves atheists, to 5% of the population, according to WIN-Gallup International, a network of pollsters. Meanwhile the proportion of Americans who say they are religious has fallen from 73% in 2005 to 60% in 2011."

In an article in *The Week* magazine, the rise of atheism is attributed to the rise of moralistic hypocrisy in religion. The Catholic priest sex scandal and the politicization of faith by the "religious right" are cited as evidence of an increasing unattractive and distasteful moralistic hypocrisy that governs today's religious experience.

These infamous events of hypocrisy within the religious community are the reason why Divine Embodiment needs to become the new religious emphasis today. People are taught that man is by nature sinful, but he must worship a righteous God in order to be free of the effects of his sinful nature. Colloquialisms like "to err is human" and "nobody's perfect" have been coined to reflect this belief. However, it is easy to see how this belief creates a built-in excuse for hypocrisy and wrongdoing, because, after all, "to err is human."

The message of Divine Embodiment is what is needed to revive religion's attractiveness. Specifically, religion can be revived by a society of men and women who aspire to be like God. This is what Jesus was teaching in the New Testament when he said "I and my Father are one." This is what he was teaching when he chided the people for "loving God whom they had never seen and hating their brothers that they saw daily." The implication being that the essence and potential of God are within the capacity of your brother to manifest, and you can bring out those divine qualities if you show him love and respect.

This is what Minister Farrakhan is desirous of producing among the violent streets of Chicago and everywhere his Peace In The Streets campaign has gone. His goal is to inspire the Black community to aspire to be like God. His message is that the true worship of God is found in the human beings striving to submit to Him and give up every artificial character trait, mental attitude and behavior that violates man and woman's innate goodness.

In fact, when the children aspire to be doctors, lawyers, policemen, firemen, scientists, engineers or any other nation-building profession, they are aspiring to professions that demonstrate man's ability to be like God. A good example of this are the 99 Attributes or Names of Allah (God) found in Islam. The 99 characteristics of Allah (God) reflect the noblest of qualities and abilities. They represent the perfect ideal for human beings to aspire to. It is even customary in Islamic culture for Allah's attributes to be used as the personal names of Muslims.

All this points to there being a hidden message in religion—that is, that man and woman can become gods. And since we have proven that we can be devils that destroy our communities, don't you think it is time now to go from "N@#8!%*s to Gods."

"The Earth Swallows The Flood": Minister Farrakhan, Hip-Hop Controversy & End-Times Prophecy

"But the earth helped the woman, and the earth opened its mouth and swallowed up the flood which the dragon had spewed out of his mouth."- Revelations 12:16-NKJV

"The ultimate aim of this world should be known to everyone; especially the righteous…The (arch-deceivers) ultimate aim is to do as their people have done-try to destroy the preacher of truth and those who believe in him. This was the aim of Cain when he slew his brother, Abel, and the aim of the dragon when he sought to destroy the woman (Messenger), as it is written in Revelations 12:4" -Hon. Elijah Muhammad April 30, 1965

The Honorable Minister Louis Farrakhan's July 4th message, which offered divine guidance and pastoral comfort in the midst of a global pandemic to millions of men and women throughout the world, at the same time generated a flood of negative news coverage from various publications within the Jewish community.

Popular YouTube vlogger DJ Vlad joined the Jewish press in attempting to scandalize the Minister's divine message. His insistence that Minister Farrakhan had used his July 4th message to call for violence against Jews was met with scorn and rebuke from many in the Black community, many of whom took to social media to register their condemnation of DJ Vlad's false statements against our beloved Minister.

In reaction to the Black community's righteous indignation against DJ Vlad for slandering Minister Farrakhan, the popular YouTuber and member of the Jewish community released the following statement detailing his actions:

> "On Friday, Vlad TV posted an interview with D.L. Hughley where I referenced part of Farrakhan's speech about Jews. After our interview was released, I was made aware that there was a later part in Farrakhan's speech where he clarified those points. Based on that new info, we removed that part of our interview, changed the title and removed the social media posts. Although I don't agree with some of Farrakhan's statements, Vlad TV has always reported on people accurately and will continue to do so."

Vlad's statement however, angered many due to the fact that it failed to include an apology to Minister Farrakhan. This anger undoubtedly arises from the Black community having taken notice that when Blacks are alleged to have offended the Jewish community, public apologies are required from the offending Black person. They are also expected to allow Jewish organizations to educate them on Jewish suffering. And often times they are expected to donate large sums of money to Jewish institutions and causes. And all of this is done to demonstrate contrition and sincere sorrow for having offended the Jewish community. It is also required so that the Jewish community will refrain from using its influence to ruin the offending Black person's career and reputation. The most recent example of this is the talented entertainer Nick Cannon. To put it plainly, many in the Black community feel that if Jews are going to require Nick Cannon et.al. to undergo a step by step process to make amends for offenses to the Jewish community; DJ Vlad should do the same to make amends to the Black community.

One of the most vocal voices of condemnation against DJ Vlad has been Detroit based rapper Royce Da 5'9". He took to his Instagram account to record a powerful statement in support of the Honorable Minister Louis Farrakhan. Royce Da 5'9" boldly stated:

> "I think you need to understand, that as an associate of yours, when you misquoted Minister Farrakhan, that is highly offensive to me...It's reparable to me, between me and you. But nothing like this can ever happen again. It's making my brain go somewhere else. I'm starting to get that abused feeling again.... We're being nice. We're a kind forgiving people. Minister Farrakhan is a very regal, deep, intellectual, cerebral, great man. My respect love and admiration for him will never waver, ever...So you can't have a relationship with me, if you don't respect the Minister."

He has been joined in his stance against DJ Vlad by legendary Hip Hop artist and podcaster Lord Jamar and Comedian Godfrey. Activist MC Mysonne the General and Nation of Islam member, the legendary artist West Coast KAM have also used their social media platforms to call out DJ Vlad and issue forth the call to boycott his YouTube podcast.

Spiritual Intersection

That these popular Hip-Hop artists are uniting on the occasion of DJ Vlad's attempt to assassinate the character of the Honorable Minister Louis Farrakhan is very significant. It draws our attention to the scriptures of the Bible, particularly the scriptures that use poetic language to detail the End-Times prophecies concerning the last days and years of the present global civilization of the Caucasian or European people. These prophecies include a reference to the presence of a divine Messenger of God who is symbolically described as a woman who is pregnant with a child of destiny. Commonly referred to as "the woman and the dragon prophecy", this dramatic passage of scripture includes Satan who is described as a great and powerful dragon.

The passage from the Bible's Revelation's chapter 12 that leads into this article reveals that the dragon sought to drown the pregnant woman in his attempt to kill the woman and the child she was about to deliver, a child whose destiny it is to rule the nations of the Earth. But instead of being successful in the destruction of the mother and child of destiny in her womb, the dragon's flood is rendered non-effective because **the Earth swallowed the flood and helped the woman escape to a safe place with God.**

This poetic and symbolic portrait of one of the Bible's major end-times events is explained by the Most Honorable Elijah Muhammad and the Honorable Minister Louis Farrakhan. The "woman and the dragon" episode has deep and profound meaning. This "woman" is a symbolic reference to the Most Honorable Elijah Muhammad's national representative, the Honorable Minister Louis Farrakhan. He is anointed and authorized by Allah (God) through the Most Honorable Elijah Muhammad to deliver the Black man and woman of America from our present state of mental and spiritual death. Our destiny as a people is the same destiny of the child inside the womb of the woman being pursued by the dragon in Revelations 12:16. Our destiny is to replace the old wicked rulership of this present civilization of the white man, with the righteous rulership and civilization of Allah (God); to fill the earth with righteousness and the praises of Allah (God).

A careful study of Minister Farrakhan's conflict with the Jewish community on behalf of Black people in America reveals that this "woman and the dragon" episode found in Revelation 12:16 is prophetic prediction of the Minister's conflict.

Minister Farrakhan has been unique as a leader of Black people in that his efforts among us are always fueled by his demonstration of an unconditional love for us. For even when other Black leaders have repudiated the Minister, he has forgiven them and refuses to retaliate against them. His love for us is divine. And it is both paternal and maternal. He is therefore a consummate leader. As a father, his love of his people is on display in his long history of sharing guidance and profound knowledge, wisdom and understanding to the Black community. And he has been a great provider for our people in the way he has worked to create a model of solutions to many of the social ills we suffer from in the Black community, solutions that if followed en masse would make the Black people of America one of the healthiest and wealthiest in the world. His unconditional love is like the maternal love of a mother, and it is frequently seen in his ability to defend even the worst among us. Yet despite Minister Farrakhan's beneficial impact on Black people, his conflict with the Jewish community causes mainstream media outlets to denigrate him and victimize him with false propaganda. The purpose of their propaganda is character assassination which is itself purposed to incite physical assassination.

There is a lot that can be expounded upon and extracted in this passage whereby relevant parallels can be drawn to current events to open up more and more of the scripture's inner meaning for those who are courageous enough to study it.

Royce Da 5'9", Lord Jamar, West Coast KAM, Mysonne the General and Godfrey's collective stance against the flood of propaganda aimed at Minister Farrakhan is an encouraging sign of the "earth swallowing up the flood" to help the modern messenger of Allah (God)-the Honorable Minister Louis Farrakhan.

These strong brothers and their stance signify that Allah (God) is with Minister Farrakhan. While these brothers are standing in support of Minister Farrakhan, other prominent Black celebrities are similarly refusing to repudiate and condemn the Minister even though they are being pressured to do so by Jewish organizations. In recent times Nick Cannon, Stephen Jackson, Ice Cube and others have resisted the evil suggestion by Jewish political organizations to repudiate Minister Farrakhan.

Again, these are encouraging signs. They help us to see that Allah (God) is involved in these controversial current events. They are signs that the people, symbolically referenced as the "earth swallowing up the flood", are willing to help the Messenger of Allah (God) by standing against the modern dragon's flood of propaganda.

Empathy: Minister Farrakhan, Conflict Resolution & The Restoration of Brotherhood

Every morning that I turn on my television to watch the local news, I am frequently saddened to learn of shootings and deaths that have taken place during the previous night. In the Black community deaths resulting from gun violence have become a disturbing phenomenon. All too often, we make the decision to react violently to those with whom we have disagreements. News stories abound that reveal that we have reached a time where even a minor disagreement or interpersonal dispute can result in someone being shot and killed.

The inability to peacefully resolve conflicts that exist between husbands and wives; parents and children; brothers and sisters; co-workers and colleagues; neighbors and friends has, at this point, produced rivers of bloodshed within the Black community. We have a great need to make peaceful conflict resolution a Black cultural norm. Our survival as a people depends on it.

An important aspect of peaceful conflict resolution is the development of the ability to empathize with those whom we have a disagreement with. I am studying the characteristic of empathy based upon witnessing it on display in the life of my teacher the Honorable Minister Louis Farrakhan. I learn a lot by studying Minister Farrakhan. He is my teacher and I love to share what I have learned from him. He is an unusual man, and I think that we all should carefully study his life, his work, his words and how he has been greatly mistreated and misunderstood.

One of the things that make the Minister unusual is his profound spirituality. I have seen people who represent themselves as spiritual, but time and circumstances proved that their commitment to spiritual principles was very superficial. As I understand it, spirituality or spiritual awareness is when we can respect the fact that each and every human being is so much more than mere flesh and blood. Spiritual awareness is the recognition that man and woman exist as a unique configuration of mind, body, soul and spirit. Spiritual awareness is the appreciation of the fact that no man or woman is who they once were; and neither is any man or woman who they will become in the future. We are all growing and evolving. Ultimately spiritual awareness or spirituality is the understanding that Allah (God) is the only true reality. Allah was; Allah is; and Allah will always be. The rest of us are passing and temporary realties who occupy time and space for a season within all of eternity. The spiritually aware and awakened man or woman seeks to live life, our short season within all eternity, acting in harmony with the Creator and His Creation.

The critics of Minister Farrakhan don't see him as spiritual. They attribute pejorative attributes to him all the time. They call him angry and hate-filled. Yet, what they misconstrue as hate and anger is the passionate expression of courage born out of his deep and profound capacity to love. This is a very important fact to appreciate. For, when the Bible states that **"perfect love casts out fear"** it presents courage and bravery as the fruit of love. Courage then must not be seen or viewed as arising out of vanity; nor must it be thought of as the result of hatred. The Minister's long history of "speaking truth to power" is a portrait of awe-inspiring courage. That Minister Farrakhan has been witnessed and become known for speaking powerful truths that condemn the evils of the most powerful forces within the world, is extraordinary. It is the result of his deep and profound capacity for love; the love that removes fear and produces courage.

I remember an experience that I had with the Honorable Minister Louis Farrakhan that has made me study and subsequently write this article on the importance of empathy as a characteristic feature of successful interpersonal conflict resolution. According to the Collins Dictionary of the English language, empathy is defined as:

> "the power of understanding and imaginatively entering into another person's feelings; the projection of one's own personality into the personality of another in order to understand the person better; ability to share in another's emotions, thoughts, or feelings"-Collins Dictionary of the English Language

In appreciating the importance of **empathy**, it is also helpful to differentiate between a similar concept, the characteristic of **sympathy**. According to Webster's Dictionary:

> "**Sympathy**, constructed from the Greek "sym," meaning together, and "pathos," referring to feelings or emotion, is used to describe when one person shares the same feelings of another, such as when someone close is experiencing grief or loss. **Empathy** is a newer word also related to "pathos," but there is a greater implication of emotional distance.

With "empathy" you can imagine or understand to how someone might feel, without necessarily having those feelings yourself."

Last week many in the Chicago community and others around the country were saddened to learn of the passing of Brother Munir Muhammad. Brother Munir was a very important man who built an institution dedicated and purposed to remember and promote the Most Honorable Elijah Muhammad. His center for the housing of C.R.O.E. [the **C**oalition for the **R**emembrance **O**f the Honorable **E**lijah Muhammad] also served as a television studio for his popular television program called *Muhammad and Friends*. I was blessed to be invited by Brother Munir to be a guest on his show last year. I am very grateful to Brother Munir for hosting me and so many of my colleagues and fellow helpers of the Honorable Minister Louis Farrakhan. May Allah (God) be pleased with him.

When I learned of his passing I thought about a "rough patch" in his relationship with Minister Farrakhan that was very public. Because of disagreements and misunderstandings-natural to any and all relationships-Brother Munir publicly chastised and made unflattering statements about Minister Farrakhan. However, one day Minister Farrakhan said to some of us that Brother Munir wanted to meet with him to reconcile. At that time, I did not feel that this was something that the Minister should do. I was angry and disappointed due to the way that Brother Munir was making very negative statements about my teacher, Minister Farrakhan. I don't think I expressed it verbally to the Minister, but I felt this way within my own heart and mind.

But as I watched Minister Farrakhan react to Brother Munir's request, I began to re-think my position and I learned a profound lesson. The Minister said that Brother Munir feels that *"I broke his heart."* The Minister then looked pensively out into the distance and asked the question *"How do you mend a broken heart."* The room was quiet as those of us with the Minister could see that he was deep in thought. And someone said that *"you know Brother Minister there is a song called 'How do you mend a broken heart'?"* The Minister replied *"Really, I'd like to hear it."* So, the brother found a clip of the song on YouTube and played it so the Minister could listen to it. We all listened to it for a while until someone mentioned that the version of the song we were listening to was by Al Green but that the original had been done by a group called the Bee Gee's. The Minister replied, *"Really, I'd like to hear it."* So, someone found the original version of *"How do you mend a broken heart?"* sung by the Bee Gee's and we sat listening to their original version. I remember thinking to myself that I never thought that I would have such an unusual experience as sitting listening to the Bee Gee's with the Honorable Minister Louis Farrakhan. I felt blessed and privileged to witness what I was witnessing.

I was deeply touched by what I witnessed in how Minister Farrakhan handled and reacted to Brother Munir. I watched as the Minister sat quietly thinking, reflecting and listening to songs because he was trying to see and understand Brother Munir's point of view. He was making the sincerest of efforts to empathize with his brother and to, as the definition states, to *"imaginatively enter into another person's feelings in order to understand the person better."* An ordinary man in Minister Farrakhan's position of prominence and power would not be willing to absorb the offense of his brother without retaliating. And most folks, whether in positions of power or not, aren't willing to sincerely try and see things from the viewpoint of a complaining friend, colleague or family member. Our communities are filled with examples of when misunderstandings and rather minor disagreements rapidly escalate into "World Star-esque" scenes of violent savagery.

Brother Munir's passing brought this important episode in my life back to my remembrance. And though saddened by his passing, I felt inspired because Brother Munir was able to leave this world having participated in a process of reconciliation and a restoration of brotherhood between himself and Minister Farrakhan. Both he and Minister Farrakhan are to be commended for providing this demonstration of empathy, conflict resolution and reconciliation that we all can learn from and emulate.

Facebook Punishes Minister Farrakhan With Slave Code Laws

"[Lord], Shall the throne of iniquity have fellowship with you, which frames mischief by a law"? (Psalms 94:20 AKJV)

"[God], Will destructive national leaders, who plan wicked things through misuse of the Law, be allied with you"? (Psalms 94:20 ISV)

Students of Black History are well aware that since the beginning of Black Life in America there has existed a separate set of harsh laws and rules established for the purpose of keeping Black people in a state of perpetual slavery. Commonly referred to as the Slave Codes and later on as Black Codes, these "special" laws and regulations were extraordinarily punitive and restrictive. Yet, they were the rules that our enslaved fore parents were forced to live under. Knowing what we know now about the phenomenon known as "epigenetics", where the traumatic effects of negative environments are passed from one generation to the next on a cellular level, we understand how the Black community's experience under such a harsh judicial system has naturally created ambivalence and an overall tension-laden bad relationship between Black folk and the American justice system.

I once read an article written by the Most Honorable Elijah Muhammad called **Separation or Death** that was published within the legendary Negro-Press publication The Los Angeles Herald Dispatch. He referenced a book called **The American Slave Code** written by William Goodell. The words of the Most Honorable Elijah Muhammad are as follows:

> "According to the American Slave Code of Law, by William Goodell—page 304, under the above title, the Negroes may be used as breeders, prostitutes, concubines, pimps, tapsters, attendants at the gaming table and as subjects of medical and surgical experiments for the benefit of science."

The quote attributed to Mr. Goodell's book describes the purpose for the slave codes. These laws were designed to ensure that Black people would never be able to have a purpose or function outside those most degrading roles. These degrading and inferior roles within American society are the only ones approved for Black people to function as. In other words, if a Black person desires or tries to be anything other than these degrading characters they are acting outside the law. It was the perspective of the white ruling class then and today, that for a Black person to be someone who is a responsible husband, wife, father, businessman, businesswoman, scholar, artist, scientist or anything of this sort, it is to commit and illegal act. To pursue roles of human dignity and nobility would make the offending Black person an outlaw. The American Slave Codes essentially outlawed universally accepted practices of righteous conduct!

I respectfully submit that an understanding of the American Slave Code is extremely important to understand the nefarious origins of the social media ban that Facebook/Instagram have executed to punish the Honorable Minister Louis Farrakhan.

If we were living in the 1700s or the 1800s, Minister Farrakhan would be considered a rabble-rouser, an abolitionist preacher. His preaching would be both feared and hated by the plantation owners and the white ruling class of slave holders. And the social media ban would be executed in compliance with the legal prohibitions or laws against slaves preaching and the laws against abolitionist speech.

Yes, there were actual laws against any slave vocally expressing or writing their disagreement with being a slave! It was the view of the slave holders that *'Blacks are our slaves, and they better not even utter a mumbling word that they are unhappy in being our slaves!'*

Mr. Goodell gives us examples of the laws against abolitionist speech and publications:

> "In Louisiana If any person shall use any language from the BAR, BENCH, STAGE, PULPIT, or in any OTHER place, or hold any CONVERSATION having a TENDENCY to promote discontent among free colored people, or insubordination among slaves, he may be imprisoned at hard labor not less than three nor more than twenty-one years; or he may suffer death, at the discretion of the Court. ... In North Carolina, 'for publishing or circulating any pamphlet or paper having an evident tendency to excite slaves or free persons of color to insurrection or resistance,' the law provides imprisonment not less than one year, and standing in the pillory and whipping, at the discretion of the Court, for the first offense, and DEATH for the second. In Georgia, the same without any reservation. In Virginia, the first offense is punished with thirty-nine lashes, and the second with death. Mr. Preston, Senator in Congress,

declared, in his place in that body, that any person uttering abolition sentiments at the South would be hanged." *(The American Slave Code pages 384-386)*

In the modern era, the spirit of these laws can be found within the regular attempts to silence Minister Farrakhan and keep him from speaking out against how Black people are still treated as slaves throughout all of America's institutions. He was censured by the U.S. Senate in 1984 for defending Rev. Jesse L. Jackson. He was banned from speaking on college campuses in 1992 as a result of the work of the Anti-Defamation League of B'Nai B'rith. And now Facebook/Instagram have banned him for life from their social media platforms.As Mr. Goodell makes it clear, one of the foundational stones of the "peculiar institution" of American slavery was the suppression of the speech of slaves. He describes how it was written into law that no slave could even provide testimony in a court of law against the crimes committed against him by his mater or any other white person. According to Goodell:

> "Slavery is upheld by suppressing the testimony of its victims. Allow slaves to testify, and the hitherto unimagined secrets...would explode like an earthquake. Universal humanity would unite in one general crusade, and break down its whole fabric."

According to Fredrick Douglass, slaves learned the hard way not to speak against their masters. He writes of when a slave master questioned his slave: **"Well, boy, whom do you belong to?" "To Colonel Lloyd," replied the slave. "Well, does the colonel treat you well?" "No, sir," was the ready reply. "What, does he work you too hard?" "Yes, sir."** ... The colonel, after ascertaining where the slave belonged, rode on; the man also went on about his business, not dreaming that he had been conversing with his master. He thought, said, and heard nothing more of the matter, until two or three weeks afterwards. **The poor man was then informed by his overseer that, for having found fault with his master, he was now to be sold to a Georgia trader. He was immediately chained and cuffed; and thus, without a moment's warning, he was snatched away, and forever sundered, from his family and friends, by a hand more unrelenting than death. This is the penalty of telling the truth, of telling the simple truth, in answer to a series of plain questions.** It is partly in consequence of such facts, that slaves, when inquired of as to their condition and the character of their masters; almost universally say they are contented, and that their masters are kind. The slaveholders have been known to send in spies among their slaves, to ascertain their views and feelings in regard to their condition. **The frequency of this has had the effect to establish among the slaves the maxim, that a still tongue makes a wise head. They suppress the truth rather than take the consequences of telling it....**" (The Narrative of the Life of Fredrick Douglass)

The suppression of the speech of Black people that began with the slave codes has indeed taught many in the Black community that there is great price to be paid for telling the truth. According to Harper's Bazaar writer Rachel Elizabeth Cargle this phenomenon continues up to the present day and time. Her article entitled **"When White People Are Uncomfortable, Black People Are Silenced"**, states:

"Silencing happens when, for white people, hearing the truth is too much; when the truth hangs so painfully heavy on their shoulders that they'd rather get rid of the weight, than actually face the issue head on. But why would something as virtuous as truth be a burden for some? Because when the truth is held up, it reflects the false securities that our society rests on: the elitism, the capitalism, the racism, the ableism, the sexism, the homo/transphobia, the xenophobia, the anti-blackness. And the people who benefit from those systems have a hard time letting go of their privilege within those realms. To escape these truths, silencing has very often been the answer."

Minister Farrakhan is unafraid to speak the truth. He is, for all of us, a great gift from Allah (God). As Professor Geneva Smitherman has said of him:

> "Quiet as it's kept, Farrakhan is respected by millions of African American, on all socio-economic levels, for his courage in standing up to an oppressive system and his penchant for calling white folk out. Truly "unbought and unbossed," he often says the things that many Blacks feel **but don't have the freedom to express**." (Million Man March by Haki Madhubuti page 104)

The time is now for us to unite and campaign against the ban against Minister Farrakhan, so that all who are courageous enough be un-muzzled and un-muted may be forever free to speak truth to power on behalf of all who suffer under modern forms of slavery and oppression.

The Year 1974 and Why Farrakhan Is Good For Morgan State

The recent article in the Baltimore Sun condemning the Honorable Minister Louis Farrakhan is a feeble attempt to dissuade students and members of the Baltimore/Morgan State community from attending the Minister's lecture on November 22, 2014. It was written by a member of the Jewish community seeking to assassinate Minister Farrakhan's character and to make his critical analysis of Jewish misdeeds in the Black community, a reason for not attending this historic event.

Minister Farrakhan has spoken to the students at Morgan State University on several momentous occasions and all with positive outcomes. As he is always such a well-spring of knowledge, wisdom, inspiration and motivation, the Morgan State students should be commended and congratulated for making such a wise choice of inviting the Honorable Minister Louis Farrakhan.

The Minister is, according to Jewish apologist Abraham Foxman, the last man standing. Foxman said of the Minister in the April 2013 issue of Ha'ertz Magazine

> "The only leadership that now exists in that community"—the "African American community"— "is Louis Farrakhan. Farrakhan can assemble 20,000 people several times a year,"

Why wouldn't Black college students want to listen to and be guided by the "last man standing?" It is indeed a wise choice on the part of these courageous young people. In 1974 their parents' generation came out in droves to be inspired and motivated by Minister Farrakhan. Minister Farrakhan was the keynote speaker at a Black Family Day event in 1974 at Morgan State where 30,000 students, faculty and Baltimore residents attended this electrifying event.

The Minister's message was reported on in the October 11, 1974 issue of the Muhammad Speaks (MS) newspaper. The MS coverage documented some of the highlights of the Minister's message that day as he echoed many of the powerful themes and ideas resident within the teachings of the Most Honorable Elijah Muhammad. The Minister taught the students

> "You are not a man, until you learn how to love, respect and protect, your Black woman."

128-STUDENTS OF FARRAKHAN

The Minister continued this theme of respect and protection for the woman by teaching the students that

> "The Honorable Elijah Muhammad says to us that the only way we can gain the respect of the civilized world is to take that Black woman honor her, respect her, protect her..."

Minister Farrakhan was so well received by the students at Morgan State that they invited him to come back and teach them more from the wisdom of the Most Honorable Elijah Muhammad. The November 29, 1974 issue of the Muhammad Speaks newspaper reported that nearly 1000 students filled Murphy auditorium to hear Minister Farrakhan. Muhammad Speaks reporter Lonnie Kashif documents some of the powerful guidance the Minister shared with the students. The Minister said,

> "...don't doubt the power of Allah to make something out of you; don't doubt the power of Allah to bring you from under the foot of white people and make them bow to you who once groveled in the dust at their feet."

The Jewish propagandist, who wrote the Baltimore Sun article condemning Minister Farrakhan's visit at Morgan State obviously has a problem with this kind of messaging being given to Black students. This kind of message motivates and inspires Black students toward an enlightened self-interest. It restores in the students a concern for their communities and gives the students an awakening that will prevent these brilliant young people from further exploitation.

Perhaps he would rather these gifted young Black students not know what Minister Farrakhan knows. He called Minister Farrakhan anti-Semitic. And since he opened that door, let's look inside it to see some of the things that Minister Farrakhan has made known about the hidden misdeeds of the Jews against Blacks. In the Secret Relationship Between Blacks and Jews series, Minister Farrakhan has made known previously hidden admissions from Jewish scholars, historians and rabbis. Some jaw-dropping revelations include:

> "The first two centuries of the Black-Jewish encounter in America were highlighted by a fairly extensive record of Jewish slave-holding. Indeed, during the colonial period, in the small Jewish community of the time, **almost every Jewish household of any form, North or South,**

possessed at least one slave."
-Dr. Abraham Peck, American Jewish Archives
From the exhibit "Blacks and Jews: The American Experience: 1654-1992," presented by Hebrew Union College, Jewish Institute of Religion, the American Jewish Archives, and the America Jewish Committee.

"The cotton plantations in many parts of the South **were wholly in the hands of the Jews, and as a consequence slavery found its advocates among them.**" The Jewish Encyclopedia

"In Charleston, Richmond and Savannah the large majority (over three-fourths) of the Jewish households contained one or more slaves; **in Baltimore**, only one out of three households were slaveholding; in New York, one out of eighteen.... Among the slaveholding households the median number of slaves owned ranged from five in Savannah to one in New York."
- "The Jewish Population in 1820," in Abraham J. Karp, ed., The Jewish Experience in America: Selected Studies from the Publications of the American Jewish Historical Society (Waltham, Massachusetts, 1969, 3 volumes), volume 2, pp. 2, 17, 19.

"It would seem to be realistic to conclude that any Jew who could afford to own slaves and had need for their services would do so.... **Jews participated in every aspect and process of the exploitation of the defenseless blacks.**"
-Rabbi Bertram Korn, From "Jews and Negro Slavery in the Old South, 1789-1865," Dr. Korn is a rabbi, historian with degrees from Hebrew Union College-Jewish Institute of Religion, Cincinnati.

"**The female slave was a sex tool beneath the level of moral considerations. She was an economic good, useful, in addition to her menial labor, for breeding more slaves. To attain that purpose, the master mated her promiscuously according to his breeding plans. The master himself and his sons and other members of his household took turns with her for the increase of the family wealth, as well as for satisfaction of their extra-marital sex desires. Guests and neighbors too were invited to that luxury.**"
- Dr. Louis Epstein, author of Sex Laws and Customs in Judaism

What the Jewish propagandist in the Baltimore Sun is angry over is that Minister Farrakhan has exposed this history to the Black community. It is a history that needs to be told. Because unless Black people know the history of what happened to us, we will look upon one another in our miserable condition and draw the wrong conclusion.

It is ironic that in 1974 when Minister Farrakhan was at Morgan State awakening the Black students to their duty and responsibility to God, family and community, Jewish leaders were doing something entirely different.

In 1974 the Anti-Defamation League of B'Nai B'rith (ADL) and the American Jewish Congress joined forces to legally fight against Affirmative Action. In other words, while Minister Farrakhan was giving Black college students purpose and guidance for their education, Jewish groups were working to reduce the number of Black students able to enter into college. The case entitled DeFunis v. Odegaard had been dubbed in some Jewish publications "the greatest legal battle in the history of America." The ADL had pressured a young Sephardic Jewish student Marco DeFunis Jr. to sue for entry into Washington University Law School after he had been initially denied. His argument was that the school's admission policy favored Blacks to the exclusion of qualified whites.

DeFunis v. Odegaard was at the time widely viewed as a betrayal of Black progress by supposed Jewish allies. Civil rights leaders were disappointed. Maryland Congressman Parren J. Mitchell said

> "If the court rules in favor of DeFunis, we've lost our one weapon to get Blacks into colleges and professional schools-affirmative action. No school will let us in out of the goodness of its heart, without the pressure of the law and courts backing us up."

The value of Minister Farrakhan's visit to the students at Morgan State is even more important in light of another critical event that took place in 1974. It was then that Dr. Richard Hammerschlag, a neuro-chemist working for the City of Hope National Medical Center in Duarte, California revealed ominous truths at the American Chemical Society's national meeting in Los Angeles. Dr. Hammerschlag revealed that the U.S. military was involved in genetic research to develop a weapon capable of wiping out Black people while excluding other ethnic groups.

Dr. Hammerschlag cited a November 1970 article written by Carl Larson in the magazine Military Review on the work being done to create "ethnic weapons." Dr. Hammerschlag pointed out in his presentation that new information indicates that there are "many blood proteins (known as polymorphisms) that exist in several different genetically controlled forms in human populations." And that based on this, substances can be created to adversely affect a specific ethnic population who has a particular type of polymorphism without affecting other ethnic populations. He added that as a result of "the newly developed, binary nerve gases, the possibility of genetically selective weapons becomes entirely feasible and quite probable.

What Dr. Hammerschlag pointed out in 1974 appears to have come to fruition in 2014. Minister Farrakhan said is on record warning the Black community of the creation of "race-based weapons."

The Minister said in his very popular lecture entitled Justifiable Homicide: Black Youth In Peril that

> "Another method [of depopulation] is disease infection through **bio-weapons such as Ebola and AIDS, which are race targeting weapons**. There is a weapon that can be put in a room where there are Black and White people, and it will kill only the Black and spare the White, because it is a genotype weapon that is designed for your genes, for your race, for your kind."

The Morgan State students, I am sure, are just as stunned as others are in the Black community that the only 2 people in America who have died from the Ebola virus are Black males. And the only countries around the world that are suffering from Ebola are Black African countries.

All of these critical issues of the day are well within the grasp of the Honorable Minister Louis Farrakhan to dissect, analyze, guide and instruct us on. We don't need Jewish propagandists interfering with who we listen to in the Black community. It's clear that if we let them guide us, we won't be in college classrooms; we will be back on plantations.

Farrakhan is Innocent, FBI is Guilty:
Setting the record straight in Malcolm X Assassination

"Only one movement (The Black Muslims) though looked upon by disfavor by the major black civil rights groups, remains strong, consequential, cohesive, influential..."

-Phillip E. Hoffman, American Jewish Committee, 1972

"For years the Bureau has operated a counterintelligence program against the NOI and Muhammad...despite these efforts, he continues unchallenged in the leadership of the NOI and the organization itself, in terms of membership and finances, has been unaffected."

-Chicago Special Agent in Charge FBI Memo 4/22/1968

There is no doubt; the Unites States Federal Bureau of Investigation (FBI) has been a number 1 enemy of Black America. The crowning achievement of the FBI's COINTELPRO (counter-intelligence) program, during the 60's, were the assassinations of Rev. Dr. Martin Luther King Jr. and Malcolm X.

A new film called "Betty and Coretta" that is airing on the Lifetime network is working really hard to deceive the public. This oddly timed film features the wonderful R&B singer Mary J. Blige portraying the legendary Mrs. Betty Shabazz. The writers of this film include in its script accusatory words coming from Mrs. Shabazz, portrayed by Mary J. Blige, that Minister Farrakhan was responsible for her husband-Malcolm X's death.

The desire of the writers and producers are to destroy the magnetism of Minister Farrakhan among a new generation of Black youth that are discovering the living legend for the first time for themselves on college campuses and in the streets of the hood throughout America. This film is a weak attempt to derail Minister Farrakhan's momentum.

What do they want to derail, you might ask? Minister Farrakhan at nearly 80 years of age is more prolific than ever. He has recently toured the Caribbean nations addressing the governments, professional groups and youth groups. In 2012 Minister Farrakhan visited major historically Black college campuses and even delivered a major address at the University of California-Berkeley. During the heat of the summer, Minister Farrakhan mobilized the Nation of Islam's men's class, known as the Fruit of Islam, into the streets of Chicago and America's major cities on a peace in the streets mission. And in January of this year Minister Farrakhan began a 52-week webcast lecture series entitled The Time and What Must Be Done.

These are all activities that have historically been fought by the United States Federal Bureau of Investigation (FBI). J. Edgar Hoover used untold sums of tax payer dollars to wage a war against all Black Nationalist Groups. His stated goal was to prevent the rise of a Black "messiah" who could unite Black America in a bond of brotherhood and strength. Minister Farrakhan is the modern equivalent of what Hoover feared would happen 40 plus years ago.

This movie fits rightly in the category of what Hoover described in his COINTELPRO memos as "friendly media." Consider the following quoted from the famous Church Committee Report III.:

> "Much of the Bureau's propaganda efforts involved giving information or articles to "friendly" media sources who could be relied upon not to reveal the Bureau's interests... the Division assembled a list of "friendly" news media sources -- those who wrote pro-Bureau stories. Field offices also had "confidential sources" (unpaid Bureau informants) in the media, and were able to ensure their cooperation. **The Bureau's use of the news media took two different forms: placing unfavorable articles and documentaries about targeted groups, and leaking derogatory information intended to discredit individuals.**" (Church Committee Report III)

In his very important book *Racial Matters: The FBI's Secret File on Black America 1960-1972*, Kenneth O'Reilly writes:

> "In 1968 the Miami field office of the FBI and its "friendly and reliable" media contacts began work on a far more ambitious series of **documentaries** on the Nation of Islam and other black groups."

This film "Betty and Coretta" that disrespects and mocks the great legends of Black History is straight out of the FBI playbook. It is a "friendly media" documentary that aims to ruin the Nation of Islam. But this isn't the first time that the NOI has been under attack.

It is a well-known fact that the long-term leader of the FBI, J. Edgar Hoover was a member of the Masonic Shrine. The Masonic Shriners are largely Christian white men who occupy powerful and influential positions within business, government and academic fields. They are students of the Bible, Holy Qur'an, World History and Prophecy. They are particularly known for their private veneration of Prophet Muhammad and the early history of Islam as a world conqueror.

Hoover's Shriner membership sheds light on his use of the word "messiah" in his infamous COINTELPRO memo. For in both Bible and Quranic prophecy, the Messiah is born from and is a blessing to the Children of Israel. The Messiah is to be a man like Moses. Moses liberated the enslaved Hebrews out of Egypt in the Biblical narrative. This led to the destruction of the Egyptian way of life and economy and produced the end of the rule of the wicked Pharaoh.

Ward Churchill and Jim Vander Wall write in their excellent expose *The COINTELPRO Papers* the following conclusion about the assassination of Malcolm X. This conclusion is informed by their meticulous research of the available documents on the nefarious government sabotage of Black movements.

> "By the point of Malcolm's assassination during a speech in Harlem on the night of February 14, 1965, the FBI had compiled at least 2,300 pages of material on the victim in just one of its files on him, the NOI and the OAAU." Malcolm X was supposedly murdered by former colleagues in the NOI as a result of the faction-fighting which had led to his splitting away from that movement and their "natural wrath at his establishment of a competing entity. However, as the accompanying January 22, 1969 memo from the SAC, Chicago, to the Director makes clear; **the NOI factionalism at issue didn't "just happen." Rather, it had "been developed" by deliberate Bureau actions - through infiltration and the "sparking of acrimonious debates within the organization," rumor-mongering, and other tactics designed to foster internal disputes – which were always the standard fare of COINTELPRO. The Chicago SAC, Marlin Johnson, who would shortly oversee the assassinations of Illinois Black Panther Party leaders Fred Hampton and Mark Clark, makes it quite obvious that he views the murder of Malcolm X as something of a model for "successful" counterintelligence operations."**

This may be a shocking conclusion, but it is the right conclusion. The FBI considered the assassination of Malcolm X a model for "successful" counterintelligence operations. And using Malcolm's assassination as a model, they proceeded to work to assassinate Fred Hampton and Mark Clark of the Black Panther Party!

They hope that they can assassinate Minister Louis Farrakhan. But Minister Farrakhan is a divinely guided man and a divinely protected man. He is completely innocent of Malcolm X's assassination. The FBI infiltrated and produced division within the Nation of Islam and worked diligently until their intended goal was achieved.

Black America must not allow itself to be deceived today, for this indeed is the day where the truth (the facts) shall make all free.

Farrakhan Vindicated!

Charges of anti-Semitism exposed as anti-Black racism, fear mongering and money scheme

In an interview with Democracy Now's Amy Goodman, former Israeli Education Minister Shulamit Aloni said this of the charge of anti-Semitism:

> "... It's a trick, we always use it."

What Ms. Aloni is describing is the very skullduggery used against the noble work and reputation of the Honorable Minister Louis Farrakhan and the Nation of Islam. Minister Farrakhan remains the beloved champion of truth and the heroic servant to the poor and oppressed peoples around the world. The price he has had to pay for speaking the truth is to suffer being called an anti-Semite and all that comes with that negative designation. However, those who have falsely accused the Minister have actually revealed more about themselves and their true motives and intentions.

The Most Honorable Elijah Muhammad taught that both the American slave master and the European colonizer used the artful science of "tricks and lies" to master the original people of the Earth. Ms. Aloni's statement bears witness that the Most Honorable Elijah Muhammad taught us the truth. Her statement goes to the heart of the false labeling of the Honorable Minister Louis Farrakhan. More plainly, this is a trick that has been played on the general public, who are often forced to admire, respect, support and even love Minister Farrakhan in veritable secret, or otherwise suffer by being accused of allowing their admiration to provide legitimacy for an alleged "anti-Semitic hate teacher." Some are so affected by the trick that they have developed outright negative opinions of Minister Farrakhan.

The Minister's criticisms of the Jewish community and the policies of Israel are not de facto anti-Semitism. This is what propagandists like the ADL, Simon Wiesenthal Center and Southern Poverty Law Center would like us to believe. They deliberately mischaracterize legitimate criticism as anti-Semitism to obfuscate or hide the truth of their misdeeds. These so-called anti-anti-Semitic watchdog groups have actually been criticized by avowed Farrakhan-critic Rabbi Michael Lerner. In his book, co-authored by Dr. Cornel West, titled Jews and Blacks: Let the

Healing Begin, he writes:

> "The ADL, like the Simon Wiesenthal Center in Los Angeles, has built its financial appeal to Jews on its ability to portray the Jewish people as surrounded by enemies who are on the verge of launching threatening anti-Semitic campaigns. It has a professional stake in exaggerating the dangers, and sometimes allows existing racial or political prejudices in the Jewish world to influence how it will portray the potential dangers."

A youthful Lerner in 1969 also expressed sentiments that agree with Minister Farrakhan and other Black leaders. The Tikkun magazine editor once wrote that Black criticism of Jews is "rooted in the concrete fact of oppression by Jews of Blacks in the ghetto." Lerner referred to this as an "earned" criticism.

In the mistreatment of Minister Farrakhan by these money-driven propagandist groups, Black people en masse have suffered the most. For all of the economic programs and unity efforts advanced by Minister Farrakhan to uplift Blacks in America from poverty and want have been undermined by these groups, whose efforts are no less racist and anti-Black than those of the Ku Klux Klan. Maybe this is why when in 1991 Klan wizard David Duke ran for governor of Louisiana, the ADL was mute, claiming that its tax-exempt status prevented it from intervening in a political campaign.

Tax-exempt status concerns were a non-issue in 1984 when the Reverend Jesse Jackson ran for the office of the President of the United States of America. The ADL actively engaged in sabotaging Reverend Jackson's campaign, even working to destroy his candidacy before it got started! According to Daniel Levitas of the Center for Democratic Renewal,

> "Before Jackson announced his candidacy in 1983, but aware of his impending run, the A.D.L. quietly circulated a nineteen-page memo to reporters detailing Jackson's past statements regarding Jews."

Matters got even worse when Rev. Jackson was accused by reporter Milton Coleman of using a racial slur when referring to Jews in New York. This caused Rev. Jackson to apologize publicly to the Jewish community for using the term "Hymietown," to which ADL director Nathan Perlmutter responded:

> "He could light candles every Friday night, and grow side curls, and it still wouldn't matter...he's a whore."

When Perlmutter attacked Rev. Jackson, he obviously viewed Blacks as an "underdog" people without any defense or aid or power. He cared nothing for the fact that Rev. Jackson's run for the presidency symbolized the collective hopes and dreams of all Black people at that time. His vile reference to Rev. Jackson as a whore is definitely a tongue-in-cheek remark. By his own admission, the ADL practiced Black-baiting for money. In its publication "Not the Work of a Day": ADL of B'nai B'rith Oral Memoirs, Vol. 1, former ADL director Nathan Perlmutter bragged about how much money the ADL made from the vilification of Rev. Jackson. The mailing for donations after the group made Rev. Jackson a Black boogeyman was so successful, Perlmutter wrote, that:

> "we never had the response to a mailing that we had in our July, 1984 mailing."

Author Micah L. Sifry, in his 1993 Nation magazine article titled "Anti-Semitism in America," raises serious questions about the selective use of the term "anti-Semite." In his inquiry he exposes those groups kowtowing to powerful whites who not only have spoken against Jews but have acted against the Jewish people. Sifry points out that in 1990 political commentator Pat Buchanan blamed the Israel Lobby and Jewish geopolitical strategists for America's use of force against Saddam Hussein. Sifry notes that it was anti-Semitism watchdog William F. Buckley Jr., founder of National Review, who quickly offered a defense for Buchanan by writing that he did not believe that Buchanan was anti-Semitic; he was just "attracted to mischievous generalizations." These same groups often demonize Minister Farrakhan for saying once that Hitler was wickedly great. But in 1977 Pat Buchanan had written that Adolf Hitler "was also an individual of great courage, a soldier's soldier" and possessed "extraordinary gifts." I guess comments by Buchanan are "mischievous generalizations," but a comment by Minister Farrakhan is anti-Semitism?

Sifry also notes Buchanan's orchestration of President Reagan's laying a wreath at the tomb of German SS soldiers. Sifry writes:

> "The Washington Post reported that Buchanan was "credited... with the President's characterization of World War II German soldiers and SS troops as 'victims' of the Nazis 'just as surely as the victims in the concentration camps.' And that Buchanan bluntly urged Jewish leaders visiting the White House to 'be good Americans' and stop protesting

Reagan's cemetery stop."

According to Sifry, the ADL claimed that it couldn't verify that Buchanan actually made those statements. Really?

Sifry also questions the ADL response to Fred Malek and Pres. Richard Nixon. Malek, White House personnel chief, provided for President Nixon a list of Jews in the Labor Department and some lost their jobs as a result of this. Years later Malek goes on to become a high-level advisor to Vice-President George H. W. Bush. To this the ADL's Abraham Foxman called Malek's involvement in fellow Jews losing their jobs

> "ancient history," adding that Malek had merely been "carrying out the instructions of an individual who had [prejudiced] feelings."

We might consider Foxman's response as genuine were it not for what the ADL wrote about the so-called individual "who had [prejudiced] feelings." The Watergate tapes of President Nixon reveal Nixon calling Jews "kikes" and complaining about their prevalence in the arts and advising his staff to stay away from them. Yet according to Sifry the ADL said: "Richard Nixon is indeed a friend of Israel and his views on foreign affairs merit regard."

All this evidence points to the ulterior motives of racism, fear-mongering and money-scheming on the part of the so-called anti-anti-Semitic watchdog groups. These groups falsely label Minister Farrakhan as an anti-Semite to support their economic interests, not because he is a threat to Jewish people. For when confronted with real anti-Semitism, these groups make calculated decisions based on who they think is the weakest target. It is time now to expose these tricks, artifices and devilish wiles. If what Minister Farrakhan is teaching is not the truth, why not call boxing promoter, entrepreneur and radio show host Rock Newman and schedule a showdown so the public can once and for all separate fact from fiction, truth from falsehood, the falsely labeled from the real anti-Semite.

Who Is The Original Woman?
The Mis-Education of Trump Rally Chanters

According to the research findings and conclusions of Alexander von Wuthenau, who wrote The Art of Terracotta Pottery in Pre-Columbian South and Central America, Black people were in America long before Columbus first voyaged here. He writes:

> "It is a contradiction to the most elementary logic and to all artistic experience that an Indian could depict in a masterly way the head of a Negro without missing a single racial characteristic, unless he had actually seen such a person. The types of people depicted must have lived in America... The Negroid element is well proven by the large Olmec stone monuments as well as the terracotta items and therefore cannot be excluded from the pre-Columbian history of the Americas."

Despite the facts of history cited by von Wuthenau and others, most of the American people are ignorant of these important truths. For example, over the last few days there has been much outrage and righteous indignation resulting from the ominous scenes of the recent rally in support of President Trump. As President Trump delivered a speech to his supporters and discussed his political controversy with Minnesota Representative Ilhan Omar, his crowd of adoring supporters began to chant "send her back, send her back, send her back." The chants echoed and were in obvious support for President Trump's controversial tweet that suggested that Representatives Ilhan Omar (MN), Alexandria Ocasio Cortez (NY), Rashida Tlaib (MI), and Ayanna Pressley (MA) ought to leave America instead of complaining about the corrupt laws and policies in America.

As a student of Black History, this grotesque display of ignorance and fever-pitch enthusiasm caused me to think about the lynching of Black men and women that also took place before crowds of enthusiastic supporters. The lynching of Black men and women in America was really America's first popular spectator sport. And for many years, the lynching of Black men and women was completely legal! Courageous women like Ida B. Wells and others literally had to fight to get the government to enact laws that forbade the rape, murder, mutilation, desecration and slaughter of Black people.

Original People

The Bible's Exodus 20:12 states:

> "Honour your father and your mother, so that you may live long in the land the LORD your God is giving you."

The Honorable Minister Louis Farrakhan's profound exegesis on this verse maintains that this verse of scripture serves as an exhortation to Caucasian people. It gives them the conditions under which they-as a people- might enjoy longevity beyond their allotted time; they could appeal to God for more time by honoring their parents, who are the original Black people of the Earth. The Minister brilliantly expounded upon how scripture, world history and also science, documents that the original man and woman are an ancient Black man and woman of whom the modern Black people are direct descendants from. The Minister said that the Black, Brown, Red and Yellow peoples of the Earth are original people. He quoted his teacher, the Most Honorable Elijah Muhammad who said that:

> "The Original Man is the Asiatic Black man, the maker, the owner, the cream of the planet earth, god of the universe."

Scholars who bear witness that the original Black people are the father and mother of the white race have said:

> "the process of artificial selection carried on by plant and animal breeders...[its]probable that the fairest races of White people of Europe, are descended from...Negroes."- Dr. James Cowles Prichard
> "White skin...started from an ancestor with a black skin, in whose offspring hair and iris color were suppressed more and more." - Lodewijk "Louis" Bolk

The Minister went on to discuss the Biblical passage in Psalms 24:1 that states that the "Earth is the Lord's and the fullness thereof," The Bible has also described God as being "the ancient one of days" (Isaiah 43:13 and Daniel 7:9, 13, 22). This description of God being "the ancient one" is very important. For when we search the world for the most ancient people, we discover that the most ancient human remains that have been found have been found in Africa, where Black people live!

The most ancient people descend directly from the ancient God and both are Black people! These ancient Black people are the fathers and mothers of humanity; they are the original Adam and the original Eve. In fact, a few years ago the Discovery Channel produced a documentary called the **"Real Eve."** The description for this eye-opening documentary states:

> "The made-for-cable documentary film The Real Eve is predicated on the theory that the human race can be traced to a common ancestor. The mitochondrial DNA of one prehistoric woman, who lived in Africa, has according to this theory been passed down from generation to generation over a span of 150,000 years, supplying the "chemical energy" to all humankind."

This controversy involving President Trump and his supporters proves why the average white person in America needs to study Black History just as much as the average Black person does.

Moreover, according to the Australian Museum it was the country of Somalia-the country of origin of Congresswoman Ilhan Omar-where ancient axes were discovered in the 1800s that inspired the 20th century's research discoveries that proved that **Africa is the cradle of humanity**.

According to www.australianmuseum.net.au:

> "...stone hand axes from Somalia provide important evidence, showing unity of early human species across the Old World. In addition, they asserted that Africa must be examined when the human origin is being considered. Successive research in the 20th century demonstrated that **Africa was indeed the cradle of humanity**."

The Bible again, states that you should **"honor your mother and your father..."** The Holy Qur'an says similar when it says **"do good to parents"** and don't use foul speech when speaking to them; don't say so much as **"fie to them."** These 4 courageous Congresswoman are members of the original people of the planet Earth. And as such, they are owners of the earth. President Trump and his supporters have no right to tell them where they can and cannot live on the earth! The original people are the owners of the Earth and as owners, we can go and live anywhere we choose to go!

I say to their critics, if you disagree with their politics, then submit your alternative political position and allow the public to weigh which of the 2 opposing views they agree with. But to act dishonorably towards them; to be vile and ignoble; to proceed forth with unmitigated gall and savage rancor regarding them is to position yourself on the opposite side of God and his commands!

Congresswomen Signs of God's Presence

It should be noted that Allah (God) often communicates His divine presence within a situation, set of circumstances or events through the use of signs and symbols. Allah (God) says in the Holy Qur'an (15:75):

"Surely in this are signs for those who take a lesson."

These 4 courageous congresswomen have emerged from their respective communities to challenge the status quo in American politics. I noticed that each of them was blessed by their parents with a name of spiritual significance and importance. The Most Honorable Elijah Muhammad always stressed the importance of Black people in America having names that reflect the divine attributes of Allah (God) and the Original peoples of the Earth. He frequently gave to his followers names of strength; names of power; noble names that describe the presence of God within man and woman.

This group of extraordinary women has names rich in meaning, names that provide indicators of their respective destinies and life's work in and out of American politics. The meanings of their names, like signs from Allah (God), suggest the presence of the hand of Allah (God) inside this current season of American electoral politics. Consider that the name **Rashida** means *"rightly guided"*; it is the feminine of one the 99 divine names of Allah (God) in Islam, al-Rashid. The name **Ilhan** has several profound meanings. It means *"ruler"*, *"precious"* and it means *"to have a beautiful voice"*. Within the Holy Qur'an, the believing men and women are admonished to speak their prayers in "goodly voice." They are similarly told that they should "argue in the best of manners using wisdom and beautiful preaching." The name **Ayanna** means *"beautiful flower."* Jesus is referred to in the Bible as the *Rose of Sharon* and *the Lilly of the Valley*. The name **Alexandria** is the feminine of the name Alexander. It means *"defender of the people; to defend, to help"*. There is a verse of scripture in the Bible, Psalms 121:1-2, that says "I lift up my eyes to the hills– where does my help come from? My help comes from the LORD, the Maker of heaven and earth".

These 4 courageous Congresswomen should be respected and protected. Their work and courageous stand is worthy of admiration. None of President Trump's supporters has a right to tell these courageous women to get out of America. Dissent has always been a sacred right in America that is secured by the First Amendment right to free speech. And despite that painful price that is paid to speak the truth, a price that often includes mockery, ridicule and even assassination, those who dare to speak the truth are patriots of the highest order. For, it is the courageous speakers of truth, who exist as the protectors of a society against the abuses of the powerful. Legendary Senator Carl Shurz put it like this:

> "I confidently trust that the American people will prove themselves ... too wise not to detect the false pride or the dangerous ambitions or the selfish schemes which so often hide themselves under that deceptive cry of mock patriotism: 'Our country, right or wrong!' They will not fail to recognize that our dignity, our free institutions and the peace and welfare of this and coming generations of Americans will be secure only as we cling to the watchword of true patriotism: 'Our country—when right to be kept right; when wrong to be put right.'"— Sen. Carl Schurz, "The Policy of Imperialism,"

GOD'S PROPHETS CRITICIZE, REBUKE & WARN ISRAEL: VINDICATION FOR REP. OMAR

While Minnesota Rep. Ilhan Omar is being vilified in the halls of Congress for statements that are critical of the Israeli lobby's control and influence over the American government, I am reminded of how the subject of Israel is both a religious and political subject of importance and modern relevance.

House majority leader Rep. Nancy Pelosi rushed to appease the Israeli lobby by pushing through the often-laborious process required to bring a resolution or bill up for a vote; she speedily forced the resolution through to condemn "anti-Semitism"; and after public pressure modified it to include a condemnation of so-called other forms of bigotry. And this all stemming from newly elected congresswoman Ilhan Omar's (D-MN) criticism of the power and influence of groups like AIPAC.

And while I have witnessed numerous articles written that have taken up either side of this issue, I have yet to see anyone discuss a fundamental flaw in the insistence that Israel and the Jewish people should be beyond criticism, and that all criticism of Israel must be de facto "anti-Semitism."

The flaw is that in order for the claim of the chosen people of God to be maintained; the conditions set forth to define and describe the chosen people must be met. The primary description and definition can be found in the Bible; specifically, the Old Testament or Torah.

According to numerous references in the Old Testament, Israel was a people that frequently disobeyed God and suffered painful consequences. And God, out of His love for this people, would send apostles or prophets to instruct them, warn them, rebuke them, criticize them and otherwise spell out the conditions upon which they might return to the favor of God.

The work of God's prophets to Israel was primarily to criticize their bad behavior. And since Israel's relationship with God stems from their experience with God's prophets, then we maintain that receiving and properly responding to criticism and rebuke is at the heart of what true Jewishness is all about. And those who refuse to be open to criticism are in violation of the conditions set forth in scripture that make the status of "chosen people" dependent upon receiving and accepting criticism and rebuke.

146-STUDENTS OF FARRAKHAN

Consider the following notes from the field of religious studies as it relates to the prophets' role and function as critics:

> "**The prophets boldly rebuked vice, denounced political corruption, oppression, idolatry and moral degeneracy**. They were preachers of righteousness, reformers, and revivalists of spiritual religion, as well as prophets of future judgment or blessing. **They were raised up in times of crisis to instruct, rebuke, comfort and warn ISREAL**, the nations, and the messianic kingdom." **(Freeman, Intro. to Old Testament Prophets, p. 14.)**

> "Prophets arose in Israel ...challenged the people in power—the political rulers and the economic elite. Not all the prophets were anti-establishment, however. For example, Nathan was King David's prophet, and he was financially supported by the king. But most of the prophets criticized the direction in which the people were being led by their rulers, and this often got them into trouble. They were met with hostility, ridicule, mistreatment, punishment, and exile. The prophetic message varied with the circumstances. When things were going well, the prophets warned the people about impending doom if they did not change their ways. When things were going badly, they supported the people with words of encouragement and hope."
> *(https://www.loyolapress.com/our-catholic-faith/scripture-and-tradition/scripture/prophets-in-israel?p=1)*

A sample of the strong and bold criticisms of God's Prophets is below. Israel's future destiny with God depended upon their acceptance of this divine criticism. They were supposed to accept the rebuke of the Prophets as being the rebuke of God Himself. And to demonstrate their acceptance they were expected to perform the required behavior modifications called for in the Prophets' stinging rebuke and come into alignment with God's laws of moral rectitude.:

"Ah, sinful nation, a people laden with iniquity, offspring of evildoers, children who deal corruptly! They have forsaken the LORD, they have despised the Holy One of Israel." **(Isaiah 1:4)**

"Their works are works of iniquity, and deeds of violence are in their hands. Their feet run to evil, and they are swift to shed innocent blood; their thoughts are thoughts of iniquity; desolation and destruction are in their highways." **(Isaiah 59:3-6)**

"The way of peace they do not know, and there is no justice in their paths; they have made their roads crooked; no one who treads on them knows peace." (Isaiah 59:8)

"For the people of Israel have forsaken your covenant, thrown down your altars, and killed your prophets with the sword." **(1Kings 19:10)**

"Now when the Israelites cried out to the LORD because of Midian, He sent them a prophet who said, "This is what the LORD God of Israel says: I brought you up out of Egypt, out of the house of slavery. I delivered you out of the hands of Egypt and all your oppressors. I drove them out before you and gave you their land. And I said to you: 'I am the LORD your God. You must not worship the gods of the Amorites, in whose land you dwell.' But you did not obey Me." **(Judges 6:7-10)**

"You admonished them to turn back to Your law, but they were arrogant and disobeyed Your commandments. They sinned against Your ordinances, by which a man will live if he practices them. They stubbornly shrugged their shoulders; they stiffened their necks and would not obey." **(Nehemiah 9:29)**

"They served idols, although the LORD had told them, "You shall not do this thing." Yet through all His prophets and seers, the LORD warned Israel and Judah, saying, "Turn from your wicked ways and keep My commandments and statutes, according to the entire Law that I commanded your fathers and delivered to you through My servants the prophets." But they would not listen, and they stiffened their necks like their fathers, who did not believe the LORD their God." **(2Kings 17: 12-15)**

Another over looked historical fact in the rush to condemn Rep. Omar is the nefarious legacy of the slave codes. I was introduced to the slave codes by studying the writings of the Most Honorable Elijah Muhammad. He cited the book written by William Goodell entitled **The American Slave Code**. This fascinating book exposes how the behaviors and practices that Black people are condemned for not displaying in impoverished communities today, began as practices and behaviors that Black people wanted to display but were deemed a threat to the white social order, and as such, were outlawed within the American legal system. In an article entitled Separation or Death Part V, The Most Honorable Elijah Muhammad writes:

> "According to the American Slave Code of Law, by William Goodell—page 304, under the above title, the Negroes may be used as breeders, prostitutes, concubines, pimps, tapsters, attendants at the gaming table and as subjects of medical and surgical experiments for the benefit of science."

Moreover, the Slave Code is really the inspiration for what is being done today in the case of the U.S. House of Representatives reaction to Rep. Ilhan Omar's statements about the enormous influence of the Israeli Lobby. Rep. Omar should be free to express her own conscience. She should be free to speak what she thinks and understands. Her thoughts, views and opinions should not have to agree with the ruling class of white people who have taken a pro-Israel political position. After all, Rep. Omar is not a slave.

Yet, there is a desire to punish her like she is a disobedient slave who has dared to think for herself and form her own thoughts and opinions. This kind of bold independence has always been seen as an affront to the ruling class of whites. And they let it be known in the their legally binding slave code laws. From The American Slave Code by William Goodell we learned the following:

> "But we waive and pass by all this, for the present, to affirm distinctly that "the legal relation" of slave ownership, in America, as defined by the code that upholds it, is a relation that cannot and **does not consist with the recognition (either in theory or practice) of the intellectual and religious RIGHTS of the slave.**
> The slave "is a chattel." But chattels have no literary or religious rights. He is a chattel "to all intents, constructions, and purposes whatsoever." He/she is "in the power of a master, to whom he belongs"- "entirely subject to the will of his master "- "**not ranked among sentient (able to think and feel) beings, but among things."**
> ...The American Slave Code, from beginning to end, **knows no rights of conscience in its subjects. The master is to be implicitly obeyed. His will is to be law. The slave is allowed no self-direction**...The slave master may withhold education and the Bible; he may forbid religious instruction, and access to public worship. **He may enforce upon the slave and his family a religious worship and a religious teaching which he/she (the slave) disapproves**. In all this, as completely as in secular matters, he is "entirely subject to the will of a master, to whom he belongs." The claim of chattel hood extends to the soul as well as to the body, for the body cannot be otherwise held and controlled. There is

"Un-Smiting The Shepherd"

no other religious despotism on the face of the earth so absolute, so irresponsible, so soul-crushing as this."

Rep. Omar, like Tamika Mallory and many other courageous women are being called by God to rise today and speak uncomfortable truths to the most powerful forces in the world. They represent true women's liberation; a liberation that is a part of and is permanently tied to the liberation of the oppressed peoples of the world, whom God Himself has declared that today is the time of their(our) rising. I salute her courage and willingness to do as the Holy Qur'an admonishes all believers to do in traveling the "uphill road." The "uphill road" as described in Surah 90 of the Holy Qur'an involves the freeing of slaves. We pray that Rep. Omar can ultimately be a divine instrument of Allah (God), that He will use to free the U.S. Congress from the enslavement to the Israeli Lobby.

"Guilty by Association"?

Defending the Nation of Islam in the Fresno Shooting Case; Exposing the Plan to Equate Black Nationalism with Extremism, Terrorism.

"We hurl the Truth against falsehood, so it knocks out its brains, and lo! it vanishes. And woe to you for what you describe!"-Holy Quran 21:18

The unfair and exclusive burden to all in the Muslim and Islamic community nowadays is that whenever a crime or heinous act is committed by anyone, the media first checks to see how many degrees of separation the perpetrator is from the religion of Islam. And if it can be established that the perpetrator ever did anything even remotely Islamic in nature, his crimes are reported as though they are the direct result of his or her association or membership in the Islamic faith. And despite the obviously unfair and dangerous position that this politically based coverage puts Muslim men, women and children in, it continues to go on uninterrupted.

As a Muslim, I will lift my voice against anti-Muslim bigotry or Islamophobia as it is commonly referred to because it is the right thing to do. Also, because accepting Islam has been the single best decision I ever made in my life. I owe a debt of gratitude to my Creator for the wonderful and transformative faith and system of belief and practice known as Islam. Some people refer to Islam as a religion and it is that. Some refer to it as a way of life and it is that. But the most important characterization of Islam is when my teacher the Honorable Minister Louis Farrakhan describes it as the nature of the human being and the nature of the Creator of all that exists, Allah (God).

Last week news reports circulated out of Fresno, California of a shooter who mercilessly took the lives of several individuals while shouting Islamic sayings and proclaiming that God is Great in Arabic-a phrase transliterated into the English language as 'Allahu-Akbar'.

The Los Angeles Times coverage of this horrible event saw fit to associate the alleged gunman, named Kori Ali Muhammad, with the Nation of Islam. In their coverage they attempted to connect the gunman's actions with the teachings of the Nation of Islam and its founder Master W. Fard Muhammad. And they did this despite the fact that the Nation of Islam has no record of violence associated with its teaching and message. We will document this fact within the scope of this report.

We are disappointed that the Los Angeles Times utilized a familiar trope in modern journalism by citing for the record the false labeling of the Nation of Islam as a hate group by the Southern Poverty Law Center. The Southern Poverty Law Center has never proven that the Nation of Islam (NOI) is a hate group. And the more than 80-year history of the Nation of Islam in America exists to deny the Southern Poverty Law Center (SPLC) the ability to prove such a false allegation. And this is why the true history and contribution of the NOI, its membership and its leadership is routinely omitted from the public view. They understand that if the truth about the Nation of Islam becomes widely known, the general public will view the NOI with respect and admiration.

The Los Angeles Times calumny in question also quotes Brian Levin, director of Cal State San Bernardino's Center for the Study of Hate and Extremism. Levin attempts to make a direct correlation between the Nation of Islam's teachings and the criminal actions of Kory Ali Muhammad, saying:

> "many of Muhammad's social media postings make reference to **terms used by the Nation of Islam**, which has been labeled a racist hate group by the Southern Poverty Law Center. Pointing to **Muhammad's repeated references to "white devils" and "Yakub"** — **the villainous figure responsible for creating white people, according to Nation of Islam lore** — it is likely Muhammad thought he was taking part in a race war against whites...We're living in an era of violent reciprocal prejudice, and there are references on his website to **Fard Muhammad, the founder of Nation of Islam, and Nation of Islam uses the term 'white devils' quite prolifically, as did this shooter**," (http://www.latimes.com/local/lanow/la-me-fresno-shooting-20170418-story.html)

So, in the interest of truth, justice and the advancement toward a more enlightened electorate let's review the facts of history of the Nation of Islam in America as we document why we disagree with the coverage of this heinous act by the Los Angeles Times et.al.

Not our teaching; Not our practice
The question is "What do the actions of Kory Ali Muhammad have to do with the Nation of Islam?" The answer is "Absolutely

nothing!"

All members of the Nation of Islam are forbidden from carrying any weapons on our person or in our homes. We aren't even allowed to possess a pen knife.

We are forbidden from being the aggressor in any altercation for the Holy Qur'an teaches all Muslims that Allah (God) stands against the aggressor and only allows fighting as a defense against aggression.

Within the Nation of Islam, we have been given a modified version of the Islamic world's shariah law. It was given to us by the Great Mahdi, Allah (God) in person, Master W. Fard Muhammad, under the titling "The Restrictive Law of Islam." On page 94 of the book The Restrictive Law of Islam we are directed to **"obey those in authority among us and obey non-believers in authority over us as long as it does not conflict with our religion."** This handy reference book contains a list of our guiding moral principles. In it, Nation of Islam members are also directed to **"be kind and do good to all."** Another point directs **"no lying; we are to speak the truth regardless of the circumstances."**

The Restrictive Law of Islam also tells the Nation of Islam members **"do not commit acts of violence on ourselves or others."**

Again, these are our internal teachings to all Nation of Islam members. And these teachings and guidance is what has made us a group of persons who eschew violence as a means to an end. In fact, as we will document, the Nation of Islam's history is one where we have developed a noble reputation for working very hard to end violence and to produce peace amidst social, political and economic conditions that routinely cause the Black community to be overrun with violent incidents.

Mental illness not religion lies at the root

An important fact that the Times article did include was documentation of Kori Ali Muhammad's prior mental illness. It documented that in 2005; he spent 4 months in a court ordered mental health facility. (http://documents.latimes.com/judge-commits-accused-fresno-shooter-facility-because-he-was-mental-health-issues/)

Mental illness in the Black community is often a taboo subject. No one wants to talk about the various emotional and

psychological maladies plaguing the Black community. The recent advances in genetic understanding have yielded what many see as a direct connection between behaviors in the Black community today that originated with the traumatic experience of chattel slavery. The field of study known as epigenetics has taught scientists that traumatic experiences leave an imprint within an individual all the way to the depth of the cellular level. The eye-opener for most has been that the trauma- produced gene modifications are able to be transferred or passed down from one generation to the next.
(http://www.huffingtonpost.com/darron-t-smith-phd/the-epigenetics-of-being-_b_4094226.html)

Kory Ali Muhammad suffered from mental illness and he also has a record of prior drug use. His actions are more consistent with mental illness than with being inspired or motivated by the religious teachings of the Nation of Islam.

Catholicism isn't blamed for pedophilia; Islam shouldn't be blamed for terroristic acts

I don't know any member of the Catholic faith that condones the sexual abuse of children by priests. I don't know any member of the Islamic faith that condones the killing of innocent people by members of ISIL. I don't know any member of the Protestant faith that condones the killing of Black people by the Ku Klux Klan. The point is that, it is understood that any religion must be judged based upon the ideas, beliefs and teachings of that religion; and on the practice or actions of the predominant majority of adherents that make up that religion. It is understood that just as there are deviants and 'bad actors' in all faiths; no religion or group should be falsely generalized and labeled based upon the extreme actions of the minority of deviants who are associated with that religion. Yet as we have already stated, there is a historical pattern of media coverage that delights in highlighting and showcasing a criminal's religious affiliation when that religious affiliation is any of the various sects of Islam.

The Nation of Islam's hidden history of courageous crime fighting

To promote the ugly picture of the Nation of Islam, the great achievements of the Nation of Islam are routinely and deliberately hidden from the public view. One such episode in our history is the heroic victory over crime and drugs brought about by the Fruit of Islam-the men's class of the Nation of Islam.

The following is excerpted from our article devoted to this history located here : (http://researchminister.com/stop-the-mischief-making-setting-the-record-straight-on-the-nation-of-islam-the-police/)

During the rebuilding of the Nation of Islam under the guidance of the Honorable Minister Louis Farrakhan, the Nation of Islam developed a community security force affectionately known as the "***Dopebusters.***" From the Nation of Islam Research Group article entitled **How Farrakhan Solved the Crime and Drug Problem** we see the Dopebusters described in the following description:

> "In 1988, the Black men of the elite Fruit of Islam, under the training and guidance of Minister Farrakhan, formed into units and began to conduct security patrols in some of the most drug-infested public housing developments. Armed with only a deep love for their own people and a determination to improve their condition, they became known as the "Dope Busters." The Muslims in Washington DC marched unarmed into a veritable drug gang war at the Kenilworth Parkside and Mayfair Mansions housing projects and a remarkable thing happened. The Muslims closed open-air drug markets and brought peace and quiet to those neighborhoods. It was a condition that had never been seen in that area since those projects were built."

And just like the Most Honorable Elijah Muhammad, Minister Farrakhan has students and followers that have achieved wide acclaim for their work and success. A sample of some of glowing commendations bestowed upon the Dopebusters includes the following:

> "I am currently a lieutenant in the Metropolitan Police Department, assigned to the 7th District as the Commander of the Special Emphasis Unit and Support Coordinator of all vice, detective and tactical operations. I have been employed with the Department for 26 years in a sundry of assignments. It is most noteworthy that the areas of the city which they [Dopebusters] have contracted to provide security have shown drastic reductions in crime. This, within itself, speaks to the basic tenets of community empowerment policing. Some of the communities in which I personally know that crime has been reduced by their presence are the Clifton Terrace Apartments, the Mayfair Mansion Apartment Complex, the Paradise Gardens Apartment Complex, the Atlantic Street Apartment Dwellings and the surrounding areas. I have had the occasion to observe some of their security training and to participate in the training as a volunteer instructor. I

have found them to be professional, courteous and committed to the delivery of service to the communities in which they patrol and provide security." -*President DC Black Police Caucus, Lowell Duckett*

"The founders [of the Dopebusters] formed the company after volunteering their services during that period to secure the Paradise/Mayfair community of over 1200 apartments, which had become the largest open-air drug market in the Mid-Atlantic States in the mid-1980s. At the time, no security firms were willing to work in the neighborhood; in fact, the police came into the neighborhood only in force because of the very dangerous conditions. The volunteers patrolled the two complexes, confronted dangerous individuals, and testified in court about the activities of accused felons; all at great personal risk. Their leadership allowed the police to become more effective and encouraged the residents of the neighborhood to work for a safer community. Both Paradise at Parkside and Mayfair Mansions are now healthy, vibrant and safe communities' thanks in good part to the efforts of the [Dopebusters]." -Deputy Assistant Secretary for Enforcement and Investigations Office of Fair Housing and Equal Opportunity U.S. Department of Housing and Urban Development, Ms. Susan Forward

"In terms of bottom line results, they are doing such a good job and the living environment in public housing developments has so markedly improved that I would be reluctant to remove NOI security from those developments."- Baltimore, MD Kurt L. Schmoke, Mayor

Minister Farrakhan's message and ministry is totally opposite the crimes alleged to Kori Ali Muhammad

The male members of the Nation of Islam are organized into a brotherhood known as the Fruit of Islam. And based upon our creed and training, we would be more accurately considered a real **"salvation army."** And this is not because we are necessarily a charity organization. Although the men of the Nation of Islam that you see in neighborhoods across America are volunteering and donating their time, talent and resources to present themselves as a moral force and true manhood alternative to the savage bestial representation of Black manhood promoted and imposed upon the impressionable minds of Black youth by Hollywood.

But we can be dubbed a "salvation army" because we are trained to be saviours of the fallen and downtrodden poor man and woman. Take a look at our guiding manual of instruction which is really a publicly available transcript of a speech delivered by the

Honorable Minister Louis Farrakhan:

"We must see what kind of concept we as Fruit of Islam should have in our minds about this army that we have joined. Those who think in terms of any army running with rifle practice, an army that knows their M-16, an army that studies maneuvers in killing and what-not No, I am sorry. This is not that kind of army. I am not saying that we won't have to someday or under some circumstances deal with an enemy and if necessary destroy. But you must look at the first Fruit, the first Fruit whom we now know as the Christ. One of the titles of Christ is "The Saviour." Another title of Christ is "The Redeemer." Another title of Christ is, "Christ, the Lord." Another title of Christ is "Christ, the King." Well, since we are subjects of the King-or as the scripture calls us, the body of the Christ-then the body does not make the decision, Christ makes the decision. He gives the direction. He's the sole boss.

Well, if Christ is "The Saviour," that's the number one title of Christ. When he becomes God, He exercises that power to save people. From what? From their sins, the scripture says. "And He shall save His people from their sins." And the Messenger of Allah said He's not here to save us from our sins, he's here to save us from the sins of white people that we have adopted.

So, the army that is going out there, is not an army of gangsters. They are not going out there with the face of a thug.... You are a Saviour, Blackman. You are not a destroyer, you are a healer. You're not a killer, you're a Saviour.

You know that [our people have been made into] savages. So, we got to be patient with our people. But brothers, you got to study. And the more you study the words, the teachings, the very spiritual roots of his Word and the program of the Honorable Elijah Muhammad, you grow into the mind of a Saviour. And when people see you coming, they act as though a Saviour has come into their midst.... We are an army raised by God through the Messenger to save our people....

Now, what about killing the devil? ...did you know that every time you save a Blackman you have in that same act of salvation killed a devil'? ...Every time you save a Blackman you have killed a devil because when truth comes in, falsehood goes out. And the only way the Whiteman has been able to rule our people is through the field of falsehood and ignorance. So, you replace the field of falsehood and ignorance with truth and knowledge. And there is no devil anymore there, we just killed one."

So, if you think that you can't qualify to be in that kind of an army, then I would hope to receive your letter or resignation from the FOI because you won't be a part of this. We're not having thugs, we're not having gangsters, we're not having little pseudo-cleaned up criminals. We are righteous men, with a righteous purpose"

In addition, the Honorable Minister Louis Farrakhan has taught us of the need to exorcise the **"Satan of self"** as the primary means of ridding the world of evil. He has advanced our understanding of the devil by making us to see that **whenever any human being uses deceptive intelligence to rationalize disobedience to that which is right and true, such a person is acting as a devil.**

The Nation of Islam has been falsely accused of having a race-hated doctrine. But the facts of history do not support such a false characterization of our divine teachings. The founder of the Nation of Islam, the Great Mahdi, Master W. Fard Muhammad- Allah (God) in person- was born of a white mother and a black father. And there are many bi-racial members of the Nation of Islam, who love, honor and respect their parents even though they are Caucasian. The Honorable Elijah Muhammad also had relationships with many white Muslims whom he taught to us were our brothers and sisters in faith. In over 26 years in the Nation of Islam, I have never been encouraged or required to hate white people or to do harm to them.

White devil teaching nothing compared to Black devil teaching

The media reports have sought to connect Kori Ali Muhammad's crimes to the teachings of the Most Honorable Elijah Muhammad that examines and describes the evil history of American and European global dominance as being the manifestation of pure evil.

In discussing this aspect of the Nation of Islam's teaching, it must be noted that the description provided by a victim in coping with the crimes of their victimizer are never to be invalidated. In fact, the conviction of crimes often begins with the victim's description of their victimizer.

But the Honorable Elijah Muhammad never claimed to arrive at his designation of the white man as the devil on his own. He says that this teaching is a part of what was revealed to him by Allah (God) in the person of Master W. Fard Muhammad.

To refer to a people who have purposed to victimize others as devil is not an alien concept in religion. Jesus in the New Testament referred to his enemies as devils. In the Gospel of St. John in the 8th chapter we read Jesus saying **"Ye are of your father the devil, and the lusts of your father ye will do. He was a murderer from the beginning, and abode not in the truth, because there is no truth in him. When he speaketh a lie, he speaketh of his own: for he is a liar, and the father of it. And because I tell you the truth, ye believe me not." (John 8:44-45)**

In fact, Jesus even referred to his beloved disciple Peter as Satan. In the Gospel of St. Matthew, the 16th Chapter it is recorded that "Jesus turned and said to Peter, "Get behind me, Satan! You are a stumbling block to me; you do not have in mind the concerns of God, but merely human concerns." (Matthew 16:23)

So, referring to a person or a people as devil is not an alien concept, nor does it automatically make such one(s) the target for violence. In fact, the Bible says, "resist the devil and he will flee from you." (James 4:7) And this is exactly the message of the Honorable Elijah Muhammad. For as he taught Black people that the whites who had enslaved, tortured, victimized and dehumanized them were devils, he simultaneously taught Black people to separate themselves from whites. And as Minister Farrakhan is referenced above in his training of the Fruit of Islam, to become educated and enlightened as a means of killing the devil within our own selves. The full quote of James 4:7 is quite harmonious with the overall message of the Most Honorable Elijah Muhammad and the Honorable Minister Louis Farrakhan: **"Submit yourselves, then, to God. Resist the devil, and he will flee from you. Draw near to God, and He will draw near to you. Cleanse your hands, you sinners, and purify your hearts, (James 4:7-8)**

The history of the Nation of Islam's constructive interpretation of the "white man is the devil" teaching can be summed up by the comments of Professor Martha F. Lee who said of the Nation of Islam's non-violent history **"In many ways then, the Nation of Islam provides a case study of why and how a religious movement with a radical belief system did not engage in violence related to its doctrine. ...The movement's doctrine and history, suggest that the Nation of Islam was not particularly concerned with a violent overthrow of the American state. Its members waited in faith for Allah to** destroy the forces that oppressed them. Instead, it was law-enforcement agencies that more actively fostered violence in the hope of destroying the Nation of Islam."

In Professor Lee's powerful admission, the question arises is the current "dishonorable mention" of the Nation of Islam in connection with the Fresno shooting once again the result of a high-level hidden government plan to destroy the NOI?

The reader should remember that in 2007, the Department of Homeland Security was exposed revealing that they were carrying out covert plan of espionage against the Nation of Islam. These contemporary discoveries brought back to public attention how it was under J. Edgar Hoover's COINTELPRO policy of the 1960s that such domestic espionage on the part of the U.S. government was specifically designed to destroy what the FBI dubbed **"Black nationalist hate type groups"** of which the Nation of Islam was of their greatest concern and as a result suffered the most infiltration sabotage and negative publicity.

By contrast, the history of negative appellations and false designations attached to Black humanity has not only been insulting it has resulted in the tremendous loss of the lives and property of Black men and women and the associated obscene amounts of wealth generated from the centuries long trade in Black flesh.

The "Black devil" teaching is actually commonly known as the teaching of the Hamitic Curse. It does not expressly designate the "Black man is the devil." However, to the degree that one of the primary meanings of the term devil is "the accursed one" this ubiquitous ideology portrays Black human beings as being divinely proscribed to servitude, evil morals and the harshest of human existence-accursed.

The Hamitic Curse or the Curse of Ham is a religious ideology that grew out of the Jewish Babylonian Talmud. Rabbis of the Babylonian period crafted a religious teaching that sought to explain the origin of Black people as being the evil spawns of Noah's cursed son Ham. Unsuccessful Nation of Islam critic Dr. Harold Brackman has even admitted that:

> "There is no denying that the [Jewish] Babylonian Talmud was the first source to read a Negrophobic content into the episode by stressing

Canaan's fraternal connection with Cush.... The more important version of the myth, however, ingeniously ties in the origins of blackness -- and of other, real and imagined Negroid traits -- with Noah's Curse itself. According to it, Ham is told by his outraged father that, because you have abused me in the darkness of the night, your children shall be born black and ugly; because you have twisted your head to cause me embarrassment, they shall have kinky hair and red eyes; because your lips jested at my exposure, theirs shall swell; and because you neglected my nakedness, they shall go naked with their shamefully elongated male members exposed for all to see."

In her excellent article entitled **The Hamitic Hypothesis; Its Origin and Functions in Time Perspective** author Edith R. Sanders discusses the power of the Hamitic Curse as a rationalization for nations to get involved in the Trans-Atlantic Slave Trade; a power to obtain 'ill-gotten gains.'

"Talmudic or Midrashic explanations of the myth of Ham were well known to Jewish writers in the Middle Ages, as seen in this description by Benjamin of Tudela, a twelfth-century merchant and traveler south of Aswan: **There is a people... who, like animals,** eat of the herbs that grow on the banks of the Nile and in their fields. They go about naked and have not the intelligence of ordinary men. They cohabit with their sisters and anyone they can find... **they are taken as slaves and sold** in Egypt and neighboring countries. **These sons of Ham are black slaves.** Ideas have a way of being accepted when they become useful as a rationalization of an economic fact of life. As Graves and Patai put it: **'That Negroes are doomed to serve men of lighter color was a view gratefully borrowed by Christians in the Middle Ages; a severe shortage of cheap manual labor caused by the plague made the reinstitution of slavery attractive'.**"

Sanders, again makes the point that it was the lust for money that served to perpetuate and keep in circulation this most harmful ideology and evil invention of Jewish rabbinical imagination.:

"By and large, however, the Negro was seen as a descendant of Ham, bearing the stigma of Noah's curse. This view was compatible with the various interests extant at that time. **On the one hand, it allowed exploitation of the Negro for economic gain to remain undisturbed by any Christian doubts as to the moral issues involved.** 'A servant of servants shall he be' clearly meant that the Negro was preordained for slavery. Neither individual nor collective guilt was to be borne for a state of the world created by the Almighty."

Such a history when viewed not only in light of slavery but all of the horrors that slavery produced which includes lynching, destruction of Black towns and cities and centuries of systemic oppression from all American institutions powerfully contrasts against any negative effects whites may have experienced by the Nation of Islam's "white devil" teaching.

No if you want to point to any group who has experienced the negative effects of religious ideology consider the Black people of America during the last 460 years.

Conclusion: Minister Farrakhan, Black Nationalism Set-Up For Take-Down

Is the Fresno shooting a false flag event designed to seed the minds of the American public with hatred for the Nation of Islam? Most see the image of an Islamic terrorist as some foreign born radical or immigrant. Popular Islamic stereotypes seek to broad brush the immigrant Sunni and Shia Muslims as the new American boogey-men. Could it be that the generally positive view of the "Black Muslims", the Nation of Islam, is now being dragged into the milieu of Islamic boogey-men that good patriotic Americans must be on the look-out for?

What about Minister Farrakhan? Could the Fresno killing serve those who hate him and fear the widespread proliferation of his message?

Students of the Nation of Islam history have observed that in the early history of the Nation of Islam in Detroit, such an incident as the Fresno shooting was used to justify the expulsion of Nation of Islam founder Master W. Fard Muhammad.

It was November of 1932, a little over 84 years ago, that a mentally ill member of the early Temple of Islam committed a murder that was reported in the media as a "human sacrifice to the Gods of Islam." Robert Harris murdered his roommate James Smith. This savage act committed by a mentally ill person was used as "just cause" for the Detroit police to arrest Master W. Fard Muhammad, have him psychologically evaluated and ordered to leave Detroit, being told to never come back.

The Honorable Minister Louis Farrakhan will soon, by the will and blessing of Allah, celebrate his 84th birth anniversary on May 11,

2017. Is the Trump administration preparing to arrest the Minister and outlaw his teachings?

These are all serious and important questions.

The Los Angeles Times used this horrible incident to tie in the ennobling and empowering philosophy of Black Nationalism with criminal terrorist-type activity. In doing this they are skillfully maneuvering to install within the thinking of the American public the fear of all who subscribe to the various schools of thought that may be defined as "Black Nationalism." **They want to make Black Nationalism the American equivalent of Wahhabism in Saudi Arabia.** Wahhabism is believed to be the extreme version of Islam promoted by groups like al-Qaeda and ISIL. In other words, Black Nationalism will come to be seen as the ideological seed-bed for the growth of home-grown extremists and terrorists.

This is designed to further marginalize and isolate Black Nationalist groups, to make them the new American menace. Ultimately the plan is to arrest and imprison leaders of Black nationalist movements. And to create a negative view of Black nationalist groups within the law enforcement community. If the plan can be executed, the future will be bleak for all in the Black community who subscribe to the ideas of **Marcus Garvey, Martin Delaney, Malcolm X, the Hon. Elijah Muhammad, the Black Panther Party et.al.** Going forward, any organization that is of a Black nationalist orientation will also be deemed a de facto hate group. And members of these organizations will be subject to "enhanced sentencing" if they are ever convicted of a crime.

Again, careful consideration of the Los Angeles Times articles reminds us of that Black Nationalism's most well-known and popular leader today is the Honorable Minister Louis Farrakhan. In fact, any bibliography on the subject of Black Nationalism will include at the top of the list the book entitled "Black Nationalism" written by Essein Udom. Udom's book may have well been titled "A Sociological Study of the Nation of Islam" because such a title would more appropriately describe the scope of Udom's work. Udom was a Nigerian scholar who received permission from the Most Honorable Elijah Muhammad to conduct an objective and in-depth study of the Nation of Islam in 1962. Udom obviously understood that Black Nationalism's most recognizable and most significant manifestation in America was and is the Nation of Islam.

Udom's 384 pages seminal work is described by the University of Chicago Press as:

> "One of the first studies of the organization, life and meaning of the Nation of Islam and, by extension, all Black Nationalist movements, this classic work dispels the still common conception that the movement functioned primarily for political purposes. By observing the daily life of its members, Essien-Udom demonstrates that the Nation of Islam served primarily as a means for poor urban blacks to attain a national identity, a sense of ethnic consciousness, and empowerment in a society that denied them these privileges."

And just as Udom equated Black Nationalism with the Nation of Islam, the Los Angeles Times means the same in its article's headline covering the Fresno shooting. Udom's cover even includes the image of the Nation of Islam's eternal leader the Most Honorable Elijah Muhammad.

When J. Edgar Hoover was spending vast sums of the tax payers' dollars spying and sabotaging the Nation of Islam as a part of his COINTELPRO efforts, he made regular use of his "friends in the media" to serve as the character assassination apparatus of the FBI. Hoover's "friends" would set-up potential take-down targets with negative media attention. This was designed so that when the take-down was carried out Hoover's victims would receive little to no public sympathy at all. And Hoover's evil war against Black Nationalists groups and leaders would go undetected.

Today the work to destroy Black Nationalism is the work to destroy Louis Farrakhan and the Nation of Islam. And it is not only being aided and abetted by the current government's "friends" in the media; groups such as the Southern Poverty Law Center and the Anti-Defamation League of B'Nai B'rith are key co-conspirators.

Here is how they are working together to destroy the Nation of Islam. The Southern Poverty Law Center labels and designates the Nation of Islam as a hate group. Again, this has nothing to do with any documented history of the Nation committing any hate crimes or violence against any one. They claim it is solely based on our teachings; the same area of focus of the Los Angeles Times articles covering the Fresno shooting. The SPLC's hate crimes lists are frequently cited and repeated in all main stream media stories the mention the Nation of Islam. And most importantly, their lists are consulted by law enforcement agencies around the country. The reader should note that there is currently no legal definition for "hate." So, the SPLC's designation of a "hate" group is purely at their discretion. They have the power to at will and without explanation label any group they desire to be a "hate" group.

The ADL, in the meantime, and in its role as an accomplice to the SPLC, uses its considerable influence and access to power to sponsor "hate crime" legislation. According to the ADL's website:

> "For more than three decades, **ADL has spearheaded the drafting, enactment and implementation of hate crime laws**, working in partnership with other civil rights and religious organizations, law enforcement groups, civic agencies and business leaders. Today, the federal government and 45 states and the District of Columbia have their own hate crime laws. We have had considerable success, **but we need to do more.**"

This is the same ADL that since the early 1980's has dogged the trail of the Honorable Minister Louis Farrakhan falsely labeling him as an "anti-Semite." This is also the same ADL that collaborated with the South African government to spy on the Nation of Islam. This is also the same ADL that colluded with the KKK and been a party to an entire history of nefarious acts.

These two groups who oppose Minister Farrakhan have positioned themselves in the eyes of the American public and law enforcement as the "go-to" experts on "hate speech", "hate crimes" and "extremism." They are working to do the necessary ground work in preparation for the destruction of Minister Farrakhan, both his person and his ideas.

And just to be clear, their assault on Minister Farrakhan, the Nation of Islam and all Black Nationalist groups doesn't mean that they view the rest of the Black community as their cherished and beloved brothers and sisters. Quite the contrary, they oppose Minister Farrakhan while simultaneously acknowledging that he is the "only" leadership present in the Black community!

In 2013 ADL head Abraham Foxman said that:

> "The only leadership that now exists in that community"—the "African American community"— "is Louis Farrakhan. Farrakhan can assemble

20,000 people several times a year,"

The vilification of the Nation of Islam uses negative publicity to intentionally to sow seeds of hatred in the American people for the "Black Muslims." To achieve this nefarious objective, heinous acts of violence are associated to our teaching through deliberate media distortions. This was the case when Dallas shooter-Micah Johnson- killed local police officers in 2016. This was also the case when the first stories emerged about the bombing of the federal building in Oklahoma City in 1995. The strategy seeks to paint Black nationalist organizations and leaders as having a "radicalizing" influence on Black youth. But the Minister's impact and influence on Black youth has been the opposite of radicalization. On the contrary, His long record is not one of radicalization, but one of salvation and restoration!

For some perspective on Minister Farrakhan's value and impact in the Black community numerous scholars and historians can be consulted. The Fresno shooter who had a history of drug use, mental illness and legal troubles is no example of what Minister Farrakhan and the Nation of Islam teach or represent. But the SPLC and the ADL would love for you to believe that. This is because they want to destroy a man whom they themselves have identified as **"the last man standing."** The Minister and the Nation of Islam stand in the way of the sophisticated and scientific plan of destruction of the Black community. Minister Farrakhan's message seeks to purify and dignify Black people, while the enemies of the Black community seek to negatively influence Black people into savage behavior that makes us worthy of extermination.

Swedish professor of theology Professor Mattias Gardell writes of the Minister's uncommon power with Black men in his book **In the Name of Elijah Muhammad: Louis Farrakhan and The Nation of Islam**. Professor Gardell exclaims:

> "Farrakhan has a unique capability...He is able to reach deeply into the souls of black youths...He is able to talk to them in a way that really makes them listen...this rapport enables Farrakhan to criticize and redirect destructive behavioral patterns."

In another testimony, Professor Gardell acknowledges:

> "Minister Farrakhan and the NOI clearly have been instrumental in

bringing the gangs together and redirecting their activities toward community improvement and political empowerment"

Author and academician Dawn Marie Gibson is another scholar who is on record documenting the meaningful and positive effect of Minister Farrakhan's message on men. She writes in her new book **The Nation of Islam, Louis Farrakhan and the Men Who Follow Him** that:

> "Conversion to the Nation impacts men in various but nonetheless meaningful ways. Those men who embrace the dietary laws of the organization find that their food habits change in significant ways. Likewise, those men who fully embrace the protocol of the FOI and its teachings appear to find a new appreciation for authority and discipline."

And despite the serious, credible and substantial praise from scholars, the true history of the Nation of Islam remains hidden from the masses within the American electorate. The Fresno shooting is a tragedy as are all crimes where innocent human beings lose their lives. Yet everything about it and about the alleged shooter is in direct opposition to the teachings of the Most Honorable Elijah Muhammad, the Honorable Minister Louis Farrakhan and the Nation of Islam. The truth of this fact is what we have documented in this special report. We pray that it is helpful to all who seek the truth.

Happy September 17th! : Theology, Ufology and Black Liberation in Minister Farrakhan's Vision-Like Experience

Part 1

A Special Day in the Nation of Islam

Happy September 17th!

What is so special about today? Well today is the anniversary of a vision that Minister Farrakhan experienced in 1985. It has since been described by Nation of Islam theologian Jabril Muhammad as a "vision-like" experience. This experience is very special to all students of Minister Farrakhan and the Nation of Islam. It is special because it is this "vision-like" experience that the Minister credits with furnishing him with the guidance and instruction for the work he has done from that point onward.

The Minister has frequently over the years described his vision to us. He explains that while he was on a retreat to fast and pray and commune with the spirit of Allah (God) in a village near the town of Tepoztlan, Mexico he had a unique experience with what some call a UFO. Within the Nation of Islam, one might regularly hear discussions regarding so-called UFOs. This is not because the Nation of Islam is necessarily filled with sci-fi enthusiasts. Instead it is because of a profound history and teaching that we have received beginning all the way back in the 1930s when the Nation of Islam was founded in America.

The Most Honorable Elijah Muhammad taught us what his teacher Master W. Fard Muhammad taught to him. And part of that broad message and teaching aimed at the total liberation of the Black people of America includes a profound teaching on the aerial phenomenon that is now commonly known as UFOs. A 2012 ABC News report revealed that nearly 36% of Americans believe UFOs exist; that's nearly 80 million people. Yet to this date, the American government has refused to declassify its UFO files so that the public can know what it knows.

I strongly recommend taking a little time to watch Minister Farrakhan's treatment of this subject that can be found online at http://www.noi.org/thetime/ . For 5 weeks, the Minister used the subject of UFOs to create a series within the larger series "The Time and What Must Be Done." Beginning in part 51 and continuing through part 55, the Honorable Minister Louis Farrakhan delivers the most complete treatment of this subject to date. And using very strong sources of empirical information, he brings this obscure subject out of the realm of science fiction and conspiracy theory. And he places it within the context of scripture, theology, prophecy and the liberation of the Black people of America.

The Minister's series on this subject is nothing short of amazing. It is an awe-inspiring and breathtakingly profound series of messages that deserves the widest possible audience and careful study. From my vantage point, the Minister is uniquely qualified to speak on the subject of UFOs. Of course, the Nation of Islam does not refer to these objects as UFOs, because we don't consider them to be "unidentified." We look at them as being manifestations of what we have been taught regarding the Bible and Holy Qur'an and their respective theology and eschatology. *Theology* is the study of God and *eschatology* is the study of end times prophecies. And we have been given a lot of wisdom on these areas.

What makes the Minister uniquely qualified to offer this guidance to us in this critical time in history is first of all his position as the most popular, effective and committed student of the Most Honorable Elijah Muhammad's teachings. Second, his "vision-like" experience with these "wheels," as the Honorable Elijah Muhammad describes them, gives him the authenticity and authority of an eye witness.

Theology

As far as theology goes, most people outside of those within religious studies departments or seminaries aren't too versed in all that a "study of God" provides. That is not to say that most people don't believe in God. However, to believe in God and to have knowledge of God, that is borne of one's study of God in an academic way is altogether quite different. As a believer, one may conceive of God in whatever way they choose. But a study of God will quickly reveal if one's own personal belief and concepts agree with primary sources and sacred texts.

With that in mind, one should re-visit the Nation of Islam's (NOI) teaching on the reality of God. The NOI theology that can be best summed up in these words by the Most Honorable Elijah Muhammad in his seminal work "Message to the Blackman in America":

"God is a man, and we just cannot make Him other than man..."

And despite the criticism that the NOI has routinely experienced based on this aspect of its teaching, a study of God reveals that Mr. Muhammad and Minister Farrakhan are 100% correct. And you don't need to be a religious scholar to have an appreciation for this simple and basic, yet profound theological point. Just consider that all of the major figures within the Bible, commonly used by Jews and Christians, had encounters with God as a man.

Adam's God was surely a man because Adam is first of all said to be in the "image and likeness" of God (Genesis 1:26). But Adam also hears God walking about in Garden

> When the cool evening breezes were blowing, *the man and his wife heard the Lord God walking about* in the garden. So, they hid from the Lord God among the trees. Then the Lord God called to the man, "Where are you?"-Genesis 3:8-9(NLT)

Abraham's God was also a man. Abraham is a very special case. Abraham is special because he is considered to be the father of the kind of monotheism (worship of one God) practiced by Jews, Christians and Muslims. So, Abraham is definitely intimately connected with the Jewish Christian and Muslim concept of God. He is a major theological figure. Yet in chapter 18 of Genesis, he bows down and prostrates before a man whom he calls "Lord". This man is travelling with 2 other men who are angels.

> And the LORD appeared unto him in the plains of Mamre: and he sat in the tent door in the heat of the day; And he lift up his eyes and looked, and, lo, three men stood by him: and when he saw them, he ran to meet them from the tent door, and bowed himself toward the ground, And said, My Lord, if now I have found favour in thy sight, pass not away, I pray thee, from thy servant: Let a little water, I pray you, be fetched, and wash your feet, and rest yourselves under the tree: And I will fetch a morsel of bread, and comfort ye your hearts; after that ye shall pass on: for therefore are ye come to your servant.-Genesis 18:1-5(KJV)

The God of Moses was a man who talked to Moses face to face according to the Bible in its book called Numbers. In the 12th chapter of Numbers we read:

> At once the Lord said to Moses, Aaron and Miriam, "Come out to the

tent of meeting, all three of you." So, the three of them went out. Then the Lord came down in a pillar of cloud; he stood at the entrance to the tent and summoned Aaron and Miriam. When the two of them stepped forward, he said, "Listen to my words: "When there is a prophet among you, I, the Lord, reveal myself to them in visions, I speak to them in dreams. But this is not true of my servant Moses; he is faithful in all my house. With him I speak face to face, clearly and not in riddles; he sees the form of the Lord. Why then were you not afraid to speak against my servant Moses?"-Numbers 12:4-8(NIV)

Moses also has tremendous significance. He is the prophet of God whose responsibility it was to liberate an enslaved mass of people- the Children of Israel. Moses is also the most mentioned prophet in the Holy Qur'an. His name occurs 524 times in the deluxe edition of the English translation of the Holy Qur'an translated by Maulana Muhammad Ali.

Professor Albert J. Raboteau in his book Slave Religion discusses the belief system of the African slaves on plantations in America. He quotes a Union Chaplain named W. G. Kiphant on his work among freed slaves in Decatur Alabama:

> "There is no part of the Bible with which they (slaves) are so familiar as the story of the deliverance of the children of Israel. Moses is their ideal of all that is high, and noble, and perfect, in man. I think they have been accustomed to regard Christ not so much in the light of a spiritual Deliverer, as that of a second Moses who would eventually lead them out of their prison-house of bondage."

This is an amazing admission. For it powerfully demonstrates that our enslaved ancestors, many of whom could not read the Bible for themselves, yet drew appropriate parallels from the plight of the Children of Israel in the Bible to their own plight in bondage in America. So much so, that they believed God too would bless them with a deliverer. This is astonishing because today the work of the Honorable Minister Louis Farrakhan to teach this is made difficult due to the Black community's own disbelief that they would receive a prophet or messenger from God to deliver them from their suffering in America.

Jesus God was also a man. He demonstrated his concept of God in the Bible's book of John. John's chapter 8 records the following:

> Then spake Jesus again unto them, saying, I am the light of the world:

he that followeth me shall not walk in darkness, but shall have the light of life. The Pharisees therefore said unto him, Thou bearest record of thyself; thy record is not true. Jesus answered and said unto them, Though I bear record of myself, yet my record is true: for I know whence I came, and whither I go; but ye cannot tell whence I come, and whither I go. Ye judge after the flesh; I judge no man. And yet if I judge, my judgment is true: for I am not alone, but I and the Father that sent me. It is also written in your law, that the testimony of two men is true. I am one that bear witness of myself, and the Father that sent me beareth witness of me. -John 8:12-17

This passage shows clearly that Jesus' concept of God-the Father was a man! Jesus believed that this Man-God could come and testify before his enemies that Jesus was in fact the Light of the World as he claimed.

All of this points to the fact that the Prophets and Messengers of God as they are recorded in the Bible had an altogether different concept of the reality of God from what most Bible based believers have today. Therefore, we ask the question, "Are the Prophets correct, or are the religious teachers of today correct?"

Happy September 17th!! : Theology, Ufology and Black Liberation in Minister Farrakhan's Vision-Like Experience

Part 2

The major religions today teach a belief in a shapeless, formless and immaterial God. But in part 1 of this article we demonstrated that the sacred texts of Judaism and Christianity describe God as a man. In the Bible, Adam's God was a man. Abraham's God was a man. Moses God was a man. And Jesus God was a man.

As far as Classical Islam is concerned, they also teach that Allah (God) is shapeless, formless and immaterial. The problem with this position is that since the Holy Qur'an and Prophet Muhammad are chronologically after the Bible, and Prophet Muhammad claimed to believe in the same God as the God of Abraham, Moses and Jesus, Classical Islam naturally inherits the same Man-God of those former prophets and the former scriptures.

This is clearly the reason why the Holy Qur'an in Surah 2:2-4 reads:

> "This Book, there is no doubt in it, is a guide to those who keep their duty, Who believe in the Unseen and keep up prayer and spend out of what We have given them, And who believe in that which is revealed unto thee (Muhammad) and that which was revealed before thee, and are certain of the Hereafter."

The only reason Muslims could be said to believe in the scripture revealed to Prophet Muhammad and the scriptures revealed before him (Bible) is because both the Holy Qur'an and the Bible were revealed by one and the same God. Abraham's God is Prophet Muhammad's God. If Abraham's God was a man, so is Prophet Muhammad's God.

Ufology

The question could be asked, at this point, what does all of this have to do with the modern field of study known as Ufology?

Well consider that God is always described as being "above." Most theologians agree that the Judeo-Christian-Muslim God is conceived of as being omnipresent yet he primarily occupies an "elevated" place. Scripture describes Him as having a geospatial position equal to being in the air or in the heavens. He is even colloquially referred to as "the man upstairs."

But how would a Man-God be up in the heavens or up in the clouds? He would occupy the heavens above our heads just as any other man would travel in the clouds. The Honorable Minister Louis Farrakhan eloquently pointed out to us. "Men don't travel in the clouds unless they are in planes." The Honorable Minister Louis Farrakhan's series of internet broadcasts entitled The Time and What Must Be Done contains a wealth of in-depth analysis and commentary on this vitally important subject. They can be viewed here from the archives: http://www.noi.org/thetime/

Let's take a look at the God of the Bible and the various descriptions of Him being in the clouds.

God Rides Upon A Cloud

> The burden of Egypt. Behold, the LORD rideth upon a swift cloud, and shall come into Egypt: and the idols of Egypt shall be moved at his presence, and the heart of Egypt shall melt in the midst of it.
> (Isaiah 19:1)

> And the LORD said unto Moses, Lo, I come unto thee in a thick cloud, that the people may hear when I speak with thee, and believe thee forever. And Moses told the words of the people unto the LORD.
> (Exodus 19:90)

> He bowed the heavens also, and came down; and darkness was under his feet. And he rode upon a cherub, and did fly: and he was seen upon the wings of the wind. And he made darkness pavilions round about him, dark waters, and thick clouds of the skies.
> (2Samuel 22:10-12)

> And the LORD came down in a cloud, and spake unto him, and took of the spirit that *was* upon him, and gave *it* unto the seventy elders: and it came to pass, *that*, when the spirit rested upon them, they prophesied, and did not cease.
> (Numbers 11:25)

> And he rode upon a cherub, and did fly: yea, he did fly upon the wings of the wind.
> (Psalms 18:10)

Who layeth the beams of his chambers in the waters: who maketh the clouds his chariot: who walketh upon the wings of the wind
(Pslams 104:3)

The Mother Plane

All of these passages of scripture which have amazed, perplexed and intrigued scholars and Bible believers for centuries have finally been clearly explained and vindicated through the teachings of the Most Honorable Elijah Muhammad.

The Honorable Elijah Muhammad's groundbreaking teachings on the aerial phenomenon called UFOs, has made him a pioneer in the field of ufology. For it was Mr. Muhammad who is the first to teach to the masses the knowledge he was given of these objects more than a decade before public fascination over the sighting of pilot Kenneth Arnold in Washington state made the term UFO a household word.

In fact, when the federal government had Mr. Muhammad arrested in 1942 to quell his preaching that Blacks should abstain from America's war efforts in World War II, it was Mr. Muhammad's knowledge and teachings on UFOs that occupied a great deal of the interview and interrogation of Mr. Muhammad by federal agents. We know this because of Mr. Muhammad's description of his arrest.

> "I sat down and I talked with them years ago about it. They asked me questions. They have the drawing on a blackboard that they'd taken from us when they arrested us and I had drawn the plane and written explanations on the blackboard, and they took it to the F.B.I. office. They have it there today. They know this to be true and they admitted to me that it is true."
> (Theology of Time Lecture Series July 2, 1972)

The Honorable Elijah Muhammad said of his teacher, the Great Mahdi Master Wallace Fard Muhammad that,

> "He pointed out a destructive dreadful-looking plane that is made like a wheel in the sky today. It is a half mile by a half mile square; it is a humanly built planet. It is up there and can be seen twice a week; it is no secret."
> (Message To The Blackman pages 17-18)

The Honorable Elijah Muhammad would go on to describe these objects more accurately by introducing a new nomenclature for these objects, an act reflective of his position as an authority on this subject that from the 1940s onward, baffled scores of prominent Americans in government and science. From his teachings we learned that the large "humanly built planet" that his teacher pointed out to him is called the "Mother Plane" or "Mother Wheel.'" This Mother Wheel he said was so large that it contained within itself 1500 smaller spheres called "baby planes."

More important than the status of the Most Honorable Elijah Muhammad as being the first to introduce and explain a definitive knowledge of UFOs to the public, is that within his teachings is the harmonizing and intersecting of the seemingly non-related subjects of scripture, Black Liberation and the aerial phenomenon of UFOs. That these popular subjects could be interconnected and co-related is an uncommon premise that provides intrigue and beauty to Mr. Muhammad's teachings. In his teachings on this subject he brilliantly provides for us the context, a definite Black Liberation Theology context, for the appearance of these "flying saucers" inside of America.

Consider some important quotes from Mr. Muhammad's catalog of teachings on the great Mother Wheel.

> "It will be the work of the wheel. The wheel is the power of the four creatures, namely the four colors of the Black man (Black, brown, yellow and red). The red Indian is to benefit also from the judgment of the world."
> (The Fall of America page 239).

> "As Ezekiel saw and heard in his vision of it (Chapter 10:2) the plane is terrible. It is seen but do not think of trying to attack it. That would be suicide!"
> (Message To The Blackman page 291)

> "He [Prophet Ezekiel] said he saw a wheel in a wheel and that this wheel rose up from the Earth. He didn't say nothing about where it was made at on the earth, but he said a wheel rose up from the earth and that it got so high that it looked dreadful."
> (Theology of Time July 9, 1972)

> "The like of this wheel-like plane was never seen before. You cannot build one like it and get the same results. Your brains are limited. If you would make one to look like it, you could not get it up off the earth into

outer space. The similar Ezekiel's wheel is a masterpiece of mechanics." (Message To The Blackman page 290)

"Allah (God) Who came in the Person of Master Fard Muhammad, to Whom praises are due forever, taught me that this Plane is capable of reaching a height of forty miles above the earth. His words could have been a sign meaning forty years, in which the Plane would go into action and not referring actually to forty miles. Allah (God) does not speak one word that does not have meaning. Every word that He speaks has meaning." (Fall of America page 237)

"They (devils) see the end of their world and they see the signs of the Son of Man coming in the sky with power and great glory (the great Ezekiel's wheel and the unity of the Muslim world and the distress of nations)." (Message To The Blackman page 293)

On this wheel in a wheel here that Ezekiel prophesy of, that it got so high up in the air that it look dreadful. This wheel is up in the air now. This is what they're trying to locate from the moon, if they could get a good stationary place on the moon and watch for this plane. Drop that bomb on the Earth and that his height would be something about twenty miles above the Earth when he dropped it, not getting too far out the atmosphere because he wants to use the atmosphere to help guide his bombs. So that this bomb, when it strikes the Earth, it will start right into the Earth. It has a bomb that is timed and that it has a little motor to the bomb that when it strikes the Earth that motor automatically goes on and takes that bomb one mile into the Earth before ever it explodes. When it explodes, it set up a mountain one mile high. That's a powerful bomb.

Allah taught me that that's the same type of bomb that God used to make mountains on the Earth. It's the same thing. It goes into the Earth with a very speedy motor taking it right on through like an air hammer. It doesn't dig out. It just sucks itself right on into the Earth like an air hammer chiseling down into the Earth and when it gets its time, it's not to explode until it gets a mile into the Earth. They have in this bomb, the type of dynamite that they used to bring up the mountains of Everest mountain range.

Powerful dynamite. It's more powerful than America is using.

America uses 30% dynamite. These people have their bombs equipped with 100% dynamite today to blast just a few mountains across the continent of North America. And that these mountains pulling up out of the Earth from that blasting away bomb, it will kill people for fifty miles around. That crater it makes pushing up the mountain on each side, and this will go into action when America start using her high explosives, dropping it from the air. This thing will come out and get us. It carries fifteen hundred, or rather this thing carries fifteen hundred of these small bomb planes.

Each one of these bomb planes carries three bombs and these three bombs will take these bombs over an area of just what I said. Everyone that's dropping a bomb at the covering to destroy us for one hundred and fifty miles that it was dropped. Excuse me for my lengthy time but I want you to try and understand this and I want you to be looking out for it any day. I have seen that plane. This is no perfect drawing of it but the brother did the best he could. That's a powerful plane. It can dart in the sky. It's just like you see what they call those wheels—those flying saucers.

Right through the plane measures one mile. Allah showed me this thing. As I tell you, if you find me lying on what I tell you He said, I'll give you $10,000 out my brother's vest pocket. If he don't happen to have it, I'll ask you to loan it to me then I'll pay you back. I saw this plane. This thing can move about into space so wisely until their way of trying to shoot him out of the sky never touch this one. There is a scientist, more than a scientist, I think there are four or five on this Plane. It's a ½ a mile by ½ a mile. And this Plane will make these look like us here but it been can dart out your eyesight so fast until it didn't look like nothing was there. You will see this Plane one day because this Plane have a civilization on it. They stay up there a year and sometimes a year and a half in that Plane. It's a wonderful thing. Dreadful looking Plane. I'm not trying to deceive you, I'm trying to show you what you're going to see pretty soon. (Theology of Time July 2, 1972)

The more we look at and critically analyze the Honorable Elijah Muhammad's teaching on the prophecy of Ezekiel's wheel, we come to the glorious conclusion that he is indeed the man to whom the God of the Bible and the Holy Qur'an gave special knowledge about the most fascinating and important of all developments in human history! I would imagine that our enslaved fore-parents, who toiled and suffered the inhumane treatment of chattel slavery, would rejoice over Mr. Muhammad's teaching and agree that Ezekiel's wheel and the Mother Plane were one and the same "Sweet Chariot" of God, that so many of them sang about. "Swing low sweet chariot, comin' for to carry me home..."

Hidden History: NAACP's Black Face & White Mind

In the city of Philadelphia, Pennsylvania the Nation of Islam's Regional Student Minister Rodney Muhammad has proven the wide and broad-based appeal of, the message of the Most Honorable Elijah Muhammad and the ministry of the Honorable Minister Louis Farrakhan. His simultaneous leadership of both the local mosque of the Nation of Islam and the local chapter of the NAACP is historic. For many years, the Nation of Islam has been portrayed as a group whose ideas and membership exist in the margins of society. The Nation of Islam has deliberately been obscured, hidden and prohibited from access to most things considered "mainstream." The media often speaks **"about"** the Nation of Islam, but rarely speaks **"to"** the Nation of Islam. And despite our salvific, redemptive and well- known work within and among Black communities throughout America and the world, the public is made to think that the bold message of Elijah Muhammad and Louis Farrakhan has been rejected by the majority within Black America. But to this popular notion, the Philly NAACP's election of Regional Student Minister Rodney Muhammad, demonstrates just how respected and integral the Nation of Islam's core message is to the overwhelming majority within Black America.

In history, the NAACP and the NOI have been situated almost at polar opposites of one another. Consider the viewpoint of legendary white supremacist J.B. Stoner. Stoner wrote a letter of appeal to the police chief in New York City, Stephen P. Kennedy on August 6, 1959, asking for a partnership between his KKK and the NYPD. He observed of the two groups the following:

> "The NAACP is a bad gang but I assure you that the Muslims are ten times more dangerous. The NAACP is a cream puff compared to Black Islam. The NAACP likes White people so much that its members try to associate with us Whites every day, but the Muslims think they are better than us Whites even though everybody knows that we Whites are superior.... I guess you know that the NAACP is headed by a man who is not a n*gger, but there is a bad n*gger at the head of the Muslims."

Minister Farrakhan & Muslim – Christian Unity

Brother Student Minister Rodney's ascendancy to the leadership of both groups in Philadelphia powerfully highlights the magnificent and historic approach to re-building the Nation of Islam demonstrated by the Honorable Minister Louis Farrakhan. In the re-building of the Nation of Islam, Minister Farrakhan established strong ties to the Black church, the place where most NAACP members consider as their spiritual home. And Minister Farrakhan has said that *"the Nation of Islam has room in it for churches."* The Minister has also been fond of expressing the fact that *"a true Muslim is a true Christian; and a true Christian is a true Muslim, if you understand."* Minister Farrakhan remains a beloved leader who is recognized, admired and followed by many in the Black Church. When Minister Farrakhan called for a million men to meet him in Washington D.C. on October 16, 1995, nearly 2 million men showed up and 80% of them self-identified as Christian.

Recently, Minister Rodney has been publicly attacked for posting a meme in social media that some Jewish organizations consider to be anti-Semitic. And despite a long record of being a strong and committed spiritual leader and activist in the city of Philadelphia, the NAACP national offices made an extraordinary move to dissolve the local chapter in Philadelphia, so that they might re-constitute it without Minister Rodney as the local head.

NAACP Infamous President Joel Spingarn

This move by the NAACP, to take such drastic action to oust Minister Rodney, because of hurt Jewish feelings, reminds us of this organization's very controversial history. It reminds us especially of the NAACP's nefarious white founders who sought to keep the NAACP perpetually under white control.

An excellent history of the early days of the NAACP and Urban League can be found in the doctoral dissertation of Yvonne DeCarlo Newsome, entitled *A house divided: Conflict and cooperation in African American-Jewish relations. (Volumes I and II)* Newsome noted:

"Measurable racial disagreement over who should lead the organization, what its goals should be, and how it would pursue them were apparent at the founding conference of the NAACP. Significantly, two prominent African American leaders who attended the National Negro Conference, anti-lynching activist **Ida B. Wells-Barnett and the radical editor of the Boston Guardian, Monroe Trotter, refused to join the organization because they were "distrustful of white leadership**"… In later years, the African American press protested when the NAACP Board chose Joel Spingam to be president...".

Moreover, Newsome writes:

> "Final decisions about control of finances remained in the hands of the predominantly white Board, and there is evidence that decision-making about long-term goals and agenda also remained in its hands. In addition, NAACP Board members who were authorized to sign checks and disburse money, including the treasurer, were almost always white…. Because of their monopolization of power, whites were able to exert undue influence over determining agenda, programs, strategies, and finances"

The NAACP, from 1915-1938, had a nefarious Jewish board chairman and president named Joel Spingarn. Spingarn became known for advancing the NAACP's philosophy of "**non-economic liberalism**". Newsome documents how, over and over again, Spingarn and the whites who dominated the early board of directors at the NAACP, fought against W.E.B. Dubois who wanted *"to put segregation to positive use by helping blacks to build a strong economic foundation on which to uplift themselves."*

Not only was Spingarn opposed to the NAACP helping Blacks do as Jews have done in overcoming oppression through using group economics and monetary strength, he also actively opposed other Black leaders, like Marcus Garvey, who championed Black economics. Spingarn's NAACP participated in a "Garvey Must Go" campaign in its Crisis Magazine.

Spingarn also infamously ran a military intelligence unit. He was given the rank of major in 1918 and was in charge of a group of undercover agents in the army's Military Intelligence Unit (MID). This unit spied on and opened 100,000 pieces of mail each week in its espionage activities against Black leaders and organizations. Spingarn remained working in this capacity during his tenure as the head of the NAACP. Spingarn's history as an espionage agent of the U.S. military taints his work in the NAACP and shows how one of the most well-known and popular Black organizations in America was once run by someone whose job it had been to spy on Black people and violate our right to privacy and free speech.

The history of the NAACP as a "Black-faced, White-minded"

organization provides insight into its decision to dissolve an entire chapter because of a cartoon posted in social media by chapter president and Nation of Islam Regional Student Minister Rodney Muhammad of Philadelphia, PA.

NAACP Has Never Wanted Black Leadership It Didn't Control

It is a rather startling reality, when one considers how the NAACP has become so synonymous with Black causes, and yet this Black looking organization, has been primarily led by white people, many of whom have been Jews. In fact, it was only with the death of Jewish patent leather manufacturer Kivie Kaplan, who was NAACP president from 1966-1975 that the NAACP was able to have its first Black president; some 64 years after its founding!

The history makes it clear that the whites and Jews of the NAACP were never going to get used to a Black Muslim leading one of its most important chapters. I close this article by showcasing a brief review some of the powerful criticisms from giants in the Black struggle that exposes the NAACP's history of being the organizational equivalent of a Black face minstrel show.

Adam Clayton Powell, "There are no Negroes in the American Jewish Congress or in the national organizations of Italians-and show me a Black Irishman if you will. The NAACP has white people in high positions. We should boycott it."

Malcolm X- "The Jew is always anxious to advise the black man. But they never advise him how to solve his problem the way the Jews solved their problem. The Jew never went sitting-in and crawling-in and sliding-in and freedom-riding, like he teaches and helps Negroes to do. The Jews stood up, and stood together, and they used their ultimate power, the economic weapon. That's exactly what the Honorable Elijah Muhammad is trying to teach black men to do. ...But the Jew that's advising the Negro joins the NAACP, CORE, the Urban League, and others. With money donations, the Jew gains control, then he sends the black man doing all this wading-in, boring-in, even burying-in—everything but buying-in. Never shows him how to set up factories and hotels. Never advises him how to own what he wants."

Jackie Robinson- "We (the NAACP) are not meeting the needs of the masses. We don't know the people; the people don't know us. I have been asked by many people to form another organization that would be closer to the masses. I'm all for a new organization if we can do it without interfering with what the NAACP is doing."

Hidden History:
200 Black Leaders Unite Against Jewish Pressure, Threats

Black Leaders Unite Summon Courage

In an extraordinary show of courage and unity, that has been heretofore like a footnote in modern Black history, 200 courageous Black leaders came together in 1979 to present a Black united front to push back against Jewish opposition. As reported by Thomas A. Johnson for the August 23, 1979 edition of the New York Times, Black leaders converged in an unprecedented show of force to *"air their grievances"* against Jewish pressure relating to the criticisms and ultimate forced resignation of American United Nations Ambassador Andrew Young. Johnson writes:

> "A statement called "Black/Jewish Relations" was read at the news conference by Julian Bond, a Georgia state senator, who said: "There is no question that individual Jews and Jewish organizations and their leaders have worked as part of the liberal coalition with blacks and organized labor to form a powerful political force for social and economic reform in the U.S. It is also clear that Jewish organizations and leadership have done so when it is in their best interests to do so, as do we."
>
> He said: "However, it is a fact that within the past 10 years some Jewish organizations and intellectuals who were previously identified with the aspirations of black Americans for unqualified educational, political and economic equality with all other Americans abruptly became apologists for the racial status quo. They asserted that further attempts to remedy the present forms of discrimination were violative of the civil rights laws."
>
> The original draft of the document said that "such powerful organizations as the Anti-Defamation League (ADL), the American Jewish Congress and the American Jewish Committee opposed the interest of the black community" in court cases involving affirmative action programs. But the reading by Mr. Bond and the statement released omitted the names of the Jewish groups.
>
> The statement said: "Black America is also deeply concerned with the military alliance that exists between Israel and the illegitimate and oppressive racial regimes in South Africa and southern Rhodesia. That relationship, in our view, imposes upon Jewish organizations in this

country an obligation to insist that the state of Israel discontinue its support of those repressive and racist regimes."

The 200 leaders represented the "National Urban League, the Congressional Black Caucus, the Southern Christian Leadership Conference, organizations of black clergymen and political caucuses from such states as New York, Wisconsin, Georgia, and California." Dr. Kenneth B. Clark, a psychologist, and the Rev. William Jones used the phrase "declaration of independence" to express the sentiment of the group of 200 who had previously been afraid to offend the aforementioned Jewish groups, by taking an opposing position on Israel and Mid-East politics. During this same time period Washington Post writer Warren Brown reported in their October 25, 1979 edition that:

> "Some prominent Blacks have been the targets of death threats and financial pressures in the Black-Jewish dispute that has developed over the last few months. These threats have come mostly from extremists in the American Jewish community..."

This hidden history is important to frame and view the current controversy involving the Honorable Minister Louis Farrakhan and the Jewish backlash against his worldwide July 4, 2020 message entitled **The Criterion**. Minister Farrakhan is frequently blamed for being the "stumbling block" that causes Black-Jewish relations in America to remain troublesome. However, this hidden history helps us to see that the Black-Jewish relationship was problematic long before the name Louis Farrakhan became a house-hold word.

In addition to this hidden history of Black defiance against Jewish pressure, consider the host of academic elite scholars who have published unvarnished accounts of the problematic "secret relationship" between Blacks and Jews.

Scholars Bust Myth of Black Jewish Relationship

"The major role [that Jews] once played in the civil rights movement, [is a] myth ... [that] enhances the self-image of a Jew as a caring and sensitive minority selflessly contributing to improve the lot of other minorities."

SOURCE: *Two Worlds of Judaism: The Israeli and American Experiences* by Charles Liebman and Steven M. Cohen

"For many years, certain Negro intellectuals have been unable to face the Jews realistically. Among the many myths life and history have imposed on Negroes (such as that of Lincoln's "freeing" the slaves) is the myth that the Negro's best friend is the Jew."

SOURCE: *The Crisis of the Negro Intellectual by Harold Cruse*

"[Jewish] loyalists," declared Thelma Thomas Dalevy, president of the mostly Black Delta Sigma Theta sorority in 1979, "are not compatible with the struggle of black Americans for equal opportunity under the law. Indeed, we question whether their loyalties are first with the state of Israel or the United States."

SOURCE: *The Black-Jewish Coalition, Shaken but Still Alive After Young Incident by* Rochelle Stanfield

"Jewish leaders, representing different socio-economic classes, ideologies, and cultural experiences committed themselves to black betterment and gave time, money, and energy to black organizations. The spectrum was so wide and the involvement so extensive that one must conclude that these leaders acted out of peculiarly Jewish motives ... The book demonstrates that Jewish ends were secured by involvement with blacks."

SOURCE: *In the Almost Promised Land: American Jews and Blacks, 1915-1935 by Hasia Diner.*

"I would be hard pressed to find examples of where Blacks and Jews worked together as equals and in harmony. Whenever the Jews were involved they wanted to control the situation. Although altruism cannot be discounted, self-interest and patronization were much more characteristic than equality. Moreover, while many Jews served on the boards of African-American organizations, I can think of no Jewish organization where African Americans served in similar capacities. So, to argue[otherwise] strikes me as a divergence from reality."

SOURCE: *Review of Melnick's Black-Jewish Relations on Trial: Leo Frank and Jim Conley in the New South by Leonard Dinnerstein*

Jews Silent On Trayvon et. Al.

Moreover, we have witnessed many Blacks in social media cry out against how in the midst of Black people's grieving over the recent spike in police brutality resulting in the deaths of George Floyd and Breonna Taylor, Jewish groups like the Simon Wiesenthal Center choose to renew their baseless claim of anti-Semitism against the Hon. Min. Louis Farrakhan. Popular celebrity Nick Cannon was essentially "fired" from Viacom because of alleged anti-Semitic statements that offended Jewish political groups. Yet Viacom and the Wiesenthal Center have yet to get any officers charged in the death of Breonna Taylor fired. Their silence in the midst of our suffering is consistent with the pattern of history as the above scholars attest to.

The May 4, 2012 edition of the *Jewish Advocate* included a stinging article by author Jason M. Rubin, who chided the Jewish community in his piece entitled *The Jewish Silence On Trayvon Martin*. Mr. Rubin wrote:

> The lack of words speaks volumes. Trayvon Martin is shot dead by George Zimmerman, a watchman in a multiethnic, gated community in Sanford, Florida, and Jewish American has nothing to say about it.... I visited the websites of major Jewish organizations and searched for the term "Trayvon." The organizations, which ranged from fundamentalist to progressive, Zionist to pluralist, political to congregational, were: The Anti-Defamation League, Central Conference of American Rabbis, Hadassah, Jewish Council for Public Affairs, Jewish Federation of North America, J Street, Orthodox Union, Union for Reform Judaism and the United Synagogue of Conservative Judaism. Nine organizations. All but two of my searches yielded the words, "No Results."

Minister Farrakhan deserves Black leadership to close ranks around him

This very revealing episode of Black history helps us to properly view the current controversy surrounding the Hon. Min. Louis Farrakhan. It shows that Minister Farrakhan is not alone as a Black leader who saw the need to rise up and challenge powerful Jewish groups over the needs and concerns of the Black community. This history is a reminder to us. And it should motivate Black America to close ranks around Minister Farrakhan like these courageous leaders did in 1979 around Ambassador Andrew Young. Back then it is clear that Black leadership understood that our integrity and self-respect as a people demands that we disallow those outside our community to dictate to us what to think and who to follow or support. This is the kind of unity, intelligence and courage that we need today. Minister Farrakhan deserves better from Black leadership. Professor Andre C. Willis candidly and boldly admitted that no one defends the Black community like Minister Farrakhan. Prof. Willis reported:

> "There is simply no Black person in the world that has — over so many years — been as consistent, as unrestricted, and as forthright in defending the humanity of Black people throughout the world against its attackers."

Now then, with this in mind, let us all be motivated to do for Minister Farrakhan what he has always done for us.

"In Good Company": Hon. Min. Louis Farrakhan Among Great Black Leaders Opposed By Jewish Groups

The magnificent message delivered by the Honorable Minister Louis on July 4, 2020 watered the souls of millions of people in America and around the world. Within 24 hours, the Minister's message had been viewed by an estimated 1.8 million people. And the reactions to his bold and divinely inspired message have been profoundly positive.

And while the common man and woman praised God for the likes of a man like Louis Farrakhan, Jewish periodicals abound in a campaign to injure Minister Farrakhan and to douse the enthusiasm of those who were so edified by his message.

Prominent public figures like DeSean Jackson, Nick Cannon, Stephen Jackson, Allen Iverson and others have been pressured to apologize and explain their love and respect for one of Black America's greatest champions, the Hon. Min. Louis Farrakhan.

The current fury with which Jewish periodicals are pursuing their daily character assassination of Minister Farrakhan has created a teachable moment. In fact, it is cause for an important lesson in history.

The Oppressor Can't Love The Liberator

It is worth saying, and it is worth emphasizing that "Pharaoh didn't love Moses." Pharaoh hated Moses, because the oppressor does not and cannot love the liberator. And Black people in America have been and continue to be oppressed by both Gentile and Jewish groups who rule over American institutions using White supremacy and Black inferiority as governing principles. One of the problems is that most in the Black community have been acquainted with Gentile white oppression; but this same group is all but oblivious to the harm and hurt caused by members of the Jewish community. And it is this previously hidden oppression that Minister Farrakhan exposes and exclaims.

Again, the oppressor cannot love the liberator. Black people have never had a true leader that was loved or approved of by the same people who have oppressed and enslaved us. This fact should empower all of us to refrain from apologizing for associating with or admiring a Black man or woman that the white power structure doesn't like (i.e. Minister Farrakhan). How could an enslaved people realistically think that their slave master would approve of a man whose purpose it is to liberate the enslaved. Never has there been a greater conflict of interests than that which naturally exists between an enslaver and a liberator.

Allah (God) has reared, nurtured and elevated Minister Farrakhan to say things, to expose things and to reveal to the public previously hidden truths and realities that 85% percent of the general public remain oblivious to. He is like Jesus in that he is now known for certain "hard sayings" of truth. Author F.F. Bruce discusses the controversial sayings of Jesus in his book **The Hard Sayings of Jesus**. Examples of Jesus hard sayings include the following:

> "You brood of vipers, how can you who are evil say anything good? For the mouth speaks what the heart is full of." -Matthew 12:34

> "You belong to your father, the devil, and you want to carry out your father's desires. He was a murderer from the beginning, not holding to the truth, for there is no truth in him. When he lies, he speaks his native language, for he is a liar and the father of lies." -John 8:44

Jesus

It is because of Jesus's hard sayings along with the New Testament's exposing of the plot between the Roman and Jewish authorities to crucify Jesus, that the New Testament is considered the most anti-Semitic book of all time! The Jewish Virtual Encyclopedia states:

> "The gospel story, which has generated more anti-Semitism than the sum of all the other anti-Semitic writings ever written..."

Prophet Muhammad

Minister Farrakhan is therefore in the good company of Jesus. The reaction to Jesus and the New Testament is analogous to the reaction to Min. Farrakhan and the **Secret Relationship Between Blacks and Jews**. Like Jesus, Prophet Muhammad (peace be upon him), also had problems created by his Jewish opponents. According to famous translator of the **Glorious Holy Qur'an** Marmaduke Pickthall, Prophet Muhammad's death is connected to his Jewish opposition. He notes:

> "In the first year of this reign at Yathrib (Medina) the Prophet made a solemn treaty with the Jewish tribes, which secured to them equal rights of citizenship and full religious liberty in return for their support

of the new State. But their idea of a Prophet was one who would give them dominion, not one who made the Jews who followed him as brothers of every Arab who might happen to believe as they did. ....In the seventh year of the Hijra the Prophet led a campaign against Kheybar, the stronghold of the Jewish tribes in North Arabia, which had become a hornet's nest of his enemies. The forts of Kheybar were reduced one by one, and the Jews of Kheybar became thenceforth tenants of the Muslims until the expulsion of the Jews from Arabia in the Caliphate of Umar. On the day when the last fort surrendered, Ja'far, son of Abu Talib, the Prophet's first cousin, arrived with all who remained of the Muslims, who had fled to Abyssinia to escape from persecution in the early days. They had been absent from Arabia fifteen years. It was at Kheybar, that a Jewess prepared for the Prophet poisoned meat, of which he only tasted a morsel without swallowing it, then warmed his comrades that it was poisoned. One Muslim, who had already swallowed a mouthful, died immediately, and the Prophet himself from the mere taste of it, derived the illness which eventually caused his death."

Marcus Garvey

Along with being in the good company of the powerful prophets and messengers of Allah (God), Minister Farrakhan is in the good company of the "Black Prophets" of the 20th Century struggle for justice in America. The one Black man who organized the largest Black movement in American history is the Hon. Marcus Mosiah Garvey. He described his Jewish problem in the following when he stated:

> "When they wanted to get me, they had a Jewish judge try me, and a Jewish prosecutor. I would have been freed but two Jews on the jury held out against me ten hours and succeeded in convicting me, whereupon the Jewish judge gave me the maximum penalty."

Malcolm X

The February 25, 1966 edition of the Detroit Jewish News carried an article entitled, **Tragic Tale of Malcolm X: Autobiography Denies Anti-Semitism, But Is Filled With It**. In the article Malcolm is lambasted for being an anti-Semite:

> "Much is said about Jews, Negros relationship with them, and there are many charges against them. Malcolm played an interesting game, predicting that he would be accused of anti-Semitism and resenting it. Yet there is so much evidence of his dislike for Jews that it is impossible

to view him other than anti-Semitic."

Hon. Elijah Muhammad

Author Marc Dollinger discussed the opposition of the Jewish leaders to the Most Hon. Elijah Muhammad when he wrote:

> "Despite the Nation of Islam's political marginalization, American Jewish Committee officials still feared [Elijah] Muhammad. His charismatic personality, willingness to confront racism in the most dramatic rhetorical terms and ability to inspire even non-believing African American listeners concerned Jewish leaders. The Nation of Islam leader, they feared, could earn the respect of his black audiences, even if they chose not to join his movement."

Minister Farrakhan

The ADL, whose claims to represent the Jewish community are in jeopardy due to the growing number of Jewish people who agree with Minister Farrakhan, actually planned their current tactics way back in 1994. Forcing celebrities like DeSean Jackson and Nick Cannon to apologize and be publicly humiliated for associations with Minister Farrakhan come out the ADL's playbook. Their report entitled **Mainstreaming Anti-Semitism The Legitimation of Louis Farrakhan** proposed:

> "ADL is not going to make Farrakhan go away. What we can and should do is impose an obligation on those who deal with him, or, as in the case of universities, give him a platform. In each case, the burden should be on those who give Farrakhan some measure of credibility."

As I have documented, Minister Farrakhan is a victim of character assassination. The Black community should not be surprised. This has not only happened to our heroes and heroines from the past, but it also happened to the Prophets of Allah (God). The opposition to Minister Farrakhan, is therefore a defining moment in our history as a people. Each of us then, have to ask ourselves will we be on the right side of history when today's events are written down for future generations. If you feel in your heart that you would have stood for Jesus, or stood for Prophet Muhammad, or stood for Garvey, Malcolm and Messenger Elijah Muhammad, then I say you can easily prove it, by finding the courage within yourself to stand and support the Honorable Minister Louis Farrakhan!

Jesus Is the Name of The Messiah(s)
The Bible, The Holy Qur'an & Black Liberation Theology

In Part 2 of his extraordinarily profound Saviours' Day message the Honorable Minister Louis Farrakhan discussed the subject of **"Jesus Is the Key."** This message is a message that is rich with wisdom, understanding and revelatory insight. And the areas of the message where the Minister boldly discussed his own life's history that parallels with both Biblical and Quranic scripture deserves deeper study and acknowledgement by believers of all faith traditions.

It is a common belief among the 3 Abrahamic religions of Judaism, Christianity and Islam that at some point at the end of this present world of sin and transgression, a divine man called the Messiah will be born from the womb of a righteous young woman. The Messiah is very important to the overall scope and outlook of all 3 of these great faith traditions. According to the Catholic Dictionary, the word Messiah has a denoted meaning that states the following:

> "Messiah is the Hebrew word for "Anointed One." The equivalent word in Greek is Christos. In the Old Testament it was sometimes applied in a general sense to prophets or priests (Exodus 30:30), but more specifically it referred to the coming of one who would usher in a period of righteousness and conquer sin and evil (Daniel 9:26). In the New Testament the Evangelists made it clear that they knew Jesus was the long-anticipated Messiah (Acts 2:36; Matthew 16:17; Galatians 3:24-29)."

Jesus: Basis for Muslim – Christian Unity

Within the Christian and Muslim sacred texts-The New Testament & The Holy Qur'an-Jesus is the name of the Messiah. Both Christianity and Islam are in agreement on the fact that Jesus is worthy of respect, honor, and that all righteous people should emulate his sterling example of obedience to Allah (God). The Jewish faith does not share this honor and respect for Jesus. While Jewish religious tradition maintains a belief in an expected Messiah, Jewish belief subscribes to the notion that the Messiah is yet to arrive. The New Testament famously documents that the historical Jesus' most ardent foes were the Jewish leaders of his day-The Pharisees, Sadducees & The Scribes- who disagreed that he was the promised Messiah and as a result organized his crucifixion. Some of the New Testament scriptures that highlight

Jesus as the Messiah include the following:

> "But Jesus remained silent and gave no answer. Again, the high priest asked him, "Are you the Messiah, the Son of the Blessed One?" "I am," said Jesus. "And you will see the Son of Man sitting at the right hand of the Mighty One and coming on the clouds of heaven"" (Mark 14:61-62).

> "The woman said, "I know that Messiah" (called Christ) "is coming. When he comes, he will explain everything to us." Then Jesus declared, "I who speak to you am he"" (John 4:25-26).

Characteristic ayats/verses that serve as samples of the Holy Qur'an's high regard for Jesus-the Messiah include the following:

> "When the angels said: O Mary, surely Allah gives thee good news with a word from Him (of one) whose name is the Messiah, Jesus, son of Mary, worthy of regard in this world and the Hereafter, and of those who are drawn nigh (to Allah)." (Surah 3:45)

> "And for their saying, 'We did slay the Messiah, Jesus, son of Mary, the Messenger of ALLAH;' whereas they slew him not, nor did they bring about his death upon the cross, but he was made to appear to them like one crucified; and those who differ therein are certainly in a state of doubt about it; they have no certain knowledge thereof, but only pursue a conjecture; and they did not arrive at a certainty concerning it." (Surah 4:157)

The Historical Jesus Was A Sign of The Messiah

According to the teachings of the Most Honorable Elijah Muhammad, the work of the Messiah was not completed 2020 years ago by the "historical" Jesus. For certain, the man whose name was Isa in Arabic and Yeshua in Hebrew is the man commonly referred to in English as Jesus. And he was an important prophet of Allah (God). However, the work that is described as being done by the Messiah, was not done by that man. But that man's name and life have been preserved in world history to serve as a sign of the Messiah. The Holy Qur'an states in Surah 23:50 the following:

> "And We made the son of Mary and his mother a sign..."

Moreover, the Most Honorable Elijah Muhammad wrote on

September 21, 1957 in the Pittsburgh Courier Newspaper that what is contained in the New Testament about Jesus the Messiah or Christ does not refer to the "historical Jesus." He writes:

> Nearly 75 per cent is referring to a future Jesus, coming at the end of the white races' time, to resurrect the mentally dead, lost members (so-called Negroes) of the Tribe of Shabazz.

And it might surprise many who don't really examine religion from an academic or empirical perspective to learn that some of the most esteemed Biblical scholars in the world have done research and drawn conclusions that agree with the writings of the Most Honorable Elijah Muhammad. On March 4, 1991, The Los Angeles Times published the following:

> The provocative Jesus Seminar on Sunday concluded six years of voting on what the Jesus of history most likely said, ruling out about 80% of words attributed to him in the Gospels and emerging with the picture of a prophet-sage who told parables and made pithy comments.

Modern Black Messiah to End Satan's World

The fact that the world's leading Biblical scholars have concluded that the historical Jesus did not perform 80% of what the New Testament attributes to being the actions and sayings of the Messiah has extraordinary implications!

It obviously and sadly makes clear the fact that the masses of the people don't know the truth of Jesus and have been deceived about the true role and function of the Messiah. To this sad fact, the Most Honorable Elijah Muhammad noted the following on July 7, 1957 in the Pittsburgh Courier Newspaper.

> "I do believe that if my poor, blind, deaf and dumb people could be taught the true knowledge of the true history of Jesus, they would awaken at once."

The awakening that the Most Honorable Elijah Muhammad makes mention of is actually one of the most important events to take place at the end of this world and civilization; referred to in the scriptures as the "resurrection of the dead." And it is the Messiah whom Allah (God) uses to bring about the resurrection. The Holy Qur'an makes mention of this in Surah 3:49 when it states:

> "And (make him) a messenger to the Children of Israel (saying): I have come to you with a sign from your Lord, that I determine for you out of dust the form of a bird, then I breathe into it and it becomes a bird with

Allah's permission, and I heal the blind and the leprous, **and bring the dead to life with Allah's permission**; and I inform you of what you should eat and what you should store in your houses. Surely there is a sign in this for you, if you are believers."

The Holy Qur'an also helps us to understand why the Messiah, while being loved by the poor and oppressed, is at the same time, hated and vehemently opposed by the wicked rulers of nations and societies. The Messiah's role *in "bringing the dead to life with Allah's permission"* is the major end-times event that is the Holy Qur'an's signal indicator of the permanent doom and punishment of Satan. For the time provided to Satan/Shaitan is called a respite, which is defined as *"a short period of rest or relief from something difficult or unpleasant; postpone (a sentence, obligation, etc.)"*, and it is to only last until the day of the resurrection of the mentally and spiritually dead. This eschatological picture is discussed in the Holy Qur'an 7:14, 15:36, 17:62 and 38:79.

The Messiah then, according to scripture and the history of religions is to perform a work of resurrecting the mentally and spiritually dead, who have been rendered such as a result of the evil influence and teaching of Satan. Satan, according to the Book of Revelation 12:9 deceived the whole world, thus making mental death widespread.

In America, the divine work of the Messiah can be witnessed in the work of the Nation of Islam. J. Edgar Hoover of the FBI infamously documented within his nefarious counterintelligence memos that he wanted to prevent the rise of a messiah among Black people in America. And further research has revealed that he devoted most of his anti-Black Messiah resources (time, money, manpower and strategic focus) towards sabotaging the Nation of Islam and its divine leadership.

This suggests that FBI Director J. Edgar Hoover understood the Black Man and Woman of America to be a people from whom the Messiah would be born. And he saw the Most Honorable Elijah Muhammad and the Nation of Islam as best fitting the description about the true role and function of the Messiah. So, like Pharaoh and Herod of the Bible, he sought to kill the Messiah before he could grow to fulfill his purpose of ending Satan's world. In a future article, I hope to go further the research that buttresses and supports Minister Farrakhan's bold claims!

4 Murdered Black Girls and a Christmas Boycott

Denise McNair, Carole Robertson, Cynthia Wesley and Addie Mae Collins were murdered by Alabama racists in 1963 as they attended Sunday school at the 16th Street Baptist Church in Birmingham. Their sweet innocent faces grace many a Black History bulletin board in schools and churches throughout the Black community. We love them and we miss them even though most who are alive today never got to know them. But we do know that the trajectory of their lives, had they not been brutally massacred by white terrorists, would have carried them to wonderful destinations. And all would have benefitted from their growth, maturation, and achievements. They were "church girls" who obeyed their mothers and fathers and studied hard in school and were respectful of their elders. Yes, these four precious children would have been a blessing to their people and to this nation. And according to the predominant custom within the Black community at that time, they would most likely have married their male counterpart among the "church boys" of their peer group and created families. Who knows what their children would have achieved and accomplished. Perhaps, as Minister Farrakhan has taught, the cures for debilitating diseases or great technological advances would have been the outcome of their sons' and daughters' achievements. We can only reflect upon their important but short lives and wonder what might have been.

While we can only imagine who these young princesses might have become, a good indicator of the greatness, brilliance, tenacity, and intelligence of the Black girls of Birmingham, Alabama, in the early 1960s can be found in the life story of Condoleezza Rice. Madame Secretary Rice was a childhood friend of Denise McNair. They played with dolls together. Secretary Rice went on to accomplish great things in her life, earning a Ph.D. in political science and becoming a Stanford University professor. She also served as an advisor to the Joint Chiefs of Staff and held other weighty positions in government before becoming the first Black woman to serve as Secretary of State for the United States of America. Secretary Rice and her accomplishments represent the caliber of human beings that were murdered when the 16th Street Baptist Church was bombed by racist anti-Black terrorists.

These young women are martyrs of the Black man and woman's struggle for liberation in America. And it was in response to this act of savagery and barbarism that Dr. Martin Luther King Jr. and numerous young popular artists and entertainers united to call for direct action. Specifically, they sought to rally the entire nation of Black people to convert their nickels, pennies, dimes, quarters, and dollars into "weapons of mass destruction." The idea they had in mind was a complete economic withdrawal from the most prosperous season of the year in America's capitalist economic system. Dubbed by Dr. Martin Luther King Jr. as a "sacrificial Christmas," the primary call to action was for all Black people to withhold their usual billions of dollars spent on Christmas shopping, in an act of revolutionary defiance. Congressional legend and Black activist Adam Clayton Powell Jr. was a supporter of this idea and even offered a thematic catch phrase to capture the sentiment of the time when he suggested that Black people "hold your dollar and make the white man holler."

Secretary Rice offered a priceless service as America's chief diplomat, a role that helps American businesses gain lucrative contracts abroad while preserving the lives of American service men and women through successful international negotiations that avert wars and conflicts. If we multiply her contribution by a factor of four, we only approximate the value that we were deprived of in the terroristic murder of Denise McNair, Carole Robertson, Cynthia Wesley and Addie Mae Collins. So, Dr. King and the call for a "sacrificial Christmas" in 1963 was a well-conceived strategy. It was the idea that since Black people had lost an inestimable value in the murder of four precious Black girls, our oppressors should lose an equivalent amount as a direct result of our boycotting their biggest money-making season. This idea of "redistributing the pain" was born out of an enlightened attitude among many in the Black community and reflected the zeitgeist of the times, which was that we simply must stop using our money to financially support the murderers of our children.

Christmas Boycott Theologically Justified

Dr. King's activist strategy of boycotting the Christmas shopping season makes all the sense in the world. However, there is a peculiar aspect to Dr. King's decision; Why would Dr. King, as a Christian minister, make a call to boycott Christmas? And Christmas is claimed to be the celebration of the Christian Savior. This could not have been an easy decision for Dr. King. Or was it?

First of all, we must remember that "Dr. King" is called "Dr." for a very good reason. Most people forget that he received a Ph.D. in

Systematic Theology from Boston University. He is therefore a scholar of religion. As a religious scholar, he was a possessor of knowledge about religion that the average person is not privy to. Within the realm of religious or spiritual knowledge, there is a hierarchy that has God (the Supreme Being) at the top. He reveals some of His secret knowledge and wisdom directly to the prophets, and after the prophets religious knowledge is found among the scholars of religion. The scholars of religion are the teachers of the preachers of religion, who in turn preach of religion to the "laymen and women." In Dr. King's case he occupied the position of both scholar and preacher, or academician and evangelist. But most have not been acquainted with Dr. Martin Luther King Jr. in his important but often overlooked role as Religious Scholar.

The reason he, as a Christian pastor, was comfortable with calling for a Christmas boycott may surprise some and shock others: Dr. King—religious scholar—acknowledged the pagan origins of the Christmas holiday. What I am specifically referring to is Dr. King's research conducted while a student at Crozer Theological Seminary. His 1949 paper titled "A Study of Mithraism" received an academic letter grade of A. His professor Morton S. Enslin wrote of Dr. King's paper: "This is an exceedingly good paper. You have given a very complete picture of the essential details and you have presented this in a balanced and restrained way. And furthermore, you know how to write. You should go a long way if you continue to pay the price."

Dr. King writes:

> "It is well-nigh impossible to grasp Christianity through and through without knowledge of these cults. That there were striking similarities between the developing church and these religions cannot be denied. Even Christian apologist had to admit that fact. For an instance, in the mystery-religions identification between devotee and the Lord of the cult was supposed to be brought about by various rites of initiation; the taurobolium, or bath of blood; the eating of flesh of the sacrificial beast and the like. Now there was something of this in Paul too, for he thought of the believer as buried with Christ in baptism and as feeding upon him in the Eucharist. This is only one of many examples that I could give to prove the similarity between the developing Christian Church and the Mystery Religions."

In Dr. King's discussion of the specific cult religion known as Mithraism, he documents that Mithra was believed to be the "genius of celestial light," who in his chariot "goes through heaven with a team of four white horses... 'ever watchful'" and that "Mithra was the god of wide pastures and the giver of gifts." What Dr. King documents is that the modern Christmas tradition of light decorations and an all-seeing (all-knowing) Santa Claus with reindeer originates in an entirely different religion and has nothing at all to do with Jesus the Christ!

As a scholar, Dr. King cites his sources. He refers often in his paper on Mithraism to the earlier more expansive work of Franz Cumont titled The Mysteries of Mithra. Referencing Cumont's work, Dr. King writes about the "Syrian merchants who established trading posts throughout the [Roman] empire." These merchants were primary transmitters of the cult of Mithra. Citing Cumont, Dr. King notes that

> "most of these Syrians belonged to the upper classes and were not true worshippers of Mithra.... [I]t was the slaves and servants of these merchants who were followers of Mithra..."

Again, knowledge of this history enabled Dr. King to draw clear and strong parallels between the slave followers of Mithra and the Blacks in America who were chattel slaves during the antebellum period and the economic slaves to the modern merchants in his own lifetime. The belief of the Roman slaves in a gift-giving celestial god of light that traveled the night sky in a chariot drawn by horses is no different from Blacks in America ritually displaying Christmas lights and indoctrinating their children in the belief that Santa Claus travels the night sky with reindeer, giving gifts.

It is a marvel that Dr. King remained a devoted minister of Christianity as the true religion of God when we consider his study and knowledge gained as a religious scholar. For as we see from his own academic research, astute writing, and powerful documentation, the main teachings and practices of Christianity originated in the early "mystery religions" like Mithraism—the same religions that most Christians today would consider heathen and pagan cults!

In the section of Dr. King's paper titled "The Influence of Mithraism on Christianity," he writes:

> "When Mithraism is compared with Christianity, there are surprisingly many points of similarity. Of all the mystery cults Mithraism was the greatest competitor of Christianity. The cause for struggle between

these two religions was that they had so many traditions, practices and ideas that were similar and, in some cases, identical."

Dr. King goes on to highlight the fact that because of these similarities **"many believed the Christian movement itself became a mystery cult."** He then lists 6 areas where Mithraism and Christianity are virtually indistinguishable from each other:

(1) Both regarded Sunday as a holy day.
(2) December 25 came to be considered as the anniversary of the birth of Mithra and Christ also.
(3) Baptism and a communion meal were important parts of the ritual of both groups.
(4) The rebirth of converts was a fundamental idea in the two cults.
(5) The struggle with evil and the eventual triumph of good were essential ideas in both religions.
(6) In both religions only initiates who passed through certain preliminary phases of introduction were admitted to the mysteries which brought salvation to converts.

We get a sense of Dr. King's feeling about these non-traditional histories of the origin of Christianity in his acknowledgment that there are so many similarities between Christianity and Mithraism that "the general effect is almost startling."

Dr. King concludes his short essay with a bold confession. He writes:

"That Christianity did copy and borrow from Mithraism cannot be denied.... Many of the views, while passing out of Paganism into Christianity were given a more profound and spiritual meaning by Christians, yet we must be indebted to the source."

It is a shame that we have not been properly introduced to Dr. King as a religious scholar. For as a religious scholar we see him come into agreement with the Most Honorable Elijah Muhammad, who taught for many years that the celebration of Jesus' birth on December 25th is of pagan origin.

King, Muhammad, and Christian Scholars Agree

And as Dr. King's research led him to the pagan god Mithra as the source of the December 25th celebration of Jesus' birthday, the Honorable Elijah Muhammad introduces us to the role of the pagan worship of Nimrod. Consider now some of the teachings of the Most Honorable Elijah Muhammad on the pagan origin of

Christmas. In his illuminating book Our Saviour Has Arrived, Messenger Muhammad writes:

> "So, you go out and spend your hard-earned money to worship with white people. They force you under disguise and defraud you into worshipping the birthday of that wicked old Nimrod on December. And if you knew the truth of him, you would not dare to worship it." ...

Nimrod gets a great ovation on the 25th day of December; one of the most wicked leaders that ever lived....

The great false worship of December 25 is a lie. The worship of Jesus' birthday, which they claim is on the 25th of December, is one of the most open lies against the truth. And the authors of their religion, Christianity, know that they are wrong in trying to tell the world that that is the day Jesus was born on....

God taught me that the 25th day of December is the day of the birth of Nimrod, and that the scientists know that that is Nimrod's birthday. Nimrod was a leader, born as an opponent of Moses' teachings....

Notice that the Most Honorable Elijah Muhammad is exposing knowledge to the public from the highest level of the religious knowledge hierarchy. In these passages He lets us know that Allah (God) taught him the truth of Christmas and that the religious scholars are in agreement with that truth, which he is exposing to his deceived and manipulated people!

As proof that the "authors" and "scientists" of the Christian faith know the truth of what Mr. Muhammad and Dr. King have attested to, we bring to the "witness stand" noted scholar, author, and evangelist Ralph Woodrow, who wrote the book Babylon Mystery Religion. On page 151, Woodrow quotes from James George Frazer's book The Golden Bough:

> "The largest pagan religious cult which fostered the celebration of December 25 as a holiday throughout the Roman and Greek worlds was the pagan sun worship-Mithraism...This winter festival was called 'the Nativity'—the 'Nativity of the SUN.'"

Woodrow continues,

> "Was this pagan festival responsible for the December 25 day being chosen by the Roman Church?"

Woodrow cites The Catholic Encyclopedia to provide a definitive answer to that question:

> "The well-known solar feast of...Natalis Invicti [the Nativity of the Unconquered Sun] celebrated on 25 December, has a strong claim on the responsibility for our December date [of Christmas!]"

Moreover, Woodrow writes:

> "As pagan solar customs were being 'Christianized' at Rome, it is understandable that confusion would result. Some thought Jesus was Sol, the sun-god!"

Woodrow's research and admissions even strike a blow at the gross consumerism of the Christmas "winter festival." He condemns the rationalization that gift exchanges should be the primary way to celebrate the birth of Jesus. According to Woodrow,

> "[S]ome have sought to link Christmas gifts with those presented to Jesus by the wise men. This cannot be correct. By the time the wise men arrived, Jesus was no longer 'lying in a manger' (as when the shepherds came), but was in a house (Matthew 2:9-11). This could have been quite a while after his birthday. Also, they presented their gifts to Jesus, not to each other!"

On the use of Christmas trees Woodrow states:

> "The Christmas tree, as we know it, only dates back a few centuries, though ideas about sacred trees are very ancient. An old Babylonish fable told of an evergreen tree which sprang out of a dead tree stump. The old stump symbolized the dead Nimrod, the new evergreen tree symbolized that Nimrod had come to life again..."

In addition to Ralph Woodrow, popular 20th-century Christian evangelist and scholar Herbert Armstrong ruffled many feathers when he published his popular The Plain Truth About Christmas. In it he notes that

> "recognized historical authorities show Christmas was not observed by Christians for the first two or three hundred years—a period longer than the entire history of the United States as a nation!"

The Rev. Herbert Armstrong's scathing revelations about Christmas' true origin also agrees with those by the Most Honorable Elijah Muhammad and the Rev. Dr. Martin Luther King Jr. On page of 11 of his pamphlet-size exposé, the Reverend

Armstrong discusses Nimrod. We read:

> "From many ancient writings, considerable is learned of this man, who started the great organized worldly apostasy from God that has dominated this world until now. Nimrod was so evil, it is said he married his own mother, whose name is Semiramis. After Nimrod's untimely death, his so-called mother-wife, Semiramis, propagated the evil doctrine of the survival of Nimrod as a spirit being. She claimed a full-grown evergreen tree sprang overnight from a dead tree stump, which symbolized the springing forth unto new life of the dead Nimrod. On each anniversary of his birth, she claimed, Nimrod would visit the evergreen tree and leave gifts upon it. December 25th was the birthday of Nimrod. This is the real origin of the Christmas tree."

The history of Christmas' true origins made it a lot easier for Dr. King, the religious scholar, to call for a complete economic withdrawal from the Christmas shopping season. In his example we see the value of academic knowledge as a guide for social activism. Looking at Dr. King as a scholar of religious knowledge opens up an entirely new vista through which to explore his thinking, strategies, and evolution. It seems as though this side of the great leader of the Civil Rights Movement has been omitted or kept hidden from most discussions about him. From my perspective, this is done intentionally by those who would like to keep Dr. King in a box and deny the fact that he had much in common with the Most Honorable Elijah Muhammad and other revolutionary thinkers.

Dr. King was not able to convince the masses of Black people to join him in his call for a "sacrificial Christmas." Yet despite the fact that only a few cities participated, the boycott injury to their local economies was significant. This year we encourage all to support the call for a **"sacrificial Christmas,"** a call that has been renewed by the heir to Dr. King's role as the most respected Black leader in America—the Honorable Minister Louis Farrakhan. For just as the murder of 4 innocent Black children served as the context and inspiration for such a call in 1963, the senseless and barbaric murders of Black men, women, and children today give us the motivation we need to pick up Dr. King's brilliant idea of economic withdrawal and execute it for maximum impact.

Master W. Fard Muhammad Revealed Supreme Wisdom, Evidence Now Comes Forth

A Teachable Moment

In thinking about the introduction of the name **Master Fard Muhammad** into the current wave of popular culture, the phrase *"teachable moment"* comes to mind. This colloquial phrase is defined in various ways. One education writer for *ThoughtCo.Com* described a teachable moment as

> "an unplanned opportunity that arises in the classroom where a teacher has a chance to offer insight to his or her students. A teachable moment is not something that you can plan for; rather, it is a fleeting opportunity that must be sensed and seized by the teacher."

This current teachable moment has been provided courtesy of Hip-Hop legend Busta Rhymes. His song entitled **Master Fard Muhammad** is a lead single from his new music project *Extinction Level Event 2*. And it is providing the Nation of Islam an opportunity to educate and to provide insight into the true history, significance and on-going work of Master W. Fard Muhammad.

The current moment of heightened interest in Master W. Fard Muhammad will inspire more and more study of him and what he taught to the Most Honorable Elijah Muhammad, for it is my belief that His teachings should be categorized as divine revelation.

The Bible and Holy Quran are books that fit within the category of divine revelation. Consider the harmony of both the Bible and Holy Qur'an when they speak on Allah's (God's) revealing of secret wisdom to Prophets and Messengers.

> "The Knower of the unseen, **so He makes His secrets known to none except a messenger whom He chooses**. For surely, He makes a guard to go before him and after him, that He may know that they have truly delivered the messages of their Lord; and He encompasses what is with them, and He keeps account of all things."
> -Holy Qur'an 72:26-28 M.M. Ali Translation

> "Surely the Lord God does nothing, **Unless He reveals His secret to His servants the prophets**. A lion has roared! Who will not fear? The Lord God has spoken! Who can but prophesy?"
> -Amos 3:7-8 NKJV Translation

These 2 passages of scripture stand out within these sacred texts, as they highlight the encounter that the Most Honorable Elijah Muhammad had with His teacher Master W. Fard Muhammad. He only spent 3 ½ years among us, yet the Supreme Wisdom that he left with us contained powerful and previously hidden truths, much of which had not been known before. He was sharing with the Most Honorable Elijah Muhammad the private or secret thinking of Allah (God).

Master W. Fard Muhammad and What He Revealed
On page 16-18 of the book **Message To The Blackman In America**, the Most Honorable Elijah Muhammad provides a beautiful overview of the major content areas that help us to see the scope of what Master W. Fard Muhammad revealed. He writes:

> "Allah came to us from the Holy City Mecca, Arabia, in 1930. He used the name Wallace D. Fard, often signing it W. D. Fard. In the third year (1933), He signed his name W. F. Muhammad which stands for Wallace Fard Muhammad. He came alone."

> "He began teaching us the knowledge of ourselves, of God and the devil, of the measurement of the earth, of other planets, and of the civilization of some of the planets other than earth. He measured and weighed the earth and its water; the history of the moon; the history of the two nations, black and white, that dominate the earth. He gave the exact birth of the white race; the name of their God who made them and how; and the end of their time, the judgment, how it will begin and end." ...

Evidence For The Truth of Revelation
In 2014, The Honorable Minister Louis Farrakhan spent an entire year delving deep into every aspect of what Allah (God), in the person of Master W. Fard Muhammad, revealed to the Most Honorable Elijah Muhammad. Through the **Time and What Must Be Done** Lecture Series, Minister Farrakhan presented an abundance of evidence that supports and proves the truth of the Supreme Wisdom revealed by Master W. Fard Muhammad.

In part 39 of this series Minister Farrakhan stated:

> "Guess what? The scientists are now agreeing with the Honorable Elijah Muhammad about the time of the White race's appearance on our planet, and their nature! Oh, so many have mocked and ridiculed

Mr. Muhammad's Teachings about "Yacub"; that he said, "Allah taught him" that the White man first appeared 6,000 years ago on an island in the Aegean Sea called Pelan, or "Patmos"—but White scientists are now confirming the reality of this event in their history, and this revelation from Allah to the Honorable Elijah Muhammad! Dr. Jonathan Pritchard, with other researchers at The University of Chicago, had found "where genes appear to have been reshaped by natural selection ... within the last 5,000 to 15,000 years." Incredibly, Dr. Pritchard estimates that the point in time when the genes of the Asian and European populations were altered was "6,600 years ago"—the exact date that the Honorable Elijah Muhammad taught that Mr. Yacub began his Patmos Island grafting process!"

Master W. Fard Muhammad revealed to the Most Honorable Elijah Muhammad that Allah (God) has always been Black, not White. This explosive truth proved iconoclastic in the lives of the American Black man and woman who have been conditioned to hate their Blackness by preachers of religion and religious imagery that communicated that God and God's people were white.

Yet nowadays, more and more evidence exists to vindicate the Supreme Wisdom of Master W. Fard Muhammad that Allah (God) has always been Black. A fascinating commentary on theology that is relevant to this point is the powerful preaching of legendary Bishop Henry McNeal Turner. In his writing **God Is A Negro**, he states:

> "We have as much right biblically and otherwise to believe that God is a Negro, as you buckra, or white people have to believe that God is a fine looking, symmetrical and ornamented white man. For the bulk of you, and all the fool Negroes of the country, believe that God is white-skinned, blue-eyed, straight-haired, projecting-nosed compressed-lipped and finely-robed white gentleman sitting upon a throne somewhere in the heavens.
> Every race of people since time began who have attempted to describe their God by words, or by paintings, or by carvings, or by any other form or figure have conveyed the idea that the God who made them and shaped their destinies was symbolized in themselves, and why should not the Negro believe that he resembles God as much as other people? We do not believe that there is any hope for a race of people who do not believe that they look like God."

Added to Bishop Turner's wisdom is the scholarship of Dr. Wesley

Muhammad who devoted nearly 500 pages to the effort of evidence finding that supports Master W. Fard Muhammad's Supreme Wisdom. Dr. Wesley's **The Book of God: An Encyclopedia of Proof That the Black Man Is God** includes a brilliant feast of religious history that makes the Nation of Islam theology impervious to mockery. He notes:

> "The Creator was a Man-a Black Man. This was acknowledged by all of the ancient spiritual traditions of the Original People. This was acknowledged by the original Hebrews (and Jews), the original Christians, and the original Muslim followers of Prophet Muhammad ibn Abdullah (saw). This understanding of God is the hallmark of Traditional Aboriginal Religion and Philosophy as well as the original orthodoxy of the three Hebraic religions. It was the later Greek philosophers who introduced the Spook God to the world."

Dr. Wesley quotes Godfrey Higgins' *Anacalypsis* which further states:

> "We have found the Black complexion or something relating to it whenever we have approached the origin of nations. The Alma Mater, the Goddess Multimammia, the founders of the Oracles, the Memnon of first idols, were always Black. Venus, Jupiter, Apollo, Bacchus, Hercules, Asteroth, Adonis, Horus, Apis, Osiris, and Amen: **in short, all the...deities were Black**. They remained as they were first...in very ancient times."

These brief samplings of evidence are literally the tip of the proverbial iceberg of what now exists to powerfully demonstrate that the teacher of the Most Honorable Elijah Muhammad and Founder of the Nation of Islam in America, is exactly who the Most Honorable Elijah Muhammad said that He is, Allah (God) in person. He visited America and revealed unto the Black man and woman of America a controversial and profound truth, which only now is being privately acknowledged and borne witness as true by the rich and powerful. And in light of these discoveries we can rejoice like Jesus did in the New Testament when it is written of him these words:

> "I thank You, Father, Lord of heaven and earth, that You have hidden these things from the wise and prudent and have revealed them to babes." (Matthew 11:25 NKJV)

Master W. Fard Muhammad: An Introduction To The Theology of The Nation of Islam

During a period of time when many platforms are being closed to the Honorable Minister Louis Farrakhan and his representatives, it has been encouraging to notice and witness overtures of support, solidarity and appreciation emerging from the world's most popular and significant cultural expression; Hip-Hop. For in the aftermath of the Honorable Minister Louis Farrakhan's worldwide July 4th message, his and our enemies have become more enraged. They now callously dog the trail of Minister Farrakhan seeking to extirpate him and the Nation of Islam from all platforms, including the digital spaces and social media.

Over the past few days, the world has been taken by storm with the release of the much-anticipated new music project from Hip-Hop legend, the multi-talented Busta Rhymes. Not only does this new project, **Extinction Level Event 2**, include amazing features and collaborations from noteworthy artists like Kendrick Lamar and Rakim, but the project comes with tributes to and content from, the Honorable Minister Louis Farrakhan.

To add to that already impressive and courageous inclusion of Minister Farrakhan's ver batim words, is another track that is simply titled "Master Fard Muhammad". At the time of the writing of this article, that song has over 2 million views on YouTube.

As a student of the Honorable Minister Louis Farrakhan, I am very appreciative of Busta Rhymes in what he has done with this new project. And I see in it a teachable moment for the Nation of Islam.

Theology 101

Master W. Fard Muhammad is – simply stated- the God of Louis Farrakhan, Elijah Muhammad and the Nation of Islam. And for his name to be on the lips and hearts and minds of millions of people throughout the world is no small achievement.

Some religious prudes might recoil at the notion of referring to Master Fard Muhammad as God. However, religious scholarship maintains that throughout the Judeo-Christian and Islamic sacred texts, over and over again Allah (God) is depicted as a man.

But don't take my word for it. Go to Genesis 18 of the Bible and read where **"3 men stood before Abraham and one of them was the Lord"**. Or go to Numbers 12 to read where God told Aaron and Miriam that He speaks to Moses **"face to face as a man**

speaks to his friend". The New Testament continues with Jesus in John 8 telling his Jewish adversaries that 2 men are witnesses of his divine authority and one of those men was **"the Lord"**. Prophet Muhammad was the successor to these Prophets who preceded him. So, if the preceding Prophets' God was a man, the God of Prophet Muhammad was also a man. And the Holy Qur'an is filled with references that outline its own "man-God" theology. For example, Surah 55:27 states in the English translation **"And there endures forever the person of thy Lord, the Lord of glory and honor."** The Arabic word that is translated as "person" is actually the word **"wajhu"**, which means **"face"**. So, the God of the Holy Qur'an has a face. And ayats/verses 59:2 and 89:22 discuss the coming of Allah (God).

A review of the Bible and the Holy Qur'an powerfully demonstrates that the most important characters to be found in the sacred texts of Jews, Christians and Muslims all had encounters with the divine supreme being, Allah-God, in human form. Abraham's God was a man; **Moses' God was a man; Jesus' God was a man and Prophet Muhammad's God was a man.** The Most Honorable Elijah Muhammad, who is also in spiritual lineage of divine Messengers of Allah (God) maintained that his God was a man; Allah in the person of Master W. Fard Muhammad.

The Holman Bible Dictionary discusses the hidden history of God in human form in its entry for the word **"theophany."** Consider the following extract of that Bible Dictionary entry:

> "THEOPHANY-Physical appearance or personal manifestation of a god to a person. The basic postulate here is that to see God could be fatal. "He said, "You cannot see My face, for no man can see Me and live!' "(Exodus 33:20. ...Yet the record is unmistakable that people did see God, such as Moses and others at Sinai (Exodus 24:9-10); the Lord's rebuke of Aaron and Miriam (Numbers 12:4-8); and the majestic vision to Isaiah (Isaiah 6:1,6:5). ...Without question the theophany in Exodus 24:10 involved the appearance of a human being, for the text clearly states that a pavement of sapphire appeared "under His feet." At Peniel, Jacob testified that he had seen God face-to-face (Genesis 32:30). On Mount Horeb it was the experience of Moses to speak to God "face to face, just as a man speaks to his friend" (Exodus 33:11). In the same passage when Moses begged God to show him His glory (Exodus 33:18), the Lord graciously granted Moses a vision of Himself, saying, "I will take My hand away and you shall see My back, but My face shall not be seen" (Exodus 33:23). ...God in His wisdom does not

restrict Himself to one method of self-revelation."

OUR SAVIOUR

Who is Master W. Fard Muhammad? As an answer to this important question, consider a sampling of some of the profound statements made by the Most Honorable Elijah Muhammad:

SEPTEMBER 22, 1956- "THE REVELATOR saw (Rev. 18:1) an angel come from Heaven (from the Holy Land) having GREAT POWER, and the earth (the so-called Negroes) was enlightened with His Glory (wisdom, knowledge of the truth). This angel can be no other than Master W. F. Muhammad (the Great Mahdi), who came from the Holy City Mecca, Arabia, in 1930. He is the most wise and powerful being on earth or ever will be (God in Person). He, who with a strong voice announced the immediate doom of America. He said that there was no punishment great enough to repay the slave masters for their evils done against the so-called Negroes of America. He also said that the country is filled with devils and every kind of evil. His voice was strong and mighty, and to everyone who believed and accepted the TRUE religion, ISLAM, he gave them a holy name of Allah's (God). Every word that he said is true. He came for the salvation of the so-called Negroes, warning them to join on to their OWNKIND (the nation of Islam)."

JULY 20, 1957- "One of the main things that one must learn is to distinguish between the history of Jesus two thousand years ago and the prophecy of the Jesus who is expected to come at the end of the world. What we have as a history of the birth of Jesus 2,000 years ago often proves to be that of the Great Mahdi, the Restorer of the Kingdom of Peace on Earth who came to America in 1930 under the name of Mr. W. D. Fard. Later, he admitted that he was Mr. Wallace Fard Muhammad, the one whom the world had been looking for to come for the past 2,000 years. According to the Holy Qur'an chapter and verse we have under discussion, the name Messiah, the meaning fits that of the Mahdi more than any other man.

The Mahdi is a world traveler. He told me that he had traveled the world over and that he had visited North America for 20 years before making himself known to us, his people, whom he came for. He had visited the Isles of the Pacific, Japan and China, Canada, Alaska, the North Pole, India, Pakistan, all of the Near East and Africa. He had studied the wild life in the jungles of Africa and learned the language of the birds. He could speak 16 languages and could write 10 of them. He visited every inhabited place on the earth and had pictured and extracted the language of the people on Mars and had a knowledge of all life in the universe. He could recite by heart the histories of the world as far back as 150,000 years and knew the beginning and end of all things.

The names Christ, Jesus, Jehovah, God, Allah and many other good names, rightly are His names and He came to give divine names to the whole of the 17 million so-called Negroes, Jesus was made an example for the Jews (Holy Qur'an 43:59). Jesus and his mother were made as a sign (23:50)."

OCTOBER 5, 1957-"THE HISTORY of Jesus and His mother is a sign of the history of the so-called Negroes, who have been lost from their people for 400 years - who now are found and must be returned to their own; or else every Western (Christian) government will be brought to an aught by the Great God, Allah, under the name of Mr. W. F. Muhammad, "The Mighty Mahdi, the Son of Man," Allah in person."

Minister Farrakhan as The Defender of Black People

Throughout the years Minister Farrakhan's love for Black People has been witnessed as he has looked beyond their faults and ministered unto their needs.

Quotes

"But what is Farrakhan's role in the political realm today? First, he is a prosecuting attorney on behalf of this nation's poor and oppressed minorities. He understands his role to be one of forcefully pointing out discrepancies between American political rhetoric and the reality of black American life. His eloquence and analytic gifts, extraordinary memory, and refined debating skills uniquely qualify him to represent the cause of the unemployable masses which most civil rights organizations and churches have not consistently advanced."-former Morehouse President Robert Michael Franklin

"The best of the legacy of Farrakhan is twofold. First, he has demonstrated a deep understanding of and shown an unswerving courage to publicly detail the lived reality of anti-black racism. There is simply no Black person in the world that has — over so many years — been as consistent, as unrestricted, and as forthright in defending the humanity of Black people throughout the world against its attackers."-Prof. Andre C. Willis

Quiet as it's kept, Farrakhan is respected by millions of African American, on all socio-economic levels, for his courage in standing up to an oppressive system and his penchant for calling white folk out. Truly "unbought and unbossed," he often says the things that many Blacks feel but don't have the freedom to express. According to a poll reported in Time, 59% of Blacks believe Farrakhan is a good role model for Black youth and that he speaks the truth. -Prof. Geneva Smitherman

Jewish Acknowledgement

These episodes in the history show Minister Farrakhan using his good name and reputation to defend prominent Blacks who have found themselves in trouble. Jewish author Daniel Pipes commented on this phenomenon in a blog post on his website; an excerpt from his blog post is below:

> "The New York Post reports today that "Michael Jackson last night became a member of the Nation of Islam." Of course, this development

takes place in the aftermath of Jackson's being arrested on Nov. 20 in connection with child-molestation charges and now being out on $3 million bail.

If this report of his conversion proves to be accurate, it would fit a well-established pattern of African-Americans who, finding their reputation in tatters, turn to the Nation of Islam, which then provides them with solace and help. This phenomenon is most apparent in jails, where blacks since the late 1940s have been converting in large numbers. Famous converts in trouble include:

- Tawana Brawley, who converted after her much-publicized claim of being raped by a gang of white men
- Mike Tyson, the heavyweight champion jailed for rape,
- Benjamin Chavis, who converted after his eviction from the National Association for the Advancement of Colored People, in large part for having paid off a mistress with NAACP funds.
- Kenny Gamble, the music producer whose life fell apart as he faced a payola investigation in 1975.

Other blacks in disgrace do not make the full step to conversion but become closely affiliated with the NOI, which provides them too with political and moral support. Prominent beneficiaries include:

- Alcee Hastings, an impeached Federal judge;
- Marion Barry, the mayor of Washington, D.C., convicted for drug-taking;
- George Stallings, a Catholic priest accused of child molestation; and
- Gus Savage, a U.S. congressman from Illinois charged with sexual harassment.

Finally, some blacks in difficult straits merely dip into Islam, without developing a formal relationship – such as O.J. Simpson, who read the Qur'an while incarcerated."

-Daniel Pipes; December 18, 2003, updated Jun 27, 2010
http://www.danielpipes.org/blog/2003/12/michael-jackson-and-blacks-in-stress-who

The Short List of Black leaders, groups and prominent men and women who have benefitted from Minister Farrakhan defending them in the court of public opinion and privately pastoring them through serious life trials and tribulations.

1. Mayor Marion Barry
2. Mike Tyson
3. Rev. Jesse Jackson
4. Michael Jackson
5. O.J. Simpson
6. Rep. Alcee Hastings
7. Julian Bond
8. Rep. Cynthia McKinney
9. Rep. Earl Hilliard
10. Tawana Brawley
11. David Dinkins
12. President Barak Obama
13. Rev. Charles Coen
14. Rev. Eddie Carthan
15. Qubilah Shabazz
16. Malcolm Shabazz
17. Charles Rangel
18. Congressman Mel Reynolds
19. Mayor Willie Herenton
20. Congressional Black Caucus
21. Mayor Kwame Kilpatrick
22. Benjamin Chavis
23. James Luther Bevel
24. Father Michael Pfleger
25. Rev. T.L. Barrett
26. Alderman Dorothy Tillman

27. Harold Washington Cultural Center
28. Imam Jamil Al-Amin (H.Rap Brown)
29. Bloods and Crips
30. Vice Lords and Gangster Disciples
31. From Gangs to Street Organizations
32. Hip-Hop Community
33. Stan Tookie Williams
34. Sistah Souljah
35. Bishop George A. Stallings
36. Rep. Bobby Rush
37. Steve Cokely
38. Arsenio Hall
39. Bill Cosby
40. Oprah Winfrey
41. Harold-Washington

The Minister has stood and defended our people. When are we going to return the favor? Surely after 63 years of service to our people, Minister Farrakhan is more than worthy.

Minister Farrakhan Visits Monroe, a city of Lynching

The Honorable Minister Louis Farrakhan recently graced the city of Monroe, Louisiana with his presence. The Minister's visit to the commencement exercises of Grambling University, a historically Black university, brought him to the Monroe area.

During the Minister's short stay, he was honored by his supporters, Grambling officials, civic leaders and the members of the local mosque of the Nation of Islam in Monroe. A great honor was bestowed on the Minister by the city Mayor Jamie Mayo when he gave the Minister the key to the city of Monroe.

And despite the noble reputation of the Minister and his work, local news outlets have questioned the Mayor's decision to bestow such an honor on the Minister. It is as if the Minister is supposed to be persona non-grata in the city of Monroe. However, a news source has compared the Mayor's accommodation of Minister Farrakhan with police escort and city services to past occasions where they did the same for white racists like David Duke.

The problem here is that the Honorable Minister Louis Farrakhan should never be compared with known bigots and race haters. The Minister's record proves him to be a beautiful man who has devoted his life and sacrificed many years of his life in devotion to the cause of the complete liberation of Black people and all oppressed people throughout the Earth.

In contrast, the city of Monroe and the Ouachita Parish have a history of shame and infamy over its treatment of Black people.

According to the research of the **Equal Justice Institute (EJI)**, who published the groundbreaking study on lynching in America:

> "During the period between the Civil War and World War II, thousands of African Americans were lynched in the United States. Lynchings were violent and public acts of torture that traumatized black people throughout the country and were largely tolerated by state and federal officials. These lynchings were terrorism. "Terror lynchings" peaked between 1880 and 1940 and claimed the lives of African American men, women, and children who were forced to endure the fear, humiliation, and barbarity of this widespread phenomenon unaided. Lynching

profoundly impacted race relations in this country and shaped the geographic, political, social, and economic conditions of African Americans in ways that are still evident today.

The largest numbers of lynchings were found in Jefferson County, Alabama; Orange, Columbia, and Polk counties in Florida; Fulton and Early counties in Georgia; Caddo, Ouachita, Bossier, Iberia, and Tangipahoa parishes in Louisiana..."

The EJI Report entitled **Lynching in America: Confronting the Legacy of Racial Terror Second Edition** goes on to document that the state of **Louisiana had 559 lynchings of Black people from 1877-1950. The Ouachita Parish, where Monroe Louisiana is located, had 37 lynchings during this time period.**

Author Ralph Ginzburg writes in his book 100 Years of Lynching that on October 22, 1913 in Monroe Louisiana,

> "Warren Eton, a negro, who made an insulting remark to a white woman Monday, was taken from the jail here early this morning by a mob and hanged to a nearby telegraph pole. Two masked men held up the jailer with pistols, but other members of the mob made no attempt to conceal their identities."

Ginzburg also documents that on April 29, 1919 near Monroe Louisiana

> "A Vicksburg, Shreve-port and Pacific train was held up by an armed mob about five miles from Monroe, La., today, and George Holden, negro, accused of writing an insulting note to a white woman named Onlie Elliot, was taken from the train and shot to death. Holden was taken from a stretcher in the baggage car. He had been wounded in two previous attempts to lynch him. Holden was being sent to Shreveport for safekeeping. He was shot in the leg Monday night by unidentified persons shortly after the woman received the insulting note. Later he was beaten into insensibility. When the local sheriff heard of this, he placed Holden aboard the V, S&P train for the purpose of taking him to Shreveport for safekeeping. Local citizens, hearing of this, raced ahead of the train in automobiles and reaching the next station pulled the helpless negro from the train, took him to a nearby tree and riddled his body with bullets. The note sent to Mrs. Elliot was written in plain handwriting. Acquaintances of the Negro state that he

had no education and could hardly write his name."

In addition to the Monroe legacy of lynching Black people is the history of its role in the attempted lynching of Nation of Islam Minister Troy X Cade-now known as Minister Abdul Bey Muhammad. As discussed on the occasion of Minister Bey's 80th birthday in 2010 in the Final Call newspaper we learned that:

> "In March of 1960, the Monroe, Louisiana Temple was stormed by police, who brutally beat men, woman and children; killing one Muslim brother and attempting to lynch Minister Bey by his necktie over a rafter in the Temple.
> Among those Muslims who fought for their lives that day were Minister Bey's then pregnant wife, Lureatha, and his nine-year-old daughter. Toward the end of the violent struggle, which required the intervention of the United States National Guard; there were three police casualties also among the injured.
> The Muslims of the Monroe, Louisiana Temple were arrested and required medical treatment. While many of the Muslims were charged fined and later released; Minister Bey was charged with inciting a riot, overthrow of the United States government, desecration of a United States flag and murder. In the book Message To The Blackman, on page 211, under a section entitled "The Persecution of the Righteous," The Most Honorable Elijah Muhammad wrote: "If Troy X Cade [as he was called before receiving the holy name Abdul Bey Muhammad] is guilty of teaching insurrection against the government, then I am guilty, because I am Troy's teacher. I would rather go to prison in place of Troy if this is the justice for the truth Allah gave me."
> Sentenced to six years in prison in the Louisiana State Penitentiary; isolated from other inmates; forced to sleep on a concrete floor and drink from a commode in his cell; Minister Bey awaited a Louisiana Supreme Court Decision to overturn his conviction.
> Before this decision would take place, however; prison guards, at approximately two o'clock one morning, removed Minister Bey from his cell, shackled him, and turned him over to police and state troopers who drove him to the Louisiana/Mississippi state line.
> Once there, Minister Bey was again brutally beaten within an inch of his life by scores of officers who then attempted to drown him by standing on his body in a swamp until they thought he was dead.
> Only his faith in Allah kept Minister Bey alive, and the fact that he had been a lifeguard, a frogman, and an excellent swimmer with the ability

to hold his breath under water."

Monroe's history of lynching may be the real reason why certain interest groups in the city are concerned over Minister Farrakhan's visit. Whites who kill Blacks have historically feared the day their evil against their former slaves would be made known. Minister Farrakhan has dubbed this fear as **"the mind of Cain."** In the Bible, when Cain killed Abel he feared that *"now every man that sees me will slay me."*

But contrary to the fears, the Honorable Minister Louis Farrakhan has always channeled the energy and talent of his audiences toward the dual purpose of giving up moral vices and towards the cleaning up of the Black community of its negative elements. And the Minister's work is well documented.

It is appalling that news media cite the dishonest reports of the Southern Poverty Law Center and the false claims of the Anti-Defamation League when reporting about Minister Farrakhan to their audiences. These are only 2 groups out of scores of groups, elected officials, spiritual leaders, celebrities and scholars who have testified of the Minister's beneficial impact.

In a book entitled **Who Do They Say I Am: The Vindication of the Honorable Minister Louis Farrakhan** numerous well-known men and women and groups have their testimonies of Minister Farrakhan documented. For example, in 1997 Philadelphia Mayor Edwin Rendell invited Minister Farrakhan to Philadelphia to calm racial tension within the city. As an introduction to the Minister's speech in Gray's Ferry Mayor Rendell said:

> "I would like to thank the Nation of Islam here in Philadelphia. To thank you for what you stand for and what you stand for all the good it does to so many people in Philadelphia. And if there is anybody out here...who doesn't know, this is a faith that has as its principles, the family. This is a faith that doesn't just talk about family values, it lives family values. This is a faith where men respect their women and children and they manifest that faith by staying in the home with them. This is a faith that doesn't just talk about being against drugs but is out there every single day and night fighting against drugs. This is a faith that just doesn't talk about the value of education, it imbues in their children and schools that education is the way to opportunity."

Minister Farrakhan's work to eradicate juvenile delinquency is another element of his work and history that makes him a worthy presence in all cities. Professor Mattias Gardell has noted that "Minister Farrakhan has a unique capability ...able to reach deeply into the souls of black youths...is able to talk to them in a way that really makes them listen...this rapport enables Farrakhan to criticize and redirect destructive behavioral patterns".

The broad and universal message of Minister Farrakhan was what journalist Debra Hananiah Freeman reacted to when she referred to Minister Farrakhan as **a national asset**. On the occasion of Minister Farrakhan's 1993 press conference entitled A Torchlight for America, Ms. Freeman wrote:

> "Hearing Farrakhan in person for the first time was clearly startling to many of those gathered who had only read news accounts of him circulated by his enemies. But Farrakhan's wit, vitality, and most importantly, his humanity, were irrepressible. Farrakhan is, without question, a far different man than the sound-bite target that the Anti-Defamation League (ADL) of B'nai B'rith has constructed...
> Clearly, Farrakhan came to Washington to deliver a message and to offer his help to a troubled nation. He is a national asset whose voice should be heard."

We conclude that if the truth of the Minister's history is put on display, it becomes clear why Mayor Mayo and every mayor in America should welcome Minister Farrakhan and create avenues where he and his representatives can teach and bring the Nation of Islam's beneficial impact to their citizens.

Like Farrakhan Dr. Martin Luther King Jr. Attracted Jewish Opposition

If you listen to the folks at the Anti-Defamation League of B'nai B'rith (ADL); or the folks at the Simon Wiesenthal Center; or perhaps you have read the dubious publications of the Southern Poverty Law Center. If so, you might have come to the conclusion that Minister Louis Farrakhan is an anomaly, an outlier, a freak of nature, some wild eyed anti-Semitic radical departure from the good, well-mannered Black leaders that white America and the Jewish leadership now approves of. However, nothing could be farther from the truth. Black leaders in America are only approved of by the white power structure after they are dead. This reminds me of a quote from Russian leader Vladimir Lenin who stated in *The State and Revolution* the following:

> "During the lifetime of great revolutionaries, the oppressing classes constantly hounded them, received their theories with the most savage malice, the most furious hatred and the most unscrupulous campaigns of lies and slander. After their death, attempts are made to convert them into harmless icons, to canonize them, so to say, and to hallow their names to a certain extent for the consolation of the oppressed classes and with the object of duping the latter, while at the same time robbing the revolutionary theory of its substance, blunting its revolutionary edge and vulgarizing it"

The men and women who proved to be good for the cause of the liberation of Black people in America faced vehement opposition from White gentile leadership as well as White Jewish leadership. And the exposure of the hidden history of the great Black leaders in America importantly reveals that the Honorable Minister Louis Farrakhan is not an anomaly or outlier; he is in the good company of his predecessors within the struggle for liberation.

Frequently I have witnessed commentators and panel speakers invoke the noble name and person of the great and legendary Rev. Dr. Martin Luther King Jr. His mantra of "the content of their character" and his "I have a dream" speech have been used as convenient slogans by white liberals. And nowadays, Dr. King is used by whites as an example of the kind of Black that all the other Black folks should be like if we want to be accepted by the white power structure in America. But, truth be told, most of us who really understand that "Pharaoh didn't love Moses" know that if we want liberation, we can't achieve it with a leader who is loved and approved of by the modern Pharaoh and the modern Egyptians.

Just a brief overview of some of the hidden history of the life and work of the Rev. Dr. Martin Luther King Jr. reveals that he faced serious Jewish opposition from the same groups who oppose Minister Farrakhan.

Joel Spingarn Spy Master

For starters, Dr. King was spied on by the Jewish leader of the NAACP, Joel Spingarn. Joel Spingarn, for whom the NAACP's Spingarn award is named, was a spy for the U.S. military. He specialized in spying on so -called radical Blacks and others the military had deemed "subversive." The Nation of Islam's Research Group website notes:

> "Spingarn was hired in May of 1918 and given the rank of major in the Military Intelligence Division (MID). Spingarn ran "a small unit of undercover agents" who were looking for "proof of subversion." The MID opened 100,000 pieces of mail a week and monitored Black publications. According to the Memphis Commercial Appeal: "The documents show Spingarn, who remained NAACP chairman during his tenure at MID, used his post to obtain critical information for MID, such as a list of the organization's 32,000 members.""

Among those whom NAACP chairman Spingarn spied on was the family of the Rev. Dr. Martin Luther King Jr. The *Memphis Commercial Appeal* states in its March 21, 1993 edition the following:

> "The intelligence branch of the United States Army spied on the family of Dr. Martin Luther King Jr. for three generations. Top secret, often illegal, intrusions into the lives of black Americans began more than 75 years ago and often focused on black churches in the South and their ministers. The spying was born of a conviction by top Army intelligence officers that black Americans were ripe for subversion..."

Rabbi Grafman Charges Anti-Semitism

Dr. King was called anti-Semitic by Birmingham rabbi Milton Grafman. The book entitled *to Stand Aside or Stand Alone: Southern Reform Rabbis and the Civil Rights Movement* includes the following quote from Rabbi Grafman:

> "At this meeting he [King] kept referring to the "merchants" and the role of the merchants. And I told him that in the city of Birmingham when you talk about merchants, you might just as well use the word "Jew," and that there was certainly implied anti-Semitism here by the use of the word "merchant." He kept harping on the radio, kept on harping in his talks and everything was quoted in the newspaper about the merchants, the merchants, the merchants. Birmingham, you talk about the merchants, you're talking about Jews.... I brought out the fact that [King's] continual harping about merchants was implied, if not actually anti-Semitism, because in the city of Birmingham everybody knew that the merchants were Jews."

This Rabbi Grafman is the same Rabbi who was quoted in a Harvard study conducted by Suzanne F. Nossel entitled, *Weathering the Storm: The Jewish Community in Birmingham, Alabama, During the Civil Rights Revolution,* which states:

> "agency representatives were forced to accept that Rabbi Grafman voiced a sentiment common in Birmingham when he said, "the lives of one thousand Negroes are not worth a hair on the head of a single Jew."

Dr. King Confronted Jewish Slum Lords

From the *The Autobiography of Martin Luther King, Jr* by Clayborne Carson, we learned of Dr. King's discovery and confrontation with Jewish slumlords:

> "When we were working in Chicago, we had numerous rent strikes on the West Side, and it was unfortunately true that, in most instances, the persons we had to conduct these strikes against were Jewish landlords. There was a time when the West Side of Chicago was a Jewish ghetto, and when the Jewish community started moving out into other areas, they still owned the property there, and all of the problems of the landlord came into being. "We were living in a slum apartment owned by a Jew and a number of others, and we had to have a rent strike. We were paying $94 for four run-down, shabby rooms, and we would go out on our open housing marches on Gage Park and other places and we discovered that whites with five sanitary, nice, new rooms, apartments with five rooms, were paying only $78 a month. We were paying 20 percent tax.... The Negro ends up paying a color tax, and this has happened in instances where Negroes actually confronted Jews as the landlord or the storekeeper. The irrational statements that

have been made are the result of these confrontations."

Stanley Levinson Dr. King's Jewish Advisor

J. Edgar Hoover infamously commented that Dr. King could be the "messiah" among Black people if he gave up his obedience to white liberal tutelage. No doubt, it was the likes of Jewish liberal and advisor to Dr. King, Stanley Levinson that Mr. Hoover was making reference to, as keeping Dr. King from becoming the Black "messiah." An FBI report states:

> "Stanley Levinson has told Clarence Jones, another advisor to King, that under no circumstances should King be permitted to say anything without their approving it."

ADL Espionage Against Dr. King

According to Jeffrey Steinberg in his *ADL Caught In Spy Scandal*, the organization had a fear and loathing of Dr. King. Steinberg notes:

> "Henry Schwarzschild waited a long time to go public with his personal horror story about the Anti-Defamation League of B'nai B'rith. Today an employee of the American Civil Liberties Union (ACLU), he resigned from a high-ranking position in the ADL's publicity office in the mid-1960s when he discovered, to his shock, that the ADL was spying on Rev. Martin Luther King, Jr. on behalf of J. Edgar Hoover and the FBI. It was not until the spring of 1993-nearly 30 years after he quit the ADL-that Schwarzschild came forward and told about the League's efforts against Dr. King. In an April 28, 1993 interview, Schwarzschild told San Francisco Weekly: "They [ADL] thought King was sort of a loose cannon. He was a Baptist preacher and nobody could be quite sure what he would do next. The ADL was very anxious about having an unguided missile out there."

This shocking overview of the secret relationship between Dr. King and his Jewish opponents affords us the ability to put Minister Farrakhan's Jewish opposition into proper perspective. Moreover, as we continue to search through the archives of hidden histories, we are able to conclude that the charge of anti-Semitism is a routine response reserved for the strongest and most popular Black leaders; the men and women who truly have the "messianic" potential to change the world.

Muhammad Ali's Beloved Teacher, The Most Honorable Elijah Muhammad

I join the entire world of admirers, supporters and fans of the greatest boxer that ever lived, Muhammad Ali, in expressing my condolences to his family and in declaring my sense of loss and mourning upon learning of his passing.

Ali's accomplishments in and out of the ring are legendary. He was a magnificent and talented pugilist who changed the sport of boxing forever. He is rightly credited with paving the way for the large purses that many top tier fighters earn today. And he broadened the appeal of boxing making it a universally popular sport as a result of his unusual confidence, media magnetism and unimaginable ability as a knock-out artist.

Many writers, commentators and analysts will and are expressing themselves in articles or on-air appearances devoted to the remembrance of Muhammad Ali, but so far, I have not found any that speak for me. So, I must speak for myself.

I never met the great champion, but I feel a connection to him because many years before me Muhammad Ali became a student of the Most Honorable Elijah Muhammad's teachings and a member of the Nation of Islam. And like myself, he served as a member of the Nation of Islam's male class known as the Fruit of Islam. Also, like myself he served as a student minister in the Nation of Islam representing the teachings to mosques and public audiences throughout the country.

He grew up in Kentucky. I grew up also in the South in Mississippi. In the magnificent documentary devoted to his life and struggle against the U.S. government's conscription of servicemen into the war in Vietnam, I learned more about his life growing up in Louisville, Kentucky. One aspect that grabbed my attention is the segment that talks about his mother's objection to him becoming a Muslim. I also experienced the same consternation and objection of me joining the Nation of Islam at 15 years of age by my mother who had been rearing me in the Baptist church.

So, despite never having an in-person interaction with a man that I consider my "big brother" in Islam, I feel a sense of closeness to him. I feel connected to him. And I feel a sense of personal loss knowing that his physical presence is no longer in the world. Even though, his beautiful children carry their father's physical likeness in such a wonderful way that to see them is to really see him over and over again.

Again, I have not heard any commentators speak for me. By that I mean that none have expressed either what I feel or shown forth an analysis that harmonizes with what I think is important to highlight at this time. The closest was the strong words of historian Zaheer Ali on MSNBC.

I also enjoyed and agreed with much of what Maxwell Strachan wrote in his Huffington Post article Don't Let Muhammad Ali's Story Get Whitewashed

So that only means that I have to speak for myself and in so doing, speak for the many others who feel as I feel. Specifically, obvious to those of us who share Ali's faith in Islam is the crafty strategy to portray him as an enigma and exception to the rest of Muslims. For sure, the talent that Allah (God) blessed him with from birth was and is exceptional. Yet raw talent and raw materials of any kind remain "in the raw" and remain un-cultivated unless there is someone to develop them and extract them from a raw state so that their beauty and value may be known. Such is the case with human beings. So much so that it has been suggested that the greatest travesty in the world today is the enormous waste of human potential.

In Muhammad Ali's rise as an athlete and as a trailblazer of the athlete-activist archetype, there is one man that is conspicuously absent from all recent conversations. This man is largely responsible for the cultivation and development of the man who went from being Cassius Marcellus Clay to Muhammad Ali. That man that is routinely hidden and omitted from conversations about Black history and achievement, as if he never existed, is the Most Honorable Elijah Muhammad.

So just who is the Most Honorable Elijah Muhammad? Let's take a look some descriptions of him from some of the most prominent and well-respected persons in history...

"Elijah Muhammad has been able to do what generations of welfare workers and committees and resolutions and reports and housing projects and playgrounds have failed to do: to heal and redeem drunkards and junkies, to convert people who have come out of prison and to keep them out, to make men chaste and women virtuous, and to invest both the male and the female with a pride and a serenity that hang about them like an unfailing light. He has done all these things, which our Christian church has spectacularly failed to do." **-James Baldwin, The Fire Next Time**

"We told our people, 'It's got to be done like the Muslims do it. It's got to be done person to person.' Of all the movements we know of, we have a lot of respect for you, because you have a lot of people doing things." he said referring to the constructive program of the Most honorable Elijah Muhammad and its effect on his energetic followers. **-Caesar Chavez, Mexican Farm Worker Leader**

"Approximately 30 percent of the United States' six to eight million Muslims are African American, making Islam the second most popular religion among African Americans. Although the vast majority of these African American Muslims are now Sunni Muslims, many (or perhaps their parents or grandparents) were introduced to Islam through the Nation of Islam, a movement that was exclusively Black, segregationist, and militant. Its leader for over forty years, Elijah Muhammad, was therefore arguably the most important person in the development of Islam in America, eclipsing other prominent figures such as Noble Drew Ali, Wali Fard Muhammad, Malcolm X, Louis Farrakhan, and Warith Deen Mohammed (originally known as Wallace D. Muhammad). Despite his unrivaled prominence, Elijah Muhammad is rarely treated as a major figure in Islam." **-Professor Herbert Berg, Elijah Muhammad and Islam**

"What the Negro needs first is $100 million," world famous composer Duke Ellington said last week in an exclusive interview with Muhammad Speaks. "And that is the advantage your boss (referring to the Honorable Elijah Muhammad) has over the rest of the 20 million. He urges that we get some money together." "Without $100 million there is no voice. There are 20 million Negroes and we don't have $20 million. "MONEY TALKS in our society and economics is the big question throughout the world. Every race on this earth has some money but the American Negro..." This then is the solution to the "race problem" of the famous Duke, who is universally acclaimed as royalty in the realm of American music." **-Duke Ellington interview with Muhammad Speaks Newspaper**

"We're here in honor of a man to be respected. In honor of a man who is very much deserved of the praises given to Him for His many deeds that most of us know very little about. I'm here, joining the others to give respect to a very beautiful man that I've seen do a lot with my brothers, people who I lived with; as a matter of fact – people that I am. He has most definitely been a positive influence...I've got to respect this man for His works." **-Curtis Mayfield on the Occasion of Elijah Muhammad Appreciation Banquet 1974**

"DEAR MR. MUHAMMAD,

An engagement of long standing in Madison, Wisconsin prevents my accepting your invitation to attend your testimonial dinner on March 29th. I do, however, want to extend my personal best wishes to you and my congratulations on your almost half a century of productive leadership." **-Vernon E. Jordan Jr., Director National Urban League 1974**

"These Black Muslim women looked at the Nation, and saw love and courage. To them the Honorable Elijah Muhammad was a man who loved his people so much that he designed an institution in which the primacy of women was integral, and every man in the organization was obligated to put himself on the line for them. Black Muslim women saw this as a measure of love and respect for them." - **Cynthia S'thembile West, Scholar and Author of Nation Builders: Female Activism in the Nation of Islam 1960-1970**

"I as many of you, sat at the feet of the Honorable Elijah Muhammad and shared and was taught. The Messenger made the message very clear. He turned alienation into emancipation. He concentrated on taking the slums out of the people and then the people out of the slums. He took dope out of veins and put hope in our brains. He was the father of Black consciousness. During our "colored" and "Negro" days he was Black. His leadership exceeded far beyond the membership of the Black Muslims. For more than three decades, the Honorable Elijah Muhammad has been the spiritual leader of the Black Muslims and a progressive force for Black identity and consciousness, self-determination and economic development." -**Rev. Jesse Jackson, Rainbow PUSH**

"Without question, he [Hon. Elijah Muhammad] aided many young Black Americans to gain dignity and hope and a will to survive. I have great deal of admiration for the sense of discipline he provided for many young Black men and women." **-John Lewis, U.S. Congressman, Former Head of SNCC**

"Elijah Muhammad gave Blacks new confidence in their potential to become creative and self-sufficient people. In addition, he taught his followers the efficacy and rewards of hard work, fair play, and abstinence. It has been shown beyond a shadow of a doubt that the Muslims who have followed his economic teachings and have in many cases moved substantially ahead in their economic pursuits. He gave also his people a success formula for home and family life. The rate of delinquency among Muslim children is extremely low. The rate of divorce is quite low. The stability of the Muslim home is an ideal for which the rest of America might strive." **-Dr. C. Eric Lincoln author of Black Muslims in America**

"Mr. Muhammad's life is one of peace, harmony and great integrity. He made the Nation of Islam a pillar of strength in Black communities throughout the country." - **Ralph Metcalf, Former U. S. Representative 1st District, Illinois**

"I tell people again and again and again that I know what I know not because of anything U.C. Berkeley (University of California Berkeley) taught me, but because I learned what I learned in the Nation of Islam. I learned it from the sisters who learned it, basically, from Elijah Muhammad- and it worked! It changed a people who just like my Indian people, had a terrible diet. Still a lot of work needs to be done in the African American community, but Elijah Muhammad was successful in alerting, millions probably, of African American people about pork and leading a healthier life." - **Diane Williams, MPH, Native American Social Worker**

"Whiting H & G, Hereafter, and Fruitman (songs from their album Light of the World) are meant to reflect a message of unity and seriousness from the Honorable Elijah Muhammad." **-Robert 9X Bell, Founding member of Kool & The Gang**

"The Hereafter means Freedom, Justice and Equality and I never knew anything about that until I started following the Messenger. When we first accepted Islam in Jersey City, N.J., the rest of the band was against it. They even tried everything to stop us from coming in. But now Islam is attracting them." **-Ronald 6X Bell,**

Founding member of Kool & The Gang

"Once I heard the teachings of the Honorable Elijah Muhammad; that really touched me. It was something I could relate to and made me do better. Once you have heard the teachings (of the Nation of Islam) and know the knowledge, there is no turning back." - **Larry Johnson, NBA Basketball Star**

I could go on and on. But this is just a small introduction to the magnificent man who is at the root of the great boxing champion and activist Muhammad Ali. Ali loved the most Honorable Elijah Muhammad for what he did for him in his life and trajectory that propelled him onto the world stage.

Now if that list does not drive home the importance of the Most Honorable Elijah Muhammad on the life and success of Muhammad Ali, let's consider some of Ali's own glowing words about his beloved teacher.

From Thomas Hauser's book Muhammad Ali: His Life and Times:

"The first time I heard about Elijah Muhammad was at a Golden Gloves Tournament in Chicago. Then, before I went to the Olympics, I looked at a copy of the Nation of Islam's newspaper, Muhammad Speaks. I didn't pay much attention to it but a lot of things were working on my mind. When I was growing up, a colored boy named Emmett Till was murdered in Mississippi for whistling at a white woman. Emmett Till was the same age as me, and even though they caught the men who did it, nothing happened to them. Things like that went on all the time. And in my own life, there were places I couldn't go, places I couldn't eat. I won a gold medal representing the United States at the Olympic Games, and when I came home to Louisville, I still got treated like a nigger. There were restaurants I couldn't get served in. Some people kept calling me "boy." Then in Miami in 1961, **I was training for a fight, and met a follower of Elijah Muhammad named Captain Sam [Minister Abdul Rahman Muhammad]. He invited me to a meeting, and after that, my life changed.**"

In a November 1975 Playboy magazine interview the champ stated:

"**He was my Jesus**, and I had love for both the man and what he represented. Like Jesus Christ and all of God's prophets, he represented

"Un-Smiting The Shepherd" -231

all good things...**Elijah Muhammad was my savior**, and everything I have come from him-my thoughts, my efforts to help my people, how I eat, how I talk, my name."

He went on to discuss how he would like to be remembered in the Playboy interview:

"I'll tell you how I'd like to be remembered: as a Black man who won the heavyweight title and who was humorous and who treated everyone right. As a man who never looked down on those who looked up to him and who helped as many of his people as he could-financially and also in their fight for freedom, justice and equality. As a man who wouldn't hurt his people's dignity by doing anything that would embarrass them. **As a man who tried to unite his people through the faith of Islam that he found when he listened to the Honorable Elijah Muhammad.** And if all that's asking too much, then I guess I'd settle for being remembered only as a great boxing champion who became a preacher and a champion of his people. And I wouldn't even mind if folks forgot how pretty I was."

In the excellent documentary The Trials of Muhammad Ali there is a section where his love for orange juice is discussed. And Ali is certainly not alone in loving orange juice. And it only makes sense to me that if one love's orange juice, one must love the orange that produced the sweet vitamin rich juice. And it logically follows that if one loves oranges, one must love the orange tree that produced the oranges that produced the golden pulp-filled nutritious orange juice. Perhaps this kind of logic should be applied in the case of Muhammad Ali and his beloved teacher the Most Honorable Elijah Muhammad. Because it is not logical to love the student and hate the teacher that produced the student.

Heeding Muhammad's Warning Is America's Only Way Out!

"On that day, the unjust person shall bite his hands for anguish and despair, and shall say, Oh that I had taken the way of truth with the apostle."

-Surah 25:27 (Sale Translation)

The Most Honorable Elijah Muhammad stood up and boldly declared to the world, that he met with God and was taught by Him day and night for more than 3 years. Reactions to this bold declaration varied. And though the Most Honorable Elijah Muhammad was beloved for more than 40 years by Black People in America and around the world, he and his followers were persecuted by the American government, which even recruited and duped members of the Black community to aid and abet their persecution of Muhammad.

Numerous current events point to the fact that, despite being opposed by the most powerful government in the world, Elijah Muhammad's message-His life-giving teachings-should no longer be ignored. In fact, the unraveling of the American government presents an emergency situation of such magnitude, that it compels America's leaders to adopt the solutions offered by the Most Hon. Elijah Muhammad that they have so far rejected.

Filled within the divine message of the Most Honorable Elijah Muhammad are solutions to the problems plaguing America. The presentation of these solutions has been the "meat" of the ministry of the Honorable Minister Louis Farrakhan. Minister Farrakhan's effective and prolific presentation of these solutions for the past 44 years, since he began the rebuilding of the Nation of Islam, clearly identifies our beloved Minister as the best helper and aid to the Most Honorable Elijah Muhammad.

Muhammad & Farrakhan Have Divine Authority

It's not difficult to see how the work and history of Elijah Muhammad and Louis Farrakhan parallels the history and work of Moses and Aaron described within the scriptures. The Holy Qur'an discusses a very important aspect of the relationship between Moses and Aaron that has manifested itself in the history of the work of the Most Honorable Elijah Muhammad and the

Honorable Minister Louis Farrakhan. In the 28th Surah we read:

> "28:34-And my brother, Aaron, he is more eloquent in speech than I, so send him with **me as a helper to confirm me**. Surely, I fear that they would reject me. 28:35- He said: We will strengthen thine arm with thy brother, and **We will give you both an authority**, so that they shall not reach you. With Our signs, **you two and those who follow you, will triumph**."

In this passage, Allah promises Moses, Aaron and their followers' victory over their opposition (i.e. Pharaoh Et.al.). This passage also powerfully indicates that both men were given divine authority to warn Pharaoh and divine authority to liberate the enslaved Children of Israel. According to this passage it would be the work of Aaron to confirm what Allah (God) had revealed to Moses. Minister Farrakhan and the Most Honorable Elijah Muhammad have been given divine authority. And the ministry of the Hon. Min. Louis Farrakhan has provided the confirmation of the divine message of the Most Honorable Elijah Muhammad, a message which is actually the latest installment of the divine revelation of hidden truths by Allah (God) to the human family of the Earth.

Within what Allah (God) revealed to the Most Hon. Elijah Muhammad is both warning and instructions. The American government has failed to heed the divine warnings. And now its leaders fight and contend against one another as the larger problems of the country go unresolved. The political climate in America is such that scholars-armed with the knowledge of history- are beginning to cry out in desperation, their own warnings that the country is headed for a fall!

On June 1, 2021, 100 scholars affixed their names to a document stating their serious concerns over the future destiny of America if current trends continue. The document published on newamerica.org is officially titled **Statement of Concern: The Threats to American Democracy and the Need for National Voting and Election Administration Standards.** It begins with an extraordinary statement of concern over the future national standing of the United States of America:

> "We, the undersigned, are scholars of democracy who have watched the recent deterioration of U.S. elections and liberal democracy with

growing alarm. ...When democracy breaks down, it typically takes many years, often decades, to reverse the downward spiral. In the process, violence and corruption typically flourish, and talent and wealth flee to more stable countries, undermining national prosperity. It is not just our venerated institutions and norms that are at risk—it is our future national standing, strength, and ability to compete globally."

This group of scholars are providing a warning very late into the downward spiral of the American government. Since 1985 Minister Farrakhan has been warning the government of America of both her fall, and that America's sins against Black people and the poor, have earned for her the chastisement of Allah (God). He said most recently in his July 4, 2020 worldwide address entitled *The Criterion* that the president should do all that he can to:

"try to make America safe from the wrath of God, her chastisement over the wickedness that you all have been involved in since your inception.... America, you've been weighed. Try to keep yourself out of war. Try to keep yourself away from the Judgment of God."

The Minister has brilliantly and beautifully and over many years demonstrated the striking parallels between modern America and the Biblical Egypt. He has shown the parallels between ancient Rome and modern America. He has given profound scriptural exegesis showing how modern America and ancient Babylon mirror one another. And he has made the rulers of America to know the sins of this country against Black people. And He has continued the warning of the Most Honorable Elijah Muhammad to the rulers of America that if they refuse to give justice to Black people, Allah's (God's) wrath will bring America to her doom.

What Should Black People Do?

The political tumult now on daily display has placed Black America into a quandary. The hype and excitement over the election of President Biden has all but evaporated. And once again, the Black voter has bailed out the Democratic party, only to be left disappointed and frustrated.

The time is out for Black America's over dependence on electoral politics to address and resolve our people's problems and concerns. Allah (God) has given divine authority to the Most Honorable Elijah Muhammad and the Honorable Minister Louis

Farrakhan. That authority is not only to warn the government of America. It is also divine authority to direct and guide the Black man and woman of America away from suffering and into the favor of Allah (God).

In his powerful 2016 Saviours' Day address, Minister Farrakhan made a presentation of divine commands to Black America from his teacher, the Most Honorable Elijah Muhammad. Every pastor, imam, organizational leader and elected official within the Black community should get this message and study it and begin working to implement those divine commands immediately! A sampling of those divine commands includes the following:

> "We must stop relying upon the white man to care for us. We must become an independent people.
> 1. Separate yourselves from the "slave-master."
> 2. Pool your resources, education and qualifications for independence.
> 3. Stop forcing yourselves into places where you are not wanted.
> 4. Make your own neighborhood a decent place to live.
> 5. Rid yourselves of the lust of wine and drink and learn to love self and your kind before
> loving others.
> 6. Unite to create a future for yourself.
> 7. Build your own homes, schools, hospitals, and factories.
> 8. Do not seek to mix your blood through racial integration.
> 9. Stop buying expensive cars, fine clothes and shoes before being able to live in a fine home.
> 10. Spend your money among yourselves.
> 11. Build an economic system among yourselves.
> 12. Protect your women. "

These commands are divine commands that were originally published within the pages of **Message To The Blackman in America**, written by the Most Hon. Elijah Muhammad; a book that should be read and studied by every Black and indigenous person in America. These commands are a part of what comprises the gospel message that should be preached and practiced throughout the Black community.

One of America's founding fathers, Thomas Jefferson, owned one of the early English translations of the Holy Qur'an produced by George Sale. Sale's English rendering of the Quranic Arabic for

Surah 25:27 introduces this article. Jefferson's political heirs, the current leaders of the American government, should read it and reflect. For, during this current dispensation of time, it is Minister Farrakhan who is Allah's Apostle and the way of truth is with him.

Follow the divine commands of Allah coming through Minister Farrakhan and live; reject them and mourn as the unraveling of American continues!

Muhammad's Wisdom & Warning Diagnose America's Time of Confusion

In an extraordinary display of open rebellion, white militia groups on January 5, 2021 stormed the U. S. Capitol! What is all the more confusing and perplexing is that the activities of these groups that many have condemned as an insurrection, was led and inspired by President Donald J. Trump.

Throughout Black America, there has been outrage and amazement at how kind and accommodating the U.S. Capitol Police were in their handling of the angry mob of white protestors, whose conduct threatened the lives and safety of the U.S. Congress who had assembled to certify the 2020 Presidential Election results. This is in stark contrast to how Black Lives Matter protestors were received when they assembled for the purpose of mass rallies to call for justice in the case of the numerous Black men, women and children that have been executed in the streets of America by rogue police officers.

The deferential and accommodating way some U.S. Capitol police posed for selfies and kindly escorted female militia members down the steps of the Capitol highlights the deliberately deceitful way Black protests are portrayed versus how white protests are portrayed. Whites who protest are portrayed as angry, yet patriotic Americans filled with righteous indignation. Blacks who protest are pejoratively dubbed rioters, scofflaws and rabble rousers.

As millions of Black youth join groups like Black Lives Matter, the Nation of Islam, the New Black Panther Party and other groups for the purpose of fighting injustice, they have been labeled as Black Identity Extremists in reports from the FBI. In fact, America's chief Middle Eastern ally, the state of Israel, had this to say about Black Lives Matter:

> "The major problem with Israel is with the young generation of the black community,"-Judith Varnai Shorer, Consul General-Atlanta, GA

The August 3, 2017 report issued by the FBI labeled Black Identity Extremists as those "motivated to target law enforcement officials." Yet in the same year, 2017, statistics emerged revealing the number one terrorist in America was the white male. In an

October 2, 2017 article written for VOX.com entitled *White American men are a bigger domestic terrorist threat than Muslim foreigners* Jennifer Williams wrote:

> "But in the eight months since Trump took office, more Americans have been killed in attacks by white American men with no connection to Islam than by Muslim terrorists or foreigners… In fact, between 2001 and 2015, more Americans were killed by homegrown right-wing extremists than by Islamist terrorists, according to a study by New America, a nonpartisan think tank in Washington, DC.

The series of tumultuous events throughout America in 2020 were all directly or indirectly tied to the fundamental problem of injustice and the refusal to give justice to Black people in America who have been denied justice for now 466 years. Even the COVID-19 pandemic has been enveloped by racial controversies and concerns. Numerous statistics have described the highest incidence of COVID-19 deaths as being among the Black and Brown communities. And as the year concluded we saw the campaign to vaccinate Black and Brown communities with the experimental Pfizer and Moderna vaccines.

The very serious and ominous cavalcade of events has generated much confusion and anxiety among many. Fortunately for us, there is guidance available to us. The Honorable Minister Louis Farrakhan as the representative of the Most Honorable Elijah Muhammad has for many years served as a divine warner to America and the world of the peril that exists as the result of tyranny, oppression and corrupt governments. Over and over again he has pointed us to the words of his teacher the Most Honorable Elijah Muhammad. His words give us divine insight into the true cause and diagnosis of America's woes. His words should be studied and used as a guide to understanding the perilous times in which we live. Consider the following sample of the Most Honorable Elijah Muhammad's words that although written decades ago, could have easily been written today in light of their perfect description of the events and happenings in today's world.

Review of Muhammad's Wisdom & Warning

"Now the rise of America's once slave into the knowledge of self in the spirit of Allah, in the Person of Master Fard

Muhammad (the Son of Man), the Author of the Resurrection of us, the mentally dead is causing untold confusion between the heads of state. ... America is being torn to pieces politically, as Pharaoh's political party was in the days when Jehovah went after the freedom of Israel." -September 22, 1967

"THE EVER-HOVERING DARK WAR CLOUDS OF DEATH keep the minds of the heads of nations from ever concentrating sanely concerning the way in which they should react under such a troubled and dark world of confusion. **Their vision is lost due to their confusion which causes fear. Fear has taken away the mastery of self-control. What will be the end of this confusion which has taken away the vision of the wise?**" -May 14, 1971

"**She has divided the nations and has put brothers fighting against brothers. Now she must be divided and her brother of evil put to fighting with her. This is going on at the present time.**... The white man's greatest effort to rule us was to divide one against the other. He divided Korea, as you know, with one brother against the other. He divided China, with one brother against the other. There out in Formosa he has a brother of China, sitting there to fight his brother, China, on the mainland. He divided Vietnam just like he did Korea. Then he made the two brothers fight and kill each other while he (the white man) acted as judge." -September 28, 1973

"**WAR OF CONFUSION is in America among its head officials. In the city the mayor is against the city council of aldermen and the city police department. All there have very little confidence in each other and ever disagreement with each other exists. The Congress is against the President. The President is against Congress. The state government and the Senate are against each other.** "-August 22, 1968

"Confusion among the heads of the government of the wicked is destroying the foundation of their world. 'As thou hast done so shall it be done unto thee.'...In all of America's confusion-which some may refer to as her dilemma, but her condition is beyond is beyond that word-the is a grievous confusion of the head officials. **The basis of this confusion is due to the injustice that the American white people have done to her Black once slave.**

240-STUDENTS OF FARRAKHAN

Her confusion is also due to her effort to thwart the Aims and Purposes of Almighty God, to bring about the resurrection of the blind, deaf and dumb Black man.... The world of confusion is breaking up with all kinds of disagreement between factors and factors. Take for instance-never has America had so many strikes. Everyone is against the other. If this is not a confused world then point out to me one that is more confused. In the government of America, there is nothing that is at peace in it. There is no agreement. Everybody is dissatisfied. Everybody is showing their dissatisfaction by disregarding the way that they have been going. Worker is against worker; politician is against politician. A CONFUSED WORLD, AMERICA." **-February 7, 1975**

My Disappointment with Imam Michael Saahir

As-Salaam-Alaikum,

Brother Imam Saahir I pray that this communication finds you enjoying the best of health and spirit. I read your words written to the Honorable Minister Louis Farrakhan that are dated August 14, 2015 and published for the Indianapolis Recorder.

Brother Imam, I want to first of all state my great respect and admiration for your work entitled **The Honorable Elijah Muhammad: The Man Behind The Men**. This was a wonderful documentation of various aspects of the life and work of the Most Honorable Elijah Muhammad. And even though there are conclusions drawn that I would disagree with, I have recommended this book to many people. I have cited this book in lectures that I have done and this book has been a great help to me in pointing out the grave offense of omission of the Most Honorable Elijah Muhammad from positive discussions about Black history.

I write you as a brother, admirer and student of the Honorable Minister Louis Farrakhan. And your open letter gives us the occasion for an open response that we pray will help you as well as others who share your views on the Minister's powerful and inspired message in the city of Miami wherein he provided a bold exhortation to self-preservation before a pained and trauma burdened audience.

You know Brother Imam, I am disappointed that you did not consider the totality of the message delivered by the Honorable Minister Louis Farrakhan. It is clear to me that you reacted to a sound bite and mere excerpt of a message that covered multiple themes and last several hours. Had you reached out to Minister Farrakhan's Indianapolis Representative-Student Minister Nuri Muhammad I am sure he would have secured for you a copy of the DVD for you to study the message in its entirety. Had you done so you would have been able to respond in a better more balanced way.

You would have been able to see that the Minister's message was not a blanket call for retaliation against whites for killing Blacks.

242-STUDENTS OF FARRAKHAN

The Minister's words also addressed the ever-present problem of the Black community's own internecine bloodshed. In a section of his message published by the Final Call Newspaper, the Minister is quoted as declaring:

> "How can we charge others with the crime of killing us without due process and lying about it when we are killing each other? And we won't march on ourselves, nor will we even rise up to condemn ourselves for what we are doing to ourselves. And in the gangs when we kill we don't talk, so nobody is arrested and charged with murder and brought to what is called justice."

Throughout your open letter to the Minister, you unfortunately make a straw man argument against a non-existent call for the use of guns that the Minister never made. In his message he never told his audience to seek carnal weapons for retaliatory purposes. As you point out, the Most Honorable Elijah Muhammad taught us that we did not need so much as a pen knife as a weapon against our enemies.

Yet you are incorrect in suggesting that he did not resort to "Justice or Else" theme, and that "his approach was to have faith in God." When I read that Brother Imam, it seemed as though you were seeking to water down the Most Honorable Elijah Muhammad and characterize as being the equivalent of a character that most certainly disdained among his people and that being a "scared to death Negro preacher." No sir, the Most Honorable Elijah Muhammad was the strongest voice among us to call for justice. He even painted pictures in his writings and teachings of what justice for the Black people looks like and what would be the consequences for America if she refuses to provide that justice.

In the very first edition of the Muhammad Speaks newspaper in October of 1961 includes the phrase "Justice or Else for the So-Called Negroes" on the front cover. And the theme of Justice was one of the most dominant themes running throughout all of his teachings. I am sure there were those who reacted to the Most Honorable Elijah Muhammad like you reacted to Minister Farrakhan when he said the following on page 36 of his brilliant book Message to the Blackman in America.

> "My people, you are in a dangerous position. Get that fear out of you

and stand up for your people! Who are you not to die for your people? Who am I not to die for my people! If I am shot down or cut down today, who is little Elijah Muhammad to 20 million of you! **If a million of us throw ourselves in the fire for the benefit of the 20 million, the loss would be small compared to the great gain our people will make as a result of that sacrifice.** Hundreds of thousands of Muslims gave their lives in Pakistan to get their nation's independence. They were successful. The black men in Africa are fighting and dying today in unity for their independence. We sit here like pampered babies. We cannot even stand on the floor, not to mention taking a chance of crawling out of the door. We are too careful of shedding blood for ourselves. We are willing to shed all of it for the benefit of others."

The Most Honorable Elijah Muhammad used similar language in his historic Uline Arena Message delivered in Washington D.C. May 29, 1959. Yet reviewing the full message of the Most Honorable Elijah Muhammad we can put it within the context of his overall teachings and appreciate the skill and wisdom of his approach. For after lighting a fire in his audience, he channels that fire toward acts of unity and brotherhood for the good of all Black people. So, page 36 continues with the following:

"I am not trying to get you to fight. That is not even necessary; our unity will win the battle! Not one of us will have to raise a sword. Not one gun would we need to fire. **The great cannon that will be fired is our unity.** Our unity is the best. Why are you afraid to unite?"

Again, when reviewing the Minister's Miami message in its entirety we see that the same is true of the Minister. He lit the fire of retaliation only to redirect it towards the act of an economic retaliation via withdrawal from this year's Christmas holiday, an act that would follow-up on the desire of the great Dr. Martin Luther King Jr. who proposed a Christmas boycott in 1963. Dr. King spoke of a "redistribution of pain" from the breasts of suffering Black masses to the bank accounts of white merchants and businessmen.

It is a fact opined by freedom fighter Fredrick Douglass that "power concedes nothing without a demand." The Minister's message when viewed in the light of this sage advice of Fredrick Douglass causes one to conclude that the Minister is marshaling a coalition of the willing from among Blacks, Hispanics, Indigenous Groups, Women's Groups, Muslim Groups, Veterans

Groups and even poor Whites to go to Washington and make a demand for **justice**. And as he detailed in his illuminating message in Milwaukee, the **or else** will involve mighty for of economic retaliation by targeting the obscene amounts of profit generated during the Christmas holiday where most retailers generate more than half of their yearly profits!

I am disappointed Brother Imam that you have apparently fallen for a propaganda strategy that was designed to hide the real threat within the Minister's message- "the redistribution of pain through economic withdrawal." It appears that you may have come under the influence and have been negatively impacted by the opinions of others who are either willing or unwilling participants in this planned obfuscation of the Minister's call to economic sanctions on corporate America. I reflect on the folly and utter hypocrisy contained within Milwaukee Sheriff David Clarke's condemnation of the Minister.

According to WND.com (WorldNetDaily) writer Leo Hohmann: "*Sheriff Clarke said that if Farrakhan were to come and make a similar speech in Milwaukee County, it could fan the flames of racial tensions. "I suppose if he were to come through Milwaukee I would take a deeper look at this to see if my county would be at risk of him being here," Clarke said. "He's got to know that there is a line and sometimes he has to be shown where that line is, and you know, he's a fraud in terms of a man of the cloth.""*

One wonders how the Sheriff could take issue with the Minister's exhortation to Black self-preservation when he told the National Review the following:

"As the NRA and other groups started to want to use me as a symbol of the Second Amendment — a black voice — I started reading up," he recalls. "I became fascinated. What really struck me was the black tradition of arms.... I thought, Wow. This isn't the black history I grew up reading about." Among the many thinkers to whom Clarke attributes his present philosophy are Frederick Douglass, Ida B. Wells, and — a particular favorite — Thomas Sowell. **"Once blacks were able to arm themselves to protect against kidnapping and lynching," he explains, "things really began to change in terms of black freedom."**

The Sheriff's concern that the Minister's words in Milwaukee could fan the flames of racial tension sound quite foolish when he is on record admiring the historic ability of Blacks to defend themselves against lynching. You see, brother Imam these are the kinds of misinformed and hypocritical persons who are arrayed against the Minister and the good he intends for the Black community and all of humanity.

You know Brother Imam, Minister Farrakhan spoke on June 6, 2015 to a Manhattan masjid and he addressed the growing problem of Islamophobia in America. He identified the Muslim community and particularly the immigrant Muslim community as being especially vulnerable. He invited the immigrant Muslim community to join the Justice or Else 20th Anniversary of the Million Man March observance. The Minister invites them to have spokespersons to speak out on this issue.

It would actually be a better use of time and energy if you used your influence and relationships with the immigrant Islamic community to address the issue of Islamophobia instead of the message of Minister Farrakhan. On August 13, 2015 the New York Times, America's newspaper of record, publishing a feature story entitled *ISIS Enshrines a Theology of Rape*. The article is a part of a growing body of literature that seeks to paint Islam as a religion that approves of and endorses the rape of women. I would love to read you take on that issue and the larger issue of the demonization of Islam before the eyes of the American public.

Brother Imam, I was also offended by the fact you seek to invoke the teachings and history of the Most Honorable Elijah Muhammad to publicly "correct" Minister Farrakhan. I am offended because for so many years various persons from the Sunni community have condemned Minister Farrakhan for his reliance upon and articulation of the teachings of the Most Honorable Elijah Muhammad, while they would rather he teach exclusively from the Holy Qur'an. For a Sunni leader to now use the Honorable Elijah Muhammad to condemn the Minister's message when he has based it firmly on the teachings of the Holy Qur'an is really unbelievable.

Your teacher and the illustrious Imam Warithudeen Mohammed spoke to the Nation of Islam at Saviours' Day 2000. He said this about Minister Farrakhan: "*We are to support each other in all good things.* **When the brother Muslim stands upon the**

Qur'an, the last of the revealed books and the complete book for all times and all societies, and when he stands upon faith in Muhammad as God's last prophet and Messenger to all the worlds, mercy to all the worlds, we are to support him in that."

Brother Imam you should then stand with Minister Farrakhan and not seek to condemn his ideas. The Holy Qur'an distinguishes between retaliation and aggression. It provides rules for retaliation. But it does not desire that the Muslim should seek to avoid fighting in defense of life. The English translation of the Holy Qur'an in Surah 47 ayat 20 states that And those who believe say: Why is not a chapter revealed? But when a decisive chapter is revealed, and **fighting is mentioned therein, thou seest those in whose hearts is a disease look to thee with the look of one fainting at death. So, woe to them!**

A popular hadith from the Sahih Muslim collections records the Prophet Muhammad (saw) saying **"Whoso- ever of you sees an evil, let him change it with his hand; and if he is not able to do so, then [let him change it] with his tongue; and if he is not able to do so, then with his heart — and that is the weakest of faith."**

"Of Termites & Vipers": Minister Farrakhan and the Hard Sayings of Jesus

On hearing it, many of his disciples said, "This is a hard teaching. Who can accept it?" –John 6:60

The critics of the Honorable Minister Louis Farrakhan never accuse him of telling lies. It is safe to say then that despite their opposition of him they know that he speaks the truth. However, they characterize his divine message as "hate speech" or "anti-" this or that. These characterizations that again, have nothing to do with the veracity or truth of what he teaches, are borne out of the fact that his divine message hurts the feelings of his critics. They feel offended when he holds them accountable for long histories of harm, exploitation and oppression of the Black community. That the Honorable Minister Louis Farrakhan offends and hurts the feelings of his critics is intriguing and at the same time a powerful confirmation of the divine nature of his message. For what Minister Farrakhan is accused of, is the same that Jesus was accused of in the New Testament.

Consider the following commentary of Christian scholar F.F. Bruce in his book **"The Hard Sayings of Jesus"**:

Many of those who listened to Jesus during his public ministry found some of his sayings "hard" and said so. Many of those who read his sayings today, or hear them read in church, also find them hard, but do not always think it fitting to say so.

It is all too easy to believe in a Jesus who is largely a construction of our own imagination—an inoffensive person whom no one would really trouble to crucify. But the Jesus whom we meet in the Gospels, far from being an inoffensive person, gave offense right and left. Even his loyal followers found him, at times, thoroughly disconcerting. He upset all established notions of religious propriety. He spoke of God in terms of intimacy which sounded like blasphemy. He seemed to enjoy the most questionable company. He set out with open eyes on a road which, in the view of "sensible" people, was bound to lead to disaster.

But in those who were not put off by him he created a passionate love and allegiance which death could not destroy. They knew that in him they had found the way of acceptance, peace of conscience, life that was life indeed. More than that: in him they came to know God himself in a new way; here was the life of God being lived out in a real human life and communicating itself through him to them.

One reason for the complaint that Jesus' sayings were hard was that **he made his hearers think. For some people, thinking is a difficult and uncomfortable exercise, especially when it involves the critical reappraisal of firmly held prejudices and convictions, or the challenging of the current consensus of opinion**. *Any utterance, therefore, which invites them to engage in this kind of thinking is a hard saying. Many of Jesus' sayings were hard in this sense.*

A Sample of Some of the Hard Sayings of Jesus include the following verses found in the New Testament

"Do not think that I have come to bring peace to the earth. I have not come to bring peace, **but a sword**." –Matthew 10:34

- "Woe to you, blind guides, who say, 'If anyone swears by the temple, it is nothing, but if anyone swears by the gold of the temple, he is bound by his oath.' **You blind fools!** For which is greater, the gold or the temple that has made the gold sacred?" –Matthew 23:16-17
- And the Lord said to him, "Now you Pharisees cleanse the outside of the cup and of the dish, but **inside you are full of greed and wickedness**." –Luke 11:39
- "And **cast the worthless servant into the outer darkness**. In that place there will be weeping and gnashing of teeth." –Matthew 25:30
- "Whoever causes one of these little ones who believe in me to sin, it would be better for him if a great **millstone were hung around his neck and he were thrown into the sea**." –Mark 9:42
- "**But you have not known him. I know him**. If I were to say that I do not know him, I would be a liar like you, but I do know him and I keep his word." –John 8:55
- "**You serpents, you brood of vipers**, how are you to escape being sentenced to hell?" –Matthew 23:33
- "Woe to you, scribes and Pharisees, hypocrites! **For you are**

- like whitewashed tombs, which outwardly appear beautiful, but within are full of dead people's bones and all uncleanness." –Matthew 23:27
- "You are of your father the devil, and your will is to do your father's desires. He was a murderer from the beginning, and does not stand in the truth, because there is no truth in him. When he lies, he speaks out of his own character, for he is a liar and the father of lies." –John 8:44
- "You hypocrites, rightly did Isaiah prophesy of you, saying, 'This people honors Me with their lips, But their heart is far away from Me." 'But in vain do they worship Me, Teaching as doctrines the precepts of men.'" –Matthew 15:7
- "But as for these enemies of mine, who did not want me to reign over them, **bring them here and slaughter them before me.**" –Luke 19:28
- "**Do not give dogs what is holy, and do not throw your pearls before pigs**, lest they trample them underfoot and turn to attack you." –Matthew 7:6
- "Do you think that I have come to give peace on earth? **No, I tell you, but rather division.**" –Luke 12:51
- "**And will cut him in pieces and put him with the hypocrites. In that place there will be weeping and gnashing of teeth.**" –Matthew 24:51
- "Woe to those who laugh now, for **you shall mourn and weep.**" –Luke 6:25
- "...but unless you repent, you will all likewise perish." –Luke 13:3,5
- "Then he will say to those on his left, '**Depart from me, you cursed, into the eternal fire prepared for the devil and his angels.**" –Matthew 25:41

It becomes clear from reviewing the "hard sayings" of Jesus that the Honorable Minister Louis Farrakhan is in good company as he, in the modern context, offers up inspired truths that ameliorate the hearts of the faithful and sting/rebuke the offenses of the sinful. Such is actually quite characteristic of the Hebrew notion of what it means to be a prophet. In the Old Testament Hebrew language, the word *nabi* is translated into English as "prophet". It means to *"to bubble forth, as from a fountain,"* hence *"to utter"*. According to the **Easton's Bible Dictionary** it means:

The "prophet" proclaimed the message given to him, as the "seer" beheld the vision of God. (See Numbers 12:6 Numbers 12:8.) Thus, a prophet was a spokesman for God; he spake in God's name and by his authority (Exodus 7:1). He is the mouth by which God speaks to men (Jeremiah 1:9; Isaiah 51:16), and hence what the prophet says is not of man but of God (2 Peter 1:20 2 Peter 1:21; Compare Hebrews 3:7; Acts 4:25; 28:25). Prophets were the immediate organs of God for the communication of his mind and will to men (Deuteronomy 18:18 Deuteronomy 18:19). The great task assigned to the prophets whom God raised up among the people was "to correct moral and religious abuses, to proclaim the great moral and religious truths which are connected with the character of God, and which lie at the foundation of his government." Any one being a spokesman for God to man might thus be called a prophet.

Minister Farrakhan under the inspiration and unction of the Holy Spirit of Allah (God) speaks for Allah (God) those truths that sometimes offends the ears of his listeners. This is, we see, a prophetic quality to his ministry. It is also a marker of how close he is in similitude to the Jesus of the New Testament. And this means that instead of crying out in emotionalism to condemn the Minister's words, his critics should consider it as strong medicine; an elixir of truth that is harsh upon the ears but necessary to heal the whole body.

Open Letter to Congressman Todd Rokita, R-IN

From: Demetric Muhammad, Student Minister, Nation of Islam Research Group

Re: Your U.S. House Resolution condemning Minister Farrakhan, the Office of the Pope and the Jewish ideas that have created animosity and anger toward Black Americans

Congressman Rokita, I have read the draft of your resolution to condemn the Honorable Minister Louis Farrakhan in the U.S. House of Representatives. And based upon Minister Farrakhan's profound history as a beneficial presence in the Black community, I am highly offended and disturbed by your resolution.

I am also amazed with your inability to see the connection between Minister Farrakhan's passionate words delivered in his 2018 Saviours' Day address and the sacrosanct words of your Lord and Saviour Jesus Christ.

As a Roman Catholic, you sir are a Bible believing Christian. Roman Catholicism exists as the parent denomination of all of Christendom. The Roman Catholic Pope is the Bishop of Rome and is considered to be the Vicar of Jesus, the Christ. The Holy Book of Catholics is the Catholic Bible. One of the books found inside of both the Catholic and the Protestant Bible is the Book of Revelations. In both Jesus's letter to the Church at Philadelphia and the Church at Smyrna he uses the phrase **"synagogue of Satan."** This phrase is found in Revelations 2:9 and 3:9. Revelations 2:9 reads in the Online Catholic Bible version:

> "I know your hardships and your poverty, and -- though you are rich -- the slander of the people who falsely claim to be Jews but are really members of the synagogue of Satan."

In your resolution, you identified Minister Farrakhan's use of the phrase "Satanic Jews" as problematic and cited it as the reason for your resolution stating that our beloved Minister was guilty of **"promoting ideas that create animosity and anger toward Jewish Americans and the Jewish religion."** Yet based upon the Catholic Bible's English translation of New Testament Greek, we see the Minister's phrasing arises out of the prophetic words

252-STUDENTS OF FARRAKHAN

of Jesus.

Is it safe to say then that a resolution condemning the New Testament as "**promoting ideas that create animosity and anger toward Jewish Americans and the Jewish religion**" is something that we can expect you to author sometime in the near future?

Congressman Rokita, did you know that the same thing that you condemn Minister Farrakhan for is the same thing that the Pope has been condemned for? As a Roman Catholic, I would expect you to defend the Pope, but maybe you have decided to prioritize your politics over your faith. I don't think that is wise for any believer to do. I think commitment to spiritual principles and our commitment to the truth should be the priority for all believers whether they are Jewish Christian or Muslim.

Author David I. Kertzer wrote a book entitled **The Popes Against the Jews: The Vatican's Role in the Rise of Modern Anti-Semitism**; in it Kertzer presents "shocking revelations about the role played by the Vatican in the development of modern anti-Semitism." His book promo states that while "working in long-sealed Vatican archives, Kertzer unearths startling evidence to undermine the Church's argument that it played no direct role in the spread of modern anti-Semitism."

How would you respond to Mr. Kertzer's book? He is blaming the office of the Pope for the rise and spread of modern "anti-Semitism." Congressman Rokita, the same folks who have sent you out to condemn Minister Farrakhan are the same people who have routinely condemned the Pope.

The sad fact is that the words of Jesus and the story of his life are widely condemned by the Jewish community as being anti-Semitic. So, to condemn Minister Farrakhan for using the phrase "satanic Jews" is to condemn Jesus for using the phrase "synagogue of Satan" because "satanic Jews" is only a reference to those who are the members of the place your Lord and Saviour Jesus Christ dubbed as the "synagogue of Satan."

Congressman Rokita, did you know that according to the **The Jewish Virtual Library**

"The gospel story, which has generated more anti-Semitism than the

> sum of all the other anti-Semitic writings ever written, created the climate in Christian Europe that led to the Holocaust. Long before the rise of Adolf Hitler, the gospel story about the life and death of Jesus had poisoned the bloodstream of European civilization."

What do you think about this? Do you know that it was reported that one of your Israeli counterparts who is a member of the Knesset, Michael Ben Ari, was gifted with a copy of the Bible by the Bible Society of Israel? Afterwards he was photographed ripping it apart and throwing it in the trash?

I am sure your friends at the ADL are behind your sponsorship of H.R. 772. But did you know that the former head of the ADL Mr. Abraham Foxman said the following:

> "For almost twenty centuries . . . the church was the archenemy of the Jews—our most powerful and relentless oppressor and the worlds' greatest force for the dissemination of Anti-Semitic beliefs and the instigation of the acts of hatred. Many of the same people who operated the gas chambers worshiped in Christian churches on Sunday. . .. The question of the complicity of the church in the murder of the Jews is a living one. We must understand the truths of our history."

So just to summarize this issue for you, **you have placed the Honorable Minister Louis Farrakhan in the company of the Pope of Rome, the New Testament Scriptures and Jesus the Christ**. How then sir are you able to condemn the Minister, when he has done nothing more than lift words from a book you hold to be sacred and given it a necessary modern context and application?

I have enclosed a copy of my latest article that I would like for you to read also that addresses your concern over the promotion of ideas that create anger and animosity for Jewish people.

Pharaoh's Fears Alive in Jamaica:
Black Islamic Caribbean Leaders Prevented From Meeting With Farrakhan

While reading the news reports that revolutionary Islamic leaders Gerald Perreira and Imam Abu Bakr were blocked from entry into Jamaica to meet with the Honorable Minister Louis Farrakhan several thoughts came to mind.

First of all, I reflected on how Minister Farrakhan has a long history of working to produce the unity of all Blacks in the diaspora, powerfully articulating it as the ultimate solution to the lingering effects of colonialism and imperialism. Caribbean critics of the Minister charged that he is divisive, yet his history paints a picture of him a great unifier. Careful observation of the alleged divisiveness of Minister Farrakhan will reveal that it is only those who seek to maintain the status quo of Caribbean weakness and subjugation to the governments of Europe and America that make this charge.

The Bible says in Hebrews 4:12 that the word of God is divisive.

> "For the word of God is alive and active. Sharper than any double-edged sword, it penetrates even to dividing soul and spirit, joints and marrow; it judges the thoughts and attitudes of the heart."

And since Minister Farrakhan's message is really just the word of God applied to the problem of Black suffering, it is no wonder that the oppressors of Black people falsely label him as divisive.

I then thought about who could give the orders to prevent Minister Farrakhan from meeting with these strong Black Islamic Caribbean leaders. It was then I remembered an account provided by Minister Farrakhan about some of his early global travels particularly to Africa. He went to Nigeria in 1986 in the aftermath of Nigeria joining the OIC. The Minister had prepared to encourage unity and tolerance between the dueling Islamic and Christian majorities of Nigeria. But the Minister was not permitted to speak. His aides were met at the place where his speech was to be held by armed military personnel who threatened to shoot them if they proceeded to enter the facility. It was later disclosed to the Minister that the U.S. State Department had circulated false propaganda against the Minister that falsely claimed he was a communist who was in league with Russian and global communist leaders and that he had come to stir up trouble in Africa.

During this same global tour, U.S. Attorney Edwin Meese said that Minister Farrakhan "should be prosecuted" if he traveled to meet with another strong Black Islamic leader-the patron saint of Africa- Muammar Ghaddafi in Libya. The Minister had condemned then President Ronald Reagan's travel ban to Libya. The Minister's plans to meet with the Libyan leader were not borne out of any outlaw tendencies within his character. Instead it was the Minister's commitment to the higher principles of his faith in the religion of Islam, specifically the principle of *ummah* or the universal community and brotherhood of all Muslims. The Holy Qur'an makes this principle clear in the following words of Surah/Chapter 49 ayat/verse number 10.

> "The believers are brethren so make peace between your brethren, and keep your duty to Allah that mercy may be had on you."

The Minister's profound commitment to the idea and principle of unity and reconciliation has been noted by the brilliant and renowned Muslim scholar Dr. Aminah McCloud, who wrote of the Minister,

> "When Farrakhan visits leaders in Iran or Libya, an uniformed observer might see only that the Minister is willfully consorting with America's enemies, rather than recognizing the visit as an **expression of his commitment to ummah**...In the same way that the five-times-daily prayers erase one set of class and gender issues, the notion of ummah obscures nation-state borders. This detail is critical in beginning to place some of Farrakhan's thoughts and actions within a larger Islamic context. For instance, by his **continual condemnation of neocolonialism on the African continent and in the Caribbean, Louis Farrakhan demonstrates an understanding of the notion of ummah**, however unorthodox his methods of expressing this understanding."

But America and the western powers in general have always feared the power of Islam among Africans and the Blacks of the diaspora. 20th century eugenicist and Harvard scholar Lothrop Stoddard makes a striking assessment within his book The Rising Tide of Color against White World Supremacy. Stoddard wrote this tome to warn the Caucasian world powers of the erosion of their global influence due to an awakening among Black Africa, Brown Arabia and India and Yellow China and Japan. Stoddard, therefore in the early 1900s is the "white man's watchman on the wall." He laments on page 97

> "Certainly, all white men, whether professing Christians or not, should welcome the success of [Christian] missionary efforts in Africa. ...all Negroes will someday be either Christians or Moslems. In so far as he is Christianized, the Negro's savage instincts will be restrained and he will be disposed to acquiesce in white tutelage. In so far as he is Islamized, **the Negro's warlike propensities will be inflamed**, and he will be used as the tool of Arab Pan-Islamism seeking to drive the white man from Africa and make the continent its very own."

Stoddard's boldness in sounding the alarm to alert the global Caucasian and European minority of the awakening of the global Black, Brown and Yellow majority generated another thought as I reflected over the moves to thwart Minister Farrakhan's meeting with strong Black Islamic Caribbean leaders.

This thought was of the Holy Qur'an and what it describes as Pharaoh's fear that Moses and Aaron would change the religion of the enslaved Children of Israel who were under his oppressive rule. In Surah 40 ayat 26, the Holy Qur'an reads:

> "And Pharaoh said: Leave me to slay Moses and let him call upon his Lord. Surely **I fear that he will change your religion** or that he will make mischief to appear in the land."

Pharaoh feared Moses would change the religion of the Children of Israel and based on this fear, he desired to kill Moses. The fact that murder was in Pharaoh's mind for Moses leads us to believe that what Pharaoh feared was not what we commonly consider as religion being the rather innocuous rituals, rites, ceremonies, and dogmas of a particular faith.

If the modern Pharaoh's, which include the American government and the European colonizers of Africa, are studied, it is clear that their fear and response to Islam-with its strong Black nationalist leaders- is the equivalent of Pharaoh's fears found written of in the Holy Qur'an.

The skillful prohibition of the meeting with the Honorable Minister Louis Farrakhan, Imam Abu Bakr of Trinidad and Brother Gerald Perreira of Guyana by Jamaican authorities was a reaction to the fear that Black Nationalism and Islam might become popular throughout the Caribbean islands. For it was the Caribbean Islands, that gave birth to many Black revolutionaries in history. And as the Minister pointed out in his speech, the Caribbean is located in a strategically critical area of the globe, being a neighboring region to Cuba, Central and South America and the United States. It is not hard to imagine America and Europe would want to prevent the birth and popularity of Black Islamic Nationalism in such an area, where the Caribbean islands might draw strength and mentorship from revolutionary pioneer Fidel Castro and the island nation of Cuba. Islam in the Caribbean could one day be like Socialism in Cuba. And America as the leading power in the Western Hemisphere is poised to fight the Eastern Hemisphere's most dominant religion from establishing a beach head in its backyard.

But again, the fear is not of the tenets of Islam or its classical "5 Pillars." It is a fear of the effect that Islam has historically had on improving the condition of Blacks who were under oppression and giving them power to develop and control their own economies- economies based on harnessing the wealth and treasure of the natural resources buried within the land.

According to Caribbean writer Edward Wilmot Blyden while writing in his book *Christianity, Islam and the Negro Race*, Islam produces unity and economic independence:

> "Mohammedanism (Islam) in Africa counts in its ranks the most energetic and enterprising tribes. It claims as adherents the only people who have any form of civil polity or bond of social organization...It produces and **controls the most valuable commerce** between Africa and foreign countries.... there are numerous Negro Mohammedan (Islamic) communities and states in Africa which are **self-reliant, productive, independent, and dominant, supporting**, without the countenance or patronage of the parent country, Arabia..."

Therefore, it is clear that a Caribbean region with strong Muslim beachhead would do today what it did in Africa during Blyden's time and that is produce an economic shift in power. And the Minister's Jamaica message highlighted the need and value of economic strength and independence. According to Minister Farrakhan:

> The unity of the Caribbean region could produce enough wealth to develop industries out of the resources that are here. And instead of sending what you naturally produce, like bauxite, somewhere else to be turned into aluminum and then sold back to you at exorbitant prices, you could turn your own resource into its final product and be the seller of it throughout the world.

The Magnificent & Brilliant Professor Toni Morrison: An Oracle For Her People & Their God

"It does not befit Allah to address any human being except by inspiration, or from behind a veil, or He sends a messenger who then reveals by His permission whatever He wills. He is indeed Most High, All-Wise." –Holy Qur'an 42:51 Aisha Bewley Translation

"I am more interested in local interventions that Black people themselves are doing with each other as a consequence of I don't what, is it Million Man Marches? There is an enormous and wonderful wave after wave of personal interventions in communities which is very encouraging." –Toni Morrison

Throughout the breadth and scope of the teachings of the Most Honorable Elijah Muhammad there is a great reverence for the achievements and accomplishments of Black people. And ever since I became a student of his teachings under the guidance and example of the Honorable Minister Louis Farrakhan, I have had an increase in my own awareness of the infinite number of esteemed and awe-inspiring brothers and sisters who have mastered their respective disciplines and fields of endeavor.

I became aware of Professor Morrison's work years ago while I was in college. And I had always wanted to learn more about her and her work, but I never got around to it. She was among a growing list of inspiring examples of Black excellence that I always tell myself, that one day I am going to learn more about them. As a student of Minister Farrakhan, I know that the more I learn about the greatness of my people is the more I learn about the greatness of God. For the Minister has for years trumpeted the fundamental idea and truth of his teacher, the Most Honorable Elijah Muhammad, that forthrightly states, elucidates and explains the Black man and woman's capacity for divinity. So, I believe that my people are uniquely and innately configured to be reflections of and vessels for the presence of Allah (God).

A few years ago, Professor Morrison came back on my radar when I attended one of my family reunions. There I learned about the work of my cousin Dr. Carolyn Denard who worked closely with Professor Morrison as a friend and colleague. She founded and presides over the Toni Morrison Society. It is the 41st author society affiliated with the American Literature Association; it is the fourth dedicated to a Black author. I said to my cousin that I was going to follow up with her to learn more about Professor Morrison and her work to study and preserve her work. But once again, I didn't get around to it.

Over the past few days, however I have paused to try and learn as much as I can about Professor Morrison since hearing the news of her passing. I have read academic journal articles; reviews of her books and watched hours of her interviews. And I have an order of her books. Watching her interviews was for me particularly educational and inspiring. It reminded me a lot of watching the interviews of my teacher, Minister Farrakhan. Watching interviews of prominent Black people by major mainstream news organizations is like watching a championship boxing match. There is always a question or several questions posed to the Black luminary by the white interviewer that is hostile, obtuse or belittling. But I have to say that in the case of both Minister Farrakhan and Professor Morrison, their brilliant responses to such questions are like the masterful combinations of knock-out punches executed by the likes of Muhammad Ali or Mike Tyson against the "glass-jaw" of an unworthy opponent.

Professor Morrison was just so regal, strong, unapologetic and armed with indefatigable intellect. As I watched this beautiful sister be both heralded and critiqued in reviews and interviews I began to think about how Minister Farrakhan has taught me to always look for the hand of God in everything. So, I began to look into Professor Morrison to see if I could see Allah (God). And it didn't take long for me to see her as an instrument of Allah (God) that had been gifted to her people and also gifted to America by Allah (God) Himself.

I fastened on to a short section of an interview with National Public Radio (NPR), where she talked about her mother and that her mother was named "Ramah." When I looked further into it I saw that her mother's name was Ella Ramah Wofford. The name *Ella* and the name *Allah* are related. According to the *C.I. Scofield's First Study Bible* the English word "God" in Genesis Chapter 1 requires the following explanatory note:

> "Elohim (sometimes El or Elah), English form "God," the first of the three primary names of Deity, is a uni-plural noun formed from El=strength, or the strong one, and Alah, to swear, to bind oneself by an oath, so implying faithfulness."

Legendary Islamic Scholar Maulana Muhammad Ali writes in the book *The Religion of Islam* that the 2 most oft repeated attributes or names of Allah (God) found within the Holy Qur'an are Rahman (The Beneficent) and Rahim (The Merciful & Compassionate). These two names introduce every Surah or Chapter of the Holy Qur'an except Surah 9. He explains that:

> "Rahman and Rahim are derived from the one root rahma, which means tenderness requiring the exercise of beneficence, and thus comprise the ideas of love and mercy."

Professor Morrison's father was named George, a name that morphs out of the Greek Georgios and means *"farmer or earthworker"*. Farming and Horticulture was the first occupation that God gave to Adam in the book of Genesis in the Bible.

Professor Morrison's name at birth was not Toni. It was Chloe, which means *"verdant, young green shoot"*. It too is Biblical, as it draws attention to verses such as found in the Bible's books of Isaiah and Jeremiah:

> "to provide for those who grieve in Zion— to give them a crown of beauty for ashes, the oil of joy for mourning, and a garment of praise in place of a spirit of despair. So, they will be called oaks of righteousness, **the planting of the LORD**, that He may be glorified."-Isaiah 61:3

> "But blessed is the man who trusts in the LORD, whose confidence is Him. **He will be like a tree planted by the waters** that sends out its roots toward the stream. It does not fear when the heat comes, and its leaves are always green. It will not worry in a year of drought or cease producing fruit."-Jeremiah 17:7-8

Names mean a lot. The Bible speaks of how *'a good name is better than gold'*. The Holy Qur'an speaks of how it is Allah (God) that has the best of names. And the names of Professor Morrison and her parents are indicators of what became her marvelous destiny, not just a literary destiny-which is what most perceive her accomplishments as. No, Professor Morrison's was and is a divine destiny.

I say it is divine for several reasons.

In the classical Islamic view, Allah's (God's) first act of creation was the pen and He commanded it to write. So as a writer of immense skill and immeasurable talent, I see Professor Morrison as beautifully, eloquently and powerfully plying her trade in the most ancient and divine of occupations. That Allah (God) is a Writer and Teacher is borne witness to in how the Bible and Holy Qur'an record His intervention into the affairs of men and nations. Over and over again we read of Him consistently giving to specific people and nations a man and a book; albeit a prophet and a prophecy; a messenger and a message; a teacher and a teaching. What the people of religion relish and delight in of sacred texts from God today was first written by Allah (God) on the heart and minds of humble and divine servants-the prophets and messengers-long before it was ever written on paper.

When I listened to Professor Morrison talk about how she wanted to write to her people-Black people- and how she wanted to create a world through books where Black people would be free of what she called the *"white gaze"* I knew that she was being guided and used by the spiritual power of Allah (God). Because for many years it was the policy of the Most Honorable Elijah Muhammad and the Nation of Islam to create a "white-free" sanctuary for Black people within Muhammad's Temples of Islam. No white person was allowed inside Muhammad's Temples of Islam because the "white man's gaze" would not allow Black people to feel free of white people's control and judgment. For 400 years in America, Black people never felt free to be ourselves in the presence of a people who had the unchallenged power to judge us and punish us if our actions and conduct did not meet their approval.

It is this aspect of her brilliant writing that seemed to inspire the envy of many interviewers and critics of her work. They seemed to envy the fact that a woman who was being celebrated and dubbed 'the best writer that America ever produced' could write so beautifully, so powerfully, so richly, so imaginatively, so descriptively and exclude the dominant race of people in America-the white race. And she remained gracefully unapologetic about her choice to exclude white people from having any centrality within her books.

I particularly enjoyed watching a BBC documentary about Professor Morrison. It was in those interviews where I first heard her talk about her parents. She loved her parents so much; and her parents loved her so much. She mentioned how as a little girl she felt so protected when she saw her father throw a white man down a flight of stairs who was bothering their family; which was no small thing to do during the dangerous days of Jim Crow laws that didn't respect a Black man's right to defend the honor of his women and children. But most significant to me was her describing the way in which the characters in her books lived inside her own mind and would speak to her. She didn't spend a lot of time on that thread of the conversation with the interviewer, perhaps because most artists and creative people are rather shy and guarded about their private process.

But I thought about these characters, these "fictional" Black characters, having a life inside the mind of Professor Morrison such that she described them as speaking to her. The Most Honorable Elijah Muhammad told Minister *Farrakhan 'brother speak for the whole of our people.'* He told him also, *'brother just stand and let Allah speak through you.'* And the Minister has captured the hearts and minds of men and women around the world following the guidance of his beloved teacher. He speaks for the living; he speaks for the dead; he speaks for the unborn; he speaks for the whole. And what he speaks is from Allah (God).

Professor Morrison's words have captured the hearts and minds of men and women from around the world. And she has drawn praise from both the oppressor's class and the oppressed. I would have loved to have been able to ask Professor Morrison if she had ever considered the divine implications of her work and whether or not she ever perceived herself as an oracle, a living vessel that our enslaved ancestors could speak through; that God could speak through. God made the prophets story tellers, masters of dramatic narrative and artful communicators who used parables.

Professor Manning Marable wrote *The Meaning of Faith in the Black Mind in Slavery* and stated that:

> "The God of the Old Testament communicated with slaves on a regular basis to tell them the methods they could use to deliver themselves"

Literary fiction is creative writing. But when we demystify the creative process we learn that there is no such thing as something as profound and impactful to people as Professor Morrison's words have been, that just come out of nowhere. My teacher, Minister Farrakhan said profoundly that "there is only one Creator, Allah (God)". The Minister went on to say that "all acts of creation originate within Him." I believe that Professor Morrison's writings about slavery and the Black experience in America have their origin in Allah (God). I am thankful that Allah blessed our people with such a glorious human pen who, poured into our lives rich ideas and thought-provoking dramas and hope for a better world to come. May Allah be pleased with her life and contribution to the liberation of our people.

Rabbi Bertram Korn: Considering the Sources of Minister Farrakhan's Research

Who is Rabbi Bertram Korn? Why is he important?

Rabbi Bertram Korn is important because he is a cited source within the 3-volume work published by Minister Farrakhan entitled **The Secret Relationship Between Blacks and Jews**. And in recent months several high-profile critics like Joy Behar, Angela Rye and Meghan McCain have criticized our beloved Minister by attacking his claims that there was heavy Jewish involvement in the enslavement of Black people in America. Neither of these critics are scholars. So, they have offered criticisms of Minister Farrakhan that are fact less and void of truth. Their criticism of Minister Farrakhan adheres to no standards of truth or scholarship, only popularity. Minister Farrakhan's critics frequently appear from outside the ranks of professors, academicians, scholars and researchers. And the only reason that they merit a response is because of the enormous audience that they command. Popular culture's mammoth influence in the modern era trumps the influence of religion, education, family and government combined. Minister Farrakhan in his extremely important book A Torchlight for America documented more than 20 years ago, the hidden campaign to **"dumb down the American people."** The fact that uninformed, non-scholar celebrities are allowed to pose as experts on subjects as important as the history of slavery in America, is proof that the American public is being skillfully dumbed down.

Scholars are people who literally have to prove what they say and prove what they believe. They function as safeguards to the presence of truth within a society. In religion they fit within a hierarchy of divine knowledge that places Allah (God) at the top, followed by the angels, who are followed by the prophets and messengers, who are followed by the scholars, then the preachers of religion, and lastly the religious "lay-person" or believer. Prophet Muhammad (peace be upon him) said that *"one learned man or woman is harder on the devil than 1,000 ignorant worshippers."* Meaghan McCain, Joy Behar and Angela Rye are not scholars and should not be taken seriously when they talk about fields of study that require a scholar's informed perspective. Minister Farrakhan is a Messenger of Allah (God), which means he has divine knowledge that Allah (God) reveals to him, however the Minister uses the knowledge and research of scholars to bear witness to what Allah (God) has revealed to him.

Let's consider one of hundreds of scholars from the Jewish community that serves as a source and witness bearer to the controversial aspect of Minister Farrakhan's message wherein he identifies certain Jewish persons as playing a significant role in the destruction of Black life in America (i.e. the Black Holocaust)

According to Professor Marc Lee Raphael in his June 1980 eulogy for Rabbi Korn written in the journal of American Jewish History:

"Bertram Wallace Korn was a rarity; a rabbi who served the largest Reform congregation in the state of Pennsylvania for thirty years and a native-born historian who had no rivals as the most prolific and celebrated interpreter of ante-bellum and Civil War period American Jewish life. Ordained at the Hebrew Union College in 1943, ...From 1946-1948 he studied with Jacob R. Marcus, and the Hebrew Union College awarded him the Doctor of Hebrew Letters degree in 1948 for his dissertation on "American Jewry and the Civil War." Following one year as an assistant professor at the Hebrew Union College, Korn chose the rabbinate as a career, and accepted the pulpit at Kenesseth Israel in Elkins Park where he remained until his death in 1979. Rabbi Korn was honored during his lifetime in a variety of ways: he received honorary degrees from Temple University, Delaware Valley College, Hebrew Union College and Dropsie University; he was promoted to Rear Admiral, Chaplain Corps, United States Naval Reserve - the first Jewish chaplain to attain two-star rank in any military service - and was awarded the United States Navy Legion of Merit when he retired from active service in 1978; and he served as president of the Association of Jewish Chaplains of the Armed Forces of the United States, the Alumni Association of the Hebrew Union College, the American Jewish Historical Society, and the Chamber Symphony of Philadelphia."

As his great accomplishments convey, Rabbi Korn was a man distinguished and well respected by his religion; he was a decorated U.S. military serviceman; and he was a scholar whom enjoyed the admiration of his peers. He certainly would not be considered an anti-Semite. But because Minister Farrakhan cites his stellar scholarship, the Minister is branded an anti-Semite.

In 1974 Rabbi Korn spoke at a Black college in Nashville, Tennessee. Consider a sample of some of Rabbi Korn's research-based scholarly statements excerpted from his Fisk University presentation:

"In this work in which I've been engaged for twenty-five years or more, I've had a lot of objections tossed at me on the part of Jews, scholars, and lay people, including my wife, ah, who think that it's best to sweep things under the rug. That, ah, the suggestion that any Jews owned any slaves or had anything to do with the slave trade is, ah, putting a gun in the hands of the enemy. This kind of attitude towards academic work is to me, to say the least, regrettable. And I think that if we achieve anything in our meetings this week, we'll at least begin to come to an understanding of what the realities are. Jews are no enemies to misconceptions about themselves and Jews are not immune to self-righteousness."

"...the outstanding Jew of Newport, Rhode Island, Aaron Lopez, perhaps the most outstanding colonial Jew of all the colonies, had at least one slave ship on the seas each year during the 1760s, more in the 1770s, as many as 3 a year. He used Negro workers in weaving and [unintelligible] grinding, which were 2 of the many commercial enterprises in which he was involved and had 6 domestic slaves in his home."

"Altogether you can say that Jewish individuals in the colonial period revealed no record of ideological opposition to slavery. Even a synagogue, Shearith Israel of New York City, in 1729, hired two slaves from a widow and used other black people in the building of a new synagogue building."

"It has to be stated without any attempt to cover up that leaders of Jewish communities participated in the slave system without apology."

These statements by Rabbi Korn to a Black college audience are very significant. They are especially significant when we consider how Rabbi Korn is not deemed an anti-Semite who should not be allowed to speak to Black students and faculty. But Heidi Beirich said of Minister Farrakhan's college speaking engagements that *"anytime Farrakhan is on the road speaking to groups, we are afraid those ideas are going to spread."* And it is the Southern

Poverty Law Center that is always dogging the trail of Minister Farrakhan to prevent colleges from allowing him to speak to the study body.

This article is specifically purposed to expose Minister Farrakhan's critics as woeful and lacking in scholastic competence. And it is also to unsheathe the veritable tip of the iceberg of strong, unimpeachable and mainly Jewish sources that lay as a base and foundation for the Minister's message regarding the Jewish involvement in the Black Holocaust. I close this article with another series of jaw-dropping quotes from Rabbi Korn:

Excerpted from Jews and Negro Slavery in the Old South 1789-1965 by Rabbi Bertram Korn:

"Slave-dealing obviously did not disqualify Jews from receiving the friendship and esteem of their co-religionists any more than it disqualified Christians; engaging in business transactions in Negro flesh was not regarded as incompatible with being a good Jew."

"It would seem to be realistic to conclude that any Jew who could afford to own slaves and had need for their services would do so…. Jews participated in every aspect and process of the exploitation of the defenseless Blacks."

"Even in the days of the secession crisis, and the subsequent prolongated war and eventual defeat, many Southern Jews believed slavery to be indispensable to their happiness and security."

"Jews in the towns and cities appear to have been quite content to abide by the excessively cruel punishments meted out to blacks who were caught by the law…In 1798, Polly, a mulatto slave, was tried for taking a loaf of white sugar worth two dollars from Benjamin Solomon's home, and was sentenced to five lashes on her bare back and ordered to be branded on her left hand….Benjamin Wolfe's store was broken into in 1797, and $500 in merchandise was stolen. Three slaves were tried for the crime, but only one was convicted. He was sentenced to be hung. Jews were among the many Southern citizens who appealed for the apprehension and return of runaway slaves.

The Roots of Injustice: The American Slave Codes, Laws that Criminalized Black Life in America

"Can wicked rulers be allied with you, those who frame injustice by statute? They band together against the life of the righteous and condemn the innocent to death."
- (Psalms 94:20-21)

As the Honorable Minister Louis Farrakhan mobilizes the victims of the American "injustice" system, we reflect over the historical record of this system and its harmful intentions regarding the very existence of Black and Indigenous people.

Let's begin by noting that one of the most wicked uses of law in America can be witnessed in America's denying her Black slaves the God-given **freedom** that every human being is created to enjoy.

What is especially evil is the history that reveals how far this country went to ensure that Blacks in this country would be forever denied such freedom. To ensure that Blacks in America would exist as perpetual slaves a new separate legal system was created with laws that applied only to the Black slaves stolen from Africa. Historians commonly refer to these laws as the **Slave Codes**.

One particular area of special slave laws or codes that is especially fascinating to me due to all of its nefarious implications is the area of slave religion. I remember reading once where the Most Honorable Elijah Muhammad wrote that the **"white man would never give you a religion to free you"** (paraphrase). And while some have dismissed Mr. Muhammad's bold teaching, the history of our enslaved ancestors actually serves to vindicate his message.

Professor Albert J. Raboteau discusses this in his excellent book *Slave Religion*. According to Professor Raboteau,

> "One of the principal reasons for the refusal of English planters to allow their slaves to receive [religious] instructions was **the fear that baptism would emancipate** their **slaves**. The notion that if slaves were baptized, "they should, according to the laws of the British nation, and the canons

270-STUDENTS OF FARRAKHAN

of its church" be freed was legally vague but widely believed. Repeatedly, would-be missionaries to the slaves complained that slaveholders refused them permission to catechize their slaves because baptism made it necessary to free them. **Thus, it seemed that the Christian commission to preach the gospel to all nations ran directly counter to the economic interest of the Christian slave owner. This dilemma was solved by colonial legislation.** In 1664 the lower house of Maryland asked the upper house "to draw up an Act obliging Negroes to serve durante vita (during life) . . . for the prevention of the damage Masters of such Slaves would sustain by such Slaves pretending to be Christian; And [then pleading for their freedom on the basis of] the law of England." **By 1706 at least six colonial legislatures had passed acts denying that baptism altered the condition of a slave "as to his bondage or freedom."** Virginia's was typical of the statutes enacted in expressing the hope "that diverse masters, freed from this doubt, may more carefully endeavor the propagation of Christianity," among their slaves."

What makes this particular law so representative of the wicked desire to legally codify the permanence of Black suffering is the fact that the most sacred text in Christianity-the Christian Bible-makes the claim that freedom is in fact the intended result of Baptism. **According the Bible "And all who have been united with Christ in baptism** have put on Christ, like putting on new clothes. **There is no longer Jew or Gentile, slave or free, male and female. For you are all one in Christ Jesus.** And now that you belong to Christ, you are the true children of Abraham. You are his heirs, and God's promise to Abraham belongs to you." (Galatians 3:28)

Yet, as we see from the records of history, **white slave masters only consented to their Black slaves becoming Christians after they had created laws to ensure that there would be nothing within Christianity to secure freedom for their slaves!** What a startling historical fact!

Throughout the history of the Nation of Islam in America, the Most Honorable Elijah Muhammad and the Honorable Minister Louis Farrakhan have repeatedly made the case and justified the call and plea for justice for Black and Indigenous peoples in America. And both men have courageously followed in the tradition of the Biblical and Qur'anic prophets by making it known that America's continued denial of justice to Black people is an offense to God and will ultimately bring about God's judgment/punishment against America.

In an article entitled *Separation or Death*, the Most Honorable Elijah Muhammad identified the wicked separate justice system for Blacks known as the Slave Codes. In this article the Most Honorable Elijah Muhammad writes that

> "According to the **American Slave Code of Law, by William Goodell**-page 304, under the above title, the Negroes may be used as breeders, prostitutes, concubines, pimps, tapsters, attendants at the gaming table and as subjects of medical and surgical experiments for the benefit of science..."

Goodell's book is indeed very enlightening and should be required reading for every Black family in America and for anyone who wants to understand the history of injustice in America. Goodell documents powerfully that the criminal justice system in America is founded upon the criminalization of even the noblest aspirations of Black people.

Goodell surveys the various state laws that were created to criminalize the existence of Black men and women. Section headings within Goodell's 433-page encyclopedia of wicked Slave Laws include the following chapters and subject headings:

> "Slaves Cannot Possess Anything (page 89); Slaves Cannot Marry (page 105); Slaves Cannot Constitute Families (Page 113); Education of Slaves is Prohibited (Page 319); Slaves right to practice religion is controlled or prohibited outright (Page 326)."

And what makes Goodell's survey vitally relevant to Minister Farrakhan's call for Justice in the aftermath of the murders of scores of Black men and women by police and angry whites is Goodell's examination of laws pertaining to the murder of slaves. I could not help but think about Ferguson, Missouri police officer Darren Wilson when I read Goodell quote North Carolina slavery era Judge Thomas Ruffin. Ruffin is quoted as rendering a judicial ruling that said **"cruel and unreasonable battery on a slave" by his owner or hirer is not an indictable offense, and that "there have been no prosecutions of this sort."** I thought of George Zimmerman, who lynched the beautiful young man, Trayvon Martin. And I remembered Michael Slager-the murderer of

Charleston, South Carolina citizen Walter Scott. I thought of both of these modern day lynchers when I read on page 195 of Goodell's book the words of Judge George Stroud who said **"the master may, at his pleasure, inflict any species of punishment on the person of his slave."**

As I continued to read what Messenger Muhammad directed in this article, I reflected on our beautiful sister Sandra Bland whose mysterious death while in police custody was ruled a "suicide". And though Sandra's lifeless body was found hanging in a Waller county jail cell on July 13, 2015, Goodell discusses the death of a young Black woman from the Washington, D.C. area in 1823. On page 181 Goodell notes the death of a "slave girl" in Alexandria, Virginia. It was there that **"a slave owner chased his female slave, whip in hand, in open daylight, before multitudes, to the end of a wharf, where she jumped in and was drowned. Verdict of the coroner's inquest: "Death by suicide to escape deserved punishment."**

I am grateful for the Most Honorable Elijah Muhammad's review of Goodell's **Slave Code history**. It has made me keenly aware of this important history and its direct connection to the attitudes and behaviors of the modern descendants of our former slave masters who murder and terrorize the Black community today.

In the light of this history, it is no surprise that descendants of the slave masters have evolved to imitate their slave holding ancestors. American founding father Thomas Jefferson wrote in his Notes on Virginia "The whole commerce between master and slave, is a perpetual exercise of the most boisterous passions the most unremitting despotism on the one part, and degrading submissions on the other. **Our children see this, and learn to imitate it; for man is an imitative animal.** If a parent had no other motive, either in his own philanthropy or his self-love, for restraining the intemperance of passion towards his slave, it should always be a sufficient one that his child is present. But generally, it is not sufficient. **The parent storms, the child looks on, catches the lineaments of wrath puts on the same airs in the circle of smaller slaves, gives a loose to his worst passions, AND THUS NURSED, EDUCATED, AND DAILY EXERCISED IN TYRANNY, CANNOT BUT BE STAMPED BY IT, WITH ODIOUS PECULIARITIES."**

The Most Honorable Elijah Muhammad warned America of what

awaits her if she refuses to give justice to his beloved Black and indigenous people. So, as we move forward to study and operationalize the Minister's magnificent message delivered just days ago on October 10, 2015 (10.10.15) we should also be aware of the bold and ominous warning made by Minister Farrakhan's teacher-The Most Honorable Elijah Muhammad.

In his article titled **The End**, the Most Honorable Elijah Muhammad details the **"Or Else"** that awaits America if she remains a **"throne of iniquity"** for her ex-slaves.

> "The American white race is the number one people whom Allah's anger is directed against as Jehovah's anger was against Egypt in the time of Moses. Jehovah's weapons of war used against Pharaoh and His people were the forces of nature: flies, frogs, lice, diseases, rains, hailstones, fire, water and finally the drowning of Pharaoh and his armies in the Red Sea. The same forces of nature are prepared to be used against America with the following additions: terrifying storms (which now harass America); the loss of friendship of the nations; a specifically prepared enemy people under the name "Gog" and "Magog," whose skill and power will cover the earth for a while; there will be no friends for America; snow, ice and earthquakes, even droughts and dust storms, the natural power of water, wind , terrific cold out of the north, fire from the sun, agitation of the high seas by the magnetism of the moon and sun (which will aid in the destruction of America's sea power.)"

Stop the Mischief Making! Setting the Record Straight on the Nation of Islam & the Police

"Unless the LORD protects a city, guarding it with sentries will do no good."
-Psalms 127:1

Several on-line bloggers, conservative talk-show hosts and media outlets have begun a wicked, mischievous campaign to paint a picture in the minds of the American people that the Nation of Islam and its illustrious and honorable Minister Louis Farrakhan are radicalizing young Black men and turning them into "cop killers."

Reports have even circulated that former prosecutor Larry Klayman has filed a class action lawsuit that names Minister Farrakhan along with President Obama, Rev. Al Sharpton and former Attorney General Eric Holder. In his complaint he maintains that the aforementioned prominent Black men have used their large platforms to incite a race war and are ultimately to blame for the shooting deaths of police officers in Dallas, Texas and Baton Rouge, Louisiana.

As I have watched the news stories-one after another-exposing the reality of Black life in America, particularly the deaths coming from the hands/guns of "bad apple" police officers, I have been horrified. It has been equally disturbing to witness news reports of police officers who had nothing to do with the murders of Alton Sterling, Philando Castile et.al. lose their life via vigilante lone-wolf assassins.

All of what has and is taking place, is making the condition of the American Black man and woman the leading issue of our time. It harkens to my memory something that I once read from the Most Honorable Elijah Muhammad. The November 22, 1963 edition of the Muhammad Speaks newspaper records the following from Messenger-Muhammad.

> "You have not realized how precious you are in the sight of God today. You don't realize that you are the real problem of the civilized world. You don't realize that without the solving of the so-called Negro problem today there will be nothing done. It is your problem today that

the whole world fears. It is your problem that troubles America."

The violence, police brutality, protests and civil unrest in 2016 is reminiscent of the 1960s. And in 1968 the Most Honorable Elijah Muhammad published a series of 4 articles devoted to outlining in the plainest and simplest terms just what the proper relationship between the Black community and the police should be.

Divine Wisdom For Policing

In providing guidance and divine wisdom to the police officer, especially Black officers, Mr. Muhammad directs the officer toward policing in the most respectful and noble way. Consider a few excerpts from his magnificent 4 article series:

> "If the Black policeman arrest his Black brother who has broken the law that he is out here to enforce, he should not provoke his prisoner to say something or to do something just for the sake of beating him under arrest and shooting him after having already arrested the man, or before he arrests him, for nothing but for the sake of his office, as the officer of law over his Black bother...
>
> It is an injustice and is out of the due process of law to arrest a man and handcuff him and then take him to jail, beating him while he is under arrest and then inside of the jail, going in his cell, beating him up."
> "Tell the judge the truth, officer, on your Black brother and do not think of telling other than the truth and do not think of striking your Brother when you have him helpless in your custody." ...
>
> "If he curses you or swears at you, he cannot harm you. He is behind bars. The judge will deal with him. You will tell the judge how you were treated by the lawbreaker, but just remember now you have him under control. He has submitted to your arrest, what do you care about him talking? He cannot harm you." ...
>
> "BLACK POLICE officers, we do not want you to break the law to show sympathy for us, but we want you to remember the justice of the law in dealing with us. And, Black people will be your friends and obey you and there will not be any hiding behind homes and in the streets to do bodily harm to his Black officers. You are our people, officer, and not our aggressive officer; therefore, when we look and see you we expect you to bring about peace and not increased trouble. That is destroying

our peace." ...

> "If he shoots at you, certainly you should shoot him, try and conquer him. If he runs from you in the streets, do not aim at his body and head; aim at his legs. If you are trying to shoot him, shoot him in the leg, not the head. If you do this, you are trying to murder him. Officers practice target shooting and they can stop a person without killing them."

The Most Honorable Elijah Muhammad then turns his attention to instructing the Black community on how we should relate to those who police our communities. And since, in times past it was only Black officers who were assigned to Black neighborhoods, the Black community is here encouraged to embrace the Black police officers as "brethren" and to view them as valued assets to the community. Consider these excerpts:

> "We, of the Black community must treat Black Officers in such a way that they would not dare think of doing injustice to us. Once in their power, we should respect the Black Officer with all sincerity, because he is supposed to be our peace officer and not our aggressive officer." ...

> "Respect the officer. Approach him with a smile and not so with a sour cursing face and murder in our eyes for him, as he is our protector against foreign trouble." ...

> "A good police officer is loved. Let us love our Black Brother. He is our Brother. And, let us help him by having as little trouble in our community as possible." ...

> "Obey our Black Officer. Love him as yourself, for we all are brothers. And let us show the world that we can control our Black community as white communities are controlled by white officers."

With these statements coming from the leader of the Nation of Islam, it becomes crystal clear that, the Nation of Islam has no policy of antagonism or hatred for police. And this is

the Nation's position, despite a long record of suffering harassment, sabotage and even NOI members being killed by rogue elements within the police department.

Last August, the Honorable Minister Louis Farrakhan visited the city of Memphis to promote the 20th anniversary of the Million Man March and the commencement of the Justice or Else movement. During a moment of reflection, the Minister praised the Memphis Police Department for their professional and extensive protective detail that they provided for his safety during his stay in Memphis. The Minister's stay in Memphis was the occasion for a photo taken by social media professional Jesse Muhammad. The viral photo is a beautiful scene of local police officers standing hand in hand with one another and with Minister Farrakhan during a moment of prayer. The officers were Black, white, old, young, Muslim and Christian. Such a photo is indicative of how the Nation of Islam has always considered itself as an ally of all who want a society that is orderly, peaceful and free of violence and crime.

Nation of Islam Lauded By Law Enforcement
Over the long history of the Nation of Islam in America, which is now 86 years, many police officials have lauded the Nation for its crime reducing presence in the many cities where it is established. A sampling of such complimentary testimonies includes:

"The Muslims have done more to rehabilitate narcotics addicts than any corrective agency in the country."-NY State Senator Basil Patterson from Harlem at the National Society of Afro-American Society of Policemen's tribute to the Nation of Islam (July 5, 1969)

"They stand out; they're conspicuously trying to do something positive, and that's different in many parts of the community. They have been unfairly harassed in the past." - Edward L. Kerr, Police Director of Newark, New Jersey (January 1974)

"Religious philosophies such as the Muslims' can go a long way toward reducing crime even in the most adverse circumstances." – Sherriff Richard J. Elrod of Cook County (January 1974)

"Compton has become an example relative to the Muslims in that overall attitude of respect. I for one am glad that the Muslims moved into Compton." -Officer Saul Lankster (November 1974)

"That's one of the reasons I've always respected Mr. Muhammad even before now that they've gained a measure of respectability. When everybody else was trying to condemn Him. I had some pretty close friends who belonged to the Nation. They kept themselves clean, they worked and they looked out for themselves. You have to admire the man for the way those people conduct themselves." -*Chicago Deputy Police Superintendent Mitchell Ware (November 1974)*

"As a large group of people, the Muslims tend to be law abiding and seem to have a rehabilitating influence in the community." -*Thomas W. Chochee, Police Chief Compton California (February 1974)*

"One thing I can say-where ever Muslims go, crime goes down. We policemen are always happy to have them in a community; it makes our job that much easier." -*Chicago Deputy Police Superintendent Sam Nolan (January 1974)*

Minister Farrakhan's "Dopebusters"

During the rebuilding of the Nation of Islam under the guidance of the Honorable Minister Louis Farrakhan, the Nation of Islam developed a community security force affectionately known as the "**Dopebusters.**" From the Nation of Islam Research Group article entitled **How Farrakhan Solved The Crime and Drug Problem** we see the Dopebusters described in the following description:

"In 1988, the Black men of the elite Fruit of Islam, under the training and guidance of Minister Farrakhan, formed into units and began to conduct security patrols in some of the most drug-infested public housing developments. Armed with only a deep love for their own people and a determination to improve their condition, they became known as the "Dope Busters." The Muslims in Washington DC marched unarmed into a veritable drug gang war at the Kenilworth Parkside and Mayfair Mansions housing projects and a remarkable thing happened. The Muslims closed open-air drug markets and brought peace and quiet to those neighborhoods. It was a condition that had never been seen in that area since those projects were built."

And just like the Most Honorable Elijah Muhammad, Minister Farrakhan has students and followers that have achieved wide acclaim for their work and success. A sample of some of glowing commendations bestowed upon the Dopebusters includes the following:

"I am currently a lieutenant in the Metropolitan Police Department, assigned to the 7th District as the Commander of the Special Emphasis Unit and Support Coordinator of all vice, detective and tactical operations. I have been employed with the Department for 26 years in a sundry of assignments. It is most noteworthy that the areas of the city which they [Dopebusters] have contracted to provide security have shown drastic reductions in crime. This, within itself, speaks to the basic tenets of community empowerment policing. Some of the communities in which I personally know that crime has been reduced by their presence are the Clifton Terrace Apartments, the Mayfair Mansion Apartment Complex, the Paradise Gardens Apartment Complex, the Atlantic Street Apartment Dwellings and the surrounding areas. I have had the occasion to observe some of their security training and to participate in the training as a volunteer instructor. I have found them to be professional, courteous and committed to the delivery of service to the communities in which they patrol and provide security." -President DC Black Police Caucus, Lowell Duckett

"The founders [of the Dopebusters] formed the company after volunteering their services during that period to secure the Paradise/Mayfair community of over 1200 apartments, which had become the largest open-air drug market in the Mid-Atlantic States in the mid-1980s. At the time no security firms were willing to work in the neighborhood; in fact, the police came into the neighborhood only in force because of the very dangerous conditions. The volunteers patrolled the two complexes, confronted dangerous individuals, and testified in court about the activities of accused felons; all at great personal risk. Their leadership allowed the police to become more effective and encouraged the residents of the neighborhood to work for a safer community. Both Paradise at Parkside and Mayfair Mansions are now healthy, vibrant and safe communities' thanks in good part to the efforts of the [Dopebusters]." -Deputy Assistant Secretary for Enforcement and Investigations Office of Fair Housing and Equal Opportunity U.S. Department of Housing and Urban Development, Ms. Susan

Forward

"In terms of bottom line results, they are doing such a good job and the living environment in public housing developments has so markedly improved that I would be reluctant to remove NOI security from those developments."-Baltimore, MD Kurt L. Schmoke

"Crime at Westview Terrace has fallen drastically since the Black Muslims moved in."-New Castle, PA Police Chief Louis Piscitella

We pray that what we have shared here of the facts of the Nation of Islam's history, record and true relationship with police will inoculate the mind of the reader against the flood of propaganda and slander aimed at de-magnetizing the Honorable Minister Louis Farrakhan and the Nation of Islam. For we believe that this is the ultimate aim of this present manifestation of a long-standing commitment by those in the most powerful positions within America to maintain the status quo of "White supremacy/Black inferiority" and its more contemporary goal of "White existence/Black extinction." To do this, they have determined they must get rid of the Nation of Islam. And negative propaganda (i.e. lies) about the Nation must be implanted into the minds of an unsuspecting public as a prelude to an onslaught against the Nation of Islam and the Honorable Minister Louis Farrakhan. If they can be successful in turning the public against the Nation, the public will be made to feel that any and all actions made to "neutralize" the Nation and the Hon. Min. Louis Farrakhan is justified.

The Censorship of God's Ideas and Perspective

"For My thoughts are not your thoughts, neither are your ways My ways," declares the LORD. "For as the heavens are higher than the earth, so My ways are higher than your ways and My thoughts than your thoughts." - Isaiah 55:8

"(We take) Allah's colour, and who is better than Allah at colouring, and we are His worshippers." - Holy Qur'an 2:138

The recent social media censorship of the Honorable Minister Louis Farrakhan was a very bad move for the leaders of Facebook and Instagram to make. In one fell swoop, they destroyed the large and growing audience of over 1 million people who had happily became Facebook followers of Minister Farrakhan; and more than 600,000 who had chosen to become Instagram followers of the Honorable Minister Louis Farrakhan. Many have raised the very valid point that questions why the company would have to make such a move when it already has built in features that allow its users to block any content they might deem offensive or inappropriate. In fact, the Facebook algorithms already use programming and machine learning to limit and control what posted information each user sees in their personal newsfeed. The algorithms ensure that instead of posting your information from a "mountain top" for the whole world to behold; most users are only posting their views and opinions to a much smaller audience that the algorithm has allowed them to have; this place most Facebook posts inside an echo chamber with others users that already agree with them on most issues.

Banning Minister Farrakhan was a bad move because it places the behemoth company within an ignoble historical context, one where the giants of the secular world have frequently sought to censor the giants of the spiritual world in an effort to silence and censor the word of God, which is so often critical of how the secular world's leaders exercise their leadership.

On the back page of this newspaper appears a regular addendum to all the articles, photos and news stories that are brilliantly presented each week for The Final Call's readership; it is called the Muslim Program. Within it is a statement made by the Most Honorable Elijah Muhammad that says:

282-STUDENTS OF FARRAKHAN

"WE BELIEVE in the truth of the Bible, but we believe that it has been tampered with and must be reinterpreted so that mankind will not be snared by the falsehoods that have been added to it."

The tampering or manipulation of the scriptures has historically been a method of censoring the ideas and perspective of God, when God's ideas and perspective differs from the perspective of those who run governments and rule over nations and institutions.

Very recently National Public Radio (NPR) published a story about how the British and American slave masters manipulated the Bible to ensure all passages that contained verses in favor of freedom from slavery were removed. The standard Bible was pared down from 1,189 chapters to a meager 232 chapters to make the "Slave Bible." This was done to censor God's ideas and perspective on the "peculiar institution" of American chattel slavery. The God of the Bible fought the enemies and enslavers of His people. The God of the Bible promised to topple tyrants and destroy despotic dictators. So out of fear, the oppressors and enslavers of the Black man and woman of America stripped the Bible of its liberation theology. The fear of the ideas present in the standard Bible are the same fears of those who are in control of traditional media, social media and government today. This fear lies at the heart of why Minister Farrakhan has been the principal target of the ban. It is not because there is a record of hate crimes, violence or murders resulting from the preaching of our beloved Minister.

But another way of censoring the ideas and perspective of God was to ban or prohibit slaves to become preachers. This was done in the aftermath of the Nat Turner rebellion. In Virginia, the Richmond Enquirer published the editorial sentiment of time when it wrote: **"No black man ought to be permitted to turn preacher throughout the country."** Virginia was also one of the first states to make it illegal for Black people to read.

It is remains critically important to understand that the problem that Facebook, The Anti-Defamation League of B'Nai B'rith (ADL) and the Southern Poverty Law Center (SPLC) have with Minister Farrakhan is not because of anti-Semitism. They really are angry with God. They really have a problem with the word of God as it is written in the scriptures of the Torah, Gospel and Holy Qur'an.

If Minister Farrakhan was a hate teacher, his teaching would have produced hate crimes everywhere that he has preached. And the Minister has been preaching for more than 6 decades and hate crimes are never the product or end result of Minister Louis Farrakhan having visited a city to preach to its residents. In fact, cities like Tuskegee, Alabama; Memphis, Tennessee; and Monroe, Louisiana have all given Minister Farrakhan the symbolic "key to the city." In other words, they wanted to express in gesture that "Minister Farrakhan is always welcome in our town."

I would suspect most of our readers would be surprised to learn that long before Minister Farrakhan, many Jewish leaders had targeted the New Testament-the Gospel of Jesus Christ as being the most anti-Semitic of all publications. This means that they see Jesus' life story as more anti-Semitic than Adolph Hitler's Mein Kempf! It is interesting that you can purchase Mein Kempf from Amazon.com; but Amazon.com has banned Minister Farrakhan's book series **The Secret Relationship Between Black and Jews**. Mein Kempf by Adolph Hitler produces sympathy for the Jewish Holocaust by exposing to the world the mind of the man that produced their Holocaust and suffering. The Secret Relationship Between Blacks and Jews produces sympathy for the Black Holocaust; and it organizes and presents together for the first time ever, what Jewish historians, rabbis and scholars offer as evidence of the Jewish role in the Black Holocaust and suffering.

According to **Removing Anti-Jewish Polemic from our Christian Lectionaries: A Proposal** by Norman A. Beck, the following is a break-down of the anti-Semitic content contained within the Gospel of Jesus:

- Gospel of Mark contains 40 Anti-Semitic verses
- Gospel of Matthew contains Anti-Semitic 80 verses
- Gospel of Luke contains Anti-Semitic 60 verses
- Gospel of John contains Anti-Semitic 130 verses
- Acts of the Apostles contains Anti-Semitic 140 verses

I argue that if the Gospel of Jesus can be deemed anti-Semitic, how can anyone who believes in that Gospel not be deemed anti-Semitic? If the New Testament is accused of being anti-Semitic, all Muslims and Christians stand to one day be dubbed as anti-Semites simply for believing in the word of God. This is eye-opening truth that really shows how the anti-Semitism censors are really angry with God and his ideas and perspective which are found throughout the scriptures.

Lastly, the reader should note that it was in November 2018-about 6 months ago when a convention of Jewish leaders and scholars in Europe gathered together to address the problem of anti-Semitism. They recommended that both the Bible and the Holy Qur'an go through an editing process and that verses critical of Jewish misconduct be labeled within the text as anti-Semitic.

Wow! So, God was censored in November and God's strongest Minister was censored in May! Who's next? Are we moving towards a day when it will be illegal to own a Bible or Holy Qur'an? Perhaps we are seeing the negative variant of the meaning of the name Israel, which means to "contend with or wrestle with God." If so, I must advise those who believe that they can fight God and win as my grandmother advised me many years ago when she said

> "Baby, your arms are too short to box with God."

The Criterion (Standard) of Love & Leadership

Reflections On The Significance of Minister Farrakhan's 88th Birth Anniversary

"Blessed is He who sent down the Criterion upon His Servant that he may be to the worlds a warner"

-Holy Qur'an Surah 25 (al-Furqan) Ayat 1

On May 11, 1526, the Spanish monarchy issued forth a formal decree forbidding the importing of Muslims into the Western Hemisphere. According to esteemed scholar Sylvianne Diouf:

> "After the first slave uprising in the New World, led by the Wolof in 1522, a royal decree of May 11, 1526, specifically forbade the introduction of "Gelofes" (Wolof), negros (blacks) from the Levant (or Middle East), those who had been raised with the Moors, and people from Guinea without a special license from the Casa de Contratación, which regulated the slave trade and put levies on the slaves. **All the groups that the decree prohibited were either completely or mostly Muslim. Within fifty years, five decrees were passed to forbid the introduction of African Muslims to the Spanish colonies.** This insistent reissuing of the prohibition shows that Muslims nevertheless continued to arrive and to cause concerns and problems in the New World. **The colonists claimed that the Muslims incited the other nations to rebellion, and it was feared that they would take Islam to the Indians."**

It was 407 years later, on May 11, 1933 that a baby boy was born in New York City to parents Sarah Mae Manning and Percival Clark. The baby boy named Louis Eugene Walcott would grow to become known all over the world as the Honorable Minister Louis Farrakhan.

On May 11, 2021 we celebrate and reflect upon the magnificent life and work of the Honorable Minister Louis Farrakhan. This is the 88th anniversary of his birth, and it is important to look at the life of Minister Farrakhan through the lens of history. It is even more important to look at Minister Farrakhan's life through the lens of prophecy. In truth, it is within the life of Minister Farrakhan wherein we have observed an extraordinary and profound intersection of history, prophecy and current events.

286-STUDENTS OF FARRAKHAN

The May 11th historic prohibition against Islam's entry into the Americas is a component part of the overall enslavement and oppression of Black people throughout the Western Hemisphere, especially in North America. Students of the cyclical nature of historical events bear witness to what the Most Honorable Elijah Muhammad said when he stated that *"there is no such thing as a coincidence."* On this, the 88th anniversary of his birth, we can look at his life and begin to appreciate the fact that the life of Louis Farrakhan is a very significant aspect of Allah's (God's) response to Black suffering.

The cornerstone of the Nation of Islam's theology is that we believe that Allah (God) has heard the cries, the prayers and the woe-filled mourning of the Black man and woman of America, and has intervened in our affairs in the person of Master W. Fard Muhammad. The Bible supports our belief when it states in Exodus 3:7-8:

> "And the LORD said, I have surely seen the affliction of my people which are in Egypt, and have heard their cry by reason of their taskmasters; for I know their sorrows; **And I am come down to deliver them out of the hand of the Egyptians...**"

As the National Representative of the Most Honorable Elijah Muhammad, Minister Farrakhan has, since 1977, been the foremost in spreading Islam within the Black community as a salvific force that is powerful enough to address and cure the many pathologies that our enslavement and oppression produced among us.

And within this same time period Minister Farrakhan has been the one Black leader that the white power structure has hated the most, and consistently targeted for destruction. This is significant, especially when we consider that there is a fundamental adversarial relationship between the real leaders of the oppressed and the oppressors. In fact, it can be deemed an indicator of strength and authenticity for a supposed leader of the enslaved to be hated and condemned by the slave masters. And by contrast, those supposed leaders of the oppressed that are approved of and celebrated by the oppressors cannot be the authentic leaders of the oppressed. And these most certainly cannot be a leader that reflects Allah's (God's) promised deliverance out of the hand of the oppressors.

In other words, our heroes are not the heroes of our former slave masters and their children.

Leadership

The vicious campaign to discredit and malign the noble name and person of the Honorable Minister Louis Farrakhan, for over 35 years, identifies him as the standard or criterion of Black leadership that reflects Allah's (God's) promise to deliver us. Consider some candid unsolicited statements from critics and observers.

"To a great extent, in other words, Farrakhan now is **the black leadership**—the cutting edge, the storm center, the presence against which others are measured." – **National Review Magazine**

"The appearance of Louis Farrakhan at Madison Square Garden on October 7 demonstrated, without doubt that **he is now America's preeminent black leader.**"-Julius Lester, Journalist & Critic

"Smart and super articulate, Minister Farrakhan is perhaps the best living example of a black man ready, willing and able to 'tell it like it is' regarding who is responsible for racism in this country …. **every black person important enough to be interviewed is asked to condemn Minister Farrakhan…**"-Prof. Derrick Bell

"For the first time in African American history; a non-Christian leader is a significant, if not **the significant leader within Black America.**" -**Professor Michael Eric Dyson**

"I believe Minister Farrakhan is **the most important Muslim leader in the world**, who can best represent the concerns of the Islamic world to our government. I have spent countless hours with him."-**Jude Wanniski, Advisor Pres. Ronald Reagan**

Infamous FBI Director, J. Edgar Hoover wrote that he was working to **"prevent the rise of a messiah"** among Black people. For a leading law enforcement official to invoke religious terminology within his descriptions of his counterintelligence program is strange.

Love

It is significant because Messianic leadership brings together in the leader who possesses it, the most desired attributes of both secular and sacred models of leadership. Minister Farrakhan's life and leadership exemplifies this more than any other public figure. In fact, famous attorney William Kunstler said that in the modern context, Minister Farrakhan is the Messianic Black man that J. Edgar Hoover feared. He noted:

> "During his tenure and prior to the murder of Malcolm X, Director Hoover often spoke of the need for preventing the rise in this country of what he called "a Black Messiah." **Today, Minister Farrakhan, in my opinion, would be so considered, placing him in great jeopardy**."

However, far too often examinations and analysis of Minister Farrakhan's unique and phenomenal life fail to account for his sacred qualities. And I would argue that these hidden aspects of Minister Farrakhan's character need to be the leading considerations when his life, work and significance to Black people are weighed and measured. So, I close this article with more candid, yet profound testimonies from respected figures within Black America. Their testimonies help sum up the spiritual or sacred side of Minister Farrakhan's messianic role and leadership of his people.

"There is simply no Black person in the world that has — over so many years — been as consistent, as unrestricted, and as forthright in defending the humanity of Black people throughout the world against its attackers."-**Prof. Andre C. Willis**

"Louis insisted on getting down on his hands and knees on the floor to take my shoes off. You know, I'm overweight, and it's a difficult task to get shoes and socks off. And so, Louis said, 'I will do that.' And I said, "No, no.' And Louis said, 'No, I want to do it.' He took my shoes off and rubbed my feet to get the blood circulating."-**Prof. C. Eric Lincoln**

I said, "Minister let me just be honest with you. I'm broke. SCLC is broke. We don't have no money. But if you just help me and loan me a few dollars. In terms of my plight of SCLC. I promise you that I will multiply it and I will pay you back."

And the Minister looked at me and he said "My brother, you got my attention." He said, "Just one thing that I want you to realize. I'm going to give you the money that you asked for because I know you mean well and you are going to do what is right to uplift the organization." He said, "You must realize you can't pay me back. You just go and be successful with Dr. King's organization and make it work for our people and I will be proud and I will commend the fact that you had enough motivation to come all the way to Chicago and to share with me your vision and your strategy." - **Rev. Charles Steele, SCLC President**

"The Crucifixion of Lazarus":
Jewish Leaders Punish Black Celebs and Politicians over Minister Farrakhan

Inside the memos of J. Edgar Hoover's COINTELPRO memos he specifically said that he wanted the FBI to prevent the **"rise of a messiah"** who could unite Black people. As a member of the AAONMS (Ancient Arabic Order of the Nobles of the Mystic Shrine), Mr. Hoover's language is very significant. For, the Shriners are students of both Bible and the Holy Qur'an. And in both books a man named Jesus is referred to as the Messiah.

And both Bible and Holy Qur'an describe this man Jesus as being opposed by the Jewish leaders of his day. The Bible speaks of the chief priests, the Pharisees, the Sadducees and the Scribes as being the enemies of Jesus. And the New Testament of the Bible describes how these groups used their collective influence with the Roman government to have Jesus killed.

These wonderful scriptures when considered alongside the nefarious efforts of J. Edgar Hoover's FBI are key lenses through which we can see clearly the current chapter of what has been a long controversy of modern-day Jewish leaders' opposition to the ministry of the Honorable Minister Louis Farrakhan.

In 1994 the ADL's Steven Freeman wrote a report expressing the despair and anger of his organization that resulted from the growing appeal of the Hon. Min. Louis Farrakhan among a bevy of prominent Black celebrities, polticians and organizations. Freeman writes:

> "ADL is not going to make Farrakhan go away. What we can and should do is impose an obligation on those who deal with him, or, as in the case of universities, give him a platform."

Freeman's coded language saying "impose and obligation" is reminiscent of the infamous line in the Godfather movies, "make him and offer he can't refuse." And thus, the plan to punish and publicly crucify anyone who added to the fame and popularity of Minister Farrakhan was activated. This is the modern-day equivalent of the plan to crucify Lazarus. In the Bible, the New Testament Book of John includes the following verses.

> "When all the people heard of Jesus' arrival, they flocked to see him and also to see Lazarus, the man Jesus had raised from the dead. Then the chief priests decided to kill Lazarus, too, for it was because of him that many of the people had deserted them and believed in Jesus." – John 12: 9-11

Jewish leaders fear that the Honorable Minister Louis Farrakhan's message will become universally accepted and their control of Black organizations, and Black talent will cease. Freeman opens his report by stating the reason for his report:

> "Minister Louis Farrakhan, leader of the Nation of Islam (NOI) and long a voice of religious intolerance and racial divisiveness in this country, has recently attained a new level of acceptance among certain mainstream Black organizations and leaders. His "legitimation" has been reflected most notably by his participation last summer in the Parliament of the World's Religions, his obtaining federal funds for NOI's anti-AIDS efforts and the security services it has been providing at several federal housing projects, and his warm reception at the annual legislative meeting of the Congressional Black Caucus (CBC) last fall."

News that ADL head Jonathan Greenblatt wants former President Barack Obama to repudiate Minister Farrakhan broke this week. Greenblatt's act of intimidation is in reaction to the emergence of a beautiful photo of the Minister and then Sen. Obama while the two enjoyed a moment in one another's company at the 2005 Congressional Black Caucus conference. The photo was recently published in Askia Muhammad's very moving autobiography.

These news developments come at a time also when famed Black music icon Erykah Badu is being crucified in the media for refusing to repudiate Minister Farrakhan. And there are also rumors floating that Jay-Z's Grammy snub is connected to his mention of Jewish economic strength in his highly acclaimed 2017 project entitled "4:44."

What is taking place currently follows a pattern of behavior by Jewish leaders who intimidate and pressure high-profile Blacks and Whites to distance themselves from Minister Farrakhan. This wicked historical practice that has includes the plot to kill Jesus has taken place in America with the likes of the Rev. Jesse L. Jackson, Actor Bruce Willis, Philadelphia Mayor Ed Rendell, U.S.

Congressman John Conyers, Comedian Arsenio Hall, Memphis Mayor WW Herenton and Monroe Mayor Jamie Mayo among others.

Again, the scripture explains this behavior of Greenblatt, Foxman, Freeman and the Jewish leadership. Consider the following sample of Biblical verses found within the New Testament Gospels.

John 7:1

> "After this, Jesus traveled throughout Galilee. He did not want to travel in Judea, because the Jews there were trying to kill Him."

John 7:11

> "So, the Jews were looking for Him at the feast and asking, 'Where is He?'"

John 7:15

> "The Jews were amazed and asked, 'How did this man attain such learning without having studied?'"

John 9:22

> "His parents said this because they were afraid of the Jews. For the Jews had already determined that anyone who confessed Jesus as the Christ would be put out of the synagogue."

John 12:42

> "Nevertheless, many of the leaders believed in Him; but because of the Pharisees they did not confess Him, for fear that they would be put out of the synagogue."

John 19:38

> "Later on, Joseph of Arimathea, who was a disciple of Jesus (but secretly for fear of the Jews), asked Pilate's permission to take away the body of Jesus. Pilate granted it, so he came and removed His body."

John 20:19

> "It was the first day of the week, and that very evening, while the disciples were together with the doors locked for fear of the Jews, Jesus

came and stood among them. "Peace be with you!" He said to them."

The behavior of Jewish leaders show that they view Minister Farrakhan as a Messiah. Abraham Foxman said as he was on his way out of the leadership over the ADL that it is Louis Farrakhan who is the only leader in the African American community. In other words, Minister Farrakhan is the last man standing.

"The Godfather of Harlem" And The Corruption of Black History

According to the divine words of the Most Honorable Elijah Muhammad, there is an extraordinary power and value that results from the study of history. He noted in the very early years of his ministry, as he was giving guidance to those within his ministry class the following:

> First: History is above all our studies. The most attractive and best qualified to reward our research. As it develops the springs and motives of human actions and displays the consequence of circumstances which operates most powerfully on the destinies of the human being...

I cite these powerful words of the Most Honorable Elijah Muhammad, as Minister Malcolm X frequently did, because these words emphasize several important aspects of the value of history to the liberation struggle of Black people in America. And it is within the context of history's extreme importance to the Black community that I must look critically at the new Epix TV program series called "The Godfather of Harlem", and categorize it as another manifestation of a wicked and evil strategy known as The Corruption of Black History.

This, admittedly fictional series has chosen several legends from the history of Black people's struggle for liberation in America for the purpose of creating a drama about Harlem gangsters. However, the series portrays Black History luminaries Malcolm X, the Most Honorable Elijah Muhammad and Adam Clayton Powell in such a negative light, that it threatens to completely alter the positive and noble image of these men for many years to come.

This series demonstrates how under the guise of creative license and artistic expression, the entertainment industry is able to corrupt the history of Black people in America. Completely false and artificial narratives are created and delivered through the powerful delivery systems of films, music and television. What we are witnessing is the feeding of lies to the youth of the Black community, all in the name of "harmless entertainment."

The Black community should be morally outraged that many of those who opposed our leaders during their lifetimes are now in charge of their history and legacy!

This reminds me of the experience of the Honorable Minister Louis Farrakhan with certain Jewish rabbis with whom he had a dinner meeting with. They told Minister Farrakhan that "no one who is not deemed a friend of the Jewish people is ever written of well in history."

Is this the reason why the 3 Black leaders who are being negatively portrayed in The Godfather of Harlem are receiving such an ugly historical makeover? Is this revisionist history, that is being done through cinema, to tarnish 3 heroes of Black America who were at various times in their history falsely accused of anti-Semitism? It is no coincidence that 3 men who angered the Jewish community are now being repackaged as flawed, troubled and uninspiring.

The Most Honorable Elijah Muhammad was blamed for the problems in the Black-Jewish relationship

> Another potent generator of anti-Jewish attitudes is the new Negro Moslem or Negro nationalist movement. This movement is essentially a nationalist drive emphasizing the African background of the Negro and repudiating Christianity as the white man's religion. The cult does not stop here. It has become pro-Arab and openly anti-Jewish. Elijah Muhammed himself was given a weekly column in the Pittsburgh Courier to display his hatred of the white man, of Christianity and of Jews.
> -Negro-Jewish Relations by Will Maslow

Malcolm X was considered an anti-Semite even up until the end of his life

> Along with this newer, sanitized version of Malcolm X has come a whitewashing of his attitudes toward Jews. And whitewashing it is: the man currently portrayed as a fighter for racial justice was an anti-Semite who promoted virtually every antisemitic stereotype and whose legacy as a Jew-hater continues to be felt in the form of Black youth who justify their own bigotry toward Jews because even "Malcolm" denounced them.
> -Malcolm X and the Jews by Alan Shelton

Adam Clayton Powell was accused of making inflammatory anti-Semitic speeches

> Rev. Powell said "There are no Negroes in the American Jewish

Congress or in the national organizations of Italians-and show me a black Irishman, if you will. The NAACP has white people in high positions. We should boycott it." The inflammatory speeches by a Black Muslim or by a man like Powell get the widest attention among Negro masses.
-Jewish Groups Accentuate Positive In Fight Against Negro Anti-Semitism by Saul Carson

With clear eyes, we see how The Godfather of Harlem and the phenomenon of the corruption of Black History exposes the "the springs and motives of human actions and displays the consequence of circumstances which operates most powerfully on the destinies of the human being."

The motive of the entertainment industry today is to use entertainment as a weapon against the rise in youth activism that followed the killing of Mike Brown, Eric Garner and others, that ultimately gave birth to groups like Black Lives Matter. The desire is to disconnect today's activist and leaders from those of the past to destroy the continuity of the movement for liberation. It is to break the chain of intergenerational knowledge sharing that would result and give the power of the elder generation's wisdom to go along with the younger generations energy and vitality. On this aspect, Russian leader Vladimir Lenin observed:

> What in the course of history, has happened repeatedly to the theories of revolutionary thinkers and leaders of oppressed classes fighting for emancipation? During the lifetime of great revolutionaries, the oppressing classes constantly hounded them, received their theories with the most savage malice, the most furious hatred and the most unscrupulous campaigns of lies and slander. After their death, attempts are made to convert them into harmless icons…robbing the revolutionary theory of its substance, blunting its revolutionary edge and vulgarizing it.

The Corruption of Black History witnessed within The Godfather of Harlem comes at the same time that we learn of a major movie production on the life of Harriet Tubman involved producers making recommendations that the role of our great heroine be played by the popular white actress Julia Roberts. What an outrage!

The Corruption of Black History witnessed within The Godfather of Harlem comes at the same period of time when we are witnessing the Black Holocaust, also known as the Trans-Atlantic Slave Trade, undergo major revisions on the pages of High School history textbooks. According to Rachel Higson of The Prindle Post:

> In McGraw-Hill's "World Geography" textbook, a caption, overlapping a map of the United States, points generally to South Carolina and reads: "The Atlantic Slave Trade between the 1500s and 1800s brought millions of workers from Africa to the southern United States to work on agricultural plantations." The page is titled: "Patterns of Immigration." There is no mention of the violent removal of Africans from their homes and families. The caption uses the verb "brought," a euphemism that atrociously misrepresents the inhumane and deadly transportation of Africans across the Atlantic. The caption does not even present the existence of slave owners or traders; rather it converts slavery's malicious pillage, cruel exploitation, and inhumane treatment of Africans into an opportunity for employment on plantations.

The entire premise of The Godfather of Harlem is an outright lie. Malcolm X and Bumpy Johnson were not friends and close associates. According to Bumpy Johnson's wife the 2 men met in 1963 near the end of Malcolm's life, due to Bumpy's admiration for Black militants. She writes:

> In 1965, it was Bumpy who went around to all of the businesses, sporting men, and the East Side Italians to pay for the funeral of a man whom he'd just met but he truly admired. Bumpy was in prison in 1943 when this man, who then called himself "Detroit Red," moved to Harlem. Red was a fast talker who sported flashy zoot suits, flaming red conked hair, and ran numbers for West Indian Archie. By the time Bumpy got out of Dannemora in 1947, Detroit Red had fled Harlem for Boston. But when Bumpy came out of federal prison in 1963 the two finally met.... Bumpy was impressed with Malcolm, and one of those who supported Malcolm's new organization after he left the Nation of Islam in 1964. When he was assassinated while giving a lecture at the Audubon Ballroom in 1965, Bumpy was devastated. After delivering the funeral money he raised along with his own contribution to Malcolm's widow, Betty Shabazz, he bitterly told Junie, "I offered him protection, and he turned it down. Said he didn't want men with guns around him because it would be like he was trying to provoke something. He shoulda listened to me."

-Mayme Hatcher Johnson and Karen E. Quinones Miller Harlem Godfather: The Rap on my Husband, Ellsworth "Bumpy" Johnson

This phenomenon represents a "wickedly wise" and shrewd way of "ideological birth control." Destroy the image of those who have fought for justice among Black people, and you ensure that their revolutionary ideas won't be reborn among the youth generation. That this wicked plan is ever-unfolding is a call to action for scholars, teachers, preachers, parents and students. We must fight to take back control of our own people's history and legacy. The future of the Black community depends on it!

The Messiah Is A Black Woman's Son

The End Times Messiah
In the Jewish Christian and Islamic faiths, there is an expectation that the end of the world will be marked by the presence of a man referred to by the title of Messiah. This man called Messiah is greatly anticipated and expected because he will bring about justice throughout the earth. All of these faiths have what religious scholars refer to as an eschatology or "end time" prophecy and viewpoint. The prophecy regarding a man called Messiah is a common element among all of these-the Abrahamic faiths.

The Holy Qur'an, the Muslim book of scripture, says that the Messiah will bear a similitude and likeness to Jesus who lived 2,019 years ago. According to the Holy Qur'an, Jesus and Mary are a sign of something of great significance and vital importance. The Quranic scripture reads in Surah 23:50, **"And We made the son of Mary and his mother a sign, and We gave them refuge on a lofty ground having meadows and springs."**

Nowadays modern archaeology has borne witness to what the Hon. Elijah Muhammad, historians and Black nationalists have been teaching for years, that Jesus was a man of color, that Jesus was a Black man. And the Most Hon. Elijah Muhammad has taught that the Jesus of yesterday is a sign of the Messiah who comes at the end of this world. This means that as Jesus was the son of a Black woman; the end times Messiah is also the son of a Black woman.

These religious and spiritual ideas have great relevance to the current controversy of the Women's March on Washington.

Women's March Farrakhan Controversy
There have been many news reports that this movement for equality and justice led by a powerful group of women is being fractured due to the insistence on the part of many white feminists that the non-White women in the movement leadership, repudiate and disavow the Hon. Min. Louis Farrakhan. And so far, sisters Tamika Mallory, Linda Sarsour and Carmen Perez have refused to engage in the old 1980s era politics of "repudiate Farrakhan or else."

The opposition and hostile posture towards Minister Farrakhan is outrageous and reminds us of how fundamentally different is the struggle, history and experience lived by Black women and white women.

The opposition on the part of white feminist groups to Minister Farrakhan, which is based on the false charge of anti-Semitism, fits a pattern of history where white women have opposed the sons of Black women, especially the sons of Black women who were outspoken, bold, courageous and of a revolutionary spirit.

Minister Farrakhan is many things, an anti-Semite he is not. He is a however, a magnificent leader, teacher and guide to millions of people. He is the last national Black leader in America capable of galvanizing the masses. He is talented musician. He is extraordinarily charitable. He is strong, courageous and bold. To some he has been the father that they never had. To others he has been the source of inspiration that helped them to achieve their life's goals and dreams. Still for others he has been a deep and profound teacher of religion, scripture and theology. For many he has been the personification of manhood and brotherhood. He would probably prefer to just be considered a servant of Allah (God).

The Honorable Minister Louis Farrakhan is also "the son of a Black woman." And this aspect of who Louis Farrakhan is significant in understanding why he is being opposed so strongly by a very vocal element of the white feminist activists.

Black People's Suffering & Expectation For A Deliverer
Truth be told, it is the condition and destiny of the Black woman and her sons that is the key relationship that defines and frames the struggle of women of color in this country. The American Black woman and her son typifies the Mary and Jesus salvation symbolism described in the Christian and Muslim scriptures.

We should never forget that Black people in America have, since we were brought here to be made into chattel slaves, been the most oppressed of all people in America. Our suffering as a people has given birth to a yearning among us that a liberator and a deliverer and a savior would be borne among us to free us from the terrible oppressive control of the white ruling class. Religious scholar and Professor, Albert J. Raboteau quotes in his narrative entitled Slave Religion, Union Army Chaplain W. G. Kiphant on his work among freed slaves in Decatur Alabama. According to Chaplain Kiphant, **"There is no part of the Bible with which they (slaves) are so familiar as the story of the deliverance of the children of Israel. Moses is their ideal of all that is high, and noble, and perfect, in man. I think they have been accustomed to regard Christ not so much in the light of a spiritual Deliverer, as that of a second Moses who would eventually lead them out of their prison-house of bondage."**

Enslaved Black men and women had a real practical use for religion. They put their hope and faith in God to bless them with a son who would be a Moses and a Jesus for Black people. They yearned for a son who could both free them from the cruelty of their slave masters and punish the slave masters for their unyielding evil. And in their pure, simple and righteous faith, they didn't look for such a Moses and Jesus to float in on a cloud. They looked for their Moses and Jesus to be born from the blessed womb of a Black woman. In this way, enslaved Black women shared a common belief and hope for a Messiah that the Jewish women have shared. Rabbi Efraim Goldstein noted that **"It was the hope of every Jewish mother that her child might be the key to Israel's future. With the pain of labor came the comforting thought, 'Maybe my child will fulfill God's promises to the nation. Maybe my boy will be Messiah'."**

This historical truth has been dramatically depicted in the classic film The Autobiography of Miss Jane Pittman, Miss Jane played by film great Cicely Tyson says to her interviewer: **"We was always looking for somebody to lead em'. They did it during slavery, they did during the War, and they doing it now. They always do in the hard times, and the Lord always obliges 'em. When a child is born, old folks look at him and ask, Is you the one? When Lena had her baby boy, all the folks looked at him and say, You the one, Jimmy? Is you the one?"**

The knowledge of this expectation and yearning for a deliverer and liberator among Black people in America helps us to see clearly how the environment of Black people's suffering eventually gave birth to men like Nat Turner, Denmark Vesey, Gabriel Processor, Fredrick Douglass, Marcus Garvey, Paul Robeson, Malcolm X, Elijah Muhammad, Martin Luther King Jr., Stokely Carmichael (Kwame Toure) and Minister Louis Farrakhan.

These men are the fruit of the womb of Black mothers. They

represent the growth and gestation of the "seeds of yearning" from Black fathers. And all of these men have been hated by the white ruling class in America. All of these have been strong Black men, who were given birth to by strong Black women; men who grew to become thorns in the side of the white ruling class where the sons of white women are perched at the top.

The Divine Rise of Women

Again, this understanding is critical to properly frame the women's movement within the context of destiny and universal change. Black women must understand that their struggle is a divine struggle. It is not a struggle to make some small incremental change in the laws of America. It is not just a struggle to gain higher wages on par with men who work the same jobs that they do. And it is certainly not a struggle to have diversity within behemoth corporations who exploit the earth's natural resources and economically oppress poor people all around the world. The rise of women is being orchestrated by Allah (God), who appeared in the person of Master W. Fard Muhammad. The rise of women is a part of what the scriptures speak of when various passages and verses describe "the resurrection" of the dead.

Minister Farrakhan has taught that the resurrection of the dead is a symbolic reference to the mental and spiritual resurrection of humanity. He said that his teacher the Hon. Elijah Muhammad told him that the resurrection begins with Black people in America. And he said that the overwhelming majority of the work of the resurrection –some 75%-involves the protection, education, refinement, development and empowerment of women. And in 1985, Minister Farrakhan said before the world the following:

"Whenever a people disrespect the womb, they cut off their creative powers. When you disrespect woman, you disrespect that which absolutely shows you a part of the nature of God himself. This is why the oft repeated words of the Qur'an, Bismillah Ir-Rahman Ir-Rahim, you have Rahman and you have Rahim. You have the part coming out of the nature of God. Out of the love of the creator, he creates and does good for all his creatures. Then there is another part out of his love called Rahim or mercy, undeserved kindness, where he gives to you and you don't deserve anything. A mother will love her child when it is wrong; she will love it and be kind to

it when it doesn't deserve it. This is part of her nature.

When man denies woman, he denies a part of his own nature that gives him balance. This is why the world is messed up today! You have denied woman and you have denied the quality of mercy in your own self! So, I have sisters around me to say to the whole world; the woman must play an important part in the development of the nation or the nation will go to hell. The woman must not be looked at brothers as an object of pleasure and something to bear babies with no intelligence. Any nation that has an uncultivated woman becomes an uncultivated nation. It is a foolish man who denies the mosque to the woman. The woman should be in the mosque because when she knows the Qur'an, studies the Qur'an, takes the Qur'an and internalizes it. She takes your children and she nurtures them in the Quran. But when you push her out and make her to feel like she's not wanted, that she's not as good as the man, then there's a dislike in her and she passes it on to the children. And so, the children go away from Allah rather than coming toward Allah.

You mistreat your woman you mistreat yourself. You push your woman down you push yourself down. You pick your woman up; you and I go up. Are you speaking about Black women? I am speaking about all women no matter what their color is. And let me say this, those who condemn me, who call me a bigot; who call me a racist; who call me a hater; who call me an anti-Semite; I want you to listen to me real carefully tonight. And if anything like that comes out of my mouth raise your hand and stop me, hear. But you'd only be raising your hand no matter what your color is and cheering me on. Because that is what they say I am; but tonight, you judge for yourself."

Fear of A Black Messiah With An Iron Rule

There is an old saying **that "the hand that rocks the cradle is the hand that rules the world."** This phrase is taken from a poem written in 1865 by William Ross Wallace; a poem that celebrates the power of motherhood.

According to the Biblical eschatology, it is the Messiah who will triumph at the end of this present system of things. He will lead the resurrection and He will defeat Satan. But the Bible says that

His rule is "with a rod of iron." In the book of Revelation, chapter 2 verse 27 we read **"And he shall rule them with a rod of iron; as the vessels of a potter shall they be broken to shivers: even as I received of my Father."** An important commentary on this verse is found in Barnes Notes On The Bible:

"And he shall rule them with a rod of iron - There is an allusion here to Psalm 2:9; "Thou shalt break them with a rod of iron; thou shalt dash them in pieces like a potter's vessel." ...The allusion in the Psalm is to the Messiah as reigning triumphant over the nations, or subduing them under him; and the idea here, as in the previous verse, is, that his redeemed people will be associated with him in this dominion. To rule with a scepter of iron, is not to rule with a harsh and tyrannical sway, but with power that is firm and invincible. It denotes a government of strength, or one that cannot be successfully opposed; one in which the subjects are effectually subdued.

As the vessels of a potter shall they be broken to shivers - The ironic here is that of the vessel of a potter - a fragile vessel of clay - struck with a rod of iron and broken into fragments. That is, as applied to the nations, there would be no power to oppose His rule; the enemies of his government would be destroyed. Instead of remaining firm and compacted together, they would be broken like the clay vessel of a potter when struck with a rod of iron. The speaker does not intimate when this would be; but all that is said here would be applicable to that time when the Son of God will come to judge the world, and when His saints will be associated with him in his triumphs."

This Biblical description of the rule of the Messiah "with a rod of Iron" to break into pieces the wicked reminds me of a cartoon published in Harper's Weekly back during the 1800s. It was a cartoon that express the fear of the white ruling class. They feared the growing political and economic power of Blacks during reconstruction, and that one-day white people would be under the rule of Black people-their former slaves. And in the horrific image, it shows a white man having shot and killed a Black boy-the son of a Black mother. The caption read **"If I hadn't killed you, you would have grown up to rule me."**

The fear that Blacks will one day rule over whites is rooted in the fear of retaliation. It is like what Cain said in the Bible when he feared that because he killed Abel, he would be retaliated against and himself be killed, once what he did to his brother Abel was exposed.

And this is the reason why there is a Farrakhan Litmus Test. This is the reason why white feminists are drawing a line in the sand and telling Black women that if they want to receive their support, they have to disavow Minister Farrakhan.

Minister Farrakhan is the son of a beautiful West Indian mother the late Mother Sumayyah Farrakhan; the former Sara Mae Manning. Once the Minister told me about how his mother, while working as a domestic worker for a wealthy white family, saw him on television inside the home of the wealthy white family. This was during the early days of his ministry. But the news coverage of Minister Farrakhan's speech was on the television and both Minister Farrakhan's mother and the white woman who was her employer saw it. The Minister said that the white woman said in an angry manner, "I wonder who his mother is?" And Minister Farrakhan's mother said **"that is MY son!"**

The white employer was concerned as to who the fiery and revolutionary young man's mother was. She obviously knew that what she was witnessing in a young man who was fearlessly speaking truth to power and holding the white ruling class accountable for their offenses against the Black community was a product of how he was reared. She knew that what she was looking at was the offspring of a strong Black mother.

Are white feminists comfortable with Black women who give birth to revolutionary sons? Their reactions to Minister Farrakhan demonstrate that many of them are not. They ought to know that Black women are no longer raising their sons to be docile and malleable to an oppressive society out of fear that they may be killed. Those days are over, and we witness in the youth of today a courage and boldness unlike ever before.

J. Edgar Hoover looked for the Messiah among Black people. And like Pharaoh and Herod, in the Bible, he didn't look for him to honor and help him. **He looked for the Messiah among the sons of Black women for the purpose of neutralizing him**. In February 1968, Hoover wrote that one of his primary objectives of his new counterintelligence program was to: **"Prevent the RISE OF A "MESSIAH" who could unify, and electrify, the militant black nationalist movement. Malcolm X might have been such** a "messiah;" he is the martyr of the movement today. Martin Luther King, Stokely Carmichael and Elijah Muhammed all aspire to this position. Elijah Muhammed is less of a threat because of his age. King could be a very real contender for this position should he abandon his supposed "obedience" to "white, liberal doctrines" (nonviolence) and embrace black nationalism. Carmichael has the necessary charisma to be a real threat in this way."

I find it intriguing that Hoover noted that in order to be the Messiah, Dr. King for instance, would have to give up obedience to white liberals. In Hoover's estimation, you can't be the Messiah if you're beholden to white liberal ideas. Hoover understood that the Messiah would be of a Black Nationalist orientation.

White feminists don't want the hand on the cradle of the world rulers to be the hand of a Black mother. White feminists want Black women to help them do what New York Times editor Brent Staples said is their goal; to seek **"parity with their husbands and brothers."** Staples in his piece titled How The Suffrage Movement Betrayed Black Women points that in the history of the struggle for the right to vote, we can see the fundamentally different struggles of Black women versus that of White women. He notes how Black women were struggling to find "a means of empowering black communities besieged by the reign of racial terror that erupted after Emancipation."

That the White female's motive and reason for their struggle for equality was to achieve **"parity with their husbands and brothers"** is to say that they wanted take a greater role in the systems of oppression that advanced by their husbands and brothers. In other words, they wanted to be co-equal colonizers; co-equal imperialists; co-equal slave masters; co-equal exploiters; co-equal oppressors. Again, this is the real reason they want Black women to disavow a man that their own wombs have produced-the Hon. Min. Louis Farrakhan.

In closing, could you imagine Harriett Tubman being asked to repudiate Nat Turner or Rosa Parks being asked to disavow Martin L. King Jr.; or Angela Davis to repudiate Malcolm X.? It sounds ridiculous to suggest such foolishness. Nevertheless, it is what is being demanded by white feminists who are separating themselves from Women's March Leaders like Tamika Mallory, Linda Sarsour and Carmen Perez because of Minister Farrakhan.

I am grateful that they have not succumbed to it, because as long as they stand on principle, they will be victorious despite the opposition of their critics.

The Mis-Education of Yvette Carnell et.al.

Popular social media commentator Yvette Carnell recently took to the World Wide Web to utilize the YouTube platform to make an attempt to stall the growing momentum of the Justice or Else Movement and the increasing appeal and acceptance of the message of the Honorable Minister Louis Farrakhan. Brother Demetric Muhammad who serves on the Honorable Minister Louis Farrakhan's Research Team and is an Assistant Student Minister of Muhammad Mosque No. 55 provides the following points and documentation to refute her subsequent claims made in her 40-minute conversation with Dr. Boyce Watkins. In responding to Ms. Carnell, we take the opportunity to respond to those who may share her views, views that we reject as unjustified by the facts of Minister Farrakhan's magnificent history of service to the Black community and oppressed people throughout the Earth. We thank Dr. Boyce Watkins for giving us an opportunity to put forth critical facts to better educate Ms. Carnell and the general public.

1. Carnell claims that Minister Farrakhan has called for a race war.

This claim evaporates when one actually reviews the entirety of the Minister's Miami message. The quote in question reads as follows:

"Death is sweeter than to continue to live and bury our children while White folks give the killers hamburgers. Death is sweeter than watching us slaughter each other to the joy of a 400-year-old enemy. Death is sweeter. The Qur'an teaches persecution is worse than slaughter then it says, retaliation is prescribed in matters of the slain. Retaliation is a prescription from God to calm the breasts of those whose children have been slain. ***If the federal government will not intercede in our affairs****, then we must rise up and kill those who kill us, stalk them and let them feel the pain of death that we are feeling,"*

This statement is a conditional statement and points to an obvious conclusion since self-preservation is widely considered a primal and first of the laws of nature. If federal protection for the Black man dissolves or is absent, then Black people are left without any guarantee of safety in a society that daily reminds us of our status as an unwanted former slave.

Historians know of the horrific effects of the infamous Compromise of 1877. This compromise was arrived at to settle the Presidential election of 1876, a race that was tied between Rutherford B. Hayes and Samuel Tilden. Its effect on Black people came as a result of federal troops being pulled out of the South as a stipulation of the compromise that allowed for candidate Rutherford B. Hayes to become the 19th President of the United States. The removal of federal troops from the South ended Reconstruction and paved the way for the birth of the Ku Klux Klan and other anti-Black terrorist groups who seized upon vulnerable Black communities without any protection from their government. Popular stories of the destruction of Rosewood, Florida and Greenwood, Oklahoma (aka Black Wall St.) are just the tip of the iceberg. There are many hidden histories of the Black man's time as a self-respecting, entrepreneurial, civic minded, industrious builder of Black Towns and cities. It was the Black man and woman's early adoption of what we see today as the "immigrant model." Yet the survival of these municipalities was like any nation or state, dependent upon having a defense force and protective apparatus to secure its people and property.

Carnell's worries that the Minister will inspire the murder of all the "good white folk" are actually unnecessary. Particularly when you consider that the Minister's beautiful hours long message in Miami included the following truths: **"How can we charge others with the crime of killing us without due process and lying about it when we are killing each other? And we won't march on ourselves, nor will we even rise up to condemn ourselves for what we are doing to ourselves**. And in the gangs when we kill we don't talk, so nobody is arrested and charged with murder and brought to what is called justice."

In this unmentioned passage of his message, The Minister reacts to the Black victimizers of the Black community which if we are to "kill those who kill us" should also be targets of retaliatory justice.

No, Minister Farrakhan wasn't calling for a race war; he was giving to his pained and grief-stricken Black audience an exhortation toward what is the first law of nature, self-preservation. And the fact that he has to remind us of this law is a woeful indicator of just how un-natural our oppressors have made us.

An unlikely source is available to help Ms. Carnell et.al to see that Minister Farrakhan's history of peace mitigates against any legitimate concern over a Farrakhan-led race war. In 1997 Rabbi Bruce Khan offered his observations in the aftermath of his attending of the Million Man March in 1995 in these words: ***"people who listen to him do not go chasing down Jews, or gays or Whites or Koreans to beat them and murder them."***

As for as the main action directive put forth by the Minister-which was curiously absent from Ms. Carnell's critique- is his call for a Christmas holiday boycott. Similar to Dr. Martin Luther King Jr.'s insistence that Black people "re-distribute the pain" of injustice, Minister Farrakhan prescribed to his enthusiastic audience the idea of massive economic withdrawal from the merchants and bankers who make their largest profits each year during the Christmas season. We might describe it as 'Retaliatory Economic Justice.' He instructed that we buy no gifts and presents beginning with the 'Black Friday' sales holiday. He made a powerful case that this year we make Christmas once again about the love and sacrifice of Jesus Christ. His call was essentially a "mass" of Black people for the adoption of the principles of Jesus- the Christ. This is the same Jesus who is pictured in scripture as running the corrupt merchants or "money-changers" out of God's holy temple. From Minister Farrakhan's point of view, justice for the Black man and woman will remain ever elusive until the modern merchants and "money-changers" experience the pain of economic loss and injury.

2. Carnell claimed Minister Farrakhan is not a leader of Black people in America

Again, Carnell's claims evaporate before what has been the documented reaction to Minister Farrakhan's uncompromising leadership from Jewish leaders, academics and even critics. Consider the following sampling of testimonies.

"The only leadership that now exists in that community"— the "African American community"— "is Louis Farrakhan. Farrakhan can assemble 20,000 people several times a year..." -Abraham Foxman

For the first time in African American history; a non-Christian leader is a significant, if not the significant leader within Black America." -Professor Michael Eric Dyson

"The appearance of Louis Farrakhan at Madison Square Garden on October 7 demonstrated, without doubt, that he is now America's preeminent black leader."-Author Julius Lester

3. Carnell claimed that Minister Farrakhan is not a threat to white supremacy because he isn't dead yet.

This is one of the most ridiculous assertions I have ever heard. It comes from the same school of thought that tells articulate, intelligent and well-mannered Black children that they are acting white, because to be authentically Black you must be the opposite of all those worthy character traits.

According to Unitarian Universalist minister and scholar the Rev. Dr. William Alberts, PhD of Boston University, Minister Farrakhan **"represents a serious threat to America's racial hierarchy**. *The hierarchy cannot control or buy his accommodation or "integration" as a Black leader. He dares to point out and challenge the "white supremacy" of the "founding fathers," forcing White America to recognize and deal with the fact that many of the signers of the Declaration of Independence, which declared freedom and equality for all, were themselves slave holders, and that even "Honest Abe" had a racist "wart" or two that can no longer be covered up. Farrakhan also has the power to initiate a call that led to at least twice and possibly three or more times as many African American men to respond as the U.S. Park Police counted-in spite of all the print aimed at discrediting the Nation of Islam leader and derailing the March."*

Ms. Carnell should study the thoughts of noted Professor Derrick Bell who spoke on how the white power structure is so threatened by Minister Farrakhan that they have developed what some have called the "Farrakhan Litmus Test." According to Professor Bell: *"Smart and super articulate, Minister Farrakhan is perhaps the best living example of a black man ready, willing and able to 'tell it like it is' regarding who is responsible for racism in this country ....* **every black person important enough to be interviewed is asked to condemn Minister Farrakhan..."** -Prof. Derrick Bell

To have a further appreciation for the fact that Minister Farrakhan's redemptive work among Black people is deemed an ever-present threat to the status quo of American white supremacy consider that in 1984 the Honorable Minister Louis Farrakhan was censured by the highest legislative body in world—the United States Senate—in a 95 to 0 vote.

Minister Farrakhan's international influence among African and Islamic leaders is an area where he is deemed a particular threat. The American government fearing the potential of Minister Farrakhan's ideas being backed by financial resources forbid the Minister from receiving the 1996 International Human Rights Award given by the people of Libya. The award worth $250,000 was going to be accompanied by a billion-dollar donation to the work of the Nation of Islam by Libyan leader Muammar Gadhafi.

I wonder what Ms. Carnell would think of Cuban revolutionary Fidel Castro who is reputed to have survived an estimated 638 assassination attempts! According to her logic Commandante Castro's longevity disqualifies him as a true revolutionary.

4. Carnell claimed that the Million Man March didn't accomplish anything for Black people in America

According to an October 10, 1996 USA Today article written by reporters Gary Fields and Maria Puente the Million Man March was directly or indirectly responsible for the following positive results

- **One million new voters.**
- **Up to 15,000 new applicants wanting to adopt black children**
- **A decrease in black-on-black crime.**
- **Increased child support payments by black fathers.**
- **Increased interest among black men in serving their communities.**

5. Carnell said Minister Farrakhan is responsible for the assassination of Malcolm X

This is a sensitive issue and exposes that Carnell has "drank the

Kool-Aid" of the anti-Farrakhan propagandists who have worked to position a dead Malcolm X against a living Louis Farrakhan at the expense of Black youth. And there are many facts that we have prepared in two 2-hour Power Point Presentations that completely destroys the old propagandist narrative aimed at demagnetizing the Honorable Minister Louis Farrakhan among the young within the Black community. This strategy is borne out of decades old COINTELPRO objectives that explicitly documents their goal of preventing the Nation of Islam and other Nationalist groups from gaining "youthful adherents."

Carnell should be educated in the fact that according to a January 22, 1969 memo the FBI takes credit for the assassination of Malcolm X. Jim Van derWaal and Ward Churchill discuss this memo in their book The COINTELPRO Papers. They write: *"the accompanying January 22, 1969 memo from the SAC, Chicago, to the Director makes clear;* **the NOI factionalism at issue didn't "just happen."** *Rather, it had "been developed" by deliberate Bureau actions – through infiltration and the "sparking of acrimonious debates within the organization," rumormongering, and other tactics designed to foster internal disputes – which were always the standard fare of COINTELPRO.* **The Chicago SAC, Marlin Johnson, who would shortly oversee the assassinations of Illinois Black Panther Party leaders Fred Hampton and Mark Clark, makes it quite obvious that he views the murder of Malcolm X as something of a model for "successful" counterintelligence operations.**

Furthermore, those close to Malcolm X have gone on record to make the point that Malcolm X had evolved to regret his pointing the finger at the Nation of Islam as being out to kill him. His secretary, Ms. Sarah Mitchell, wrote of her experiences with Brother Malcolm in her manuscript entitled **Shepherd of the Black Sheep**.

"His philosophy was evolving almost on a weekly basis," Mitchell said. *On Feb. 20, 1965-the eve of his assassination- Malcolm X told aides that he should not have criticized Elijah Muhammad, leader of the NOI, Mitchell said. Malcolm had severed ties with the Muslim sect and had accused it publicly of the recent bombing of his house.* **"He said now anyone could kill him and everyone would blame the Muslims,"** *Mitchell said.* **"He said, 'We've been set up, and they succeeded.'"** *Malcolm X planned to*

recant his criticism of Muhammad at the Harlem rally that afternoon, Mitchell said, but he was gunned down before he could do so. She disputes a widely held belief that angry Muslims were behind the assassination."

6. Carnell claimed that Minister Farrakhan has not done anything for Black people and has no record of leadership

Leadership among people is analogous in function to that of a head on a body. Thusly a good leader provides sight or vision; thought and guidance as well as speech and hearing. The Minister's long history of leadership is too numerous to enumerate his most significant accomplishments in such a short treatise. But the record is clear he has been an effective head.

Some commentators make a case for the Million Man March as being the most significant achievement of his leadership. Pastor Jamal Bryant recently spoke at a seminar on the subject of *The Black Church and Social Justice.* In his comments to a predominantly Christian audience he pushed back against the criticism he received for hosting Minister Farrakhan on his televised and webcast WORD Network program. He reminded his audience of the fact that no Christian leader has ever assembled a million people.

The Minister's accomplishments are numerous and the Million Man March is an easily identified victory. But when we consider all of the casualties in America's so-called War on Drugs, the Minister's work to end this scourge is another strong contender for his top accomplishment.

His male followers, as a result of his inspiration and guidance, organized themselves to form what became known as the Dopebusters. The Dopebusters, which were members of the Nation of Islam's men's class known as the Fruit of Islam, operated in in 5 states, as different chapters of the NOI Security Agency won bids to patrol-crime and drug-infested housing projects in D.C., NYC, LA, Baltimore, Philadelphia, Pittsburgh and Chicago.

The Dopebusters were very successful as evident by the reduction of crime in the public housing apartment communities that they served. In New York at Ocean Towers, vacancy was routinely 30%

as a result of the high rates of crime. After the Muslim security did their work that vacancy rate dropped to 1%. They were so effective Jewish resident Bonnie Kirshtein told the New York Times that, **"They did the best security I've seen in 20 years. If they were doing their job, what was the problem? I don't hide what I am and they treated me with the utmost respect."** Their work in Los Angeles brought about a 75% reduction in crime in the Holiday Venice Apartment Complex.

There are numerous stories that document that Minister Farrakhan's work to eradicate drugs and crime wherever the presence of his followers and his message have gone. There is a serious value in re-viewing the Dopebuster's history not just to vindicate the leadership of Minister Farrakhan, but to serve as a tried and true model that courageous Black men around the country can adopt to begin to patrol and protect their own communities.

If there was unlimited time and space I could go on and on in educating Ms. Carnell in why her views, feelings and perspective on the Honorable Minister Louis Farrakhan are wrong. What I have provided does not discuss the Minister's role in producing gang truces between rival street organizations. I haven't discussed his impact in Hip-Hop to influence the creation of socially conscious rap groups and lyrics, or the settling of "rap beefs." I haven't even discussed his single-handed rebuilding of the Nation of Islam that began in 1977 with Minister Farrakhan and only one other brother (Jabril Muhammad). His international work has also not been brought forth. Yet we have given enough for Ms. Carnell to do an about face if she is to be moved by facts and empirical data.

Whether she will or not remains to be seen, but at least she cannot say that we did not make an effort to educate her in an area where she was ignorant.

The Strategy of Ritual Defamation: Chicago Sun-Times & Chicago Tribune Unite Against Minister Farrakhan

As each day passes, we are witnessing the work product of a powerful group of entities that have privately agreed to work together for the common goal of the defamation and character assassination of the Honorable Minister Louis Farrakhan. It is my belief that the ultimate goal of this defamation and character assassination campaign is to inspire and provide a justification for a literal physical assassination of Black America's most ardent and beloved champion, the Honorable Minister Louis Farrakhan.

This week both of the major Chicago based news organs-Chicago Sun Times and Chicago Tribune-showcased editorials lambasting Father Michael Pfleger and the Honorable Minister Louis Farrakhan. One article was written by Rabbi Ari Hart (Chicago Tribune) and the other was written by Jay Tcath (Chicago Sun Times).

Such false and opinion-based commentaries brought back to my remembrance an essay written by political archivist and researcher of political movements, Mr. Laird Wilcox. Mr. Wilcox's famous **Wilcox Collection of Contemporary Political Movements** was housed at the University of Kansas' *Kenneth Spencer Research Library* where Mr. Wilcox was honored in 2005 for his research and archivist work.

Consider how what Mr. Wilcox defines and explains as the practice of **ritual defamation** applies to the smear campaign that currently targets Minister Farrakhan. Mr. Wilcox states:

"Defamation is the destruction or attempted destruction of the reputation, status, character or standing in the community of a person or group of persons by unfair, wrongful, or malicious speech or publication....the central element is defamation in retaliation for the real or imagined attitudes, opinions or beliefs of the victim, with **the intention of silencing or neutralizing his or her influence, and/or making an example of them so as to discourage similar independence** and "insensitivity" or non-observance of taboos. It is different in nature and degree from simple criticism or disagreement in that it is aggressive, organized and skillfully applied, often by an organization or representative of a special interest group, and in that it consists of several characteristic elements.... Like all propaganda and disinformation campaigns it is accomplished primarily through the manipulation of words and symbols. **It is not used to persuade, but to punish.** Although it may have cognitive elements, its thrust is primarily emotional. **Ritual Defamation is used to hurt, to intimidate, to destroy, and to persecute, and to avoid the dialogue, debate and discussion upon which a free society depends.** On those grounds it must be opposed no matter who tries to justify its use."

Mr. Wilcox includes 8 elements to the practice of ritual defamation. They are listed below to show how each one has appeared as an element of the character assassination of Minister Farrakhan of which the Tribune and Sun Times are key participants within.

Elements of Ritual Defamation

1. In a ritual defamation the victim must have violated a particular taboo in some way, usually by expressing or identifying with a forbidden attitude, opinion or belief. It is not necessary that he "do" anything about it or undertake any particular course of action, only that he engages in some form of communication or expression.

Minister Farrakhan was bold enough to defend Rev. Jesse Jackson against groups like Jews Against Jackson way back in 1984. These groups firebombed Rev. Jackson's campaign offices. Minister Farrakhan warned the Jewish community against any plans it had to harm Rev. Jackson as it would provoke a negative response from the Black community. Following the Minister's defense of Rev. Jackson, Nat Hentoff of the Village Voice and Nathan Perlmutter of the ADL began calling the Minister the new "Black Hitler".

2. The method of attack in a ritual defamation is to assail the character of the victim, and never to offer more than a perfunctory challenge to the particular attitudes, opinions or beliefs expressed or implied. Character assassination is its primary tool.

This is always the case where the Minister is concerned. He is, at this point in time, simply called an anti-Semite without any proof being provided to support such a claim. And at no point have we witnessed his critics deconstructing his arguments and conducting an investigation of his sources. We only see name calling, hence "Character Assassination 101."

3. An important rule in ritual defamation is to avoid engaging in any kind of debate over the truthfulness or reasonableness of what has been expressed, only condemn it. To debate opens the issue up for examination and discussion of its merits, and to consider the evidence that may support it, which is just what the ritual defamer is trying to avoid. **The primary goal of a ritual defamation is censorship and repression.**

Over the years, Minister Farrakhan has called for an open dialogue or debate with the leaders of the organizations who have falsely labeled him an anti-Semite. Yet over and over again they refuse to debate the issues in an open forum.

4. The victim is often somebody in the public eye - someone who is vulnerable to public opinion - although perhaps in a very modest way. It could be a schoolteacher, writer, businessman, minor official, or merely an outspoken citizen. Visibility enhances vulnerability to ritual defamation.

This applies to Minister Farrakhan in the sense that he is a high profile and highly visible personality. In fact, the Minister has been regularly referred to as the most important leader within the entire Black community

5. An attempt, often successful, is made to involve others in the defamation. In the case of a public official, other public officials will be urged to denounce the offender. In the case of a student, other students will be called upon, and so on.

As in the case of Father Michael Pfleger, Tamika Mallory, Rev. Jesse Jackson and others, we see how often anyone who has a high profile or a prominent place within American society is called upon to repudiate the Minister. In fact, the "repudiate Farrakhan" phenomenon has become a routine trope in Black electoral politics.

6. In order for a ritual defamation to be effective, the victim must be dehumanized to the extent that he becomes identical with the offending attitude, opinion or belief, and in a manner, which distorts it to the point where it appears at its most extreme. A victim defamed as a "racist" or "anti-Semitic" will be identified with the worst images of racism or anti-Semitism, such as lynchings or gas chambers.

This is what Rabbi Hart attempts to do in his article for the Chicago Tribune. He falsely suggests that random Black men in New York City have been inspired by Minister Farrakhan to commit an act of violence against a Jewish man. Minister Farrakhan has had a public ministry for more than 60 years and his ministry has never been accused of inspiring acts of violence or crime. On the contrary, Minister Farrakhan inspires crime fighters and people who become abstinent, chaste, teetotalers even.

7. Also to be successful, a ritual defamation must bring pressure and humiliation on the victim from every quarter, including family and friends. If the victim has school children, they may be taunted and ridiculed as a consequence of adverse publicity. If they are employed, they may be fired from their job. If the victim belongs to clubs or associations, other members may be urged to expel them.

Over the years Minister Farrakhan's economic initiatives, that were inaugurated to benefit the larger community of Black and poor people nationally, have been sabotaged by issues related to this charge. George Johnson of Johnson Products hair care and beauty line was pressured by his Jewish distributors to renege on a promise to manufacture a national Black hair and beauty product line called "Clean and Fresh."

8. Any explanation the victim may offer, including the claim of being misunderstood, is considered irrelevant. To claim truth as a defense for a politically incorrect value, opinion or belief is interpreted as defiance and only compounds the problem. Ritual defamation is often not necessarily an issue of being wrong or incorrect but rather of "insensitivity" and failing to observe social taboos.

Consider the recent ban of Minister Farrakhan's book series The Secret Relationship Between Blacks and Jews from Amazon.Com, or the ban against the physical presence of Minister Farrakhan in the United Kingdom. Both are evidence of the presence of this final element of ritual defamation. At no point, have those books been accused of being false. In fact, at no point has Minister Farrakhan been accused of telling lies or teaching falsehoods. He is simply accused of being anti-Semitic. And the only proof ever offered is a sound bite taken out of context.

For sure, there is no other public figure that the strategy of ritual defamation has been used upon more than the Honorable Minister Louis Farrakhan. And the fact that he is an anointed servant of God, makes us to see this strategy of ritual defamation as a critical part of the process of crucifixion.

The Unconquerable Nation of Islam: 90 Years of Service & Survival

"And set out to them a parable of the people of the town, when apostles came to it. When **We sent to them two, they rejected them both**; then **We strengthened (them) with a third, so they said: Surely, we are sent to you**. They said: You are only mortals like ourselves, nor has the Beneficent revealed anything — you only lie. They said: Our Lord knows that we are surely sent to you." Holy Qur'an 36: 13-16

I am so happy and grateful to be a registered member of the Nation of Islam. I join all of the many believers and supporters in wishing the membership of the Nation of Islam in America, a very happy 90th Anniversary.

I am so happy to live and be a witness to our continued growth and survival in the midst of the many forces of evil who have worked hard to destroy us, yet Allah (God) continues to demonstrate that He is with the Nation of Islam, and that He approves of the work of His servants the Most Honorable Elijah Muhammad and the Honorable Minister Louis Farrakhan. Our work is far from complete, but with such powerful and hostile adversaries, our mere survival is a triumph that is worthy of admiration and celebration.

The United States of America is analogous to the "town" referred to in the passage that introduces this article.

This passage describes 3 servants of Allah (God) who were sent to an extravagant and wicked society to warn them and deliver to them the message of repentance. Yet the people in this "town" rejected them. They opposed them and, as was the case with nearly all of the divine servants of Allah (God) described within the scriptures, sought to kill them and those who followed them.

Master W. Fard Muhammad, The Most Honorable Elijah Muhammad and the Honorable Minister Louis Farrakhan have all survived the evil onslaughts of their nefarious enemies, who are the same enemies of the masses of Black People in America. Their unconquerable spirit, which is the holy, divine spirit of Allah (God), is the root reason why the Nation of Islam has survived within the hostile American environment for now 90 years. We survive, not just for survival's sake, but to be able to awaken the sleeping masses of our people, and oppressed men and women throughout the world; to be able to share with them what has proven to be the invincible truth of God, Self, The Enemy of God and The Knowledge of the Time and What Must Be Done in these perilous times.

The United States Government has failed in its efforts to destroy the Nation of Islam. The FBI ultimately had to admit that:

> "For years the Bureau has operated a counterintelligence program against the NOI and [Elijah] Muhammad...despite these efforts, he continues unchallenged in the leadership of the NOI and the organization itself, in terms of membership and finances, has been unaffected." —Special Agent in Charge in Chicago, FBI Memo, April 22, 1968

The Anti-Defamation League of B'nai B'rith has built a reputation of targeting and tarnishing the name and work of the Honorable Minister Louis Farrakhan for many years, yet outgoing ADL head Abraham Foxman stated in his April, 2013 exit interview with Ha'aretz Magazine:

> "The only leadership that now exists in that community"—the "African American community"— "is Louis Farrakhan. Farrakhan can assemble 20,000 people several times a year..."

The American Jewish Committee noted in the early 1970s the unconquerable quality of the Nation of Islam when they stated:

> "Only one movement (The Black Muslims) though looked upon by disfavor by the major black civil rights groups, remains strong, consequential, cohesive, influential..." -Phillip E. Hoffman, American Jewish Committee, 1972

The Nation's survival, is not just a feather in the cap of the Muslims or mere source of pride for the faithful. On the contrary, the survival of the Nation of Islam means that our salvific work- serving as a literal *salvation army* within suffering Black communities continues.

To appreciate the necessary presence of the Nation of Islam among Black people in America, consider the revolutionary presence of Islam among our enslaved ancestors. European colonizers and enslavers noticed early on, the problem that the religion of Islam presented them in their quest for the genocidal commercializing of African flesh. Spain was one such European nation that made it against their law to knowingly import any Black Muslims or Latino Muslims into colonies that they controlled. The author of *Black Conquistadors: Armed Africans in Early Spanish America* Matthew Restall notes:

> "In the early sixteenth century Spanish Crown legislation aimed at reducing the incidence of slave rebellions attempted to prevent the importation into the colonies of Africans deemed most pugnacious. The Crown and its colonial officials varied on their opinions as to which Africans were the most bellicose, but two categories appeared most consistently in such commentary and legislation. These were Muslims (or anyone of African descent who may have been exposed to Islam, which periodically included mulattos, ladinos or Hispanized Blacks, and anyone from Guinea); and Wolofs described in royal legislation of 1532 as "arrogant, disobedient, rebellious and incorrigible."

Through the bold teaching of an invincible truth, along with its work to challenge the forces of oppression in America, the Nation of Islam has been an indispensable factor in the overall survival of Black America. In truth the genocidal plans against Black life in America circa the 20th Century til present have been so shrewd and scientific that it causes us to appreciate in a deep way, the Nation of Islam's frequent interference with these genocidal plans, serving as the proverbial "watchman on the wall" alarming the poor and oppressed of the wicked plans of our enemies. It certainly causes me to conclude that in the modern times, Black America has survived because the Nation of Islam has survived. The Nation of Islam's salvific work and necessary presence has frequently been cited.

Professor Andre C. Willis has called out Minister Farrakhan for being in a class by himself as a defender of Black People:

> "The best of the legacy of Farrakhan is twofold. First, he has demonstrated a deep understanding of and shown an unswerving courage to publicly detail the lived reality of anti-black racism. There is simply no Black person in the world that has — over so many years — been as consistent, as unrestricted, and as forthright in defending the humanity of Black people throughout the world against its attackers."

Author James Baldwin has proclaimed that the Most Honorable Elijah Muhammad has achieved the impossible as a reformer and restorer of Black People:

> "Elijah Muhammad has been able to do what generations of welfare workers and committees and resolutions and reports and housing projects and playgrounds have failed to do: to heal and redeem drunkards and junkies, to convert people who have come out of prison and to keep them out, to make men chaste and women virtuous, and to invest both the male and the female with a pride and a serenity that hang about them like an unfailing light. He has done all these things, which our Christian church has spectacularly failed to do."

Professor Herbert Berg has discovered that the most important Muslim in American history, is the Most Honorable Elijah Muhammad:

> "Approximately 30 percent of the United States' six to eight million Muslims are African American, making Islam the second most popular religion among African Americans. Although the vast majority of these African American Muslims are now Sunni Muslims, many (or perhaps their parents or grandparents) were introduced to Islam through the Nation of Islam, a movement that was exclusively Black…. Its leader for over forty years, Elijah Muhammad, was therefore arguably the most important person in the development of Islam in America…"

Professor Michael Eric Dyson had lauded the Nation of Islam as a legendary redeemer of Black Manhood:

> "The Nation has worked diligently to make proud men out of black prisoners, those in jail or those whose self-image is distorted because they are captives to a worship of the white world…. Long before the decline of black male life became widely apparent; and long before black males were vilified and glamorized by both the cultural right and the left, the Nation of Islam preached its own brand of salvation for black males. And from the very beginning, the core of the Nation's message has not changed. NOI followers believe that black men can be saved only by being restored as loving leaders in black families where they receive and return adoration and respect."

July 4, 2020 is our 90th Anniversary and we are by "no ways tired"; our work continues; the future is ours!

The Word of God is Dangerous:
The Real Reason Facebook Banned Our Beloved Minister Farrakhan

Long before the recent controversy between the Jewish community and the Honorable Minister Louis Farrakhan, the American ruling class of plantation owners and slave masters understood the revolutionary potential of the "word of God." Specifically, the sacred texts of Jews, Christians and Muslims all condemn slavery and oppression in all of its forms. They therefore knew that in order for the enormously profitable enterprise of enslaving Black people to remain in existence they had to completely control the religious training and instruction of their chattel slaves.

The historical context of the Black man and woman's experience in America should always frame our analysis and interpretation of current events and trends. Especially since, the newly discovered phenomenon known as epigenetics has proven scientifically that our people's traumatic and horrific suffering in the past has been passed down to us through the DNA of our parents. And so now, every member of the Black community is intimately and inextricably tied to our ancestors and their life experiences. And we must decide whether or not we will continue to be victimized as they were, or we will courageously struggle against every impediment to our liberation and independence.

What is happening to our beloved Minister Farrakhan is wicked and evil. It is a modern attempt to stop the dangerous word of God from liberating the masses of the American people. They are doing to Minister Farrakhan the same thing they did to the Bible.

According to NPR reporter Michel Martin in her December 9, 2018 report **Slave Bible from 1800s Omitted Key Passages That Could Incite Rebellion,** plantation owners feared constantly that their slaves would revolt and overthrow their wicked slave system. This fear of revolt caused them to literally castrate the Bible. They created an edited, censored and spiritually impotent text to give to their slaves, seeking to hide the elements within the scriptures that condemned slavery and oppression. Martin's article states:

> "...rare Bible from the 1800s that was used by British missionaries to convert and educate slaves...What's notable about this Bible is not just

> its rarity, but its content, or rather the lack of content. It excludes any portion of text that might inspire rebellion or liberation.... About 90 percent of the Old Testament is missing [and] 50 percent of the New Testament is missing...Put in another way, there are 1,189 chapters in a standard protestant Bible. This Bible contains only 232...passages that could have prompted rebellion were removed, for example: "There is neither Jew nor Greek, there is neither bond nor free, there is neither male nor female: for ye are all one in Christ Jesus". - Galatians 3:28"

This is important historical context through which to view Facebook/Instagram's decision to censure and ban the strongest and most effective preacher of the word of God in America-the Honorable Minister Louis Farrakhan. They literally said that they consider him "dangerous." Yet the Minister is a man who forbids all of his followers from carrying or possessing in our homes weapons. In fact, of the Nation of Islam Canadian Professor Martha F. Lee has written:

> "In many ways then, the NOI provides a case study of why and how a religious movement with a radical belief system did not engage in violence related to its doctrine. Its members waited in faith for Allah to destroy the forces that oppressed them. Instead, it was law enforcement agencies that more actively fostered violence in the hope of destroying the NOI."

No, the Minister is not dangerous to the public peace. He is not dangerous to the well-being of the American people. His ministry however, threatens all that is harmful to the future destiny of the America people. His ministry is dangerous to those who see an aware, awakened and enlightened electorate as problematic. He is dangerous to those who want white privilege and white supremacy to continue as the governing philosophy of America's institutions. His ministry is dangerous to the prison industrial complex, because he has proven the ability to take the same Black youth that might otherwise end up in jail or prison and make them productive. Swedish professor of theology Mattias Gardell said of the Minister:

> "Farrakhan has a unique capability ...able to reach deeply into the souls of black youths...is able to talk to them in a way that really makes them listen...this rapport enables Farrakhan to criticize and redirect destructive behavioral patterns."

The Minister, as a preacher of the unedited, unabridged and spiritually virile true word of God, is viewed by oppressors of all kinds as dangerous because he interferes with their plan of oppression and genocide. But he is viewed by the oppressed and their God as a hero and champion, a bold man with a salvific message and strong personal example.

Not only did slave masters tamper with the Bible to keep their slaves from rebelling. They also were deathly afraid of preachers that they didn't educate, appoint or approve. I am always fascinated and really amazed when I read the history of how plantation owners and legislators reacted to Nat Turner's rebellion. One might think that they would move quickly to prohibit any enslaved man or woman from being able to have access to guns or weapons. But instead they reacted by toughening laws against literacy and religion. The Richmond Enquirer in 1831 published an editorial that said:

> "The case of Nat Turner warns us. **No black man ought to be permitted to turn preacher through the country.** The law must be enforced-or the tragedy of Southampton appeals to us in vain."

According to W.E.B. Dubois in his **History of the Negro Church**, after Nat Turner's rebellion,

> "A wave of legislation passed over the South prohibiting the slaves from learning to read and write, forbidding Negroes to preach, and interfering with Negro religious meetings. For example, a Mississippi law said it is unlawful for any slave, free Negro, or mulatto to preach the gospel upon pain of receiving thirty-nine lashes upon the naked back of the presumptuous preacher. If a Negro received written permission from his master he might preach to the Negroes in his immediate neighborhood, providing six respectable white men, owners of slaves, were present."

Similarly, it was Nat Turner's rebellion that infamous Virginia legislator Henry Berry was reacting to when he said:

> "Pass as severe laws as you will to keep these unfortunate creatures in ignorance. It is in vain unless you can extinguish that spark of intellect which God has given them. ...Sir, we have as far as possible closed every avenue by which light may enter their minds. We only have to go one step further to extinguish their capacity to see the light and our work

will be completed. And they would then be reduced to the level of the beasts of the field and we should be safe."

Again, consider how this history sheds much needed light on what Facebook/Instagram is doing to our beloved Minister Farrakhan. The Minister's beneficial impact as both a bold, revolutionary preacher and an advocate for reading and literacy among the poor and downtrodden, has placed him in the cross-hairs of the modern enslavers of the masses. He is not a target because he intends harm or has caused harm to any man or woman. He is a target because he is a thorn in the side of the rich who earnestly desire to preserve the status quo where the top 1% controls more than 99% of the world's wealth and treasure. According to Bloomberg.com:

> "Billionaire Johann Rupert, the South African who has made billions peddling Cartier jewelry and Chloe fashion, said tension between the rich and poor is set to escalate as robots and artificial intelligence fuel mass unemployment. 'We cannot have 0.1 percent of 0.1 percent taking all the spoils,' said Rupert, who has a fortune worth $7.5 billion, according to data compiled by Bloomberg. 'It's unfair and it is not sustainable…How is society going to cope with structural unemployment and the envy, hatred and the social warfare?' he said. 'We are destroying the middle classes at this stage and it will affect us. It's unfair. So that's what keeps me awake at night.'"

Could it be that since Minister Farrakhan is universally viewed as a voice for the poor and oppressed, he is being pre-emptively silenced and denied access to the world's largest social media platforms? Social media was hailed for being the tool of choice that gave rise to the Middle East uprisings known as the "Arab spring" which toppled governments throughout North Africa and the Middle East. Do the rich in America and the international bankers fear an American and or European Spring? Is this why they fear Minister Farrakhan's message growing in its audience size?

I noticed that Facebook/Instagram decided to ban the Minister on what is celebrated in America as Holocaust Remembrance Day. This was a clear wink and nod to the nefarious adversaries of the Black community who have planned an ill-advised character assassination attempt against Minister Farrakhan. Groups like the ADL (Anti-Defamation League of B'Nai B'rith) and the

Southern Poverty Law Center have sought to paint the Minister as anti-Semitic. But these same groups have also labeled the word of God, specifically the Bible's New Testament as being an anti-Semitic text.

According to long time ADL chairman Abraham Foxman:

> "For almost twenty centuries . . . the church was the archenemy of the Jews—our most powerful and relentless oppressor and **the worlds' greatest force for the dissemination of Anti-Semitic beliefs and the instigation of the acts of hatred**. Many of the same people who operated the gas chambers worshiped in Christian churches on Sunday. . .. The question of the complicity of the church in the murder of the Jews is a living one. We must understand the truths of our history."

Moreover, Foxman's sentiments harmonize with what is documented in the Jewish Virtual Library, wherein it states:

> "The gospel story, which **has generated more anti-Semitism than the sum of all the other anti-Semitic writings ever written**, created the climate in Christian Europe that led to the Holocaust. Long before the rise of Adolf Hitler, the gospel story about the life and death of Jesus had poisoned the bloodstream of European civilization."

What then do we learn from this? We learn that the life of Jesus, commonly referred to as the Gospels, is looked upon as the source, root and seed-bed of global anti-Semitism by the same folks who label Minister Farrakhan an anti-Semite. Wow! That is amazing!

Perhaps then, Minister Farrakhan and those of us who stand with him should rejoice, because apparently, we are in good company right alongside Jesus and the scriptures.

Rabbi's Words Connect Jewish Talmud to Anti-Black Violence, Police Killings

The Bible and the Holy Qur'an describe the creation of man as a sacred act. The Holy Qur'an states that Allah (God) created man of Black mud. The Bible states that man is created in the image of God. In the Bible David states that "you are all gods, children of the Most High God." David's son Solomon states "I am Black but beautiful, oh you daughters of Jerusalem.

What emerges from these various scriptural passages is a picture of humanity as divine, beautiful and Black.

The image of Black people in America has always been a controversial. A pure and honest examination of scripture and world history condemns any negative image portrayal of Black people. However, The Times of Israel reported just a few days ago that the chief Sephardic Rabbi in Israel referred to Black people as monkeys. His office defended him by stating that the Chief Rabbi was only quoting a passage from the Talmud.

During the Honorable Minister Louis Farrakhan's magnificent Saviours' Day 2018 message, he cited instances that had taken place in Israel where graffiti words were spray painted on churches saying "Jesus was a monkey." The Minister's audience was shocked at learning of hostility for Jesus coming from Israel.

Most of the Minister's audience is oblivious to the existence of the Jewish Talmud; the place where the Chief Rabbi learned to refer to Black people as monkeys.

It was the Jewish Talmud, which is a voluminous collection of rabbinical interpretations of the Torah, which introduced to the world the Hamitic Curse as an explanation for the origins of Black skin and physical features. Even staunch critic of the Nation of Islam-Harold Brackman of the Simon Wiesenthal Center tells us in his doctoral dissertation, The Ebb and Flow of Conflict: A History of Black–Jewish Relations Through 1900, that:

> "There is no denying that the [Jewish] Babylonian Talmud was the first source to read a Negrophobic content into the episode by stressing Canaan's fraternal connection with Cush. The Talmudic glosses of the episode added the stigma of blackness to the fate of enslavement that Noah predicted for Ham's progeny..."

"Un-Smiting The Shepherd" -331

The Minister also reminded his enthusiastic audience of the many scandalous depictions of President Barack Obama, by racist cartoonists who portrayed him and his lovely wife Michelle Obama as monkeys or apes.

Indiana Representative Todd Rokita has sponsored a resolution that condemns our beloved Minister **"for promoting ideas that create animosity and anger toward Jewish Americans and the Jewish religion."**

As a Black man, I find Congressman Rokita's resolution ridiculous, offensive and wicked. It is especially offensive because he has never issued a resolution to condemn those who **"promote ideas that create animosity and anger toward Black or African Americans."**

If he did, he would understand the sentiments being expressed by Minister Farrakhan and Black Americans who know all too well that in America no group has been the victim of **"ideas that create animosity and anger"** more than the American Black man and woman.

The record of history is clear; **Minister Farrakhan's words have never produced harm, suffering or the loss of life among the Jewish people. But, the globally exported view that Jewish leaders have of Black people has been deadly!**

In fact, a direct line of correlation can be drawn from the recent police killing of Stephon Clark in Sacramento, California to the subhuman views of Black people in the Jewish Talmud.

In an eye-opening and groundbreaking 2014 study entitled **The Essence of Innocence: Consequences of Dehumanizing Black Children** we learn about how Black children, especially Black boys, are on the receiving end of harsher punishments and longer prison sentences when they enter the criminal justice system. The abstract of the study defines its scope in the following:

> "The social category "children" defines a group of individuals who are perceived to be distinct, with essential characteristics including innocence and the need for protection. The present research examined whether Black boys are given the protections of childhood equally to their peers. We tested 3 hypotheses: (a) that Black boys are

seen as less "childlike" than their White peers, (b) that the characteristics associated with childhood will be applied less when thinking specifically about Black boys relative to White boys, and (c) **that these trends would be exacerbated in contexts where Black males are dehumanized by associating them (implicitly) with apes."**

In describing a central aspect of their research and results they state:

> "In this research, White participants who were subliminally exposed to images of apes before watching a video of police beating a Black man were more likely to endorse that beating, despite the extremity of the violence. Participants did not, however, endorse the same beating when the suspect was White or when they had not been primed with the ape image. In a follow-up study, Goff et al. coded newspaper articles about death-eligible criminal cases in Philadelphia for ape-related metaphors. They found that the frequency of ape-related imagery predicted whether or not criminals were executed by the state. Of importance, in neither study was racial prejudice (explicit or implicit) a significant predictor. That is, dehumanization uniquely predicted violence and its endorsement."

The researchers, whose article appears in the **Journal of Social Psychology**, cite the histories of Emmett Till and George Stinney Jr. to highlight the importance of their study to understanding the all too frequent phenomenon of violence against Black children:

> "In 1944, a Black 14-year-old, George Junius Stinney Jr., became the youngest person on record in the United States to be legally executed by the state (electrocuted without the benefit of a lawyer, witnesses, or a record of confession; Jones, 2007). And, notoriously, in 1955, a 14-year-old Black boy named Emmett Till was dragged from his bed, disfigured, and lynched for allegedly whistling at a White woman (Crowe, 2003). What psychological context could explain this treatment of children?"

Prior to participating in this profound research report, one of the researchers Philip Atiba Goff conducted research to examine the impacts of Blacks being associated with apes and monkeys. His team of researchers produced a report entitled **Not Yet Human: Implicit Knowledge, Historical Dehumanization, and Contemporary Consequences.** Among their conclusions, they state:

> "...the implicit association between Blacks and apes can lead to greater endorsement of violence against a Black suspect than against a White suspect. Finally, in Study 6, we demonstrated that subtle media representations of Blacks as apelike are associated with jury decisions to execute Black defendants."

This scientific study brings to light the danger of the Talmudic dehumanization of Black people that the Chief Rabbi articulated. Whether it is classifying Blacks as subhuman "strange creatures" or associating Black skin with a divine curse, the Talmudic view of Black people is bizarre, ignoble and grotesque. For Black people it is a deadly view.

The danger of the Talmudic view of Black people becomes especially important when we consider the globally exported and highly influential entertainment and pop culture industry of America. At the center of American popular culture is the motion picture industry, better known as Hollywood. Author Neal Gabler discusses the history of Hollywood in his book **How the Jews Invented Hollywood**. Prof. Gabler's description of the Jewish founding, control and influence of Hollywood is illuminating. He writes:

> "What is amazing is the extent to which they succeeded in promulgating this fiction throughout the world. By making a 'shadow' America, one which idealized every old glorifying bromide about the country, **the Hollywood Jews created a powerful cluster of images and ideas—so powerful that, in a sense, they colonized the American imagination**….Ultimately, American values came to be defined largely by the movies the Jews made."

As to what role the Talmud has played in the creation of this **"powerful cluster of images and ideas"** that have **"colonized the American imagination"** we reference the words of Pulitzer Prize winning author Herman Wouk. In his book, **This is My God; the Jewish Way of Life**, he wrote:

> "The Talmud is to this day the circulating heart's blood of the Jewish religion. Whatever laws, customs or ceremonies we observe — whether we are Orthodox, Conservative, Reform or merely spasmodic

sentimentalists — we follow the Talmud. It is our common law."

These powerful images and ideas that include the Talmudic dehumanization of Black people have been referenced and described by screenwriter Dalton Trumbo when he wrote:

> "[Hollywood made] tarts of the Negro's daughters, crap shooters of his sons, obsequious Uncle Toms of his fathers, superstitious and grotesque crones of his mothers, strutting peacocks of his successful men, psalm-singing mountebanks of his priests, and Barnum and Bailey side-shows of his religion."

Jewish authors- Barry Shwartz and Robert Disch- of the book **White Racism** point exclusively to Hollywood as the fount from which the waters of anti-Black racism and dehumanization have flowed and affected the world:

> "This statement should surprise no one, since Hollywood, more than any other institution, has been responsible for the glorification of the South, past and present, and for creating the image of black inferiority. It created the lying, stealing, childish, eyeball rolling, feet-shuffling, sex-obsessed, teeth-showing, dice-shooting black male, and told the world this was the real Negro in the U.S.A. It invented the Negro "mammy" whose breasts were always large enough to suckle an entire nation, and who always loved old massa's chilluns more than she loved her own. The men of Fake-town have brainwashed America and the entire world with the brush of white supremacy."

According to a report entitled **Diversity in Film and Television** authored by the diversity monitoring entity called Media Scope, scientific studies have proven that the constant exposure to dehumanizing images of Black people in the media negatively impacts how whites view Blacks. The Media Scope report states:

> "Considerable public concern has arisen over the issue of media diversity, as it is generally accepted that mass media has strong social and psychological effects on viewers. Film and television, for example, provide many children with their first exposure to people of other races, ethnicities, religions and cultures. What they see onscreen, therefore, can impact their attitudes about the treatment of others. One study found, for instance, that two years of viewing Sesame Street

by European-American preschoolers was associated with more positive attitudes toward African and Latino Americans. Another study found that **white children exposed to a negative television portrayal of African-Americans had a negative change in attitude toward blacks**."

These disrespectful images of Black people, which permeate all forms of entertainment, serve a hidden role in psychologically programming the hatred of Black people into the thinking of all who are exposed to them. Hard wired now, into the thinking of even some in the Black community is the Hollywood created, Talmudic based image of Black humanity as subhuman, evil and shameful.

The negative stereotypes and images of Black people that have long since been staples of Hollywood movie production are mirror reflections of the Jewish Talmud's **"ideas that create animosity and anger toward Black or African Americans."** Research studies have proven the dangerous effect of these views. Yet Congressman Rokita has done nothing to interfere with the proliferation of these ideas that remain in Hollywood and the Music industry.

The significance of considering what we have presented in this essay is the role that the Talmudic view Black people has played in what happened to Trayvon Martin, Tamir Rice, Michael Brown, DeAunta Terrell Farrow and most recently Stephon Clark. All of these were young Black males who were murdered by either police or a private citizen who looked at these beautiful young men and saw them as older, menacing and threatening. And now we understand how these corrupt images of Black males got into the mind of their murderers.

I say that if Congressman Rokita, will not sponsor a resolution to condemn all who promote **"ideas that create animosity and anger toward Black or African Americans?"**, he proves that his sensitivity to dangerous ideas only applies for the Jewish community. He proves that at the heart of his condemnation of Minister Farrakhan is his hatred of the Minister for loving the long vilified and dehumanized Black people enough to challenge all who mean us harm!

The Fear of Black Manhood: Jude Wanniski Explains the Farrakhan Ban

Long before the very recent social media ban, Minister Farrakhan has been dubbed *persona non grata* by Jewish groups like the **ADL** (anti-defamation league), **JDL** (Jewish defense league) and the **SPLC** (southern poverty law center). In fact, the ADL threatened to punish any and all prominent persons and institutions, who would share their platform with Minister Farrakhan. In 1994 Steven Freeman wrote:

> "The ADL is not going to make Farrakhan go away. What we can and should do is impose an obligation on those who deal with him, or, as in the case of universities, give him a platform. In each case, the burden should be on those who give Farrakhan some measure of credibility..."

Within Freeman's report on the subject of the *"Legitimization of Louis Farrakhan"* he acknowledges that Minister Farrakhan and the Nation of Islam fill a void within the Black community, yet they-the ADL- still wanted to thwart him.

Again, the Minister has never advocated or been the reason that any violence has come to the Jewish people. The question therefore arises, "why is Farrakhan feared"?

I found an interesting perspective inside of a very fascinating interview conducted by my dear friend and brother, Cedric Muhammad on his groundbreaking website **blackelectorate.com**. He was interviewing legendary economist and former advisor to President Ronald Reagan, Mr. Jude Wanniski. Mr. Wanniski offered the following perspective that shines great light on and helps to answer the question of why Farrakhan is feared:

> "See, Minister Farrakhan is frightening to Whites, and I would surmise Blacks as well because he emphasizes the masculinity of Black America which has been crushed since slavery. Dr. Martin Luther King represented the feminine side and that is what has been permitted and what most White folks are now comfortable with."

This is a very powerful admission coming from Mr. Wanniski. As a member of the elite ruling class of white males within American society, Mr. Wanniski is qualified to provide an insider's view into how Minister Farrakhan is looked upon by the most powerful white males within American society. And as such, his candid expression to Bro. Cedric Muhammad provides for us a window into the private thoughts of men like Mark Zuckerberg and those who have closed ranks and determined to create a blockade against the message of Minister Louis Farrakhan.

I find Mr. Wanniski's comments very consistent with research that I have produced into the historical context of the condition of Black men within American society. In February of this year, I published a book entitled *Manhood Principles, Parables, Concepts and Characteristics from the Holy Qur'an*.

To contextualize and offer reasons for why Black Manhood is an important enough topic to publish a book about, I shared with the readers some quotes to document the perilous history of Black Manhood in America. Consider the following quotes on the fear and destruction of Black Manhood:

> President Lyndon Baines Johnson: "Perhaps most important—its influence radiating to every part of life—is the breakdown of the Negro family structure. For this, most of all, white America must accept responsibility. It flows from centuries of oppression and persecution of the Negro man. It flows from the long years of degradation and discrimination, which have attacked his dignity and assaulted his ability to produce for his family." (Address to Howard University, 1965)

Mark Twain: "I do not believe I would very cheerfully help a white student who would ask a benevolence of a stranger," Twain wrote Francis Wayland, the law school dean, on Dec. 24, 1885, "but I do not feel so about the other color. **We have ground the manhood out of them**, & the shame is ours, not theirs; & we should pay for it." (Edwin McDonnell, From Twain, A Letter on Debt to Blacks)

President Johnson and Mark Twain's quotes highlight the truth that the destruction of Black Manhood has been a societal norm in America. These statements, and what they admit, coming from such prominent and highly respected American icons cannot be overemphasized! They strongly punctuate and should actually frame current public discourse surrounding the issue of reparations.

The deliberate destruction of Black Manhood has always been based on the fear of the Black man's expected and justified resistance and opposition to the enslavement and subjugation of Black people in America. The fear and destruction of Black men is the foundation upon which the idea of white supremacy is established. It is the core requirement needed to completely dominate Black people and has been the achievement of American chattel slavery, global imperialism and European colonialism.

Minister Farrakhan is well known for his noble and upstanding male followers and his overall transformative impact on Black men. And it is within his inspiring of Black men to become strong fathers, husbands, community stakeholders, crime fighters and spiritual leaders that we find the strongest refutation of the false allegation that he is a teacher of hate and bigotry. What the Minister makes out of those of us who become his students-*that scares the white ruling class*-threatens the historical idea that Black men and women exist only to serve out certain degrading roles within American society.

Author William Goodell, in his very important work *The American Slave Code* states that the "Negro" slave:

> "may be used as a "breeder," as a prostitute, as a concubine, as a pimp, as a tapster, as an attendant at the gaming-table, as a subject of medical and surgical experiments."

The students and followers of Minister Farrakhan are unwilling to accept such an undignified status within American society. So, the Minister's magnificent message is feared and opposed only by those who seek to keep us perpetually serving in these degrading roles; the roles of the "Negro" (i.e. *a living dead person*).

Minister Farrakhan's identity as a Muslim in addition to him being a revolutionary leader is especially concerning to the ruling powers. T. Lothrop Stoddard, at the turn of the 20th century, wrote an epic warning entitled *The Rising Tide of Color Against White World Supremacy*. In his survey of the geo-political and global racial landscapes he wrote:

> "Certainly, all white men, whether professing Christians or not, should welcome the success of [Christian] missionary efforts in Africa. ...all Negroes will someday be either Christians or Moslems. In so far as he is Christianized, the Negro's savage instincts will be restrained and he will be disposed to acquiesce in white tutelage. In so far as he is Islamized, the Negro's warlike propensities will be inflamed, and he

> will...drive the white man from Africa and make the continent its very own."

He continued by writing about the fighting nature of the African people and it being stimulated by their Islamic faith:

> "With very few exceptions the colored races of Africa are preeminently fighters.... To them the fierce, warlike spirit inherent in Mohammedanism (Islam) is infinitely more attractive..."

Legendary Black historian Edward Wilmont Blyden is also on the record, as he described the religion of Islam as being a steward of and enhancement to the natural masculinity of the Black/African people. He wrote in his very important book *Christianity, Islam and the Negro Race* the following:

> "When the religion [of Islam] was first introduced it found the people possessing all the elements and enjoying all the privileges of an untrammeled manhood. They received it as giving them additional power to exert an influence in the world. It sent them forth as the guides and instructors of their less favored neighbors and endowed them with the self-respect which men feel who acknowledge no superior."

Mr. Wanniski's statements on how Black masculinity lies at the root of why the Minister is feared is easy to understand in light of these quotes that give us windows into history.

I wrap up this short article with the testimony of a white writer by the name of R. R. Reno who wrote an article in the magazine First Things, March 2013 edition. His article entitled *Black Power; White Fear* summarizes the fear-based reaction to Minister Farrakhan that Jude Wanniski so eloquently expressed to Bro. Cedric. The social media ban against the Minister's message leads us to believe that Mr. Wanniski and Mr. Reno's words typify the fear of Minister Farrakhan that haunts all who are uncomfortable seeing Black manhood rise and exert itself within American society and the world stage. Mr. Reno wrote:

> "I remember the Black Muslims from when I was growing up, I remember them as symbols of male self-possession and potency. In my racial imagination, they could meet me face to face, but not on my own terms. They represented something that I never otherwise encountered as an adolescent; a cultural way of being American that

was close enough to engage me, compete with me, put demands on me, but independent enough to resist me, and even ignore or mock me. I never felt so white, so contingent and vulnerable, as when I encountered the Black Muslims."

The Mysterious Death of a Muslim Minister

What Happened to Minister Robert D. Muhammad? Why we don't believe our brother just simply drowned!

Whenever I think about the death of Student Minister Robert D. Muhammad of Grand Rapids Michigan I feel the same way I did when I first heard the news- distraught, hurt and angry. We are living in troubling times and Minister Robert's death highlights the peculiar state of the world in which we all live. Pain and mourning are our frequent companions in such a time as this. However nowadays it is difficult to mourn for those whom we love due to the fact that by the time we are able to process our emotions and thoughts over the loss of a family member or friend the news of another who has been killed or died is made known to us. And another cycle of mourning begins.

Perhaps my own experience is not too different than most people today. If I'm not hearing a news report of the killing of unarmed Black men and women by police, my radio and social media newsfeed is filled with news of a 9-year-old child being gunned down by senseless gang violence. To this the Honorable Minister Louis Farrakhan has called for 10,000 fearless men and women to establish a presence in America's inner cities to serve as soldiers in a war that is on 2 fronts. The primary function of such a bold cadre of "10,000 fearless" is to provide avenues for conflict resolution to individuals and groups so that resolvable disagreements don't morph and escalate into violence and murder. This "army" of 10,000 fearless will also be teachers and instructors; guides and facilitators in the process of learning a new way of life. They will also serve as living models of that better way of life and the high degree of civilization that we should aspire to. This is so that the hurting people living in these impoverished communities, which are now saturated with violence and corruption, may have a chance to look upon and be impacted by some of their brothers and sisters; an army of living, breathing, walking, talking, saviors.

Brother Minister Robert D. Muhammad was such a brother.

And even though the idea to call for 10,000 fearless had not yet crystallized in the mind of the Honorable Minister Louis

Farrakhan before we lost Brother Robert, a study of his works and impact in his almost 40 years of life prove to me that he was a fearless brother who sacrificed much so that he might serve as a model and example of the high civilization taught by the Honorable Elijah Muhammad and the Honorable Minister Louis Farrakhan.

The thought to write about him has weighed on me since he passed away. For his death deeply impacted me. There is so much about Brother Robert that I identify with. So, this essay is dedicated to him and his wife and their 8 children. I pray that they will all grow and be what Minister Farrakhan prayed for on the mall at the 10-10-15 gathering. The Minister prayed that every unborn child now growing inside the womb of their mother, who was in attendance, would come to birth and grow up to be the generation that brings about a new world and be the answer to the prayers of our suffering people.

Again, I am not too different than most of us, we all have many priorities and responsibilities that we juggle. So, for several months Brother Minister Robert's death was not on my immediate "radar". So, I am very thankful to Nation of Islam Student National Secretary Brother Berve Muhammad and Student Assistant Supreme Captain Anthony Muhammad for organizing a group of believers to travel to Grand Rapids, Michigan to pursue justice for Brother Minister Robert D. Muhammad. This act not only put Brother Robert back on my radar, but it also officially made his tragedy a part of the Justice or Else movement.

Holes in the Official Account

This essay seeks to look at what happened to Minister Robert D. from a historical, scriptural and geo-political perspective. There is no event in life that is not a part of a larger historical context. Students of scripture and sacred texts will agree that the events and happenings of our world also fit within a definite scriptural or prophetic context.

The official report from the medical examiner/coroner is death by drowning. But we in the Nation of Islam don't believe the official story. The facts of the case give us reason to disbelieve the official explanation.

In the coverage of the Student National Secretary's speech in Grand Rapids found online at the Final Call's webpage the public learned for the first time the conflicting conclusions inside the Muskegon County official report.

According to the facts presented by Brother Berve in his address, when Minister Robert's body was pulled from the lake his face had bruises on it and showed the signs of a physical altercation having taken place. Informational brochures circulated by the believers showed gruesome photos of Minister Robert's body that was found in 28 feet of water. His right hand was clinched in a fist. And all we have to go on is the story of a group of Minister Robert's white co-workers. Their story is that while gathered together for a work-related function, they all went out on a boat and Minister Robert went into the water for a swim eventually going under the water and drowning. Brother Berve revealed that the Muskegon County police investigators did not interview any of Minister Robert's white co-workers the day of the incident. This delay in questioning of the on-scene witnesses is significant because it gave them time to corroborate their story prior to being interrogated by the police. Brother Berve went on to say that there was no forensic testing or photographs taken of the boat that they all claim to have been in when Minister Robert drowned. So, any evidence that remained in the boat could be conveniently destroyed.

We simply do not believe that our brother died this way.

A History of Murder and Attempted Murder of Muslim Ministers

Not only do the facts of the case give us reason to disbelieve the official story. History also strengthens us in our rejection of such a cockamamie story. Over the long 85-year history of the Nation of Islam's presence in America the Ministers of the Most Honorable Elijah Muhammad have been targets of hatred and acts of violence. And several have been actually murdered and serve as reminders of the covert and overt hatred of the religion of Islam by many powerful forces inside America.

The most famous murdered Muslim Minister is Brother Minister Malcolm X. Information available today 50 years after Brother Malcolm was assassinated shows that responsibility for Brother Minister Malcolm's death rest wholly in the hands of the law enforcement apparatus of the U.S. government and specifically the Federal Bureau of Investigation (FBI). Through a whole host of nefarious activities that span from the creation and development of informants and agent provocateurs inside the Nation of Islam to their refusal to release the more than 2300 pages of documents related to Malcolm X -the bureaus imprint is all over his assassination. The murder of Brother Minister Malcolm is even more diabolical in nature when we consider that the goal of the FBI was to destroy the movement of Black Nationalist Islam in America in one fell swoop. By this I mean that in murdering Malcolm X and blaming his murder on the Nation of Islam. The wicked forces behind his assassination would kill "2 birds with 1 stone."

And as Brother Malcolm's secretary would later reveal, Malcolm's last day on this earth was the day that this nefarious plot had crystallized in his own mind. And he had planned to retract his public accusations that it was the Nation of Islam who was "out to kill him." According to his secretary Ms. Sarah Mitchell,

> "He said now anyone could kill him and everyone would blame the Muslims," Mitchell said. "He said, 'We've been set up, and they succeeded.'"

And even though Malcolm was the most famous case of efforts to destroy Black Islamic leadership, he was not the first. Nation of Islam lore and legend includes an oral history of the Great Mahdi –**Master Fard Muhammad**-himself being violently hit in his mouth by a man who hated his teachings and reform of Black people in the impoverished Black Bottom areas of Detroit.

This time period of the early days of the Nation of Islam are also marked by the federal government's efforts to destroy the Nation of Islam through the imprisonment of its leader the Most Honorable Elijah Muhammad. In 1942 the Most Honorable Elijah Muhammad was arrested and served 5 years in Federal prison in Milan Michigan. His crime, according to the FBI, was none other than teaching the revolutionary message of Islam and global Black solidarity during a time when America was engaged in war with Japan.

But the plotting and executing of actual assassinations of Muslim Ministers begin in 1952 with the attempted murder of **Minister**

Troy X. Cade (aka Troy Bey and Abdul Bey Muhammad) of Monroe Louisiana. Monroe police officers beat him severely and threw him into a lake to drown. But thanks be to Allah (God) Minister Bey survived.

In the June 25, 1965 issue of the Muhammad Speaks newspaper, the Honorable Elijah Muhammad offers a $25,000 reward for information on the death of his **Minister Louis X.** of Winston Salem, North Carolina. At that time the official explanation for Minister Louis' death is that he had shot 2 persons in the head with a gun and then turned the gun on himself. Yet the persons alleged to have been shot had no head wounds neither were they under hospital care.

The Muhammad Speaks newspaper also covered the attempted murder of **Minister Clyde Rahman** of Muhammad's Temple No. 28 located in St. Louis Missouri. Minister Clyde survived being shot in the left arm and the right side of his head. The bullet entered his head just below his temple and exited through his left jaw. The gun man also shot the mosque secretary Brother Timothy X Hoffman and the first officer Brother John W. X. Moore. Brother John's wounds were fatal.

The most powerful Black man in America is **the Honorable Elijah Muhammad**, according to the popular publication Reader's Digest. This most powerful Black man and globally recognized Islamic leader was the target of an assassination plot in 1967. This plot was uncovered and foiled upon finding an assassin's lair along with an arsenal of weapons in an area across the street from the front entry of Mr. Muhammad's national residence.

The Nation of Islam was also deeply saddened by the cold-blooded murder of the Honorable Elijah Muhammad's Minister in Tyler, Texas- **Minister Joe X Pease**. Minister Joe left behind a wife and 9 children after he was shot down by KZEY disc jockey "King Byrd."

During the Most Honorable Elijah Muhammad's 5 years of incarceration he impacted the lives of many men. One such man was the late **Minister James Shabazz** of Newark, New Jersey. Minister James became a follower of the Honorable Elijah Muhammad after initially meeting him in prison. He went on to serve the cause of the liberation of Black people in several cities but his most significant work was in the building of Muhammad's Mosque No. 25 in Newark. The strong presence of the religion of Islam in the state of New Jersey today is largely due to the work of Minister James and the many Muslims in the Nation of Islam that labored there since the early days of the Nation of Islam. Minister James was violently murdered in 1973.

The murder of Minister James Shabazz was the occasion for a famous classic message delivered by the Honorable Minister Louis Farrakhan entitled the "Murderer of a Muslim." Many were reminded of that profound message during the janazah (funeral) service for **Minister Robert D. Muhammad** in Grand Rapids, Michigan which was officiated by the Honorable Minister Louis Farrakhan.

During the Minister's remarks at Minister Robert's janazah he let the audience know that the Nation of Islam would not rest until we find out exactly the truth of what happened to our brother. And he reminded us of some important and relevant words spoken by the Most Honorable Elijah Muhammad. The Honorable Elijah Muhammad told Bob Lucas in a Cavalier magazine interview that his teacher, the Great Mahdi, Master Fard Muhammad promised him that **"If they kill one of your least ones, I'll kill ten of their best ones."** And the Minister followed up that divine reminder with saying *"and Brother Robert was not one of his least ones."*

Brother Minister Robert's mysterious death by drowning is strangely similar to the death of **Brother Assistant Minister Donald X** of the Nation of Islam's Seattle, Washington mosque. Writer Vaughn Taplin covered the death of Brother Donald for the Muhammad Speaks newspaper and his report discusses the community feeling that foul play was the cause of Brother Donald's death. Brother Minister Donald, who also served as captain of the Seattle mosque, was found drowned in Lake Washington. Over 500 people attended Minister Donald's janazah to show their love for a man who was not just loved by the Muslims, but was loved and respected by all who knew him. Brother Donald was lauded by several Black Seattle newspapers. Fitzgerald Beaver, editor of the *The Facts*, wrote that Brother Donald "was loved and admired by everyone who knew him. If he walked into an office, his whole surroundings seemed to light up because of his pleasant smile and his attitude and whole outlook on life. It was the same whether he was talking to a businessman or in the Mosque or standing on 23rd Avenue and Union selling Muhammad Speaks newspaper. He was always smiling and he always had a kind word for everyone."

This is the same kind of love and respect the citizens of Grand Rapids had for Minister Robert Dione Muhammad. Brother Robert and the Grand Rapids Study Group of the Nation of Islam hosted and coordinated 2 of the most significant messages delivered by the Honorable Minister Louis Farrakhan. In these 2 events, the first in 2012 and another in 2013, we see the broad based support that Minister Robert's work produced for the Minister in Grand Rapids.

The Importance and Significance of Brother Robert's Work

Brother Minister Robert and **Sister Mary X** worked in conjunction with the students of Grand Rapids Community College to host the Minister in both of these epic messages spaced one year apart. Several of the program speakers during these events discussed the hurdles and obstacles that Grand Rapids Community College placed in the student's path to host the Minister. And when it appeared as though the Minister would not be permitted to speak to the students on the campus, the students began to seek other accommodations. Ultimately the planning group that also included Benton Harbor **Student Minister Marcus Muhammad** were able to secure Fountain Street Church in Grand Rapids to host Minister Farrakhan's address. Fountain Street Church is significant because it has a white pastor, Rev. Fred Wooden. Pastor Wooden not only was courageous enough to host the Minister twice, but he also shared encouraging words during his introductory remarks on the program.

I place a lot of emphasis on these messages by the **Honorable Minister Louis Farrakhan** in Grand Rapids, not only because Minister Robert was an integral part of its success-both behind the scenes and as the program master of ceremonies- but also because of what they represented and what is contained within them.

Consider the themes that the students requested the Minister to address. In the 2012 message, the Minister discussed the themes "Duty, Responsibility and the Need of Self-Sufficiency." In the

2013 message, the Minister's themes were "Education, Fatherhood and Self-Esteem." The Minister delivered these universal themes to some of the most diverse audiences that I have ever witnessed him speak to.

As the camera frequently panned the audience, one could see White, Black, Hispanic, and Asian audience members. There were students present as well as the general public. The audience was possessed of many nationalities, ethnic groups, religions, age groups, and both genders. The picture of the audience who came to see Minister Farrakhan in Grand Rapids was a portrait of America-a snapshot of the world. And Brother Robert was the leader of the group that made this happen-a Black group, a Muslim group.

From my vantage point, Minister Robert and the Grand Rapids group gave the powerful forces who hate Minster Farrakhan the worst picture that they could ever see. As the camera fastened its lens on the faces of many whites in the audience it found them nodding in agreement with the Minister. The camera's lens settled upon many from the "incorrigible youth" population who were applauding and nodding in agreement with the Minister's message. The camera found the smiling faces of women and elders along with "white collar" workers and "blue collar" workers in the audience-all in agreement with Minister's inspiring message.

Anyone who knows the history of Black movements for justice and equality in America understands the nefarious role that the American government has played in seeking to discredit, defame, de-magnetize and destroy these movements. Longtime head of the FBI J. Edgar Hoover wrote in internal bureau memos that he wanted to prevent **the rise of a Messiah** who could unite all the disparate elements of the Black community. This unifying Messiah among Blacks in America must be a Muslim based upon the observations of Harvard scholar and infamous eugenicist T. Lothrop Stoddard who wrote about Islam's role in the destiny of Blacks in Africa. According to Stoddard, "Mohammedanism (Islam) …can still give the natives a motive for animosity against Europeans and **a unity of which they are otherwise incapable**." Minister Farrakhan's long record of organizing and forming coalitions of diverse groups within the Black community makes him fit the description of the unifying Messiah perfectly. And there is no better example than the Million Man March (es).

Minister Farrakhan's messages in Grand Rapids were powerful portraits showing that Minister Farrakhan is not only the indispensable force for unity among Black people, but that he also has a broader more universal appeal that extends even into the white community. So, what we have in the 2 events in Grand Rapids, both of which can be purchased through The Final Call Incorporated in DVD format, is the Honorable Minister Louis Farrakhan producing agreement with the teachings of the Honorable Elijah Muhammad among a representative sampling of all of the American people! The Honorable Elijah Muhammad teaches that *"agreement is the basis of love."*

Both messages showed and proved that if Minister Farrakhan is allowed to teach the American people without hindrance or obstacle, he will convince them all of the truth of his divinely inspired ministry. The Biblical messiah-Jesus-also possessed a universal and broad-based appeal. So much so that it angered the Jewish leadership of his time. Their conspiracy to kill him is recorded in the Bible's New Testament: *"Therefore the chief priests and the Pharisees convened a council, and were saying, 'What are we doing? For* **this man is performing many signs. If we let Him go on like this, all men will believe in Him, and the Romans will come and take away both our place and our nation.'"***(John 11:47-48)*

The plot to kill Jesus is well known however what is less known is the plot to kill Lazarus. We find this plot in the book of John in the Bible. *"The large crowd of the Jews then learned that He was there; and they came, not for Jesus' sake only, but that they might also see Lazarus, whom He raised from the dead.* **But the chief priests planned to put Lazarus to death also; because on account of him many of the Jews were going away and were believing in Jesus.***" (John 12:9-11)*

As strange as it sounds, what this verse reveals is that **Lazarus was Jesus' best minister**. Lazarus produced converts by being an example of the power of God operating within Jesus that was capable of "raising the dead to life." The fact that the Sanhedrin leadership had determined to kill him because of his ability to recruit followers for Jesus makes a strong case that his mere existence alone served as the most effective minister Jesus had at that time. This certainly takes nothing away from the subsequent ministry of the Apostle Paul. But Paul's ministry is post Jesus' crucifixion; Lazarus is pre-crucifixion.

Minister Robert and all of Minister Farrakhan's ministers and students are like Lazarus. The teachings that we heard from Minister Farrakhan awakened us from a mental and spiritual slumber. Our mental and spiritual sleep made us other than ourselves and caused us to live self-destructive lifestyles. Minister Farrakhan in his penetrating ministry touched us and instilled in us a desire to get up and take off our "grave clothes." We were not physically dead, but neither was Lazarus. The Bible records Jesus reacting to the claim that Lazarus was dead by letting it be known that he was not dead but **"only sleeping."**

Black Muslim Leadership through the Eyes of the Oppressor

We were once asleep like Lazarus and now we are awakened and working to show the world the spirit and power of God operating in the person and ministry of the Honorable Minister Louis Farrakhan.

Has the Jewish leadership in America conspired to destroy the Muslim Ministers? Are the powerful forces in government who now wage war in many Muslim countries abroad planning the demise of Islam inside America? Did Minister Robert's role as a Muslim Minister have anything to do with his mysterious death? Based on the history of murder and attempted murder of men who have occupied the position of Muslim Minister, we have to strongly believe that it did. This history along with the dubious facts of the case causes us to disbelieve in the conclusion drawn by the Muskegon County officials.

It was during the height of J. Edgar Hoover's infamous COINTELPRO operations that he discussed preventing the rise of a Messiah among Black people. And while he considered all of the most prominent Black spokesmen on the scene at that time, he devoted considerable time and bureau resources into the destruction of the Nation of Islam and its leadership. As a Moslem Shriner, Hoover understood scripture, history and most importantly the future destiny of the Black man and woman of America. And his strategy of eliminating the "Black" Messiah can best be described using the words of Jesus in the Bible- *"for it is written, I will smite the shepherd, and the sheep shall be scattered. -Mark 14:27."* The "smite the shepherd" strategy is considered by popular author Robert Greene one of the most important principles or laws that are used by powerful people and groups. In Greene's popular book The 48 Laws of Power he lists it as Law No. 42 and suggests, **"One resolute person, one disobedient spirit, can turn a flock of sheep into a den of lions**...Do not waste your time lashing out in all directions at what seems to be a many-headed enemy. Find the one head that matters-**the person with the willpower, or smarts, or, most important of all, charisma**.... Finally, **the reason you strike at the shepherd is because such an action will dishearten the sheep beyond any rational measure**."

As far as the Nation of Islam, Hoover did not stop at his efforts to thwart the Most Honorable Elijah Muhammad. He actually profiled and placed under surveillance the Most Honorable Elijah Muhammad's 9 most active Ministers. Hoover placed **Minister Jeremiah Shabazz**(Atlanta, GA &Philadelphia, PA), **Minister Louis Farrakhan**(Boston, MA & New York, NY), **Minister John Shabazz**(Los Angeles, CA), **Minister Bernard Cushmeer**(San Francisco, CA & Phoenix, AZ), **Minister Lonnie Shabazz**(Washington, DC), **Minister Isaiah Karriem**(Baltimore, MD), **Minister James Shabazz**(Newark, NJ), **Minister James Shabazz**(Chicago, IL) and **Minister Wilfred X**(Detroit, MI) in the crosshairs of the most powerful law enforcement agency in the world.

In addition to the murders and attempted murders of Nation of Islam leaders that occurred prior to 1975, the period known as "the rebuilding" of the Nation of Islam under the leadership of the Honorable Minister Louis Farrakhan, has not been immune from mysterious deaths. In 1982, the Nation of Islam mourned the cold-blooded murder of Houston's **Minister Raymond X**. Another mysterious death involved the death of **Andre Jones** in a jail cell in Mississippi. Brother Andre was the son of Nation of Islam Minister Charles X Quinn and his wife Sister Esther Jones Quinn who served as the local president of the NAACP. Both of Andre's parents were activists in the struggle for the liberation of Black people in the state of Mississippi. The strange circumstances of Brother Andre's death were discussed in a presentation by Minister Charles to the Schiller Institute on April 8, 2000. Minister Charles reported that, **"On Aug. 22, 1992, our son, Andre Jones, was stopped at a routine sobriety check, or** *road block, in Brandon, Mississippi, which is located about 12 miles south of Jackson. Within 19 hours, our son was hung in a Simpson County jail, in Mendenhall, Mississippi. The officials said that he hung himself with his own shoelaces. Of course, we know that our son was taken out of that jail, on that night, and he was hung, and brought back into the jail, and hung up again in a dingy shower stall. And since that time, we have been fighting for justice on behalf of Andre".*

If Hoover were alive today he would certainly have taken note of the work of Brother Robert and the Grand Rapids group's 2 epic events; events that were profound demonstrations that provided for Minister Farrakhan a complete representative sampling of the American people to win over with his powerful arguments of truth. But, as a reflection of Hoover's posthumous influence, the Department of Homeland Security was forced to confess in 2007(just a few years ago) that they had been illegally spying on the Nation of Islam.

Moreover, we also have reason to disbelieve the official narrative based upon other information. Consider first that the Most Honorable Elijah Muhammad taught us of the careful study of scripture that takes place by the ruling powers. According to Messenger Muhammad, **"The white man of America is well informed through his scientists and scholars, who are paid just for studying the problems of prophecy and especially the future destruction of America which he knows is fast coming. His greatest mental burden and physical strain at the present time is how to prevent the spread of Islam among his ex-servitude slaves in these last days."**

In another relevant quote he wrote **"The ultimate aim of this world should be known to everyone; especially the righteous...The (arch-deceivers) ultimate aim is to do as their people have done-try to destroy the preacher of truth and those who believe in him."**

From these powerful truths and insights, we know that the Black man and woman's infamous oppressors understand scriptural prophecy and based on that understanding have determined that instead of accepting and complying with the truth, they will work to eliminate the truth by destroying the human vessels that possess the truth.

There is a history that involves the Trans-Atlantic slave trade and the Black man and woman's suffering as chattel slaves that strengthens us in our disbelief in the official report on the death of Minister Robert D. Muhammad.

We know that Muslim slaves were feared and hated. According to Professor Eugene Genovese **"Muslims were the most troublesome and rebellious slaves in the New World."** Author and scholar Matthew Restall's article Black Conquistadors: Armed Africans in Early Spanish America talks about lengths to which slave societies went to bar entry to Muslims. Restall writes,

> "In the early sixteenth century Spanish Crown legislation aimed at reducing the incidence of slave rebellions attempted to prevent the importation into the colonies of **Africans deemed most pugnacious**. The Crown and its colonial officials varied on their opinions as to which Africans were the most bellicose, but two categories appeared most consistently in such commentary and legislation. *These were Muslims (or anyone of African descent who may have been exposed to Islam, which periodically included mulattos, ladinos or Hispanized Blacks, and anyone from Guinea); and Wolofs, described in royal legislation of 1532 as "arrogant, disobedient, rebellious and incorrigible."*

Revolutionary Muslim Leadership in Haiti

T. Lothrop Stoddard in his classic work The Rising Tide of Color against White World Supremacy said that the religion of Islam has an influence and power over Black people. According to Stoddard as a believer in Islam **"the negro's warlike propensities will be inflamed."**

There is no stronger example of the truth of Stoddard's observation than in the history of the Haitian Revolution. For the record, it is a tremendous accomplishment that should never be forgotten by Blacks in the diaspora that the Haitian people are the only Blacks under slavery and European colonialism that rose up to defeat their oppressor and win freedom for their people.

Recent scholarship has unearthed the hidden Islamic presence in the history of the Haitian Revolution. Scholars such as Sylviane Diouf have done pioneering work to uncover and document the presence and importance of the religion of Islam and Muslims within the millions of Africans taken from the continent to be made slaves in the Americas. In Professor Diouf's excellent book Servants of Allah: African Muslims Enslaved in the America she provides us histories of the revolution's leaders who were also Muslims.

In Professor Diouf's book we read of the history of **Francois Macandal:** "What the French did not realize was that their most profitable colony, Saint-Dominique (now Haiti), was fertile ground for Muslim maroons and rebels. ...These Muslims were well known and feared, but the most famous of the pre-Revolution maroon leaders was without a doubt **Francois Macandal**.... an African born in "Guinea," Francois Macandal was in all probability a Mandingo. He came from an illustrious family and had been sold to the Europeans as a war captive. *He was a Muslim who "had instruction and possessed the Arabic language very well," emphasized nineteenth-century Haitian historian Thomas Madiou, who gathered information through the veterans of the Haitian Revolution. Macandal was most likely a marabout, for French official documents describe him as being able to predict the future and as having revelations*. He was also well known for his skills in amulet making—so much so that gris-gris were called macandals. *In addition, he was said to be a prophet, which indicates that he was perceived as having a direct connection to God.* Thus, besides being a marabout, he may have been a sharif, a descendant of the Prophet Muhammed; but this is only speculation, as no evidence exists to confirm or inform this hypothesis."

Professor Diouf also discusses the history of **Boukman:** "Another popular leader who attained quasi-mythical status in Haitian history was Boukman. Very little is known about him. He was not born in Saint-Domingue but came from Jamaica, smuggled by a British slaver. As a slave, he became professional and rose to the rank of driver, later becoming a coachman. Using a position that allowed him to travel from plantation to plantation, as well as his charismatic personality, he had built a network of followers in the north. He definitely entered Haitian history when he galvanized a large assembly of slaves gathered on the night of August 14, 1791, in a clearing in the forest of Bois-Caiman. During this voodoo ceremony, Boukman launched the general revolt of the slaves with a speech in Creole that has remained famous. He denounced the God of the whites, who asked for crime, whereas the God of the Slaves wanted only good. **"But this God who is so good, orders you to seek revenge," he pounded. "He will direct our arms, he will assist us. Throw away the image of the God of the whites who is thirsty for our tears and listen to freedom which talks to our hearts.** A week later, two hundred sugar estates and eighteen hundred coffee plantations were destroyed by the slaves, who were said to have cut the throats of a thousand slaveholders. At the beginning of November, Boukman was shot dead by an officer as he was fighting a detachment of the French army with a group of maroons. His severed head was fixed on a pole and exposed on a public square in Cap-Français.

There are indications that Boukman was a Muslim. Coming from Jamaica, he had an English name that was rendered phonetically in French by Boukman or Boukmann; in English, however, it was Bookman. Boukman was a "man of the book," as the Muslims were referred to even in Africa—in Sierra Leone, for example, explained an English lieutenant, the Mandingo were "Prime Ministers" of every town, and they went "by the name bookman." It is likely that Boukman was a Jamaican Muslim who had a Koran, and that he got his nickname from this."

In her conclusions on the role of Islam in the Haitian Revolution we read: **"There is thus compelling evidence that two major leaders in Haitian history—Macandal and Boukman—were not only Muslims, they did not embark on a jihad, but they were the leaders of the slave population, irrespective of religion. What they provided was military expertise coupled with spiritual and occult assurance that the outcome of the fight would be positive. Both skills were of extreme value, each in its own way; but put together, they conferred on these leaders the aura of mythical figures. Because of their marabout knowledge they could galvanize the masses, push them to action and to surpass themselves.**

Other marabouts, and **the Muslims in general, played a crucial role in the Haitian revolts and ultimately in the Haitian Revolution through their occult skills, literacy, and military traditions**. The marabouts provided protections to the insurgents in the form of gris-gris, as Colonel Malenfant recorded, and the Muslims used Arabic to communicate during uprisings.

Though their role and contribution have not been acknowledged, the Muslims were essential in the success of the Haitian Revolution."

Conclusion:

> *"Absence in the Ministers' Class must always be investigated"*
>
> *Original Rules of Instructions to the Laborers of Islam, No.6 by Master W.D. Fard Muhammad*

From what we have presented in this report, it becomes clear that the mysterious death of Muslim Minister Robert Dione Muhammad fits within a historical pattern, not a pattern of accidental deaths but a pattern of intentional deaths by murder. Thus, we cannot see his death as an isolated incident. His death is tied to the historical deaths of Muslim Ministers. His death is tied to the history of the American government's crusade to destroy Islam in America. His death is tied to the history of enslaved Blacks in the Western Hemisphere who believed in Islam and drew from this great faith the strength to fight and, in the case of the Haitian people, overcome their oppressors.

The 2 events hosted and Brother Minister Robert demonstrated to many his great value as a helper to the Honorable Minister Louis Farrakhan. It signaled that he was a critical and key representative of the Minister in the important state of Michigan.

Those events that assembled such a diverse audience of Blacks, Whites, Asians and Immigrants in the second largest city in the state of Michigan, flew in the face of COINTELPRO objectives as well as Jewish Leadership denial objectives where Black leaders like Minister Farrakhan are concerned. Consider that in 1968 the FBI's internal communications included the following stated objective: **Prevent militant Black Nationalist groups and leaders from gaining respectability, by discrediting them to three separate segments of the community**. The goal of discrediting Black Nationalist must be handled tactically in three ways. You must discredit these groups and individuals to, first, the responsible Negro community. Second, they must be discredited to the white community, both the responsible community and to "liberals" who have vestiges of sympathy for militant Black Nationalist simply because they are Negroes." *(March 4, 1968 Memo from FBI Director J. Edgar Hoover to Special Agents In Charge of 41 cities throughout America)* In the more recent history of Minister Farrakhan's rebuilding work of the Nation of Islam we find the 1994 memo written by Steven Freeman of the Anti-Defamation League of B'nai B'rith (ADL). Freeman's memo entitled **Mainstreaming Anti-Semitism: The Legitimation of Louis Farrakhan,** is a candid exposure of the reaction of Jewish groups to the growing appeal of the Honorable Minister Louis Farrakhan among Blacks in the traditional Civil Rights Movement. Freeman discussed actions that the ADL and its Jewish constituents would inflict upon all who help to "legitimate" Minister Farrakhan. Freeman is found using coded language when he writes that the Jewish community must ***"impose an obligation on those who deal with him, or, as in the case of universities, give him a platform."***

Michigan is now and has always been an important state to the Nation of Islam. Michigan is the state and Detroit is the city chosen by the Great Mahdi, Master W. Fard Muhammad, to begin the establishment of Islam in North America among the descendants of the enslaved Blacks. He chose Michigan. And today Michigan is the 5th most populous state for Islam as of 2010 Census report. Dearborn, Michigan which is a suburb of Detroit possesses one of the largest, if not the largest population of immigrant Muslims in the entire United States of America. Michigan is also a state where the Honorable Minister Louis Farrakhan has a residence. And very recently Nation of Islam Student Minister Marcus Muhammad was elected as the mayor for the city of Benton Harbor, Michigan.

So, in this historic state where the Nation of Islam was founded, Islam has grown and established itself. From Detroit to Benton Harbor to Grand Rapids to New Buffalo the Nation of Islam is a reality in Michigan. And as a pioneering Muslim reality dating back to the 1930s, it is at the root of the growing number of immigrant Muslims who see the state of Michigan as a welcoming landscape where the religion of Islam is not seen as an oddity as it is in many places in America. One of the first areas assigned to Elijah Muhammad to teach by his teacher Master W. Fard Muhammad was the small enclave called Hamtramck. A recent article forms **The Guardian** reports that the once predominantly polish enclave now had a 60% Muslim population. And according the Guardian report, the voters in Hamtramck have recently elected a majority Muslim city council, a fact considered a first in all of America. These facts let us know that while these kinds of developments are considered progress to Muslims, anti-Muslim forces in powerful positions view these achievements as "probable cause" for further efforts to "disrupt, discredit and neutralize" Islamic and Black Nationalists groups like the Nation of Islam.

The quote above is from the Original Rules of Instructions to the Laborers of Islam and is a part of a cherished sacred text used by all members of the Nation of Islam called **The Supreme Wisdom Lessons**. But this cherished text is addressed specifically to the **"Muslims of Number One Michigan."** And the word Michigan appears 7 times within the entire 40 pages of the Supreme Wisdom Lessons.

The above quote *"all absence in the ministry class must be investigated,"* is more than 80 years old. It was written by Master W. Fard Muhammad and serves a guidance to the Nation of Islam in our quest to find out the truth of what happened to our brother Minister Robert D. Muhammad. I believe that Master W. Fard Muhammad was giving us a principle and a posture to take knowing that His enemies and ours would seek the destruction of Islam through the elimination of its leaders.

Why Farrakhan Is Loved By Black America, and Is Always Welcomed Among Us!

Black people are never given a say in who white people choose to be their leaders. Black people are never given a say in who Jewish people choose to be their leaders. Black people are never given a say in who Asian people choose to be their leaders. Black people are never given a say in who any other self-respecting ethnic or racial group chooses to be their leader. And we are no longer going to allow those outside of our community to choose who speaks for us and who among the diverse array of Black community stake holders we will accept, associate with and honor. The Honorable Minister Louis Farrakhan's presence at the funeral and "home going celebration" of the Queen of Soul Aretha Franklin signified that in a mighty way. And this was despite the disapproval of many in the mainstream white and Jewish communities.

So please know and understand, we owe no one an explanation for why the Minister was graciously invited into the pulpit dais to sit as an honored guest at our dear sister's funeral and memorial services!

Yet as a student of the Minister, I wanted to take this as a significant and teachable moment. You see, I have seen many article headlines and FOX News commentary asking 'why was the Honorable Minister present at Aretha's funeral'. And most in the Black community implicitly understand why and were happy to see the Minister there. Quite frankly, most who love the Minister can't really put into words why they do. And this phenomenon as I have studied it, is indicative of a deep spiritual connection between the Minister and the Black community. And it is not just the Minister's kindness, personal humbleness and generosity, all of which are characteristic virtues of the Minister that are omitted in the media's reporting about him; the connection is deeper.

When we in the Black community hear the Minister's bold and beautiful preaching it is an experience where we feel as though he has read our minds; he says the things we feel but don't have the words to say. We see in him the courage, strength and forthrightness that we know needs to be expressed from Black people living in a white dominated society. And we have come to take comfort in the fact that he will always "keep it real" with us, teach us and risk his own life exposing to us truths and information that white America wants to hide from us. But most of all, we simply feel good, when we hear him speak. Hearing the Minister speak makes us feel secure. And as the old saying goes, often "people may forget what you have said, but they never forget how you make them feel". And the Minister makes a people who have endure so much pain to feel good. When we hear him our souls leap for joy!

In this teachable moment I also wanted to write for the benefit of the many who love the Minister but feel that they must do so privately out of fear of the reactions of powerful white and Jewish people that they may have relationships with and or do business with. So, despite their embrace of him within their hearts, they aren't prepared to offer a word in defense or public support for him. So, I want to show them how to do that. Because the Minister is not only worthy to sit on the stage at a funeral; he is worthy to be defended against the slander of his enemies.

I maintain that when you consider the good works and dedication of Minister Farrakhan to the survival and improvement of the Black community, that one cannot say that they are a friend of the Black community and yet oppose Minister Farrakhan. Our community does not have friends and allies that express disdain and act in opposition to our beloved Minister and champion. And the stronger we become as a people, opposition to Minister Farrakhan must and will become anathema to the Black community.

The Minister's Message Literally Gives Life

First, I want to cite the testimony of Bay Area journalist Fahizah Alim who is very powerful in her telling of her personal experience with the ministry of the Hon. Min. Louis Farrakhan. She writes:

> "I know Farrakhan's real-world impact on people. For example, when I started attending the University of California, Berkley, I also started taking the birth control pill. I think it was included in the registration packet. I mention the birth control pill because at the time, it was the drug of choice for most single young women. Many who were still in high school and not yet sexually active were prescribed the potent drugs, allegedly to "regulate their cycles."
> Moreover, marijuana, "drop out," and "free love" were the buzzwords of my generation. The Beatles, Jimi Hendrix, Sly and the Family Stone,

our Pied Pipers of modernity, lured us into a dark and swirling hole of hedonism. And Farrakhan, espousing the teachings of Elijah Muhammad, brought me out of the tailspin. Until that point, I had been taking birth control pills to keep from getting pregnant. But after listening to Louis Farrakhan speak about how potent a drug must be to be capable of shutting down one of nature's powerful biological functions-that of reproducing itself-I stopped.

It took me another 2 years to ovulate or produce eggs again. And some years later, the pharmaceutical companies revealed that we had been guinea pigs and the pills prescribed to some young women were about 10 times more potent than they should have been.

"You are poisoning yourself," Farrakhan has said. "Why kill the fruit of your womb and prevent maybe another great Black Leader from being born? Hasn't Pharaoh killed enough of our children?" I am glad I heard him, I stopped taking the pill. And now I am the proud mother of 4 children: a daughter and 3 sons."

Ms. Alim's powerful personal testimony is far from exceptional; it is typical of the experiences, both private and public, that many in the Black community have had with Minister Farrakhan.

Minister Farrakhan's Impact in Black America is Vast and Overwhelmingly Positive

Second, I remind the reader of the overwhelming and tremendous event known as the Million Man March. On October 16, 1995 Minister Farrakhan called for 1 million men to meet him in Washington, D.C. to rally and organize around the themes of "atonement, reconciliation and responsibility." Nearly 2 million men showed up to answer the Minister's call! Authors Gary Fields and Maria Puente wrote in the USA Today some of the early successes of the Million Man March:

> The Million Man March caused up to 15,000 new applicants wanting to adopt black children.
> The Million Man March spawned spin-offs: Million Woman March; Million Youth March; Million Fathers March; Million Hoodie March; Million Man March in Tahrir Square in Egypt.
> The Million Man March Increased interest among black men in serving their communities.
> Anecdotal evidence suggests this may be the march's most tangible

legacy. In Philadelphia, 19 men joined the Big Brother program during a November 1995 recruiting drive as a direct result of the march.

"Many of them were still on that high of 'you got to do something for the community,' " says Cheryl Dennis, head of recruitment for the Big Brother/ Big Sister Association of Philadelphia.

The Memphis Big Brother organization estimates that 33 of the 100 people picked up in last year's recruitment drive came as a direct result of the march.

In Denver, 100 black men went door-to-door in a neighborhood after a 3-year-old was killed in a drive-by shooting, seeking information. In a neighborhood not known for cooperating with police, their efforts helped lead to an arrest.

In Atlanta, the local organizing committee held a drive to encourage people to open accounts at black-owned banks. Timothy McDonald, leader of the committee, said the drive resulted in $3 million being transferred into Atlanta's black-owned banks. The committee also ran a Saturday school during the summer that helped 75 students with reading, writing, math, geography and English literature."

The Million March is important for a variety of reasons. Consider how FOX news and those who have come under the influence of the ADL and the Southern Poverty Law Center continue to slander the Minister by referring to him as being anti-Semitic. But on the largest possible stage and in front of his largest audience ever, Minister Farrakhan did not ask those nearly 2 million men to do harm or commit any offense to a member of the Jewish community. If he was an anti-Semite as he has been portrayed to be then this largest of all crowds assembled to hear him would have been rallied to oppose Jewish survival. In fact, Rabbi Brue Kahn was in attendance at the Million Man March and he offered this testimony as a reflection of his experience that day. According to Rabbi Kahn:

> I am White. I am a rabbi. I attended the Million Man March where I stood hour after hour in the midst of a sea of excited, highly principled, welcoming Black men. On that Monday, I was enveloped in an overwhelming sense of joy, pride, responsibility, thoughtfulness, hope and love. ...Yet, no one seemed to dodge one bit an awareness of what is wrong and what needs repair in the Black neighborhoods across America. Speaker after speaker, especially Minister Louis Farrakhan, confronted self-destructive behavior by too many Black males in a hard

hitting, no nonsense, clearly defined and agonizingly descriptive fashion. The people around me did the same. No cover-ups. But there was so much more that made this day unique. It was a day of atonement and affirmation. ... When it comes to reporting on African Americans in general and Minister Louis Farrakhan and the Nation of Islam in particular, this weakness [of the media] is most pronounced. Reporters are driven to take the quotes that will antagonize the reader and do not let go of those words. Convey a negative impression and generate conflict, regardless of how out of line that is with the point and mass of a presentation. There seems to be a mission, conscious or subconscious, to put before the American people as much bad stuff about Blacks as possible. ... the people who listen to him do not go chasing down Jews, or gays or Whites or Koreans to beat them and murder them. They do not do that for two reasons:

First, he warns them against such violent behavior. Second, these verbal onslaughts do not constitute the main thrust of his message. As unacceptable as they are, they are also tangential. His listeners know that. They are sufferers who know how tough it is to get a fair shake as Black people. They want that to change. They hear in Minister Farrakhan's words inspiration and instructions to begin to bring about that change. That is the message on which he focuses and on which they focus. That is not the message on which the media focuses.

Third, the reader must be reminded or introduced to the fact that the Minister's ability to transform the lives of Black youth is well documented. And for that, Black America loves him especially. The Minister directly and through his representatives have intervened in the lives of young men and women who were basically casualties in the U.S. government's War on Drugs. Professor Mattias Gardell has written of the Minister:

> "Farrakhan has a unique capability ...able to reach deeply into the souls of black youths...is able to talk to them in a way that really makes them listen...this rapport enables Farrakhan to criticize and redirect destructive behavioral patterns".

Minister Farrakhan's Generosity

Also, many in the Black community have been the beneficiaries of the generosity of Minister Farrakhan. The Minister is extremely generous with his time, his knowledge and with his money. Consider the testimony of the Rev. Charles Steele. As the incoming president of the SCLC (Southern Christian Leadership

Conference) several years ago, Rev. Steele inherited an organization that was financially in ruins. Rev. Steele said:

> "Minister Farrakhan is a great leader and I always respected that.... So, SCLC called upon me to come to the helm of the organization 2004. When I got here, it was devastation. We ran into many problems that I didn't realize existed, even though I was on the board. I was a state senator at the time. I resigned my state senate seat and came to SCLC and realized that it's one thing being on the board of SCLC. But it's another thing when you're sitting in the chair of the organization that was co-founded by Dr. Martin Luther King.... We couldn't meet payroll! The headline in the Atlanta Journal constitution said, SCLC has collapsed, it's dead. The only thing that can save SCLC is God himself!... And so, I called the Minister. I called Minister Louis Farrakhan and I didn't tell what the subject matter was. I just said, "Minister, this is Charles Steele Jr. President and CEO of the Southern Christian Leadership Conference. As you know Minister I've just taken over the helm of SCLC.
> I want to come to the palace to Chicago to just converse with you for an hour or two." And he said, "No problem my brother. Brother Steele when do you want to come?" I said, "What about tomorrow?" He said "Great, come on up tomorrow let's talk." And after talking with us for about two hours or so, along with Reverend Albert E. Love who was my special assistant at the time who accompanied me, I looked at the Minister, I said, "Minister let me just be honest with you. I'm broke. SCLC is broke. We don't have no money. But if you just help me and loan me a few dollars. In terms of my plight of SCLC. I promise you that I will multiply it and I will pay you back."
> And the Minister looked at me and he said, "My brother, you got my attention." He said, "Just one thing that I want you to realize. I'm going to give you the money that you asked for because I know you mean well and you are going to do what is right to uplift the organization." He said, "You must realize you can't pay me back. You just go and be successful with Dr. King's organization and make it work for our people and I will be proud, and I will commend the fact that you had enough motivation to come all the way to Chicago and to share with me your vision and your strategy. I encourage, you to continue and this is what I will do to help you. But. I repeat you can't pay me back." ... We were able to build a brand-new building that we are so proud of, of the mere fact that God enable us to raise the money to buy it, to pay it off debt free. We were able to keep our payroll in its existence and we were

able to take SCLC to another level and that's internationally. And again, this would not have been done had it not been for Minister Farrakhan and others. But he was the first one; he was the first one to write the check. Because we had no money; we had no encouragement. We had no financial resource that we could go to. The bank wouldn't loan us no money. We didn't have any individuals that would volunteer to help us at the magnitude that we needed.

To lift us up financially, God has blessed us to multiply the contribution that Minister Farrakhan gave us. And within three and a half years we built a brand-new building and raised a total of twenty million dollars."

It should be noted that what the Minister did for Rev. Steele and the SCLC is in keeping with the Quranic principle of "do no favor seeking gain." The Quran commands the believers to be charitable and to give both openly and secretly, but only for the glory of Allah (God) and never for self-aggrandizement or prestige. And this is also true of the Minister because if it was not for Rev. Steele publicizing the Minister's gift of financial support, we wouldn't know anything about it; the Minister never made it known publicly. It was the goodness and gratitude of Rev. Steele who wanted the world to know of the goodness and sincerity of Minister Farrakhan.

A final note on why Black America loves the Minister in spite of the disapproval of many in the White America is found in the commentary of Theology Professor Andre C. Willis who said of Minister Farrakhan:

> The best of the legacy of Farrakhan is twofold. First, he has demonstrated a deep understanding of and shown an unswerving courage to publicly detail the lived reality of anti-black racism. There is simply no Black person in the world that has — over so many years — been as consistent, as unrestricted, and as forthright in defending the humanity of Black people throughout the world against its attackers.

The Minister has defended us and unfortunately, we have not done a good enough job in defending him. But rest assured, this too is changing. And the Minister's prominent placement at the funeral of Aretha Franklin is a sign that we as a people are getting strong enough to say to the descendants of our former slave masters; **"we are free, and we will choose our own friends, family and leaders. Leave us alone!"**

The Wicked Use of Science & Chemistry to Stop Black Liberation

"...they would not teach our people the science of modern warfare (defense), birth control or chemistry."-Hon. Elijah Muhammad

"The devil desires only to create enmity and hatred among you by means of intoxicants and games of chance, and to keep you back from the remembrance of Allah and from prayer. Will you then keep back?" -Holy Qur'an 5:91

"The slave may be "used" so as to be "used up" in seven years; may be used as a "breeder," as a prostitute, as a concubine, as a pimp, as a tapster, as an attendant at the gaming-table, as a subject of medical and surgical experiments for the benefit of science..."-The American Slave Code, Goodell

The Prophet Daniel & Min. Farrakhan

In the July 4, 2020 message by Minister Farrakhan entitled **The Criterion**, the Minister declared to the American people, with particular emphasis on the Black and Latino communities, that the proposed COVID-19 vaccines should not be taken. Minister Farrakhan's rejection of the COVID-19 vaccine and his strong admonition against the Black and Latino communities receiving it has caused a controversy. Yet like the Bible's Prophet Daniel, Minister Farrakhan has been guided by Allah (God) to reject the pharmaceutical industry's COVID-19 vaccine. It was the prophet Daniel in the Bible's Old Testament who rejected the "King's meat" and the "King's drink." Daniel's rejection of what his government told him to put into his body, provides a prophetic example for Minister Farrakhan's rejection of what the American government has approved for us to put into our bodies as an experimental vaccine.

Yakub's Needles

A review of the Most Honorable Elijah Muhammad's teachings about Mr. Yacub, a great Black scientist whose divine mission it was to graft out of Black people the white race, is helpful to us in considering the Minister's admonition.

The Hon. Elijah Muhammad said that Mr. Yacub used doctors and nurses in the process of grafting the White race by using the genetic material of the original Black people. Mr. Yacub was a scientist. And contrary to popular opinion, it is not brute force that has been the secret to white supremacy's global conquest of people of color. It has been the weaponization of science.

The Most Honorable Elijah Muhammad writes in Message To The Blackman:

> "His [Yakub's] aim was to kill and destroy the black nation. He ordered the nurses to kill all black babies that were born among his people, **by pricking the brains with a sharp needle as soon as the black child's head is out of the mother.**"

Yakub's needling of the brains of Black babies more than 6,000 years ago is tied to today's push by the modern Yacoubian scientists who follow after his model. As infamous attorney Alan Dershowitz proclaimed, the government has the power to "plunge a needle" filled with COVID-19 vaccine into the arms of the Black and Latino communities et.al.

The Slave master's Alcohol
While Mr. Yacub was trying to prevent the physical birth of Black babies. Today there is a push and hidden agenda to not only curtail the birth rate and subsequent population growth of Black and Latino people; but to also mentally incapacitate us. The history of the white oppression of Black people is replete with documentation of the white ruling class's sophisticated scientific war against Black life and the revolutionary ideas that move our people towards the ultimate goal of freedom and independence.

After Nat Turner's rebellion, Virginia state legislator Henry Berry publicly expressed a desire to mentally incapacitate Black people, in an effort to prevent future slave rebellions. He stated:

> "Pass as severe laws as you will to keep these unfortunate creatures in ignorance. It is in vain **unless you can extinguish that spark of intellect which God has given them.** ...Sir, we have as far as possible **closed every avenue by which light may enter their minds. We only have to go one step further to extinguish their capacity to see the light and**

our work will be completed. And **they would then be reduced to the level of the beasts of the field and we should be safe."**

Henry Berry's passionate plea to find a way to destroy Black intellect so that white people could be safe is an extraordinary admission! He here, draws a direct line of both correlation and causation between intelligence and revolution.

That a COVID-19 vaccine has been hastily readied for a Christmas time delivery has caused me to reflect upon the words of Fredrick Douglass in his autobiography. He notes that during Christmas time alcohol was used as a chemical substance to blunt and neutralize the minds of Black slaves. Plantation owners feared that slaves would use Christmas time as an occasion to escape bondage and foment insurrection. According to Douglass:

> "We [slaves] were induced to drink...When the slave was drunk the slaveholder had no fear that he would plan an insurrection, or that he would escape to the North. It was the sober, thoughtful slave who was dangerous and needed the vigilance of his master to keep him a slave."

The CIA's Crack Cocaine

What will be the lasting side effects of the COVID-19 vaccine upon the bodies and minds of those in the Black and Latino community? We don't know. But we must maintain a vigilance that is based upon the Minister's guidance and our knowledge of the history of science and chemistry being weaponized against our fight for liberation.

In the 1960s heroin ravaged the inner-cities of America at a period of time when many youths were beginning to become politically active and joining the fight for justice and equality. During the 1980s crack cocaine appeared as a chemical scourge that victimized millions of youth at a time when many youths were becoming socially conscious and becoming members of the rebuilt Nation of Islam led by the Hon. Min. Louis Farrakhan.

Cocaine as a chemical substance used to control Black behavior is discussed by author Richard Harvey Brown in his work *Coca and Cocaine in the United States*. He writes:

> "Employers in the South had made a practice of supplying their black workers with cocaine ...plantation owners had discovered things went better with coke. Thus, they kept a steady supply on hand to increase

productivity and keep workers content. Cocaine was also a cheap incentive to maintain control of workers. A shrewd boss doling out one-quarter gram a day per man could keep sixteen workers happy and more productive for a full seven days on a single ounce"

The U.S. Government's complicity in the Black community's problems with chemical substance abuse was the subject of a 1996 public forum with CIA Director John Deutch and the Black community of South-Central Los Angeles. It was there, in a public forum, that former LAPD detective Michael C. Ruppert publicly stated:

"I will tell you Director Deutch, as a former Los Angeles Police narcotics Detective, that the Agency has dealt drugs throughout this country for a long time. Director Deutch, I will refer you to three specific Agency operations known as Amadeus, Pegasus and Watchtower. I have Watchtower documents, heavily redacted by the Agency. I was personally exposed to CIA operations and recruited by CIA personnel who attempted to recruit me in the late seventies to become involved in protecting Agency drug operations in this country."

Drapetomania

During the days of chattel slavery, in the era of Virginia legislator Henry Berry, Yacubian physician Dr. Samuel A. Cartwright invented the diagnosis known as "**drapetomania.**" for Blacks who refused to comfortably accept chattel slavery as their lot in life. And he prescribed brutal beating as the only cure.

The words of Minister Farrakhan, as THE spiritual guide and messianic presence among us should guide us. A study of history should confirm us in following the Minister's guidance. This vaccine is being pushed onto the Black community during a time where our cry for justice has reached a definite crescendo! We must reject the scientific use of yet another chemical substance that claims to heal us now, but may harm us later. The chemistry of alcohol, heroin, cocaine and various other substances have all been weaponized against our people over the years. But they have not been able to completely destroy the spark of our Allah (God) given intellect, that when properly fed propels us towards freedom and independence!

A final word from the Most Hon. Elijah Muhammad:

"This is the real trouble: the whites oppose us, the black people of

America, who were their slaves once upon a time, from ever becoming anything like self-independent. They want to keep them subject to themselves **in a more educational and scientific way**, other than their fathers. Their fathers only used the common knowledge of enslaving our people. But, **today their children can use one of the smartest scientific ways against our people to keep them subjected to them that ever were invented by a race of people** since time was."

Woe Unto Charleston! An Open Letter To The Clergy of Charleston, South Carolina

The Honorable Minister Louis Farrakhan has been recently unwelcomed in the city of Charleston, South Carolina. The Minister desired to grace the city of Charleston with his presence by including it as a part of his city to city tour in promotion of the 20th Anniversary of the Million Man March. Yet all arenas, churches and suitable spaces have rejected Minister Farrakhan and the Nation of Islam.

As a student in the ministry class of the Honorable Minister Louis Farrakhan and a member of his research group, I wanted to write to my colleagues in the ministry in the city of Charleston, South Carolina. All Black clergy whether Muslim, Hebrew, Christian or other faiths are co-workers in a unique and special vineyard filled with a burdened and pained mass of Black people that today are stunned and shocked at the new season of lynching that is manifest throughout America. As a result, we should see each other as colleagues, brothers and allies despite what may be theological or doctrinal differences. After all, the Abrahamic faiths are really more **orthopraxic** (*emphasizing the correct conduct and actions*) than **orthodoxic** (*emphasizing the correct beliefs and doctrines*). And one can easily see the grand opportunities for all men and women of faith to be united in brotherhood and sisterhood if we take to the "highways and byways" of the inner cities of America. For it is there among the pained and suffering Black community that we will find the modern Lazarus, the modern adulteress, the modern man with the withered hand, and the modern woman with the issue of blood; yes, even the modern blind man at the pool of Siloam is to be found today in the "hood."

I grew up in a wonderful Baptist church with parents who were active members of our church. My grandmother was a Sunday school teacher and church pianist. My great grandmother was the superintendent of the Sunday school, sang in the choir and coordinator of church missionaries. It was in the home of my great grandmother that I remember vividly to this day watching for the first time a movie about the life of Jesus and his crucifixion. And as a child, watching the horrible treatment being done to such a good man, I said to myself that if I had been alive during that time I would have helped Jesus; I would have been with him. Even as a child of no more than 9 or 10 years of age, it disturbed me to see the movie portrayal of the crucifixion of a man that I had been taught by my parents was the Saviour of the world. I remember dreaming about it for several days after watching that film.

I became a member of the Nation of Islam as a teenager and my membership in the Nation did not diminish my love for Jesus. In fact, it broadened my understanding of Jesus in a profound way. It helped me to understand how the suffering of Jesus in the Bible paralleled with the suffering of my own Black people inside America. It helped me understand how the suffering of Jesus served as a model for what Black leadership experienced as a result of the horrible confluence of forces seen in their being misunderstood by their own people, coupled with being opposed by the government and maligned and condemned by Jewish groups. My membership in the Nation of Islam above everything else made me to want to go beyond a posture and disposition of just being satisfied with praising Jesus. It made me to know that what God really requires is that I strive to discipline my life according to the teachings and example of Jesus.

I share this of myself so that you will understand that my letter to you is not from a place of hatred for you or a place of condemnation of any of you personally. I don't write to you as one who is not familiar with the Black Christian experience. Neither do I write to you as one who does not love, admire and see as a model for my life Jesus the Christ. I am not even writing you as a stereotypical Muslim who seeks to minimize the importance of Jesus as being just a mere 'Prophet.' Not that there is anything ordinary about a Prophet or Messenger of God, but I challenge my own Muslim brothers with what I have learned as a student of the Honorable Minister Louis Farrakhan. For it is Minister Farrakhan, who has always emphasized the Quranic teachings, that refers to Jesus in 11 different passages, as the "Messiah." In fact, Islamic eschatology focuses on the return of Jesus as one of the major events of the end of this world and the judgment of God.

I write to you as a brother.

And as your brother, I have to condemn in strong terms your rejection of the best brother that Black people have in the world today- the Honorable Minister Louis Farrakhan.

Dylan Roof killed 9 precious Black men and women who had assembled for prayer and worship at Mother Emmanuel AME church in Charleston. Yet in the immediate aftermath of this horrible act of terrorism, news reports circulated that the family members of the slain were offering Dylan Roof forgiveness. This sent a message throughout America and the world that the Black community of Charleston had literally forgiven the unforgivable. It said to the world that the Black community of Charleston was willing to accept the cold-blooded murder of some of the best members of that historic community without any demand for justice and prosecution of the guilty. It portrayed that trauma-stricken community as weak, helpless and leaderless. It showed that the Black community in Charleston, South Carolina is truly a "prey in the hand of the mighty."

And I witnessed no pastors or preachers intervening to offer the perspective of God. God's reaction to the murder of the righteous, as recorded in the Bible, is strong and fierce! Recall dear pastor the Bible's book of Isaiah and its 49th chapter. In Isaiah chapter 49 verses 25-26 we read **"For I will fight those who fight you, and I will save your children. I will feed your enemies with their own flesh. They will be drunk with rivers of their own blood. All the world will know that I, the Lord, am your Savior and your Redeemer, the Mighty One of Israel. "**

Yet there were no reports of Charleston clergy openly disagreeing with the family member's misguided reaction to the murder of their loved ones. And this silence and inability to apply the "meat" of the word of God is equal to **mal-practice** in the ministry.

The Bible is clear that even God hates and Jesus spoke of hate in what scholars describe as a class of his teachings known as the **"hard sayings of Jesus."** If as pastors and spiritual leaders of Charleston, South Carolina we did not draw the public's attention to the Bible where we read in the book of Ecclesiastes such passages as found in chapter 3, *"There is a time for everything, And a season for every activity under the heavens* **a time to love and a time to hate**...*a time for war and a time for peace."*, we are guilty of **mal-practice**.

If we didn't remind the believers of what the Bible contains about how God hates, and his Prophets hates the wicked, we are guilty of **mal-practice in ministry**. The Bible is clear that *"the Lord thy*

God is a man of war." And his vengeance, wrath, anger and hatred are preserved for the wicked who act as wolves devouring the righteous sheep-like believers in God. Be reminded brothers and sisters in the ministry of the "meat" of the word of God. The meat of his word if often deemed indigestible by weak hearted men and women. Some examples of the "meat" of the word include the following verses:

"For I, the LORD, love justice; **I hate robbery and wrongdoing***. In my faithfulness I will reward my people and make an everlasting covenant with them. (Isaiah 61:8)*

Again, and again I sent my servants the prophets, who said, **'Do not do this detestable thing that I hate!'***(Jeremiah 44:4)*

do not plot evil against each other, and do not love to swear falsely. **I hate all this," declares the LORD***. (Zechariah 8:17)*

Even Jesus instructed the new believers who were just beginning their journey through life as his disciples while their family and friends opposed their following of Jesus by uttering this "hard saying," *"If anyone comes to me and does not* **hate father and mother, wife and children, brothers and sisters--yes, even their own life--such a person cannot be my disciple***." (Luke 14:26)*

If we as men and women of God cannot teach these passages of scripture with courage and conviction when the wicked rise up to kill the righteous, we are guilty of **mal-practice in ministry** and should strongly consider another line of work!

I fear that some of you who have been so psychologically imprisoned by destructive doctrinal dogmas will dismiss Old Testament scripture as arcane, irrelevant and antithetical to the grace and salvation represented by Jesus the Christ. But I caution you in that attitude. Because you may distance yourself from the Old Testament and its emphasis on justice and the law of God, but Jesus certainly did not. He said *"Don't misunderstand why I have come.* **I did not come to abolish the law of Moses or the writings of the prophets. No, I came to accomplish their purpose.** *(Matthew 5:17)*

Your rejection of Minister Farrakhan is a grave offense! One needs only to consider your rejection of the Minister in the light of

Biblical scripture. In the synoptic gospels of Mathew, Mark, and Luke, we find the following cautionary verses on the subject of the rejection of the disciples of Jesus.

In Mark 6:11-12 we read *"And if any place will not welcome you or listen to you, leave that place and shake the dust off your feet as **a testimony against them**."*

In Matthew 10:14-15 we read *"If anyone will not welcome you or listen to your words, leave that home or town and shake the dust off your feet. Truly I tell you, **it will be more bearable for Sodom and Gomorrah on the day of judgment than for that town**.*

In Luke 10: 10-12 we read *"But if a town refuses to welcome you, go out into its streets and say, 'We wipe even the dust of your town from our feet to show that we have abandoned you to your fate. And know this—the Kingdom of God is near!'* **I assure you, even wicked Sodom will be better off than such a town on judgment day."**

Here in these passages we find that a severe punishment is to be visited upon towns and cities that reject disciples of Jesus. Sodom and Gomorrah was violently razed by God and exists today only in history as a warning and cautionary tale. Yet Jesus says that when his disciples are rejected by cities, those cities have been ear-marked by God for a worse fate than Sodom!

Dear pastors and clergy of Charleston, cannot you see that the Honorable Minister Louis Farrakhan is the best disciple of Jesus present among you today? If you can't, allow me to help remove the scales from your eyes.

Forget doctrine and orthodoxy for a moment. Because Jesus was **unorthodox**; and he never used orthodoxy as a standard of judgment. In fact, Jesus was so unorthodox that the Jews of his day strongly condemned him. Even to this day, the Jewish community holds Jesus in disgust and condemnation. While Islam on the other hand, venerates and honors Jesus and his mother Mary.

Mark 9:38-40 proves Jesus attached more value to one having the correct actions than in one merely espousing the correct doctrines. That passage documents a conversation between Jesus and the disciple John. In some Bible translations it is found under the subject heading **Intolerance Rebuked** and reads as follows: *"Teacher, we saw someone using your name to cast out demons, but **we told him to stop because he wasn't in our group**. 'Don't stop him!' Jesus said. 'No one who performs a miracle in my name will soon be able to speak evil of me. **Anyone who is not against us is for us.**"*

Consider such an enlightened perspective provided by Jesus as you reflect upon Minister Farrakhan, whom many pastors say preaches Jesus as well as or better than most Christian preachers. And he has been to the Black church a helper, a cheerleader, a friend and a companion. And some of you have personally benefitted from the Minister's love for you. Yet some of you think like John thought, that he should be stopped because he is not a part of your denomination. How foolish!

I challenge you to examine the effect of his preaching. You will find that his students and followers reflect the discipline, moral striving and a willingness to obey God just like Jesus taught and demonstrated. And while many of you struggle to bring your own congregations into what the New Testament calls a holiness lifestyle, Minister Farrakhan has modeled the way for you. The Minister is widely known for the moral reform of those who follow him. Many of us in our *pre-Farrakhan* days were drug abusers, thieves, murderers and practitioners of self-destructive lifestyles. This is the man that you have rejected.

The man you rejected made a call in 1995 for a million Black men to meet him in Washington, D.C. for the historic Million Man March. Nearly 2 million men answered that call and traveled to Washington, D.C. at their own expense. And of the nearly 2 million men, most or nearly 75% self-identified as Christian. This begs the question why did a million Christian men respond enthusiastically to the call of Muslim Minister Louis Farrakhan? As a pastor, you know that Bible scripture teaches that Jesus' sheep "know his voice" and will not follow a stranger. The Million Man March proved that **the voice for Jesus in the world today is the Honorable Minister Louis Farrakhan**!

The man you rejected has defended the most notable of Black men, women and groups whenever the white power structure moved against them to ruin their reputation and destroy their careers. In fact, the conflict with the Jewish community and

Minister Farrakhan is the result of the Minister's defense of Rev. Jesse L. Jackson Sr. in his ambitious run for President of the United States. And all while the Minister has defended Black leadership he has himself been the subject of the most vicious and wicked propaganda campaign in American history. As a result of defending Rev. Jackson, he was branded an anti-Semite by the leaders of the Jewish community. As a result of defending Rev. Jackson, he was ultimately censured by the United States Senate. Yet none of this deterred him in his resolve to defend his own Black brothers and sisters.

The man you rejected has used his good name and reputation with the masses of our people to speak well of and defend and support notable Black clergy. The Minister's resume documents his support and defense of **Rev. Jesse L. Jackson Sr.; Rev. Charles Coen; Rev. Eddie Carthan; Archbishop George A. Stallings; Rev. James L. Bevel; Rev. Benjamin F. Chavis; and Rev. T.L. Barrett**, just to name a few. Whether you know it or not, when the Minister suffers being beaten up by the media, the Jews and the U.S. government but at the same time defends, supports, guides and finds ways to help you, you are witnessing him reflect the principle in the phrase *"by his stripes we are healed."* Again, this proves that Minister Farrakhan is living the principles and character of Jesus while most are just satisfied to "praise his holy name." Maturity should teach us that praise alone is not enough. If praise is not followed by carrying the teachings and example of Jesus into practice, it is nothing more than an empty exercise in vanity.

The man that you rejected spoke at the Million Man March and refused to use the occasion as a recruitment tool for the Nation of Islam. Instead he gave the following humble instructions to the million men. *"Every one of you must go back home and* **join some church, synagogue or temple or mosque that is teaching spiritual and moral uplift***. I want you, brothers; there are no men in the church, in the mosque. The men are in the streets and we got to get back to the houses of God."* Which one of you as pastors would have enjoyed such an audience and steered your listeners to fill the pews of another congregation or religion?

The man that you rejected went into the treasury of the Nation of Islam to extend a grant of funding to the Rev. Dr. Charles Steele for the upkeep and maintenance of the Southern **Christian**

Leadership Conference. To which, the Rev. Dr. Steele exclaimed ***"I can honestly say, if it was not for Minister Louis Farrakhan, the SCLC would be out of business."***

This is just some of the sterling record of the man that you rejected –the Honorable Minister Louis Farrakhan. You know that he has been a great blessing to you. Your rejection of him is shameful, disgraceful and a manifestation of cowardice.

Brother and Sister Pastors, your rejection of Minister Farrakhan is an offense that demands repentance.

You would do well now to beg God's forgiveness for your rejection of Minister Farrakhan. Repent and become the bold and courageous man or woman of God that a time like this demands. Repent and join Minister Farrakhan along with your congregations for the Justice or Else rally in Washington, D.C. on October 10, 2015. Repent and join the Minister in having what Dr. Martin Luther King Jr. called for in 1963 which is a "sacrificial Christmas." This is a call for you and your congregations to unite with the Justice or Else Movement and show the world just "what would Jesus do" in a time like this. We are keeping our money in our pockets this year and expect you and your congregations to participate with us in an economic withdrawal of the Christmas spending season. Lastly, you should make haste in hosting the Honorable Minister Louis Farrakhan in your city at his earliest convenience. Extend to him an invitation to speak in the city of Charleston as soon as possible! This is critical, otherwise, you place your city into that horrible category that Jesus warned of-- a city whose fate is so horrible, it will make God's destruction of Sodom and Gomorrah seem mild by comparison.

The Mis-Education of Henry Louis Gates, Jr.

Abdul Arif Muhammad, Esq.
Student Minister and Nation of Islam General Counsel

In an April 23, 2010 Op-Ed piece for The New York Times titled "Ending the Slavery Blame-Game," Harvard Professor Henry Louis Gates, Jr. argues that a moral, historic, political and economic equivalency exists between the culpability and responsibility of some Africans who participated in the transatlantic slave trade with the nations of Europe and the American colonies. This article perverts history and violates what Dr. W.E.B. DuBois called "scientific truth." The article was intellectually disingenuous from the standpoint of history and scholarship.

The article is a perfect example of the "educated Negro" who has been taught to find his "proper place" at the back door, as stated by Dr. Carter G. Woodson in his book, "The Mis-Education of the Negro." Professor Gates demonstrates through this article that he has accepted his proper place at the back door, showing he is in the category of an "educated Negro" that has, in fact, been mis-educated. It is not surprising then that when Prof. Gates was mishandled by White police officers in Massachusetts, he felt it necessary to inform the police that he was a Harvard professor. This is the mind of Black inferiority masquerading as an "educated Negro" who has in fact forgotten who he is in the mind of White America.

Sadly, the "educated Negro" state of mind has been a historic problem in the struggle of the masses of Black people for true liberation because there has always been a segment within the black community who are the buffers and apologists for the evil of White America against its black citizens. This phenomenon has been discussed in several scholarly works including "The Black Bourgeoisie", by Dr. E. Franklin Frazier; "The Crisis of the Negro Intellectual", by Dr. Harold Cruse; "The Souls of Black Folks", by Dr. W.E.B. DuBois and of course the aforementioned "The Mis-Education of the Negro", by Dr. Carter G. Woodson.

Professor Gates' arguments are far below the standard of what one should expect from the Director of the W.E.B. DuBois Institute for African and African American Research at Harvard University. Dr. DuBois was the first Black man to receive a Ph.D. degree from

Harvard University in 1895. The irony of Professor Gates' article is that Dr. DuBois' doctoral dissertation was titled, "The Suppression of the African Slave Trade to The United States of America, 1638-1870." It was first published in 1896 as one of the Harvard historical studies. This study properly placed the culpability and responsibility for slavery on Europe and the American colonies. Whatever the role some Africans may have played, Dr. DuBois did not seem to view it as requiring research and scholarly attribution.

Professor Gates' claim that the idea of reparations is "compensation for our ancestor's unpaid labor and bondage," clearly shows the extent of his mis-education. Reparations is a cry for justice borne from the horrors of the transatlantic slave trade, over three centuries of chattel slavery where our ancestors according to Dr. DuBois were "worked to death," and the injustices suffered by the masses of black people even down to this present day. The issue of reparations is not solely based upon compensation because money alone will not solve the 400-year destruction of an entire people, who were robbed of the knowledge of themselves, the knowledge of their heritage, robbed of their names, language, and religion. The accumulative effect of slavery was that Black people were destroyed in their ability to think and do for themselves.

'When you control a man's thinking you do not have to worry about his actions. You do not have to tell him not to stand here or go yonder. He will find his 'proper place' and will stay in it. You do not need to send him to the back door. He will go without being told. In fact, if there is no back door, he will cut one for his special benefit. His education makes it necessary.'—Carter G. Woodson

Reparations have to be determined based upon the extent of the injury inflicted, and the cost must be calculated to actually repair the damage done from slavery, Jim Crow segregation, lynching, raping of women, destruction of the institution of the Black family, assassination of Black leaders, shortened life expectancy from disease, poor health care, drug abuse, gang violence, Black on Black homicide, police brutality, racial profiling and mob attacks. Prof. Gates' view that the call for reparations may be symbolic and impractical is profoundly egregious and shows his profound lack of understanding of the scientific truth of black suffering during slavery and since emancipation.

Prof. Gates' claims that Africans played a "significant role" in the slave trade and that it was "lucrative for European buyers and African sellers alike" is astounding. His view that equal culpability for the slave trade and slavery "should truly belong to white people and black people on both sides of the Atlantic" is a historic perversion of the worst kind. Prof. Gates obviously did not consider how Africa was devastated by the slave trade from the 1500s to the 1800s; then, how she was systematically underdeveloped by European colonization from 1885 through the Second World War (1947). It was not until Ghana, the first independent African nation, was established in 1957 by Osagyefo Dr. Kwame Nkrumah, that Africa began her journey to repair over five centuries of European rape and pillage of her human and material resources. Africa remains in that struggle today. An excellent source for scholarship on this point is the book "How Europe Underdeveloped Africa" by Dr. Walter Rodney.

The co-conspirators, conceivers, planners, architects and designers of the transatlantic slave trade were the European nations. The American colonies and the colonized West Indies sustained and nurtured the slave trade due to the wealth it generated. This wealth fueled the industrial revolution in Europe and America, and ultimately made the United States a world power. Where is the evidence of historical records to prove otherwise? Another excellent source of scholarship on this point is the book "Capitalism and Slavery" by Dr. Eric Williams. Africans did not know the mind of the European nations in planning the destruction of a people. Africans did not know that the Church sadly issued "papal bulls" from the pope sanctioning slavery of Africans because they were heathens, and needed to be civilized and Christianized. Africans were not aware of the peculiar institution of chattel slavery and its destructive effects that evolved over centuries in the American colonies. It is ludicrous to infer that visits to Europe by some Africans gave them knowledge of the holocaust of slavery.

Prof. Gates writes that slavery is one of the greatest evils in the history of civilization. On this point he is absolutely correct. Slavery was a crime against humanity and an entire people. America has a very narrow window to escape the consequences of her deeds; unfortunately, she has not yet shown she has the spiritual, moral or political will to repair the damage. If there was a criminal prosecution Europe and her American co-conspirators would be charged with crimes against humanity for the murder and slaughter of untold millions of African people. At best, those Africans who delivered their own brethren into the hands of their oppressors could be charged with the lesser criminal offense of being an accessory before the fact of false imprisonment. In other words, they were complicit in an aspect of an entirely different crime from the greater crime of Europe and her American co-conspirators.

But the real point here is why is Prof. Gates attempting to blunt and reduce the culpability of Europe and America in the horror of slavery? He seems to have developed a pattern of this behavior. On July 20, 1992 Professor Gates published an Op-Ed article in the New York Times to rebut the Nation of Islam's book "The Secret Relationship Between Blacks and Jews, Vol. 1." In this article, Prof. Gates attempts to minimize the role of Jewish merchants, traders, financiers and slave owners in slavery. Can we fully comprehend the contradiction and hypocrisy of describing the behavior of the perpetrator of the crime as minimal, yet the victim played a "significant role" in the crime? It is bewildering. Is Prof. Gates proving that he is a hired "educated Negro" by the rich and powerful to be an apologist against the legitimate cries for justice by a suffering people?

Finally, Prof. Gates' claim that President Obama's genetic heritage of African and American parentage makes him "uniquely positioned to solve the reparations debate." This statement does a tremendous disservice to President Obama. The question of reparations is largely a legislative issue that is the responsibility of the Congress to address. Should there ever be a Reparations Bill passed by Congress, only then would President Obama play the crucial role of signing the Bill into law. Moreover, no one person, even our President, can be the sole arbiter and reconciler on the issue of 400 years of black suffering. He could play a significant role in the discussion but the advancement of the issue of reparations is the responsibility of the more than 40-million Black people who are the descendants of slaves.

I conclude by offering to Prof. Gates the words of Dr. W.E.B. DuBois regarding the culpability of England and America for slavery, found in Sec. 96 of "Lessons For Americans in The Suppression of the African Slave Trade to The United States of

America, 1638-1870."

"It was the plain duty of the colonies to crush the trade and the system in its infancy: they preferred to enrich themselves on its profits. It was the plain duty of a Revolution based upon "Liberty" to take steps toward the abolition of slavery: it preferred promises to straightforward action. It was the plain duty of the Constitutional Convention, in founding a new nation, to compromise with a threatening social evil only in case its settlement would thereby be postponed to a more favorable time: this was not the case in the slavery and the slave-trade compromises ... and yet with this real, existent, growing evil before their eyes, a bargain largely of dollars and cents was allowed to open the highway that led straight to the Civil War...

It behooves the United States, therefore, in the interest both of scientific truth and of future social reform, carefully to study such chapters of her history as that of the suppression of the slave-trade. The most obvious question which this study suggests is: How far in a State can a recognized moral wrong safely be compromised? And, although this chapter of history can give us no definite answer suited to the ever-varying aspects of political life, yet it would seem to warn any nation from allowing, through carelessness and moral cowardice, any social evil to grow. No persons would have seen the Civil War with more surprise and horror than the Revolutionists of 1776; yet from the small and apparently dying institution of their day arose the walled and castled Slave-Power. From this we may conclude that it behooves nations as well as men to do things at the very moment when they ought to be done."

Dr. DuBois who over a span of seven decades as academic, scholar, sociologist, author, editor, civil rights activist and Pan-Africanist was truly an educated Black man. As the Director of the institute at Harvard which bears his name it is my hope that this may provide some future guidance to Prof. Gates that he might escape the syndrome of the "educated Negro" who has been Mis-Educated.

(Abdul Arif Muhammad is an attorney, historian, researcher, writer, lecturer and former Editor-in-Chief of The Final Call newspaper.

Glenn Beck:
A Minion of the Synagogue of Satan

Abdul Arif Muhammad, Esq.,
Student Minister and Nation of Islam General Counsel

An Open Letter to Glenn Beck

Woe to every slanderer, defamer! Who amasses wealth and counts it—He thinks that his wealth will make him abide. Nay, he will certainly be hurled into the crushing disaster... —Holy Qur'an 104:1-4

Although he never referenced the actual remarks of Minister Farrakhan concerning the unprecedented evil being spoken of against President Obama, he attempted to make an evil insinuation by misusing a past critique by Minister Farrakhan of the wickedness of Presidents who use lies and deception in foreign policy to start wars and assassinate leaders all over the world.

On Monday, February 27th, Glenn Beck's radio show webpage ran the headline: Farrakhan: Obama's life in danger. Glenn Beck proceeded to make slanderous comments regarding the February 26th Saviours' Day Address of the Honorable Minister Louis Farrakhan.

Minister Farrakhan, speaking on assassinations of foreign leaders and wars started based upon lies, asserted: "there are murderers in the White House." Mr. Beck in a bizarre inference to this statement made by Minister Farrakhan opined that it implied danger to President Obama from the Nation of Islam.

Mr. Beck is a minion of the Synagogue of Satan and as such represents the thinking of those used as their low-level pawns. This group, Minister Farrakhan identified in his Saviours' Day address, "...the Synagogue of Satan doesn't mean that everybody in it is Jewish. It's a combination of people, Gentiles, Jews, Black and White that agree on an idea. And some on a lesser level do not know what those on the highest level are doing, but they always give you a noble reason for what they are doing." Mr. Beck, a man who called President Obama a "racist" is now feigning concern for our Brother President.

Mr. Beck maliciously attacked not only the good name, reputation, integrity, and character of Minister Farrakhan, but also the over half century of redemptive work he has accomplished. The Holy Qur'an teaches Muslims to never be the aggressor in word or deed, but if attacked, we fight with those who fight with us.

Minister Farrakhan's actual words about the danger to President Obama were, "Never has a sitting president been spoken of in the manner that President Obama and his family have had to endure. Not just by the 'Birthers' and right-wing zealots, but those in high places, people with great influence have spoken against him in a manner that has never been accorded to even the worst of America's white presidents. They have called President Obama a 'racist,' an 'anti-Semite, a 'socialist,' a 'communist,' a 'foreigner,' an 'alien,' and they've even called him a 'terrorist.' I'm going to take a few minutes now to show you and tell you some of the things that highly influential people are saying about our Brother." Minister Farrakhan then presented a panoply of visual images and verbal insults hurled against the President by numerous prominent and influential Americans such as Republican Presidential candidates Newt Gingrich and Rick Santorum, House Majority Leader, Rep. Eric Cantor, Senate Majority Leader Harry Reid, former President Bill Clinton and Glenn Beck, himself.

In discussing the very real potential threat to the life of President Obama, the Honorable Minister Farrakhan discussed the historical comparison between President Lincoln and President Obama who both governed in a divided America. He declared, "The anger of the South, the red states, against Obama [is] the same anger the southerners had with President Lincoln. And this hatred ultimately combined with Lincoln's Emancipation Proclamation led to his assassination. A similar historical context exists with President Obama. Just as the southern states were not with Lincoln, President Obama did not win the southern states or red states in the 2008 election. The negative atmosphere and hatred created against President Obama has created a climate for his assassination."

In further discussing the Obama-Lincoln parallel, Minister Farrakhan discussed President Lincoln's strength in issuing three executive orders suspending habeas corpus in 1861 and President

Obama's struggle in signing the National Defense Authorization Act. Minister Farrakhan conveyed, "President Obama today is in a similar position [to President Lincoln], he just signed into law the National Defense Authorization Act. This Act—this Bill—f funds the military, but there is a clause in it that deprives the American people of their constitutional right to protest their government if a war goes on and the people are against it. In other words, the people's right of dissent is taken away by this Act that President Obama signed into law. When he signed it, he issued what is called a presidential statement which said that his administration would never carry out that part of the bill. He was trying to appease both sides—the warmongers and the civil libertarians. When he said that, it was like signing his death warrant." Minister Farrakhan asked, "Do you think they're wicked enough to be plotting out brother's assassination as we speak?"

Minister Farrakhan then issued a warning to those who may be planning to harm our President, "So I'm warning you, [Donald] Rumsfeld and [Dick] Cheney—I'm calling your names. [Paul] Wolfowitz, [Richard] Pearl, [Charles] Krauthammer, all of you neocons. If you harm our brother we will break our agreement with you. And our agreement with hell will be broken and our covenant with a pale horse will be annulled, and then I'll be able to call you to let's build a nation of our own."

Minister Farrakhan gave guidance and instructions to all people of good will to protect the life of President Obama. He implored, "Brothers and Sisters... it's our duty to protect the President. So, when you're at the job, listen to what people are saying. If you work in the boardroom, listen to what people are saying. Act like 'The Spook That Sat by the Door' and make mental notes, because they can't do what they're doing without talking about it [in] some way. So, you that are in the police department, listen; you that belong to the FBI, CIA, ATF, sheriff's department, listen! Keep your ear to the ground, and if you hear something that don't sound right, we've got to report it, because it is our duty to try and save the life of the man regardless of whether we agree with him or not—he's our brother, and [Michele Obama] is our sister, and those children are our daughters. And I beg you, President Obama, stand up for justice and the American people, and don't send these children to war for the sake of Israel."

Mr. Beck, contrary to your dangerous and wicked inference, it is clear that the Honorable Minister Louis Farrakhan is, in fact, seeking to protect the life of President Obama from the evil plans of the Synagogue of Satan.

Mr. Beck continuing with his nefarious inference that President Obama faces danger from the Nation of Islam stated, "I'm telling you this is a clear and present danger to the president of the United States. Will someone in the Secret Service or DOJ investigate what is happening at the Nation of Islam?"

The phrase "clear and present danger" is coded language. This term originated from a Supreme Court decision in 1919 which held that a defendant did not have a First Amendment right to express freedom of speech against the draft during World War I. It is also the title of a movie of the same name by Tom Clancy in which the President tells his National Security Advisor that a certain group represents "a clear and present danger." This authorized a covert military operation to assassinate the group.

Mr. Beck's coded language here is a call for the U.S. government to target and destroy the Nation of Islam, and in particular assassinate Minister Farrakhan. This is no different from the recently reported quote by the owner and publisher of the Atlanta Jewish Times Andrew Adler. Adler wrote a few weeks ago that Israel should consider "giv[ing] the go-ahead for U.S.-based Mossad agents to take out a president [Obama] deemed unfriendly to Israel in order for the current vice president to take his place and forcefully dictate that the United States' policy includes its helping the Jewish state obliterate its enemies."

Where was your appeal, Mr. Beck, to the Secret Service or Justice Department to investigate Mr. Adler? This is hateful and racist hypocrisy.

As a truly righteous servant of Allah (God) Minister Farrakhan even warned and admonished misguided Muslims who would seek to kill Americans. He stated, "Now, I want to talk straight into the Masjids. You sit around in the Mosque talking about Jews. And somebody hears you and gets next to you. "You know I think we can do something about this you know. After prayer we're going to talk." And they are a plant from the government of the United States. Just think about the crap that America's doing to Muslims and we're dumb enough to fit in the pattern. You want to bomb a synagogue, you stupid thing! What can you do with a synagogue when God is present? Let me tell you what He's doing and what He's going to do that makes your punk stuff like nothing. Sit down in the Mosque and pray, and go on and do the work of Allah, and leave Allah to kill whoever He wants to kill." These are not the words of a man that is a clear and present danger to the country.

This truth spoken by the Honorable Minister Louis Farrakhan is what the Synagogue of Satan and their pawn Mr. Beck fear, the exposure of their thoughts and plans against our Brother President and also against Minister Farrakhan. As he stated in his message, "... I want to talk to you and our President, because now they're pushing President Obama to strike Iran. And quietly they're pushing him to destroy Farrakhan. They want our President to deal with me and Iran and that would make the Synagogue of Satan happy. They're terrorized that somebody is bold enough to uncover them and tell the American people the truth."

We will not allow such vicious assaults on Minister Farrakhan, a man whose prescient and consistent warning could save this country. We will and must continue to respond to "anti-Farrakhan" attacks. He deserves and has earned the right to be defended. The Honorable Minister Louis Farrakhan is a divine gift raised as the Anointed Servant of Allah (God) and His Messiah, as a Warner to America, the World and Black people. He is a torchlight for America.

Atty. Abdul Arif Muhammad is General Counsel for the Nation of Islam, an historian, Student Minister and former Final Call Newspaper editor-in-chief. Contact him at arifmuhammadgc@aol.com.

Also contributing to the article were Ava Muhammad, Richard Muhammad, Cedric Muhammad and Alan Muhammad.

Unmasking Mr. Dershowitz

Abdul Arif Muhammad, Esq.
Student Minister and Nation of Islam General Counsel

Abdul Arif Muhammad, Esq., Student General Counsel for the Honorable Minister Louis Farrakhan and the Nation of Islam

Abdul Arif Muhammad, Esq., Student General Counsel for the Honorable Minister Louis Farrakhan and the Nation of Islam

Mr. Dershowitz, in writing and publishing several false claims in your article of July 8th, one of which is the Honorable Minister Louis Farrakhan "threatened" you during his worldwide address on July 4th, proves that his words are true.

"You're such a skillful deceiver; you are Satan masquerading as a lawyer. Satan, walking in full sight, deceiving whoever they can deceive. That's Satan."

As Jesus told a party of the Jews in the Bible. "You are of your father, the devil, and the lusts of your father you will do. He was a murderer from the beginning, and abode not in the truth, because there is no truth in him. When he speaketh a lie, he speaketh of his own: for he is a liar and the father of it." (John 8:44 KJV).

There was no threat to inflict physical harm upon you. In fact, his words on July 4th were directed at you, because you were the one advancing a threat, which was publicly advocating that the government could forcibly vaccinate citizens against their will. It is deceitful, how you sanitized your words in the article, that you were "urging people to take COVID-19 vaccine if a safe and effective one were developed." Here is the main thrust of your words as published in your May 19 statement:

"If you refuse to be vaccinated, the state has the power to literally take you to a doctor's office and plunge a needle into your arm."

These are your words Mr. Dershowitz. So, you were threatening to have the constitutional rights of the American people taken from them by the State. Your words prove the meaning of the Bible when it says:

"Shall the throne of iniquity have fellowship with thee, which frameth mischief by a law?" (Ps. 94:20 KJV).

The Honorable Minister Louis Farrakhan was responding to your advocacy for forced vaccinations. His true words are:

"So, Mr. Dershowitz, if you bring the vaccine and say you're going to bring your army to force us to take it, once you try to force us, that's a declaration of war on all of us. You only have this one life. Fight like hell to keep it, and fight like hell to destroy those whose heart and mind is to destroy you and take your life from you."

Like the Serpent did in the Garden of Eden, you willfully misinterpret the Honorable Minister Louis Farrakhan's words to deceive those who would listen to him. This is the way of Satan to misinterpret the context and meaning of God's words to deceive. This, the Satanic Jews, like yourself, have done, against the Honorable Minister Louis Farrakhan.

For thirty-six (36) years, since 1984, you have falsely accused Minister Farrakhan of calling "Judaism a Gutter religion"; and of calling "Hitler great" along with falsely accusing him of being "Anti-Semitic", homophobic and a misogynist none of which are true. It was in fact, Nathan Perlmutter of the ADL, and Nat Hentoff, of the Village Voice who called Minister Farrakhan a "Black Hitler," for his defense of the Reverend Jesse Jackson, whom the Jewish Defense League (JDL) was threatening to kill for his support of Yasser Arafat and the Palestinian people during his 1984 Presidential Campaign. We will not allow you anymore to continue to change history and misinterpret the truth!

The words of the Minister Farrakhan are synonymous with the words in the Declaration of Independence, issued on July 4th, speaking to the abuse of power of the Government.

"That to secure these rights,(life, liberty and the pursuit of Happiness) Governments are instituted among Men, deriving their just powers from the consent of the governed, –That whenever any Form of Government becomes destructive of these ends, it is the Right of the People to alter or to abolish it, and to institute new Government, laying its foundation on such principles and organizing its powers in such form, as to them shall seem most likely to affect their Safety and Happiness."

These words ring true today. It is an improper constitutional interpretation to place the government above the people. Governments are instituted and they derive their powers from the consent of the Governed.

The citizens of America, and especially the Black, Brown, Red and poor White, have the right to protect their lives against abuse by a government seeking to inject them with vaccines that are proven to have been injurious to populations around the world. Further we believe that the intent of the proposed COVID-19 vaccine is designed, not to relieve the people of the virus, but to carry out the Henry Kissinger doctrine, as outlined in his 1974 NSSM-200 Memorandum, which call for a massive culling of the world's population by two billion people.

We, the Black and native people are very well aware of this history of government abuse, regarding vaccines and biological experimentation. Minister Farrakhan said on July 4th;

"Remember the syphilis experiment? Remember what they did to the Native Americans with smallpox? Remember the vaccine that they gave us for polio that was cancer itself? So, how in the hell could you trust them with a vaccine after you know what they have done and that they are capable of doing it again on a bigger and broader level?"

That is why Minister Farrakhan said on July 4th; based upon this wicked History:

"We can't trust you any more White folks, not with our lives. We're not justified in so doing."

Again, Mr. Dershowitz, using your skillful deceit, you try to falsely apply the Brandenburg v. Ohio standard, to the Minister's speech.

Of course, most are uninformed of the meaning of this case. In fact, the decision in the case was the exact opposite of what you assert in the article. In brief, the facts of the case are; a Ku Klux Klan member invited a reporter to come to his KKK rally. At the rally the KKK member made several racist statements against Blacks and Jews, and said although they were not a "revengent" organization, if the government continues to suppress the White race, "there might have to be some vengeance taken." They were prosecuted and convicted under an Ohio Statute for "assemblage of persons formed to teach or advocate the doctrine of criminal syndicalism."

The Supreme Court overturned the conviction and issued the following ruling and principle of law: "These later decisions have fashioned the principle that the constitutional guarantees of free speech and free press do not permit a State to forbid or proscribe advocacy of the use of force or of law violation, except where such advocacy is directed to inciting or producing imminent lawless action and is likely to incite or produce such action."

Further, you falsely claim a "more direct threat of violence" by picking out a phrase from the Minister Farrakhan's July 4th, message, "When you see Satan pick up a stone as we do in Mecca." Your misinterpretation is a deliberate perversion. Minister Farrakhan's complete remark on that point was:

"Every Muslim when he sees Satan, pick[s] up a stone as we do in Mecca. When you know who Satan is, you don't have to kill him. No. The stone of Truth, see, that's what you throw."

The words of the Minister on July 4th and the true context and meaning of his words could never legally fit into the exception of the Brandenburg v Ohio ruling. And for the record, a few years ago, a Jewish attorney, did file a lawsuit against Minister Farrakhan in Federal Court in Texas, on this very same argument you're advancing, and the Court dismissed the action.

Mr. Dershowitz, let's address the "Anti-Black" history and actions of the Satanic Jews, who say they are Jews, and are not, but are a Synagogue of Satan. (Rev. 2:9 KJV)

Your rabbis created the Talmud, and concocted the so-called "Hamitic Curse" and claimed that Black people (Africans) were cursed by God to be "black and ugly" and punished to be your slaves forever. This wicked Jewish tale justified the Holocaust against the Indigenous people and motivated the kidnapping and enslaving of the African people, killing untold millions during the Middle Passage and beyond.

Our research, published in the Secret Relationships between Blacks and Jews, Vols. I and II quotes many Jewish scholars who admit that Jewish merchants owned, insured and financed slave ships and outfitted them with chains and shackles. Jews were slave auctioneers, brokers, and wholesalers, keeping the slave economy oiled with money, markets and supplies.

In the South Jews were significant owners of cotton plantations and slaves. There were rabbis who owned, rented and sold slaves and denounced the abolitionists. Jewish merchants and peddlers collaborated with slavery, and financed plantation operations and even bought and sold whole plantations—slaves and all. They sold to plantation masters everything from slaves, to drugs, to whips, shackles, and chains.

Jews allied themselves with the Southern Confederacy against Abraham Lincoln and the North in the Civil War. They financed the Confederacy, and the Jews' support for their pro-slavery cause was so massive that they put the face of the most prominent Jew in America—Judah P. Benjamin—on their money! Jews supported and helped set up, maintain, and strengthen America's "slave codes" and "Jim Crow" legal system through an extensive Jewish banking and financing network.

During Reconstruction Jewish merchants targeted and exploited the poor Black cotton sharecroppers growing extremely wealthy in the process. Many Jews, like the Lehman Brothers, were major dealers of slave picked cotton, as well as owners of cotton mills. Many Black sharecroppers fell into debt and lost their land to these overcharging Jewish merchants.

On February 26, 1877—the day of the Birth of our Saviour, Master Fard Muhammad—a Jewish congressman from Louisiana named William M. Levy argued for the Compromise of 1877 which saw Rutherford B. Hayes become President in exchange for removing federal troops in the Southern states. This notorious act resulted in the death of Reconstruction and the imposition of "Jim Crow Segregation" creating a condition of "defacto" slavery, which lasted until the Supreme Court Decision, Brown v. Board of Education in 1954. So wicked was Levy's plan that it is known by historians as the "Great Betrayal of the Negro."

In the post-Civil War and Reconstruction era, Jews became leaders in the trade union movement and set up racist policies that forced millions of Blacks out of employment in the skilled trades. A Jew invested in a new group of White terrorists known as the Ku Klux Klan. Jewish merchants sold sheets and guns and rope to the Ku Klux Klan and many Jews became Klan members, supporters, and even high officials.

In the early 1900s Jews attacked economics-minded Black leaders like Booker T. Washington and Marcus Garvey and financed only the Black organizations that promoted an anti-economic agenda, like the NAACP. In fact, the NAACP's first president, Joel Spingarn, who was Jewish, and also a major in the intelligence branch of the military, spied on the group for the U.S. government!

During the 1970s Jews were against Affirmative Action, and agreed with the concept of "reverse discrimination" which was used to help cripple Black progress in every field.

Most importantly, you have been "Anti-Black" in your opposition and attacks against the Honorable Minister Louis Farrakhan, who is without question, the instrument and voice of God and His Christ in our midst, bringing Salvation to His people, the Black, Brown, and Red, and the oppressed throughout the world. As he said July 4th, "God has made me His mouthpiece."

What is your aim, Mr. Dershowitz in this wicked and willful lie against the words of Minister Farrakhan?

We have been taught and know that the ultimate aim of this world is to kill the Messenger of God. Your article attempts to incite and urge the government against Minister Farrakhan, by calling him "Anti-American." and labeling his speech as "inciting to imminent lawless action."

What you fear is what Minister Farrakhan also said on July 4th, "And it's my job now to pull the cover off of Satan." As the Minister pointed to the Ayat (verse) in the Holy Qur'an: "Allah says, 'Had we wished to take a pastime from before, surely, we would have done it. Nay, we hurl the Truth against falsehood until we knock out its brains." [Holy Qur'an 21:17-18]

The throwing of the stone "of truth" is to put an end to Satan, his evil and unrighteousness that has nearly engulfed and affected the entire human family of the planet earth.

Why do you hate Minister Farrakhan? He answered the reason for your hate, on July 4th.

"The reason they hate me [is] because they know I represent the end of their civilization. I represent the uncovering of their wickedness, fulfilling the judgment that God has come to bring down on America and the world."

Your hatred of Minister Farrakhan is that the two men that have made him, God and His Christ, are producing the Salvation that God sent Jesus in the World to bring, when Jesus said, "And ye shall know the truth and the truth shall make you free." This brings Satan's world and civilization to an end.

As Minister Farrakhan on July 4th concluded with a prayer, we end this response, with his words, on that same wise.

"May Allah fill you (the righteous) with knowledge, wisdom, understanding, and power that we together may put to a perpetual flight Satan, the arch deceiver, the imposter Jews who are worthy of the chastisement of God."

"YOU DON'T HAVE MINISTER FARRAKHAN'S ASSIGNMENT"

Abdul Hafeez Muhammad

Regional Student Minister

East Coast Region-Nation of Islam, New York City-New York

The Eastern Regional Representative of the Honorable Minister Louis Farrakhan is Brother Student Minister Abdul Hafeez Muhammad. In today's post Brother Hafeez speaks to the critics of Minister Farrakhan and to the Black community. Taking the approach of spiritual teacher, Bro. Hafeez reminds the general public that Minister Farrakhan and his bold moves are not borne of personal motives or self-aggrandizement. Instead, as Brother Hafeez demonstrates, Minister Farrakhan is a man on a divine mission, and as a result, no analysis of his controversy with Jewish groups, the media or the U.S. government is complete without an appreciation of this major characteristic feature of the Minister's methodology and noble motive; and that being to complete the assignment that Allah (God) and His Messenger-the Hon. Elijah Muhammad gave to him. Read, Reflect, Share, & Act

The meaning of the word assignment is a task or piece of work assigned to someone as part of a job or course of study. An assignment is also a function, a commission, a responsibility. The Honorable Elijah Muhammad teaches us in his illuminating book, Message to the Black Man in America, on page 306, the chapter entitled, Answer to Critics. He was asked a question, "How would you describe your mission?" And he answered, "My mission is to give life to the dead." He said, "What I teach brings them out of death and into life. My mission, as the Messenger, is to bring the truth to the world before the world is destroyed."

The Honorable Elijah Muhammad did not give himself the assignment of giving life to the dead. This Mission was given to him by the great Mahdi, Master Fard Muhammad, who was born February 26, 1877 in the Holy City of Mecca. He travelled 9,000 miles from the East unto the West fulfilling the words of Jesus in the Bible in the Book of Matthew, Chapter 24 Verse 27: "For as lightning cometh out of the East, and shineth even unto the West: So, shall also the coming of the Son of Man be."

There is no other human being who has travelled from the East unto the West seeking to give life to the dead. The proof is in the next verse of this same chapter, Verse 28 that states, "For wheresoever the carcass is, there will the eagles be gathered together." A carcass is the remains of something once alive and great. Black people in America have suffered the Trans- Atlantic Slave Trade and lived under Jim Crow Laws. We have suffered the worst injustice known to the human condition. We have been robbed of our names, our culture, our country, our God, and our religion (way of life). And as the Reverend Dr. Martin Luther King, Jr. stated that under "The Emancipation Proclamation they gave the slave no land." As he stated, "Emancipation for the Negro was freedom to hunger and famine." So, the Black man and woman were used as a tool and a slave to help others become rich off our labor. We were also robbed of the ability to think and this was proven in the case of Dred Scott v. Sanford where it stated all avenues of life should be cut off to the Negro. In the case of Dred Scott v. Sanford, the Supreme Court ruled that Black men – whether free or enslaved – had "no rights which a white man was bound to respect." The scripture says the eagles will be gathered together wherever the carcass is. The carcass is a once great people. And the eagle is the symbol on the dollar bill of the American currency. This scripture in Matthew 27 and 28 in red letter print, which are the words of Jesus, is describing the arrival of one who would have to free a once great people and awaken them back to life so that the eagles (America) would not devour them in their death state. The Honorable Elijah Muhammad met this Holy one and was given his great commission of the resurrection of the dead. This is not speaking of a physical resurrection, but a spiritual one. We ask the question, "Whose stench is worst in the sight of Allah (God)?" The physically dead person who is not responsible for their odor or a spiritually and mentally dead person who is yet alive and has an odor but refuses to do anything about it. So, when we talk of raising the dead to life, this is the hardest job that any human being could have.

The Honorable Minister Louis Farrakhan serves as the National Representative of the Most Honorable Elijah Muhammad and the Nation of Islam. He does not represent himself. He represents the man of God that received his commission from God in Person. The proof that he got his assignment from God is the countless numbers of human beings that owe their spiritual life and existence to the teachings of the Honorable Elijah Muhammad. Some have moved over to other schools of thought; however, they could never escape Elijah Muhammad and the impact of his Life Saving Teachings. The Honorable Elijah Muhammad is a man who only went to the third or fourth grade of education, but confounded the wise, caused the deaf to hear, the dumb to speak and reform the lives of those off the streets of America. Many of whom no one wanted anything to do with. His teaching has and today attracts the most educated of our people that are found in the Nation of Islam following The Honorable Minister Louis Farrakhan.

In the scripture, Messengers of God are styled as women; therefore, he's the mother who has given birth to many persons' spirituality. And the Honorable Elijah Muhammad is also our father because he has impregnated us with the word and wisdom of the Almighty God.

When you critics who attack Minister Farrakhan, such as the Media or talking heads, the writers or scribes, the rabbinical scholars, Jewish philanthropists, Black politicians and weak persons in leadership positions, you don't know who you're are looking at and are maligning. And those of you who do, keep the people who are easily led in the wrong direction and hard to lead in the right direction, deaf, dumb and blind to the reality of truth. The Honorable Elijah Muhammad referred to this kind of people as the 85%. He taught us about the 10%, which are the rich: Slave makers of the Poor, otherwise known as the bloodsuckers of the poor. He taught us who is the 5% in the Poor Part of the Earth. That they are the poor, Righteous Teachers, who do not believe of the teachings of the 10% and are all-wise: and know who the living God is otherwise known as civilized people also Muslim and Muslim Sons.

The Honorable Elijah Muhammad said to Minister Farrakhan one day, "Brother, there will be two of us backing you up. Allah and myself." We must understand when you look at Minister Farrakhan; you must see him through the lens of scripture. You must view him from the perspective of the word of God. For he was born to be the chief helper of The Honorable Elijah Muhammad. Moses had Aaron as a helper and aider. In the Bible, the word is recorded as such: Exodus 4 and 16 Aaron will be your spokesman to the people. He will be your mouthpiece and you will stand in the place of God for him telling him what to say. Jesus had Peter and Paul (they both had a role at two different peaks in Jesus' ministry). Peter stands at the gate to receive those who have fallen short of the will of God. And Paul preached Christ during his departure from the people and is responsible for the letters of the Church called the Epistles of Paul. Elijah had Elisha. Elijah leaves his cloak for Elisha. Elisha prays for a double portion of the spirit of God. And Prophet Muhammad (Peace Be upon Him) had Ali and Umar, Uthman and Abu Bakr (the four companions of the Prophet).

While some great Prophets had helpers, their job was to continue the message that was commissioned to them and to make the lives of the people who are the recipients of such message improved. When you attack The Honorable Minister Louis Farrakhan, you will always receive a response from his followers, helpers and supporters who know him to represent the personification of love, character, morality and uprightness.

We must also become acquainted with this scripture, Elisha in 2nd Kings, Chapter 2 Verse 9, and it came to pass, when they were gone over, that Elijah said unto Elisha. Ask what I shall do for thee, before I be taken away from thee. And Elisha said, I pray thee, let a double portion of thy spirit be upon me. Just as Elisha prayed for a double portion of the spirit to be upon him, Minister Farrakhan was guaranteed this double portion when the Honorable Elijah Muhammad said, "Brother there will be two of us backing you up."

I am one of those whose life has been saved and prolonged by the teachings of the Most Honorable Elijah Muhammad. And the word of God that Minister Farrakhan constantly delivers into my life, which has made me a better man for myself, my family, my people, community and my nation. I am a witness bearer to the character, dignity, respect and love that Minister Farrakhan has instilled in me for my people and humanity. I will continue to write, speak, and live my life as an example of truth over falsehood and lies that the critics, detractors and naysayers have hurled at our beloved Minister and the Nation of Islam with no basis in the truth.

Minister Farrakhan doesn't have an anti-Semitic bone or vein in his body. As a matter of fact, the original meaning of the word

Semitic is "relating to or consisting a subfamily of the Afro-Asiatic language family that includes Hebrew, Aramaic, Arabic, and Amharic; of, relating to, or characteristic of the Semites." Which are not members of the Jewish community exclusively. The term includes Arabs, Akkadians, Canaanites, some Ethiopians, and Armaean tribes.

Our beloved minister, and we who follow him, are not against people of alternative lifestyles of which there are members in our families. We ascribe to the Muslim Program and what the Muslims want:

We want freedom. We want a full and complete freedom.

We want justice. Equal justice under the law. We want justice applied equally to all, regardless of creed or class or color.

We want equality of opportunity. We want equal membership in society with the best in civilized society.

The Honorable Minister Farrakhan is a life giver by the grace and permission of the Almighty God, whose proper name is Allah. He doesn't deliver speeches like a President or politician. He delivers the word of God, which brings about transformation and the lives of whomsoever receives and applies such beautiful guidance in their lives.

Whether you are Black, White, Asian, Pacific Islander, Latino, Mexican, from the Caribbean, or Central and South America when you hear the Minister and look at him through a clean lens, then the words of The Honorable Elijah Muhammad will come into view when he said, "You don't need to condemn a dirty glass, just put a clean glass next to it."

Listen to Minister Farrakhan for yourself and if you have questions, why don't you seek out his representatives and helpers in the cause of Freedom, Justice and Equality. When you are in need of an attorney, you hire one to represent your interest, not the prosecutors who are trying to sentence you to a life imprisonment. Minister Farrakhan will be cleared of all false charges. As it is written of in the 21st Surah, Ayat 18 of the Holy Quran:

Nay, We hurl the Truth against falsehood, so it knocks out its brains, and lo! It vanishes. And woe to you for what you describe!

Just as The Honorable Elijah Muhammad said, his mission is to give life to the dead. That is the same mission and assignment of Minister Farrakhan today, tomorrow and into the future.

The reason our open enemies write, speak and misrepresent his words is because you have been drawing from the mammary gland of the Black Community and you have made your American dream on the Black nightmare living in America. From the slave plantations to sharecropping to minimum wage to low income housing to food deserts in our community to more liquor stores than schools to the proliferation of gang activity to rampant police brutality and mob attacks to injustice in the Jurisprudence system even with videotape present to the slum landlords to the wearing of blackface by individuals and companies to the misuse of musical artists talents and skills and the control of the Black American economy, you are threatened that the voice of one crying in the wilderness speaking for the poor, the disenfranchised and the oppressed will awaken them to their own power that they don't need to rely on anyone else except God and themselves.

The Honorable Elijah Muhammad and Minister Farrakhan teach us that our unity is a weapon more powerful than a nuclear bomb and our unity will solve 95% of our problems. Let us unite!

MINISTER VANQUISHES NAP-TOWN CRITIC FOR "FARRAKHANSPLAINING"

Abdul Haleem Muhammad, Ph.D.

Regional Student Minister

Southwest Region-Nation of Islam, Houston-Texas

The Southwest Regional Student Minister of the Nation of Islam is Brother Dr. Abdul Haleem Muhammad. He is a spiritual teacher, community activist and scholar. He has summarily eviscerated the hollow commentary of Indianapolis writer Larry Smith. ResearchMinister. Com appreciates Dr. Muhammad's defense of the Honorable Minister Louis Farrakhan and is honored to publish it for the benefit of our readers. Read, Reflect, Act and Share.

Dear Larry,

There's an old saying: "Opinion is ultimately determined by the feelings, and not by the intellect." Therein in lies the problem with your Op-ed accusing the Honorable Minister Louis Farrakhan of anti-Semitism and bigotry. You posit that Black people have "high regard" for the Honorable Minister Louis Farrakhan because he makes his people "feel better about themselves." Note: I left off your incorrectly ordered parvum parva decent (to compare small things to great) comparison of Minister Farrakhan to President Donald Trump. Mr. Trump is a great liar, a racist and a bigot. The Honorable Minister Louis Farrakhan is a great truth teller, a lover and a humanitarian. Mr. Trump is the President of the United States; the Minister represents the Lord of the Worlds and His Christ. There is no comparison. Think.

Now back to your feeling's analysis. Are you trying to convince the readers that you, I and nearly 2 million Black men came to the Million Man March in Washington, D.C. in 1995, on a Monday, paid our own way, and stood for 16 hours because the Minister made us "feel better" about ourselves? Bloods, Crips, Gangster Disciples, El-Rukns, Alphas, Omegas, Kappas, Iotas, Sigmas, Grooves, Christians, Hebrews, Muslims, Pan Africanist, Nationalist, atheist, agnostics, June Bug, Ray-Ray and them came together in peace and unity because the Minister made us "feel better" about ourselves? Not one fight, not one Black man arrested, in addition, the mall was left cleaner at the end of the March than at the start of the March, according to the D.C. officials, because the Minister made us "feel better" about ourselves? When has making us "feel better" about ourselves ever produced such a phenomenon during our 464-year sojourn in the Western Hemisphere? To answer the above questions requires the use of intellect not feelings. Think.

Here is the genesis of the Million Man March. Misogynists (anti-women bigots) don't ask permission of women to hold a "Men's Only" meeting, do they? Did you know that's exactly what the Honorable Minister Louis Farrakhan did on December 18, 1993, at the Jacob Javitz Center in New York City? He asked and received the permission of the women in attendance if he could come back in 30 days to gather men to discuss our plight and propose solutions. On January 24, 1994, approximately 16,000 Black men came out to hear the Minister. It was at that meeting, the Minister made the call for a million men to come to Washington, D.C. Mind you, nearly 4,000 men were turned away because the venue was filled to capacity. There were no incidents of violence reported. This was repeated in city after city. For example, in Houston, Texas, on April 11, 1994, the police department estimated that 35,000 men showed up to Pleasant Grove Baptist Church which only had a capacity of 15,000. Once again, not one fight, car towed or crime committed as nearly 20,000 men were turned away. Strangers sat together in cars around the church listening to the live radio broadcast. This is more than "feeling better" about ourselves; this is the presence of mathematically provable spiritual truths after centuries of lies about the Black man and our people. Think.

Your backhanded "compliment" and explanation of Black people's "high regard" for the Minister falls flat logically, does not resonate, nor does it leave Black people "feeling better about themselves." Black people don't have "high regard" for the Minister because he makes us feel better! We have "high regard" because the facts and truths he represents from the Most Honorable Elijah Muhammad transforms the lives of countless human beings, whether they register in the Nation of Islam or not. Black people don't have "high regard" for the Minister because we admire a "purveyor of hate" or an anti-Semite! Either you don't understand the Black or Jewish relationship over the last 4 centuries or your feelings of fear won't allow you to call it what it is – a master-slave relationship. Think.

Africans, Arabs, Americans, Europeans, Christians, Muslims, and Jews all played a role in the transatlantic slave-trade. When the Minister pointed out the fact that Jews, along with others, played a role in our enslavement, he was called a liar by members of the Jewish community. What was the response of Nation of Islam under his leadership? We went into Jewish archives, libraries and found sources to defend the Minister. What did we find and publish? A "secret" relationship between Jews and Blacks has existed for centuries, not the folklore of "We marched with Dr. King," but one of enslavement and exploitation. Think.

Our documented evidence of Jewish involvement in our enslavement consists of two volumes, containing 3,037 annotated footnote citations, along with another smaller book with 283 figures of slave auction newspaper ads placed by members of the Jewish community. Our third volume related to the Leo Frank Case, wherein Mr. Frank attempted to frame a Black man for the rape and murder of a Gentile girl, has 1,227 annotated footnote citations. None of our citations come from dubious or anti-Semitic sources. Our sources are public records or the Jews themselves. Pointing out Jewish misdeeds and defending ourselves is why Minister Farrakhan and we who follow him are labeled "anti-Semites." Hate speech leads to hate crimes, right? In spite of all the evidence of Jewish mistreatment of Black people presented publicly by the Minister and the Nation of Islam, you can't point to one hate crime committed by us. Not one. Think.

Lastly, stop Farrakhansplaining, Nationsplaining or Blacksplaining to white people. The evidence found in your Op-ed, not our feelings, leads us to conclude that you are not qualified to do so. Instead, ask your Jewish and Gentile friends to accept our challenge to a public dialogue or debate about what has been said or written by the Minister or his disciples. Don't become a party to a conspiracy by colluding with Jews and Whites by comparing the Minister and the Nation of Islam to Mr. Trump's bigotry. You unknowingly are endangering Black men, women, and children. How so? The Honorable Minister Louis Farrakhan doesn't just represent a feeling; he represents the presence of God and an idea whose time has come. To get rid of that idea, which goes beyond the registered members of the Nation of Islam, you will have to round up Black people (and others), send them to reeducation camps or eliminate them altogether. That's not going to happen without a bloody revolution and God executing His final judgment on America. Why? We are Farrakhan and Black people are the Real Chosen People of God. If we're not, then who is? If America isn't the Mystery Babylon of the Book of Revelations, which nation is? Think.

So as a community leader we urge you to activate your intellect, not your feelings, as you cogitate over the above-written response to your Op-ed and this quote by Joseph Sobran: "An anti-Semite used to mean a man who hated Jews. Now it means a man who is hated by Jews." Think.

Abdul Haleem Muhammad, Ph.D.

DR. MUHAMMAD REMINDS WALL ST. OF SINS AGAINST BLACK PEOPLE, DEFENDS MINISTER FARRAKHAN

Abdul Haleem Muhammad, Ph.D.

Regional Student Minister

Southwest Region-Nation of Islam, Houston-Texas

ResearchMinister.Com publishes the following response written by Brother Dr. Abdul Haleem Muhammad. He is Minister Farrakhan's Southwest Regional Representative based in Houston, TX. He holds a Ph.D. in Urban Planning and is a community activist. He has written a response to the Wall Street Journal's Opinion piece published on January 4, 2019 by Jeryl Bier. We thank Dr. Muhammad for permitting us the opportunity to share this article that rebuts and unravels the propaganda piece published in the Wall Street Journal.

Mr. Bier added his name to the pantheon of anti-poor, anti-Black, faux conservative writers that (dis)grace the opinion pages of the Wall Street Journal.

How does a mere "accountant and a freelance writer" get published in the prestigious Wall Street Journal unless he or she fulfills the editorial board's broader agenda? The broader agenda is to destroy or marginalize any leader or social formation that seeks just compensation for fortunes made on Wall Street on the backs of Black people in particular and the poor in general. In other words, the Journal uses people like sock puppets to maintain the status quo.

Mr. Bier enumerated a litany of meetings over the past 25 years between Black political leaders and the Honorable Minister Louis Farrakhan. So, allow us to present a partial list of the centuries of Jewish and Gentile crimes against our humanity and utilize Mr. Bier's accounting language to calculate America's spiritual debits and credits.

African slavery and Black exploitation are evidenced on the general ledgers and corporate genealogies of many of Wall Street's juggernauts of finance, insurance, shipping and manufacturing. Calculate the accrued expense of Wall Street firms and Ivy League

Universities from income generated from Black slave labor and Black bodies used as capital from 1555 to 1865. Estimate the return on investment, after our "emancipation," generated on Wall Street from Black convict leasing and sharecropping when "cotton was king" and served as America's number one export.

Add the value of the wage theft of Black labor to the balance sheets of Wall Street firms during the two "Great Migrations" of 1916-1940 and 1940-1970 to the Northeast, Midwest and West. Lastly, calculate the net value of the land stolen from Black people through tax and bank foreclosures schemes, judicial misconduct, eminent domain and outright fraud over the past 154 years. This does not include the revenue generated from private prisons traded on Wall Street that house so many Black prisoners. Add it up! What is owed us Mr. Bier? Wall Street Journal? Millions? Billions? Trillions?

After all the media smears, economic sanctions, and political machinations against Minister Farrakhan and the Nation of Islam have failed, America's last resort will be an attempt to load Black Muslim men, women and children and our supporters into box cars and do to us what the monsters of Nazi Germany did to their opposition. On the other hand, the alternative is for American Jews and Gentiles to have a face to face public discussion or debate about what The Muslims Want and Believe. Defeat our arguments and ideas if you can. After all, isn't that the "American way"?

"The Farrakhan Litmus Test" for Black politicians and the ongoing Jewish and Gentile Kristallnacht against Black Muslim businesses is creating a backlash and will only increase the divide between Black and Jewish/White communities. Stop trying to place the Nation of Islam in a racial, economic and political framework or box. The basis of our existence and dispute with the Jewish community and White America is theological, not racial, economic or political. Take note, this dispute will only be resolved through dialogue, atonement and justice.

Finally, the Honorable Minister Louis Farrakhan and the Nation of Islam are Eternal Revenue Service agents (ERS not IRS) raised by Allah (God) to collect the divine debt America owes Black people and the poor of this nation. No amount of accounting wizardry or poison pen op-Eds will erase the long-term spiritual liabilities both Jews and Gentiles have accrued on America's balance sheet. The Nation of Islam led by Minister Farrakhan is pro-free market, pro-family, pro-life, pro-self-help, pro-school choice and most importantly, pro-religious freedom. Be advised, We, nor the debt owed us, are going away. In the end, America will pay its debt or be declared insolvent by God Himself.

SAN FRANCISCO MINISTER: MINISTER FARRAKHAN'S DETRACTORS, THE REAL ENEMIES OF OPPRESSED MASSES

Abdul Rashidullah Muhammad
Regional Student Minister,
Northwest Region-Nation of Islam, San Francisco-California

ResearchMinister.Com publishes below the response of Student Minister Christopher Muhammad. He is Minister Farrakhan's Representative in San Francisco, California and is an activist for justice and the rights of the poor in the Bay Area. His rebuke of Jeff Dunetz is a welcomed addition to the growing number of voices that are rising to rebut the constant barrage of propaganda aimed at injuring Black progress, and the progress of the poor throughout America, by assailing, haranguing and slandering the strongest advocate for the poor and the downtrodden – the Honorable Minister Louis Farrakhan. We are honored to be allowed to share Minister Christopher's condemnation of Mr. Dunetz's reckless opinions.

Student Minister Christopher's Reply to The Jewish Star Article by Jeff Dunetz:

"Mr. Dunetz, your "Putrid", "Hate-Filled" article on Minister Farrakhan and the Nation of Islam, repeating the timeworn, oft-repeated, "Big Lie" Propaganda quotes, "reeks" with the "Stench" of Journalistic Desperation. You even stooped so low, as to quote the ADL, the long discredited and widely condemned, Criminal, "Spy" operation, masquerading as a "Civil Rights" organization.

You (and those who Think and Write like you), are obviously at your "Wits End" over your inability to stop the Rise and Success of Minster Farrakhan and The Nation of Islam's Exemplary Work of Prison Reform. Even Sincere Critics of the Nation of Islam, readily acknowledge and praise its decades long, track record of Good Work in this vital area of Human Reformation and Development.

No sincere person of Good Will and "Sound Mind" opposes the Nation of Islam's noble work of transforming lives and making Communities safe and decent places to live. However, You (and those who Think and Write like you), are not upset with the "Prison Industrial Complex" and the "School to Prison" pipeline, that continues to plague and victimize Black and Oppressed people.

Minister Farrakhan and The Nation Of Islam is Universally recognized as the Last Hope to solve the myriad of Problems plaguing Black and Oppressed Communities, which is WHY you Oppose Minister Farrakhan and the Nation of Islam so Vehemently.

So, I encourage you (and those who Think and Write like you) to keep spewing your "Hate" and keep repeating the "Big Lies", as you have, for the last 35 years against Minister Farrakhan and the Nation of Islam. You're only helping the masses of Black and Oppressed People to see you (and those who Think and Write like you) as you really are, The Real (and last) Enemy Of their Rise.

So, Keep up the "Good" work Mr. Dunetz.

"IF THIS IS A REPRESENTATIVE DEMOCRACY; WHO DO YOU REPRESENT? A MESSAGE FOR BLACKS IN POLITICS"

Abdul Sabur Muhammad
Student Minister, Muhammad Mosque 26-B, Oakland-California

A man of wisdom, courage, commitment and strength, Brother Keith Muhammad is the Student Minister of Muhammad Mosque No. 26 and the Oakland, California representative of the Honorable Minister Louis Farrakhan. His powerful response to the recent flurry of propaganda-based attacks against Minister Farrakhan is a welcomed feature today on ResearchMinister.Com. Please read, reflect, act and share with others.

As the country celebrates the life of the Reverend Dr. Martin Luther King, Jr., let us remember that in his lifetime, he was a hated man. The FBI condemned him and followed their condemnations with investigations and counterintelligence actions which sought to disrupt, destroy and discredit him and the movement he inspired. He was convinced that he would be made to pay the ultimate price for his stand for justice, and in his final speeches, his messages were less politically expedient, and increasingly poignant in pursuit of justice for his suffering people.

The Reverend Dr. Martin Luther King, Jr. was a child of a people ensnared deeply in the web of white supremacy, oppression, violence, ignorance and fear. His intervention into the struggle would lead him to Chicago to fight oppression, not only in the segregated South, but in the segregated, concrete jungles of one of America's greatest urban cities.

He could not effectively organize in Chicago without meeting with its most prominent Black leader, the Honorable Elijah Muhammad. Muhammad's leadership was respected by friends, and enemies. His teaching and programs were considered the most effective in bringing reform to Black people and staging a new identity among those most afflicted by the effects of post slavery, Jim Crow America. Dr. King sat with the Honorable Elijah Muhammad. He defended boxing champ Muhammad Ali's right as a conscientious objector to the Vietnam war. He proved his love for his people and paid the price of redemption with his life.

Black elected officials should acknowledge that the man we celebrate with a federal holiday and a postage stamp is beloved for his faith and courage. 50 years from now, how will you be remembered? Dr. King, like you, was from time to time, questioned about the Honorable Elijah Muhammad and the Nation of Islam. Initially, before meeting Mr. Muhammad, he spoke carefully in defense of his belief in non-violence, as if this was in conflict with the often-misstated views of Muhammad as a promoter of hate and violence. When he finally sat down with Mr. Muhammad, he emerged with him forging a great understanding, and with unity to fight poverty and oppression in Chicago. I am convinced that, like you, he was a victim of media propaganda and lies against the Honorable Elijah Muhammad. He learned the truth of him by meeting with him personally.

Since that time, with legislation which gave rise to the Voting Rights and Civil Rights Acts, Blacks have been elected to the highest offices in the land. Certainly, this movement gave birth to Black mayors in major cities, Black governors, and led to the campaigns of the Rev. Jesse Jackson (1984-88) and the election of President Barack Hussein Obama in 2008. Now, with the largest membership in the Congressional Black Caucus, it is time to unite on the strength of truth.

Now America is clamoring over the direction led by President Trump, who made his name politically by falsely accusing the Central Park Five, challenging the birthright citizenship of Barack Obama (because American born slaves wear slave names, like Green or Meeks, and are not free to wear original names without permission), and winning election to the highest office in the world's greatest nation in the midst of the turmoil of alleged corruption and collusion.

Why would any Black elected official use your positions, in a representative democracy, to raise your voices against the most preeminent Black leader of the last 3 decades? Black communities throughout the country are plagued by poverty, oppression, high crime and murder rates, and injustice from the justice system. You call Dr. King's name joyfully this time of year, why don't you adopt more of his ways? Dr. King demonstrated courage to meet the Honorable Elijah Muhammad and they emerged from their meeting as brothers. Why are you afraid of Louis Farrakhan, a man with 64 years of service to our people?

Black members in the congress: most of you represent districts with strong Black populations. When you voice lies against the Honorable Minister Louis Farrakhan, did your constituents demand such statements condemning the Minister, or are you voicing concerns from someone else? If this is a representative democracy, whose interests do you really represent?

I, as a student of the Honorable Minister Louis Farrakhan, have dutifully served our community out of love from him for 28 years. I have sat in countless meetings with members of city councils, county supervisors, mayors, State Assembly, governors, and members Congress; and not once have any stated that I, or my teachers, are racists, bigots, homophobic, or anti-Semites. Every Black elected official in areas of large Black populations recognize the value of the Nation of Islam and the Honorable Minister Louis Farrakhan's impact on local politics.

As a student of the Honorable Minister Louis Farrakhan, I have been acknowledged by your contemporaries for our work on his behalf. The governments of the State of California, Alameda County, and the City of Oakland, have all given me public appreciation, passed legislation and offered proclamations that Islam, taught and led by the Honorable Minister Louis Farrakhan, has been a positive contributor to civic life in America. I am grateful for the acknowledgment, but I know that the praise belongs to Allah (God) for the Minister, whose love sent me, and others like me, to serve our people. I am Louis Farrakhan.

Many times, Muslims have worked alongside Black elected officials to participate in the democratic process with you as citizens and supporters of your campaigns. We have hosted political rallies. We have secured members of local, state and federal government. We have toured the toxicity filled wastelands called Bayview Hunters Point in San Francisco. We have walked with you to stop the violence that plagues the inner city.

Together we have fought police brutality and unnecessary uses of force. We have worked together, with Black elected officials to amend California laws relating to police accountability and oversight. We walked with the family of Oscar Grant, from start to finish, in pursuit of Justice, even taking the matter to the Congressional Black Caucus convention in 2010 in a televised event with the support of then House Judiciary chairman, the Honorable John Conyers.

Why should any Black elected officials, all of the sudden, feel the need to condemn the Minister today? What happened? The Minister has a 64-year track record of love for his people and that includes public, and private, meetings with Blacks in politics. Not once has he condemned you. Even when Black elected officials, like you, are often accused; whether the allegations prove true or false, Farrakhan defends you. He always gives you the benefit of the doubt. He never condemns you in the court of public opinion. The Minister recognizes that the same dirty tricks played against Black leaders yesterday; since the well documented FBI targeting of Martin Luther King Jr., Marcus Garvey, Malcolm X, the Black Panther Party and the Honorable Elijah Muhammad, are still if full effect today.

Tamika Mallory, when confronted by the Farrakhan Litmus Test passed in 2019; the same test failed by many Black leaders in the 1980's. The media driven lie campaign against the Minister has produced the greatest climate to kill a man, Louis Farrakhan, in the history of America.

Remember, as the Jewish Defense League led protestors and chanted, "Who do we want? Farrakhan! How do we want him? Dead!" Did you raise your voices against their threats of violence? The silence of Black elected officials voices against violence and hatred of Louis Farrakhan was/is deafening. Thank you, Ms. Mallory for not contributing to such a hateful climate.

Where were the Black elected officials' statements on the threats leveled against the life of the Minister? The lies told against the Minister are bold and horrific. Yet, you have not spoken out against them. Why? Do you really believe the lie that the Minister called for death to anyone? In fact, you really can't speak to what you charge the Minister with because you know it's not true. You know that the Honorable Minister Louis Farrakhan speaks inconvenient truths that most politicians don't see as politically expedient.

Since 1984, the onslaught against the Minister has been

consistent. If any Black elected official is concerned about things the Minister has said, call him or his representatives in your city, and get an understanding. Why participate in efforts to scourge and crucify a man that has done no wrong?

Who do you represent in this representative democracy? What is compelling you to accuse a man that you, and many others have sat down with, and dined at his table?

What is the driving force behind your sudden epiphany that the Minister, and those who follow him, are these wicked things you send out in Tweets? Why don't you come home to the district you claim to represent and face your community that elected you and make your case against the Minister? We are waiting.

This is no time for political correctness and expediency. With your false allegations, you are attempting to create a climate for the assassination and/or false arrest of our community's strongest voice of freedom, the Honorable Minister Louis Farrakhan, National Representative of the Honorable Elijah Muhammad and the Nation of Islam.

WOE TO THE SLANDERERS: A MESSAGE TO THOSE WHO CONTINUE TO ANSWER THE CALL TO SLANDER MINISTER FARRAKHAN

Abdul Shahid Muhammad

Student Minister, Muhammad Study Group Holly Springs-Mississippi

Throughout America a chorus of students of the Honorable Minister Louis Farrakhan are responding to what has become a renewed effort over the past few months to assassinate the character of the Minister. In an extensive analysis, rooted within a scriptural context Bro. Andre Muhammad rebuts the pundits, critics, weak politicians, provocateurs and who have made a cottage industry out of slandering Minister Farrakhan. ResearchMinister.Com is happy to share Student Minister Andre's bold essay with our readers. Read, Reflect, Act & Share.

"Woe To The Slanderers!"

Those Who Continue To Answer The Call To Slander Farrakhan

In 1964 the Most Honorable Elijah Muhammad wrote the following: "As you know, we have been all but universally attacked. Here for the last four or five months, especially. Universally attacked. And this attack was for the purpose of getting rid of me . . . So, I wish that you remember this: That this kind of attack that has been made on me, personally, and indirectly on you . . . This I like that you would get this in mind, ministers, as you are my helpers, that these kinds of attacks, as you are not through with them, we have something else to face yet. It may not be the same nature, but we have attacks, yet, to come on us. I don't want to excite you, now, in the very least. Don't get excited in the very least, because if I'm not excited, and I'm the hare in front of the hound, I don't think you should get excited.

The hound wants me most of all. And you should arm yourself with truth from scripture standpoints to prove my position. If you don't come out first and attack the enemy that attacks me. If you sit down and wait until I attack, then you are not much of a help. I'm just telling you frankly. Anytime that your leader is attacked, you is attacked. And you should go after the attacker with everything you have, you know, of truth to defend yourself and your leader."

To those of you who continue to bow to pressure from or seek advantage from Jewish organizations and leadership to denounce or slander the Honorable Minister Louis Farrakhan:

First: It is out of love for the Honorable Minister Louis Farrakhan, and the love that he has put in my heart for the Most Honorable Elijah Muhammad that I write this brief note. It is a love born of the nature of God in me that Minister Farrakhan's preaching has touched and awakened. Second: The love of which I speak engenders in me a strong sense of duty that I, along with my colleagues, lift my pen and voice to defend our beloved Minister Farrakhan, and in so doing, we defend ourselves. Third: The above words from the Most Honorable Elijah Muhammad are, to me, divine orders for those of us whose lives have literally been saved as a result of the transformative effect that his teachings, through Minister Farrakhan, has had on us. Love compels me to follow those orders.

The Holy Quran says in Chapter 104 entitled "The Slanderer": 1. Woe to every slanderer, defamer! 2. Who amasses wealth and counts it — 3. He thinks that his wealth will make him abide. 4. Nay, he will certainly be hurled into the crushing disaster; 5. And what will make thee realize what the crushing disaster is? 6. It is the Fire kindled by Allah, 7. Which rises over the hearts. 8. Surely it is closed in on them, 9. In extended columns.

Slander is the action or crime of making a false spoken statement with the intent of damaging to a person's reputation. Slander is an untrue defamatory statement that is spoken orally. When that false spoken statement is put in writing, it is called Libel.

Slander and libel are both types of defamation. Defamation is a false statement presented as a fact that causes injury or damage to the character of the person it is about.

In defamation law there is an important difference between stating an opinion and defaming someone. Yes, the Honorable Minister Louis Farrakhan is a "public figure", but when a person makes a statement with knowledge and facts that the statement is untrue or with reckless disregard for facts and truth it becomes a criminal act. The intent of the statement determines if it's criminal. The intent of the ADL, SPLC, the U.S. Government has been clear according to their own documents, and when you repeat from them what has been proven to be false, then you become a part of their lie and their crime! No. This is not a veiled threat. The threat is in the aforementioned verse of the Holy Quran. The question is whose threat will you fear, God's or the ADL, SPLC, and the U.S. Government? It's clear that you fear the latter.

The Hon. Min. Louis Farrakhan has so carefully taught us that God raises up a messenger or a warner with a message that is designed to guide people and nations onto a right course that they may avert God's punishment. We live in a world built upon and ruled by lies, deceit, murder and plunder. Anyone who would expose the architects who built and maintains the construct is targeted for destruction. The people at the base of such a world are always the poor, ignorant masses of the society. When the servant of God is present in such a world the ultimate aim of that world is to kill the messenger of God. The one that God raises must have this very essential attribute in his character . . . COURAGE. That courage evolves into FEARLESSNESS as God's servant embraces the message and engages in the mission that God gave to him. The onlookers from among the poor are especially drawn to the spiritual magnetism of God in His servant as he works on his mission. So, the wicked rulers move on God's servant, because those who's backs upon which their wicked rule stands are being drawn out from underneath them. The world and rule of the wicked is threatened, so they seek to frighten those who are drawn to God's servant. They know that ultimately those who are drawn to God's servant will lose their fear of them.

The Bible says in 2 Timothy Chapter 1 verse 7, ". . . for God gave us a spirit not of fear but of power and love and self-control."

It seems that most of our brothers and sisters in American politics, academia, media and entertainment are in a state of perpetual fear of members of the Jewish community, the Anti-Defamation League, and the Southern Poverty Law Center. They have them terrified to publicly speak well of, be seen in the company of, or show any sign of support of Minister Farrakhan and the Nation of Islam. They have been able to, upon demand, cower some of them into slandering Minister Farrakhan or at least put distance between him/us and themselves. We who love and help the Honorable Minister Farrakhan have grown weary of your evil treatment and talk of him. It's gotten very difficult to offer you a smile and extend our hand to shake yours in brotherhood when we see you.

Yet we, like the Minister, turn the other cheek. But, it's time to challenge you and your enemy to prove what you say about the Minister! I was happy and proud to see our sister, Tamika Mallory, stand strong and dismiss Meghan McCain's attempt to force her to denounce the Minister. You should take notice of her as she takes courage on her mission and become more and more fearless in the face of the enemies of truth.

Minister Farrakhan is a man who has been absolutely stalwart in his service to our people and black leaders. Those of you who have repudiated and denounced him at the beckoning of your open enemies, or to gain some personal advantage, did not receive a response in kind from the Minister. He responded like a true Christian would by "turning the other cheek" again and again. Some of you repudiated and denounced the Minister after he embraced and defended you! He continually humbles himself and suffers abuse and disrespect from you. You do this in a futile effort to appease your enemies, or gain personal advantage, or maintain your sick, pitiful, political relationships with our 460-year-old open enemies. In private you present yourself as a friend, but at the prompting of the ADL, SPLC, or prominent members of the Jewish community you become an enemy. You KNOW the Minister is not what they say of him, but you repeat the lies of your enemy out of fear, or because your enemy has something you want that is more important to you than principle and character. So, you're not a friend. You're a "frenemy." You exhibit both the characteristics of a friend and an enemy to the Minister and the Nation of Islam. How long will you continue to engage in this traitorous behavior?

In recent days Texas Rep. Al Green issued a statement calling Minister Farrakhan a "bigot", and likened our beloved Minister Farrakhan to Donald Trump. I was personally outraged and repulsed! My mind could not meld together Rep. Green's words and my memory of the image of Rep. Green embracing the Minister in a Texas Church.

This was a grave offense to me, because I see an attack on the Minister as an attack on my "spiritual father." He is an extension of the "spiritual fountainhead" from which I, and millions more have been blessed to drink in the wisdom and guidance of God for our lives. I'm just one of millions who see the Minister in the same or a similar light. The sad part is Rep. Green knows that he spoke a lie. The wickedness of it is the satanic puppet masters, with their hand up Rep. Green's back, have put fear in him in a futile attempt to demagnetize Minister Farrakhan and de-rail the Women's March. Even worse Rep. Green and his handlers offer NO PROOF, because they know there is NONE.

Minister Farrakhan and the Nation of Islam's Historical Research Department has offered and made available three tomes of the Secret Relationship Between Blacks and Jews documented proof of the pure evil perpetrated against black people by Jewish Americans. The first book deals with 'Jewish involvement in the Trans-Atlantic Slave Trade'. The second book deals with 'How Jews Gained Control of The Black American Economy'. The third book exposes the false basis upon which the Black – Jewish "friendship" was established in its examination of 'The Leo Frank Case'. In fact, the Minister sent Books One and Two of the research to some of our leaders. The Minister made it clear that the books contained research from Jewish libraries of what Jewish Rabbis, Scholars and Historians have said about "their involvement" in the Trans-Atlantic Slave Trade and "their control and exploitation" of the Black Economy.

Some of them didn't even have the courage to read one word of what Jews have recorded of their evil done to us! NOT ONE WORD! Some even sent the books back to the Minister! As I read his words, I wondered if Rep. Green read these books. I thought, 'if he did read the Secret Relationship Between Blacks and Jews and can still open his mouth and call the Minister a "bigot" for telling the truth, what kind of man does that make him?'

The Holy Quran says in Chapter 3 Verse 175. "It is the devil who only frightens his friends, but do not fear them, and fear Me, if you are believers."

The Holy Quran also says in Chapter 2 Verse 268. "The devil threatens you with poverty and enjoins you to be niggardly . . ."

Who is it that's frightening black leaders, and forcing them to abandon principle and exhibit poor character? Who is it that threatens to ruin your career and slam the doors of opportunity in your face to make earning a living difficult for you? Farrakhan and the Nation of Islam aren't doing that to black leaders. The Minister has repeatedly extended the hand of brotherhood to black leaders to sit down at the table of unity and solidarity to bring an end to the suffering of the masses of our people and others. Some of you hold a seat in the most powerful government in today's world and get an up-close look at America's ability to make entire nations bow to her will, yet this Government and powerful Jewish Organizations have not been able to make Farrakhan and the Nation of Islam bow. This begs the question, 'What is it about Farrakhan and the Nation of Islam that keeps us upright under the continuous onslaught of the U.S. Government and Jewish pressure?'

How could you continue to obey them when the San Francisco Police Department found that the ADL illegally spied on over 950 political organizations including the NAACP, Rainbow Push, American Civil Liberties Union and others? How could you continue to do their bidding when they infiltrated countless police and sheriff departments across the country, bribing police officials and illegally obtaining classified government data on at least 20,000 American citizens? How could you continue to do their bidding when they were caught selling information on Anti-Apartheid groups to the South African Government? How could you continue to do their bidding when they were caught passing surveillance and classified police data on Arab-Americans to Israeli authorities who then used the ADL data to illegally detain American citizens visiting Israel?

Right now, they are working to get federal legislation passed to make "fact-based criticism" of Jews and boycotting Israel a CRIME! According to "Newsweek", In May 2017, Texas became the 17th state to prohibit contractors from supporting a boycott of Israel. "Texas state law (Chapter 2270 of the Texas Government Code), currently does not allow school districts to hire a contractor unless the contract contains a written verification that the contractor does not boycott Israel and will not boycott Israel during the term of the contract. Twenty-six states now have such legislation.

The Honorable Minister Louis Farrakhan is not who most of us think he is. Wise members of the Jewish Community know who he is and whom he represents. In the Bible, Nicodemus, a ruler of the Jews, admitted that he and those he ruled knew who Jesus was and whom he represents. Even so, they opposed and sought to kill Jesus!

The Bible says in John 3:2. This man came to Jesus by night and said to him, "Rabbi, we know that you are a teacher come from God, for no one can do these signs that you do unless God is with him."

Their knowledge of who Jesus is, and who Jesus represents is also found in the Holy Quran.

It says in the Holy Quran Chapter 2:146. Those whom We have given the Book recognize him as they recognize their sons, but some of them surely conceal the truth while they know.

What kind of people would knowingly oppose a servant of God? What kind of people would knowingly and openly oppose Jesus? Jesus already answered that question in John Chapter 9 verse 44. You all should go and read it, and when you finish, ask yourself what kind of person would help them oppose Jesus by slandering a man walking in the footsteps of Jesus The Christ.

The Economic Blueprint: The Unity Of Booker T. Washington, Prophet Muhammad and Minister Farrakhan

Cedric Muhammad
Nation of Islam Research Group

When I learned that Saviours' Day 2014 would be held in Detroit, Michigan, my mind went to the steps that Allah (God) guided Prophet Muhammad (Peace Be Upon Him) to take in Arabia 1,400 years ago. I also thought in a particular way, that Booker T. Washington was the economic forerunner of the Honorable Minister Louis Farrakhan, perfectly complimenting what the Honorable Elijah Muhammad stated—that the Honorable Marcus Garvey was a forerunner of his.

One aspect of the work of Prophet Muhammad was his establishment of a market in Medina where his people would be free from taxation. M.J. Kister's "The Market of The Prophet" published in The Journal of the Economic and Social History of the Orient in 1965 documents this. One of the motives in the mind of the Prophet was his desire to benefit two different classes of his followers from two different regions in Arabia. One group of his followers, the Muhajirun—from Mecca—were primarily merchants and traders. The other group, the Ansar— from Medina - were farmers. Muhammad of 1,400 years ago wanted to see them united.

Booker T. Washington's economic work simultaneously addressed two often divided classes in Black America. In 1901 he founded the National Negro Business League focused on "commercial, agricultural, educational and industrial advancement." Its work in both the heart of the South (where agriculture shaped Black life) and the North (where manufacturing was booming) brought Black laborers, entrepreneurs, professionals and farmers together in business.

In 1972, during his Theology of Time series, the Honorable Elijah Muhammad spoke to the need for unity between the poor and the professional class. At one point he described how he had been waiting for such professionals for 40 years. During that time, he asked then-Minister of Temple #7 in New York City, Minister Louis

Farrakhan to bring a group of professionals to Chicago in order to help the Nation of Islam improve the management of its business entities. With the help of Brother Larry 4X, now known as Abdul Akbar Muhammad, Minister Farrakhan hired six Eastern Airline jets, filled with members of the learned class, who paid their own way to come to Chicago for a meeting.

Prophet Muhammad's (PBUH) market in Medina eventually was corrupted in the caliphate of Mu'awiyah. The National Negro Business League eventually 'died' and the 1972 effort initiated by the Honorable Elijah Muhammad was only a 'dry run' as Minister Louis Farrakhan explains in Closing The Gap for something that would come decades later.

I have no knowledge of what message and guidance Allah (God) and the Honorable Elijah Muhammad will bless the Honorable Minister Louis Farrakhan to deliver in February of 2014. I'm ignorant of that. But the setting of Detroit is now part of the context for that communication and therefore a vital part of understanding it. So, consider this succinct statement from Brother Jabril Muhammad in Is It Possible That The Honorable Elijah Muhammad Is Still Physically Alive???, "Among the main facts one should know about any communication, especially one of significance, whether it is spoken or written, are (1) the premise, (2) the intention, (3) the context. To put it another way, regardless to the means by which information is conveyed, or given, the more we know of the reason (the 'why' or the 'motive') for it and the circumstances involved in its production, the better we can understand and properly use the information presented to us."

Scripture better than any other written source, provides insights, hints and nods regarding the premise, intention and context in the words and actions of Minister Farrakhan. Isaiah 61: 4 states, "And they shall build the old wastes, they shall raise up the former desolations, and they shall repair the waste cities, the desolations of many generations."

Would Detroit qualify as a 'waste city?'

The Honorable Minister Louis Farrakhan has referred to Tuskegee University as both a seminal fluid and manger.

Does the Nation of Islam holding its Day of Atonement and

Saviours' Day conventions back-to-back in these two cities signify a new stage in the building of an economy, inspired by God?

In the 1983 introduction of his previously mentioned book Jabril Muhammad writes, "Now, Moses' life did not end when he went up in the mountain to meet God for the second time. After he came down and found the people involved in calf worship, he had to go back to God in order to get a second set of laws, which God gave him on his first trip. Nor did such trips end, as it was necessary for him to go up to meet God a third time. This third meeting has a profound bearing on very significant events that are happening now—which involve Minister Farrakhan—and that are yet to take place in these days of the establishment of God's complete rule."

From another perspective some scholars say Moses visited Jehovah at least 8 times. Exodus 24 and 25 pictures his seventh trip to the mountain where, after 40 days and 40 nights, the Lord tells Moses, "Speak to the children of Israel that they bring Me an offering. From everyone who gives it willingly with his heart you shall take my offering."

The contributions were to be used to make a sanctuary and tabernacle after a pattern which God gave to Moses.

The Honorable Elijah Muhammad wrote of his economic blueprint, "I have set before you a program, according to the Divine Supreme Being and his Prophets."

Every time we make a contribution to economicblueprint.org, we participate in a divine work.

Now, just imagine what would happen if college students earning degrees in urban planning, economics, international studies, engineering and agriculture—at Tuskegee University—and elsewhere, began studying the Honorable Elijah Muhammad's vision for the cities of Phoenix and Chicago, outlined in his Theology of Time series and Muhammad Speaks newspaper.

More scripture – this has everything to do with Matthew 21.

(Brother Cedric Muhammad is an Economist and Member of the Nation of Islam's Research Group.)

SUN-TIMES OPINION FAILS AS FACTS VINDICATE FARRAKHAN & PFLEGER

Dawud Muhammad

Student Minister, Detroit-Michigan

In the Op- Ed section of The Chicago Sun Times (May 20, 2019) Jay Tcath executive vice president of the Jewish Federation of Chicago wrote:

(Father) "Pfleger knows that Facebook didn't ban only Farrakhan, but several white supremacists too. Surely, he knows of Farrakhan's infamous anti-Semitic assertions: Jews are termites and Satanic; were behind the 9-11 attacks; Allah will punish them; Jews are wicked deceivers of the American people and suck their blood; are sending this nation to hell; Judaism is a gutter religion; and, at the University of Tehran, Farrakhan led chants of "Death to Israel," "Death to America!"

In this excerpt the writer assert's that Father Pfleger was indulging in hatred instead of fighting it by opening up the doors of his church (St. Sabina) to the Honorable Minister Louis Farrakhan to, in Father Pfleger's words, "come and respond to this unjust ban and his right and all of our right to the first amendment to be given protection to free speech in this country.".

Further in the same paragraph Mr. Tcath Repeats The distorted interpretations, misquotes and outright lies cast at The Minister by his detractors since 1984. Rather than address each lie or distortion one by one I would like to offer a defense by first framing it in the form of a question; Why has Minister Louis Farrakhan failed at promoting hatred, bigotry and antisemitism?

You would think in 65 years of traveling the width and breath of this country and teaching people in the thousands, the hundreds of thousands and yes- the millions there would be some evidence of the Ministers influence on the behavior of his followers, supporters and well-wishers.

What kind of influence has he had? Are there any incidents of violence against the people he has been accused of "spewing hatred" towards? No? How about vandalism? – defacing temples or synagogues etc.? He called a Million Men to a gathering in

Washington D.C (October 16, 1995). I'm sure those men who answered Minister Farrakhan's Call wreaked havoc in the Nation's Capital that day. Right? You mean no one even suffered a bloody nose?

I must ask again what kind of influence has he had on the behavior of his followers, supporters and well-wishers? I Think Father Pfleger answers the question in these remarks at the community rally at St. Sabina,

"I do not know of another man in America who can fill arenas around this country often times many of them [in attendance] if not a majority of them not Muslim-but simply want to love the Minister and hear his teaching. I don't know of another person, group or religion in this country that has done a better job in raising up strong, clean, nonviolent black men and saving lives across this country than Minister Farrakhan and the Nation of Islam."

If we were to accept Mr. Jay Tcath's and those of his ilk's characterization of The Honorable Minister Louis Farrakhan we would have to conclude that the Minister has failed at convincing his friends, supporters and followers to listen to him and follow his guidance. How else does one explain a man attempting to spread hatred but instead produces Love peace nonviolence and civility amongst those who follow and support him?

Brother Dawud Muhammad is a Student Minister of the Honorable Minister Louis Farrakhan from Detroit Michigan

THE MIS-EDUCATION OF CLARENCE PAGE

Dennis Muhammad, J.D.

Muhammad Study Group Charleston-South Carolina

The Honorable Minister Louis Farrakhan, the beloved leader and champion of the poor and the downtrodden continues to work valiantly on behalf of his suffering people. And this, much to the chagrin of those who delight in the Black community's miseries and pain. Throughout America and the world, his work has inspired committed and dedicated men and women to study him, assist him and faithfully follow his leadership. Minister Farrakhan's sincere commitment to his teacher the Most Honorable Elijah Muhammad has been a model of discipleship that is being emulated by those who have properly recognized him as a worthy teacher and extension of the Hon. Elijah Muhammad. Daily, more and more of his disciples and students are rising to rebut, disprove, hold accountable and condemn Minister Farrakhan's evil adversaries. Today, ResearchMinister.Com is happy to publish the following open letter from Attorney Dennis Muhammad as he challenges popular journalist and pundit Clarence Page. Read, Reflect, Act & Share

Mr. Page,

I am a trained lawyer, an educator by trade and one of those bow tied F.O.I. that patrol tough neighborhoods and run off drug dealers. I have been a student of the Honorable Minister Louis Farrakhan for twenty-seven years. I have studied Minister Farrakhan's words, analyzed his motives and examined his works. I have also admired and studied many other historical leaders and figures and the effect of their work in the Black community. The Honorable Louis Farrakhan has been easiest of them all to stand with and defend.

I am a beneficiary of Minister Farrakhan's Teachings and Work, but I'm always looking for critiques to understand different perspectives and viewpoints of his work and mission. When I read articles like yours about Minister Farrakhan, I often wonder what I am missing that is not making my analysis of him and his works more objective. I think it may be that I'm more concerned about my people and Black self-preservation than capitulating to false charges and allegations of bigotry and anti-Semitism.

"Un-Smiting The Shepherd" -429

I read your article addressing the question of why black politicians have a difficult time denouncing the Honorable Louis Farrakhan's for his alleged bigoted and anti-Semitic comments. Denounce means to publicly condemn as wrong or evil. What can any Black politician prove that Minister Farrakhan has said or done to Jews that is wrong or evil? Name one Jewish person whose health, interests, rights or needs have been violated by Minister Louis Farrakhan or any Nation of Islam member?

Minister Farrakhan is denouncing Jewish actions against Blacks, particularly, the control some Jewish people and institutions possess over black entertainers, athletes, politicians, preachers, and journalists like yourself. It's very difficult for Black politicians to denounce someone who is denouncing actions that ill-effect their ability to legislate for the best interests of their people and constituents. Those few feeble-minded Black politicians that are influenced by Jewish money, however, are forced to denounce Minister Farrakhan, not because of his statements, but because of Jewish control over their political careers and livelihood. Minister Farrakhan has challenged Jewish writers and apologists who accuse him of anti-Semitism for three decades to prove him wrong or his words to be lies. It is not enough to call him a bigot and anti-Semite, you have to prove what you charge.

First let me help you understand the differences between Minister Farrakhan and Donald Trump as well as the differences between their base supporters.

Trump is proven to be a compulsive and calculated liar. He is a businessman, Reality TV host, and controversial president/politician. Mr. Trump's desire is to make America a great racist nation again. Mr. Trump is not a reformer or transformer of life. He does not have a mission of redemption and restoration of a destroyed people. His message appeals to a base of white Americans that wants America to be what was in the past.

No one has proven Minister Farrakhan to be a liar. He is beyond dogmatic teaching and race-baiting rhetoric. Minister Farrakhan is a transformer of human life. To compare the two men proves you have very little interest in the truth and the real conflict between Minister Farrakhan and his Jewish opposers.

You don't understand Minister Farrakhan and the power that

upholds him. He comes in the tradition of prophets and messengers that give clear warnings to governments and nations. Minister Louis Farrakhan is a redeemer and civilizer of Black people. He has a specific mission to resurrect and transform the life of Blacks from the condition of 400 years of slavery and oppression. That mission also includes reluctant, spiritually and psychologically damaged, intellectuals from among our people. Mr. Page, there is still hope.

You, nor his Jewish enemies can calculate what motivates him to speak so boldly and truthfully; the love he has for God and his people, not hate and bigotry. Part of his work is to expose all those who are responsible for reducing a nation of black people to savages and beast in human form. We give him our allegiance and support because he helps us improve our life, not because we need someone to blame for our plight in life. Minister Farrakhan has sixty-three years of credibility among his base because of the extent and the effect of his message and his work. His work is comparable to a modern Jesus who has the ability to open the eyes of the blind, make the deaf hear, the dumb speak and raise the mentally dead to life. As his work spreads among black people it will become as difficult to get his base to denounce him and is to get Back Christians to denounce Jesus.

Anti-Semitism is foreign to the masses of our people. Black folks have enough problems to handle. They are more concerned about unemployment and raising their standard of life. It really doesn't matter to us who likes or dislikes Jews or whites. That is only a concern of those Blacks who have been indoctrinated that Jews are the Chosen People of God, and those who benefit from money and token positions offered by Jews and whites. We are just as indifferent to Jews as we are to Arabs, Koreans, and Chinese. Why don't you make assertions about Minister Farrakhan being anti-Arab (which is the same as anti-Semitic), anti-Korean and anti-Chinese?

You have admitted that you have only been an "observer", 'interviewer" and "commentator" of Minister Louis Farrakhan's remarks and controversies. Who can take you serious as a true journalist if you have not presented any facts to disprove his statements and assertions about Jewish behavior towards Blacks? Where is your research over the past three decades that proves that Minister Farrakhan is a bigot and anti-Semite worthy to be denounced by his own people?

Mr. Page, if you are making such assertions about Minister Farrakhan without valid research and proof, you are a yellow journalist. Have you researched Minister Farrakhan's "rhetoric" to verify his assertions against Jewish behavior towards Blacks? Have you read the two volumes of The Secret Relationship Between Blacks and Jews documented by Jewish historians and scholars that are the text of Minister Farrakhan's assertions about Jewish behavior towards Blacks? Have you read the Book of Revelation in the Bible that he references his assertions about the Synagogue of Satan? All of Minister Farrakhan's assertions about Jewish behavior have been authenticated. None of their assertions about him being a bigot or anti-Semite have been authenticated.

Have you done your research on chemical marijuana and its effects on the male genitalia? Our scholars have done and authenticated the research. This is why Minister Farrakhan mentioned it in his Saviours' Day 2017 message. Mr. Paige, it's only marijuana smokers and lovers that have launched an emotional retort, but they have not been able to successfully challenge the authenticated scholarly research by Dr. Wesley Muhammad in his Book: Understanding the Assault on the Black Man, Black Manhood and Black Masculinity.

Mr. Page, you mentioned Minister Farrakhan's work, but you attempt to minimize his work as though it is less important than his critique of Jewish behavior. You attempt to highlight his scathing critique of Jewish behavior and reduce it to name-calling. You fail to examine the truth of his assertions about Jewish behavior towards blacks. You fail to acknowledge that some Jewish organizations have systemic structures that ill-effect not only poor blacks, but poor Americans in general. Pointing out Jewish people's wrongs and critiquing their behavior is not anti-Semitic rhetoric. Is your critique of Minister Farrakhan for over thirty years, anti-Muslim and anti-black? I'm sure Minister Farrakhan has not said or done anything to cause harm to you or your family. Should people listen to the rhetoric spewed against Minister Farrakhan from your pen?

The majority of Minister Farrakhan's messages are for the upliftment of Black and poor and oppressed people of the planet. Are the Jewish scribes that charge Minister Farrakhan with bigotry and anti-Semitism anti-Muslim and anti-Black? Do you ever criticize the Jewish writers for unjustly attacking Minister Farrakhan, the Nation of Islam and their base? You act as though this thirty-eight-year fight between the Minister Farrakhan and some of the Jewish organizations is a one-sided, unfair assault against powerless innocent Jews. I know you are not that naïve. Minister Farrakhan is an adherent to the command in the Holy Qur'an for Muslims not to be the aggressor to anyone in words or deeds, however, we fight with those who fight with us. Minister Farrakhan did not, nor does he initiate attacks on Jews, he is responding to their attacks against him, the NOI and Black people. How do you miss that significant fact in your critiques?

Why aren't you asking Black politicians to denounce AIPAC, the Anti-Defamation League, the Jewish Defense Fund, and the Southern Poverty Law Center for their unjust attacks on Minister Louis Farrakhan and the Nation of Islam? Have you ever taken Jews to task about their scathing comments made against Minister Louis Farrakhan and other Black leaders? Are Jews above any critique or criticism at all? Perhaps, if you were not so enamored and committed to defending Jewish philanthropists and their financial contributions to control Black thought and education, you could be more conscious about some of their crimes against humanity.

In conclusion, you should be truthful about the cancellation of the Chicago Women's March that you link to Minister Farrakhan. The historic Million Man March that you mentioned in your article is the progenitor of such marches. The organizers of the Chicago Women's March are aware of Minister Farrakhan's success of the Million Man March. They should consult with and support him as did others who convened similar marches since the Million Man March. Consulting Minister Farrakhan on any matter will not hinder success, but secure success. Why don't you place blame of any Chicago Women's March organizational troubles where its rightly due, those haters of Black, Arab and Hispanic advancement; Jewish antagonists who hate and organize against anything that does not ingratiate their sickness for Jewish hegemony.

With truth,

Dennis Muhammad

MINISTER FARRAKHAN'S STERLING RECORD DESTROYS CLAIMS OF HOMOPHOBIA

Dezarae Muhammad

Muhammad Mosque No. 92, Greensboro-North Carolina

One of the many false labels attached to the ministry of The Honorable Minister Louis Farrakhan is that he's "homophobic."

The critics of The Honorable Minister Louis Farrakhan often take his words towards our homosexual brothers and sisters out of context, while selectively choosing seconds-long sound bites from the Minister's hours-long messages as a way to prove their false claims. Minister Farrakhan is not a teacher of hate. He is a beautiful man of God, who deeply loves his people, and we can prove it!

Consider the dictionary definition of the word "homophobic":

unreasonable fear of or antipathy toward homosexuals and homosexuality.

The Honorable Minister Louis Farrakhan does not have an "unreasonable fear" towards homosexuals, nor does he demonstrate "antipathy" towards them. "Antipathy" is defined as:

a natural, basic, or habitual repugnance; aversion.

Now, let's consider the evidence that proves that the Honorable Minister Louis Farrakhan does not exhibit fear or repugnance towards our brothers and sisters who identify as LGBTQI. During part 2 of the Minister's magnificent Saviours' Day address, delivered on February 25, 2018 he stated the following:

"Now, to my dear beloved brothers and sisters who are lesbian, or homosexual, or LGBTQ: I don't dislike you; I am your brother, I love you."

Let's stop there. Does that sound like an individual exuding fear, repugnance and aversion? Does that sound like it's coming from a hateful individual? Far from hate and loathing, this is a clear expression of love and compassion. The Minister's views on the subject of homosexuality and lesbianism are based upon the sacred texts of Jews, Christians and Muslims. The Minister additionally stated:

"But wait — I am a minister of the real Christ. I can't tell you that you are acceptable. I can tell you, 'You can come as you are, but with Christ, you can't stay that way.'"

As a spiritual teacher and minister, Minister Farrakhan's mind and heart is shaped and formed by the mind and heart of God that has been revealed within the word of God. To condemn the Minister's views is to simultaneously condemn the view and perspective of God that has been documented within the Torah, Gospel and Holy Qur'an. Wouldn't you agree that for the Minister to take a position that does not agree with the tenets of his faith as a Muslim, would make him hypocritical?

As The Minister stated at a press conference on May 9, 2019:

"I'm not a homophobe. Don't be angry with me if I stand up on God's word."

A representative of God teaching contrary to what God teaches — it's oxymoronic. You cannot be angry with this man for standing on what God says. To be clear and for the benefit of our readers, let's review what the Word of God has to say:

"You shall not lie with a male as with a woman; it is an abomination." (Leviticus 18:22)

Now, is God a homophobe? God is absolutely not a homophobe! He loves you just as much as He loves others who sin, yet, He condemns the unrighteous act of homosexuality just as He condemns other unrighteous acts of sinners:

"...Or do you not know that the unrighteous will not inherit the kingdom of God? Do not be deceived: neither the sexually immoral, nor idolaters, nor adulterers, nor men who practice homosexuality, nor thieves, nor the greedy, nor drunkards, nor revilers, nor swindlers will inherit the kingdom of God." (1 Corinthians 6:9-10)

The ministry of the Honorable Minister Louis Farrakhan is not purposed to hate homosexuals or to seek to harm them. The Honorable Minister Louis Farrakhan is a man that Allah (God) has raised to teach the truth and lay the foundation for the building of the Kingdom of God. A man that Allah (God) has raised to be an instrument of the mental, spiritual and moral resurrection of humanity would not view as repugnant the people whom Allah (God) has missioned him to serve and to love. The Minister understands the condition of his people. And he knows that whatever our mental, spiritual and moral condition may be, Allah (God) is powerful enough to change it and improve it.

Think about how someone in Minister Farrakhan's position-a position of great power-could inspire or instruct his many followers to carry out hate crimes against the object of his hatred. Yet the Nation of Islam has no record of hate crimes against anyone. There is no member of the LGBTQI community that can honestly say that they have been harmed or disrespected by Minister Farrakhan.

"We don't go around beating up people who say they're gay, or queer, or lesbian. I teach them with love, and they come to me." - Saviours' Day Address, February 17, 2019

If the Minister was a true homophobe, a true hateful person — why would members of the homosexual community come to him for counsel? As many young people might respond in a situation like this, "Make it make sense."

The Honorable Minister Louis Farrakhan is no homophobe. Like all men and women of God, the Minister speaks a bold truth and truth can make a person uncomfortable when the light of truth is being shone upon a part of their lives that God is displeased with. And so instead of accepting the truth and struggling to come into alignment with the truth, there are those who attack the truth and the preacher of truth.

I say to the critics of our beloved Minister, "where are your facts; where is your evidence?" Being caught up in your feelings, you react with baseless accusations to a message of pure truth. But the time has come, and we will not stand for the continued slander of a man that has been such an extraordinary blessing to us. We bear witness that Allah (God) is with him; and we are with Minister Farrakhan too!

September 17th
A Divine Sign of Min. Farrakhan's position

Ilia Rashad Muhammad

Nation of Islam Research Group

Unlike any national or world leader, the Honorable Minister Louis Farrakhan is quite distinguished in that he is virtually the only voice who has publicly and consistently expressed his connection and experiences with so-called UFOs. The blessed night of Minister Farrakhan's famous vision-like experience occurred on September 17, 1985 in Tepotzlan, Mexico from a mountain that he had climbed many times throughout his visits there. Both the time and location of this experience hold divine significance. It is from such mountainous settings that his vision was foretold in the sacred scriptures:

And he carried me away in the spirit to a great and high mountain, and shewed me that great city, the holy Jerusalem, descending out of heaven from God, – Revelation 21:10 (KJV)

After the Minister's experience with the great Mother Wheel and a smaller wheel, and the Honorable Elijah Muhammad in 1985, Tepotzlan became a haven for UFO sightings and activities. Several local inhabitants and tourists photographed and filmed some of the most credible images of these luminous circular crafts. One of such persons was Carlos Diaz who became internationally recognized for his recorded footage and photographs of these objects in and around Tepotzlan, Mexico. Mexican TV journalist and UFOlogist—Jaime Maussan, took Diaz's photographs to Jim Dilettoso, an image processing expert who concluded that his photos and videos were genuine.

Why Tepotzlan, Mexico? This location represents a spiritual journey to the ancient home of Quetzalcoatl who is considered the Christ-type figure to the indigenous people of that area associating it with a messianic-type figure and experience.

One of the most mindboggling factors associated with Minister Farrakhan's vision from Tepotzlan has to do with the Biblical calculations that signify its authenticity. Before modern Bible scholars were able to pinpoint the dates and times of Biblical events, Minister Farrakhan had been proclaiming the majesty of the vision-like experience, which occurred September 17, 1985. One of the scriptures forecasting this vision-like experience occurs in the 8th Chapter of Ezekiel. The prophet Ezekiel, who is most commonly associated with these flying wheels, was given a vision that reads in traditional Bibles in this manner:

And it came to pass in the sixth year, in the sixth month, in the fifth day of the month, as I sat in mine house, and the elders of Judah sat before me, that the hand of the Lord GOD fell there upon me. Then I beheld, and lo a likeness as the appearance of fire: from the appearance of his loins even downward, fire; and from his loins even upward, as the appearance of brightness, as the colour of amber. And he put forth the form of a hand, and took me by a lock of mine head; and the spirit lifted me up between the earth and the heaven, and brought me in the visions of God to Jerusalem, to the door of the inner gate that looketh toward the north; where was the seat of the image of jealousy, which provoketh to jealousy. And, behold, the glory of the God of Israel was there, according to the vision that I saw in the plain. – Ezekiel 8:1-4, King James Version

This vision describes a man who is being lifted in the spirit and shown the heavenly signs of God in what is understood to be the New Jerusalem. Even more astonishing is that years after the Minister's vision on September 17, Biblical scholars developed the New Living Translation Bible that was designed to offer more up-to-date calculations of Biblical dates. In this translation the same passage from Ezekiel reads as such:

Then on September 17, during the sixth year of King Jehoiachin's captivity, while the leaders of Judah were in my home, the Sovereign LORD took hold of me. I saw a figure that appeared to be a man. From what appeared to be his waist down, he looked like a burning flame. From the waist up, he looked like gleaming amber. He reached out what seemed to be a hand and took me by the hair. Then the Spirit lifted me up into the sky and transported me to Jerusalem in a vision from God. I was taken to the north gate of the inner courtyard of the Temple, where there is a large idol that has made the LORD very jealous. Suddenly, the glory of the God of Israel was there, just as I had seen it before in the valley. – Ezekiel 8:1-4, New Living Translation

Is this a coincidence that Ezekiel's foretold vision occurred on the exact same day (September 17) as the Minister's vision? The first edition of the New Living Translation was published in 1996. This happened 11 years after Minister Farrakhan's vision–like experience. The theological developers of this Bible translation did not consult with the N.O.I. for this calculation. Such mathematical precision only validates the awesome power of Allah's prophecies and the authenticity of his servant's experience.

As if that was not enough, Minister Farrakhan's September 17 communication with the (believed dead) Honorable Elijah Muhammad would hold further significance. One of the most famous international UFO abduction cases occurred on this date 12 years after Minister Farrakhan's vision. Kirsan Ilyumzhinov, President of the Republic of Kalmykia in the Russian Federation from 1993 to 2010, made international headlines when he reported being abducted by people from a circular UFO. Aside from his reputation as an international leader, Ilyumzhinov is also the President of FIDE, also known as the World Chess Federation, the world's pre-eminent international chess organization since 1995. Therefore, his friendly UFO abduction was not taken lightly. His encounter with these people occurred on September 17, 1997 while he was residing in his high-rise Moscow apartment. He told The Guardian newspaper some of this event:

They took me from my apartment and we went aboard their ship... We flew to some kind of star. They put a spacesuit on me, told me many things and showed me around. They wanted to demonstrate that UFOs do exist.

Clearly, if these UFO pilots whom Ilyumzhinov described as "people like us," wanted to show him that these planes exist, they picked a truly significant day. Obviously, they used a credible international figure to offer more credence to the Minister's September 17th experience. These types of patterns show that the Minister does not speak out of vain desire, but that he was shown some of the mightiest signs from his Lord.

Although President Ilyumzhinov has spoken publicly about his encounter to the world for several years, these reports have somehow not reached the pages of America's media. How is it that such internationally newsworthy information regarding an influential head of state has not reached the American public? Is this part of the mainstream effort to withhold prominent UFO facts from the people in order to keep them from the truth being offered by the Honorable Minister Louis Farrakhan?

Re: Your Attack on The Honorable Minister Louis Farrakhan

Jackie Muhammad
Nation of Islam Research Group

An Open Letter To Senator Mitch McConnell

April 21, 2020

On April 13 you went on the Senate floor ostensibly to pay tribute to Officer Billy Evans, a policeman who gave his life protecting federal lawmakers and visitors to Capitol Hill. Instead, you used such a solemn occasion to attempt to degrade the character of one of the most beloved leaders in the Black community, The Honorable Minister Louis Farrakhan, the National Representative of the Honorable Elijah Muhammad. You also disparaged the Nation of Islam, an institution in America for over 90 years dedicated to freedom, justice and equality for Black and Brown and oppressed people all over the world.

Your language was inflammatory and derogatory. Your fallacious diatribe was insulting and pointedly untrue. You said, "Investigators are still assessing what drove the perpetrator to attempt this attack on the Capitol and whether domestic violent extremism played a role. He appears to have been captivated by the Nation of Islam, a racist, anti-Semitic, extreme group under the openly hateful leader Louis Farrakhan".

As you are well aware The Honorable Minister Louis Farrakhan has gathered over four million people in the nation's Capital from 1995's Million Man March to the 20th anniversary of that march in 2015. Within the span of that 20-year period and 4 major marches, not one incident has ever been reported or recorded. The Nation of Islam has no history of violence against the federal, state or local governments. Law enforcement agencies are well aware of our history. Some of America's leading politicians, entrepreneurs, entertainers, and athletes have lauded Minister Farrakhan for his unmatched leadership, and the discipline of his followers.

However, on April 13 you went before the world and insidiously sought to lay the unfortunate death of Capitol Hill policeman at the doorstep of Minister Farrakhan and the faithful members of the Nation of Islam.

However, when you came under a vicious attack from former-President Donald Trump you couldn't find your voice. Mr. Trump called you a "dumb son of a b......" and, "a stone-cold loser". Over a period of the last three months he has excoriated you publicly and privately. You did not respond once to Mr. Trump demeaning you before the world. Not only that, he has also insulted your wife, former Secretary of Transportation, Elaine Chao, and her family, prominent Chinese business leaders. Even Senator Ted Cruz defended his wife when Mr. Trump hurled a barrage of insults against the senator's wife, insulting her physical attributes. However, you chose to remain silent and allowed your wife and her family to be abused.

You couldn't find your voice when Mr. Trump insulted you, but instead you engaged in an unprovoked attack again Minister Farrakhan and the Nation of Islam.

What makes your actions so despicable is the potential harm your words can cause the Nation of Islam and Minister Farrakhan, or was that your intention?

For over 65 years Minister Farrakhan has worked tirelessly to improve the quality of life of the most downtrodden community in America and throughout the world. He has visited over 110 countries and has been received as a head of state in many of the nations he visited, he has had streets named after him. I am not aware of any other independent Black man who has done more than The Honorable Minister Farrakhan has done to uplift the spirit of foreign leaders as well as the citizens of those nations. around the world to uplift humanity as Min. Farrakhan has done. He has succeeded where any combination of social service agencies, politicians and their media stooges have failed. Farrakhan's preeminence and success among the Black and Brown masses has created a firestorm of resentment. Hence your concerted efforts to attempt to degrade him.

Your hatred of Minister Farrakhan is not just limited to him. You made a pact with your Republican colleagues in the House and the Senate, upon Barak Obama's rise to become the 44th President of the United States Of America, to make him a one-term President. So, Farrakhan is not the only Black man that you have hated, he's only the latest.

Some of your fellow Republicans have not been as venomous as yourself. In fact, just the opposite has occurred. Not only have they defended him, some have befriended him. Among them are the late Jude Wanniski, and Jack Kemp, in addition to leaders in the Orthodox Jewish community, the Neturei Karta, under the leadership of Rabbi David Weiss, and Rabbi Shlomo Mordecai Hager who presented The Minister with a silver plate identifying him as the Messiah, and Christian scholars like Michael Hoffman who have vigorously defended Minister Farrakhan. You can add to that list mega stars like Bruce Willis, who told John Kennedy Jr. in George magazine, that if he were Black, "I'd be with Farrakhan, too".

Let's begin with Jude Wanniski. Mr. Wanniski was a brilliant economist, former associate editor of the Wall Street Journal, and Ronald Reagan, Steve Forbes and Jack Kemp's chief economic advisor. He coined the phrase "supply- side economics, a phrase that became the mantra of the Republican Party. His book, The Way The World Works, was named one of the 100 most influential books of the 20th century by National Review magazine. However, one of the most distinguishing aspects of Mr. Wanniski's life was his personal friendship with The Honorable Minister Louis Farrakhan. Mr. Wanniski leveraged that relationship to introduce members of the Republican brain trust to the Minister.

In March of 1997 Mr. Wanniski fostered a dialogue between The Minister and those who had labeled him an anti-Semite. At his 13th annual gathering of Republican executives and investors, sponsored by the supply-side consultant at his Polyconomics Conference in Boca Raton, Florida, Mr. Wanniski had Farrakhan address his gathering of Republican leaders that included Senator John Ashcroft, then-Representative John Kasich, Vice-Presidential nominee Jack Kemp and conservative syndicated columnist, television personality and author Robert Novak. Among the noted Democrats at the Boca Raton gathering was Senator Chris Dodd, UN ambassador, and former Governor of New Mexico, Bill Richardson, and Chinese Ambassador to the U.S. Li Daoyu.

According to Mr. Wanniski Minister Farrakhan addressed the audience for 50 minutes on Saturday morning, and answered questions for another 45 minutes. He said, on his website, Polyconomics, "The applause he (Farrakhan) received was the most sustained in the history of these events. Of the several Jewish couples in attendance there was uniform agreement on what I have been advising for the last several months-that he seems a more complex and likeable man than they expected." After the large group meeting Minister Farrakhan held small one-on-one meetings with the assembled leaders.

Congressman Jack Kemp, for his part had been impressed with Farrakhan for some time. In a private meeting I had with Mr. Kemp in New York City in 1995 following the Million Man March, Kemp said of Minister Farrakhan's speech, "I could have given that speech."

On September 6, 1996 Mr. Kemp told the New York Times he wished he had been invited to speak at the Million Man March. According to the New York Times, "Jack Kemp has praised the Nation of Islam leader, Louis Farrakhan, for emphasizing black self-reliance and family values."

In an article published in the Washington Post on March 6, 1997 titled, "Farrakhan and the GOP", Robert Novak spoke of the respect then-Representative John Kasich had for Farrakhan. Mr. Novak informed Mr. Kasich of Minister Farrakhan's positive reaction to the speech Kasich had given at the conference. He wrote, "Kasich was startled when his speech to a closed-door audience was interrupted several times by standing applause from the Nation of Islam leader. As they shook hands afterward, the congressman was floored by Farrakhan's kind words". Novak ended his article by saying, "But if they ever got together, the political landscape would be transformed". That speech was followed by Novak interviewing Farrakhan on his CNN television program, Evans and Novak.

In light of the accolades that have been bestowed on him by your Republican predecessors, by Jewish religious readers and Christian scholars, your description of Min. Farrakhan is disingenuous, insulting, and fallacious.

Your words insult the intelligence of his millions of followers, supporters and believers around the globe. Your desire to demean and demonize him is beneath the dignity of the office you occupy.

I would respectfully request that you may want to reevaluate your position and study the actions taken by Jack Kemp, Jude Wanniski and other prominent Republicans who are sincerely interested in stemming the downward spiral this nation is experiencing and her loss of world-wide acclaim and prestige. Maybe The Honorable Minister Louis Farrakhan can offer words of wisdom that could stem this downward spiral and global decline. I would advise you to listen to his Saviours' Day message on February 25, 2020 called "The Unraveling of A Great Nation", and especially his July 4, 2020 speech titled, "The Criterion".

The 2 Messiahs

Jackie Muhammad
Nation of Islam Research Group

For thousands of years the world of religion and some in government have been awaiting the arrival of the Messiah, one on whose shoulders a new government would be placed and through whom a new world order would emerge. The person identified as the Messiah is the most important person in Islam, Christianity, and Judaism.

Mystery has surrounded both the identity and the arrival of the Messiah. Believing that a Messiah was on the horizon to replace him, King Herod, the "king of the Jews," under the authority of Rome, was so protective of his throne that he killed his own son because he viewed his offspring as a threat to his kingship. Referring to Herod's Jewishness, the Roman emperor Augustus reportedly joked, "It was safer to be Herod's swine than his son" (Macrobius, Saturnalia, 2:4:11). Herod then issued orders that all first-born male children of Bethlehem were to be killed as well. His main objective was to kill the Messiah, thereby extending his own longevity as ruler.

Two thousand years later, the Government of the United States of America, along with the leadership of the Jewish community, has been obsessed with the advent of a modern-day Messiah, someone who would end the world of White Supremacy and global Jewish hegemony. The Jews, represented by the ADL, entered into a pact with the U.S. Government, represented by the FBI under the leadership of J. Edgar Hoover and later Director William Webster, to identify and destroy the one who they feared would emerge as the Black Messiah.

Definition of Messiah
What does the word Messiah mean? Who is the Messiah? Would there be one Messiah or multiple Messiahs? Where will he (they) come from? What is his (their) relationship to God? What would he (they) look like? Why should the world both rejoice and fear his (their) presence?

The word Messiah means one anointed to lead, a savior or liberator of a group who has suffered oppression; a person considered a king and a high priest. The English word Messiah is a noun derived from the Hebrew word mashach, which means "to smear with oil, anoint." In the Abrahamic religious tradition some scriptural interpretations speak of a king who is to be sent by God, and accompanied by a high priest who is also considered a part of the messiahship.

In both the early Christian and Jewish traditions, **the concept of multiple messiahs was fairly common. The Old Testament speaks of two Messiahs. In both the Book of Isaiah (chapter 53) and the Book of Zechariah (4:4) two "anointed ones" are mentioned. Zechariah foretold of a man called "the Branch." The branch was identified as one who would sit on the throne. But seated next to the kingly "Branch" would be an anointed priest. The two anointed Messiahs would stand before "the Lord of the whole earth."** In Zechariah's vision, the "two olive branches" stand before the Menorah, the seven- branched oil lamp that symbolized God's spirit and presence. Each "branch" represents an aspect of two separate individuals.

In the pre-Christian pseudepigrapha (religious writings whose authorship is unknown) the Testaments of the Twelve Patriarchs, we learn that "the Lord will raise up from Levi someone as high priest and from Judah someone as king" (Testament of Simon 7.2).

Further, according to a June 3, 2015, article in the Huffington Post titled "Waiting for the Messiahs? One, Two or Three?" written by James D. Tabor, the author questions the validity of just one Messiah to come. In his book The Jesus Dynasty, Tabor examines the concept of the two Messiahs. The topic became headline news in US News and World Report, as well as on ABC's Good Morning America, 20/20, and Nightline.

As time progressed and as Judaism underwent a transition away from the purity of the teachings of Abraham and Moses, that tradition and the concept of multiple messiahs underwent a transition also. Aspects of that transition can be traced to the leadership of Ezra, a priest and a scribe who was placed in charge of the Jewish colony that had been under Babylonian captivity from approximately 597 BCE to 539 BCE. When the Babylonians were defeated by the Persians, the king of Persia, Cyrus the Great, allowed the Jews to return to Judea. The Persian king appointed

Ezra as the new leader of the Jews. What is a factor, however, is the impact of Persian monotheism on Ezra and the Jews who had been held in captivity in Babylon. After that period a new form of Judaism emerged. Eschewing Allah's warnings in the Quran not to change the religion or modify the scriptures, the Jews did both. They integrated aspects of the Babylonian and Persian religions into their nascent practice of Judaism. Hence, the period of Babylonian captivity becomes a pivotal point in the history of messianic interpretation.

Not only did the Jews write a new scripture with their own hands, the Talmud, they also modified the Old and New Testaments to conform to their own religio-political narrative. An aspect of that narrative included the concept of a single messiah, instead of multiple messiahs. According to the Holy Quran (9:30), for example, the Jews revered Ezra so much that they called him "The son of God." Therefore, for some Jews, Ezra had reached the status in Judaism that Jesus had reached in Christianity.

Prior to their captivity in Babylon these half-hearted followers of Moses did not practice the teachings of Moses exclusively; they were not strict monotheists: they were practicing a form of monotheism called monolatrism, the worship of mini-gods in addition to a Supreme Being.

One group of believers who faithfully followed the teaching of Moses was called the Essenes. The Essenes were distinct from the Jews called the Sadducees and the Pharisees. (See The Meaning of the Dead Sea Scrolls.) The Essenes were highly influenced by the African (Egyptian) adherents of the monotheistic followers of Aton (The Mystery of the Copper Scroll of Qumran), and they were abstemious, pious, and studious. They considered the Sadducees and the Pharisees to be corrupt and sinful followers of Moses, and, quite frankly, out of their (the Essenes') league; indeed, they were enemies. The Essenes produced the purist Biblical texts ever used for Biblical translations. The text used by the Sadducees and the Pharisees was the Masoretic Text. Our King James Version of the Bible is the byproduct of the Masoretic translation. The purer, more precise, translation of the Essene documents, known as the Qumran Scrolls, predates the Masoretic text by almost 1000 years. These were original translations and original documents written by the Essenes themselves. Therefore, many scholars consider the Masoretic text to have been corrupted (redacted), and in several passages it does not conform to the purer texts of the Qumran Scrolls.

Another distinction between the Essenes and the Sadducees/Pharisees was the latter's support and justification of slavery (as evidenced in both the Torah and the Talmud). The Bible and the Talmud were referenced by the Jews as a justification for their control of the slave industry.

However, the more significant aspect of the distinctions between the groups has little to do with ethnicity or how they viewed each other's religiosity. One of the main differences between the two groups has to do with how they viewed the coming Messiah. The Masoretic scholars changed the messiahship from representing two individuals to being a single Messiah.

Aaron: The First Messiah

The Essenes believed in a Messiah of Aaron and a Messiah of Israel, in addition to a Teacher of Righteousness. All three were to make a joint appearance at the end of the rule of the enemies of God. One Messiah was to be a high priest and the other was to be a king. Ironically, according to Philo of Alexandria, also known as Philo Judaeus, the first man to be anointed as the Messiah was Aaron, the brother of Moses. Philo was a Jewish priest and a proponent of Aristotle and Plato. He bears witness to the Teachings of the Nation of Islam that speak of Christianity being a man-made religion, not of divine origin. Philo was one of the key figures who merged Hellenism with Judaism and created a new religion—Christianity. Accordingly, the biblical scholars who wrote The Interpreter's One-Volume Commentary on the Bible concluded that Philo's goal was to make Judaism acceptable to the Greeks. However, a portion of the Jewish community never accepted this. This position is exemplified in the positions adopted by the Jews under the rule of the Maccabees.

The Maccabees were a priestly family that led a revolt against Hellenism (Hellenic influence) in 168 B.C. They founded the Hasmonean dynasty, which rebelled against the Greeks and Hellenized Jews, reasserted Judaism, and reduced the influence of Hellenism and Hellenistic Judaism throughout Judea. These actions also led to a split between the rank-and-file Jews and the orthodox or traditionalist Jews on the one hand and the Hellenized Jews on the other. The Hellenized Jews sought the favor of their Greek overlords; the religious Jews never fully accepted the rule of the Hellenized Jews because the **role of a spiritual Messiah** was absent: they emphasized only the role of a political leader, not that of a religious Messiah.

With the emergence of Antiochus IV Epiphanes, the newly elected Greek ruler, the persecution of the Jews increased. With this increase in Jewish persecution, a division among the Jews was further exacerbated. The rank and file and the orthodox Jews were expecting the return of two Messiahs; the Maccabees did not. The Maccabees sought political accommodation with their oppressors; the other Jews wanted complete freedom from the Greeks.

According to Dr. Leila Leah Bronner, noted Jewish author, professor, and activist ("The Jewish Messiah: A Historical Perspective"), the Jews became wary of the idea that God was going to send a savior to redeem them. The Mishna, the Midrash, and the Talmud all downplay the role of the Messiah. Further, there is no mention of the Messiah after the failure of the Bar Kochba revolt (the second Jewish revolt against the Romans in 132 CE). The rabbis place emphasis on a "Messianic Age" and a "Messianic people" instead of a Messiah per se. The rabbinic Jewish leaders began to rely less on a Supreme Being and more on the supremacy of their own being. If God abandoned them, they were going to abandon Him.

The Concept of the Messiah and the Growth of Zionism

With the emergence of the period known as the European Enlightenment in the 18th century, Jewish thinkers stressed rational thinking and de-emphasized a belief in the supernatural aspects of the Old Testament. This led to the evolution of the Reform Judaism movement, and a move away from Orthodox Judaism. With this came the abandonment of the concept of a personal Messiah and the further adoption of a belief in a messianic people. A by-product of this movement was the emergence of modern Zionism.

The Dual Personalities of Melchizedek

Melchizedek is viewed as one of the most mysterious figures in the Old Testament. He is also viewed as the model upon which the Messiah is to be based. Melchizedek embodies a dual personage: a king and a priest. Melchizedek was the King of Salem and the "Priest of the Most High God." Like Elijah, Melchizedek never dies and he prefigures the Christ figure of the New Testament. Melchizedek is a compound noun, combining Malachi and Zadok, or Elijah and Aaron. Malachi was a prophet and "God's Messenger," while Zadok, was the chief priest of Judah and a descendant of the son of Aaron. In Ugaritic mythology Salem, or Salim, is said to have been a god identified with the evening star. In the Holy Qur'an (Surah 53) we see a reappearance of that "star," Al Najm, in its association with the cluster of stars known as the Pleiades.

God Empowers the Messiahs

What is the job of the Messiah? Where will he come from? What will he look like? Is he White, Black, Asian? According to a compilation of the character personality traits identified in the Scriptures, the Messiah will be a man of color. Daniel, Ezekiel, and John the Revelator describe him as a man with wooly (kinky) hair, an original (Black) man whose skin is the color of brass burned in an oven (black).

Daniel, Ezekiel, and John the Revelator also used the terms "Son of man," "son of man," and "one like a son of man" to depict the Christ figure. What is interesting is that each term has a different, yet similar, meaning, but they are also used interchangeably. One is a proper noun, one is a common noun, and one is indefinite; at the same time, they are all used to describe dual identities. The terms "son of man" and "one like a son of man" are subordinate to the "Son of man"; in addition, the term "Son of God" is used co-equally with the term "Son of Man" by some of the writers of the New Testament. In the English language they could be considered synonyms. Synonyms are words that may be spelled and pronounced differently, but mean exactly the same thing. The words "urban" and "inner city," for example, are used as synonyms for "Black."

In Daniel 7:13-14, the "Ancient of Days" (God) gives dominion over the earth to "one like the son of man," and this person is also given control of the "Wheel" (the ultimate weapon of mass destruction), as described in the Book of Ezekiel, to destroy the enemies of God, and bring about the final judgment of the world.

Prophet Muhammad on the Messiah

According to the Book of Malachi the job of the Messiah is to pave the way for the coming of God. He is to teach the **despised and**

rejected of the Western world (the American Black man and woman) the true knowledge of God. The despised and rejected, according to the Holy Qur'an (Surah 62), are akin to the illiterates who had been without the knowledge of God. Prophet Muhammad (PBUH) puts it this way: "He it is Who raised among the illiterates a Messenger from among themselves, who recites to them His messages and purifies them, and teaches them the Book and the Wisdom—although they were before certainly in manifest error—And others from among them who have not yet joined them. And He is the Mighty, the Wise (H.Q. 62:2-3). Hence, the Messiah is to come from a community of people who are despised, rejected, and illiterate.

Two key figures in the Book of Malachi are Elijah and Elias. Some scholars view Elijah and Elias metaphorically and symbolically as one, and they equate the reemergence of Elijah with the return of Elijah and Elias.

Malachi says the long-awaited One is to come from the East, which, according to the Book of Habakkuk, is where God Himself would reside. He is to come to America, where the dead ("the carcass") are. Daniel said he is to be a man of color. John the Revelator said the same. Ezekiel said the same thing, and he referred to the Messiah as "son of dust" (Ezekiel 3).

Prophet Muhammad said that "[e]ven if faith were near the Pleiades," a non-Arab from among the illiterates would find it. (See the exegesis of Surah 62, The Congregation.) Further, according to a Hadith, the Messiah will appear at a time when the Arabs will appear to have the letter of the law and not the spirit of the law. In Surah 53, The Star is associated with the Pleiades, which is a cluster of 7 stars in the constellation Taurus the Bull. Aldebaran, considered the Eye of the Bull, is the brightest star in the constellation Taurus and is often used as a guidepost by navigators and astronomers. Al Dabaran is Arabic for "The Follower." Taurus, by the way, is the astrological sign of the Honorable Minister Louis Farrakhan.

The Pleiades, or the Seven Sisters, are sometimes associated with the cluster of stars known as the Little Dipper. The North Star lies at the end of the handle of the Little Dipper. When the slaves were trying to find their way to freedom to the North (Canada), they just had to follow the North Star. However, in order to find the North

Star, one had to locate the Big Dipper, an asterism of the 7 brightest stars of the constellation Ursa Major that would point the wayfarer to the Little Dipper, or the North, then to eventual freedom. Thus, to find the North Star, one would first have to find the Big Dipper. The Big Dipper would then point you to the Little Dipper.

The Big Dipper was originally sighted in Africa, where it is seen as a drinking ladle and known as the Drinking Gourd; hence, the famous Underground Railroad code song "Follow the Drinking Gourd" exhorted Blacks seeking to escape enslavement to follow a northerly course. The following is a reference to a scene in the movie Django, where a White dentist shows up to free the enslaved Django. In the process he gives the other slaves a way out of their enslavement by following the North Star to freedom.

"As to you poor devil, so as I see it. When it comes to the subject of what to do next you, gentlemen, have two choices. One: once I am gone, you can lift that beast [horse] off the remaining speck [slave dealer], then carry him to the nearest town. Which would be 37 miles back the way you came. Or two: you can unshackle yourselves, take that rifle, put a bullet in his head, bury the two of them deep, then make your way to a more enlightened area of this country. Choice is yours. Oh, and on the off chance there are any astronomy aficionados amongst you, the North Star is that one [he points them to that direction]. Ta-ta."

I believe the two constellations are equivalent to the two Messiahs. I further believe that Allah is using the two constellations as metaphors for two human beings—the dual Messiahs, the two Dippers, the two Sons of Man (or ones like the son of man in the Book of Daniel): two men who will lead the people to their ultimate freedom. These two men are Black men who have been taught and trained to serve as Allah's representatives before the people. By the process of elimination, there are only two human beings that these metaphors, these synonyms, apply to: they are the Honorable Elijah Muhammad and the Honorable Minister Louis Farrakhan. It is my opinion that the high priest is the Honorable Minister Louis Farrakhan and the worldly king is the Honorable Elijah Muhammad, and in many ways their roles are interchangeable.

In the Book of Daniel in the Old Testament, the Son of man, the

Christ, the Messiah, has an encounter with the Supreme Being, the Lord of the Worlds. God, while on His throne on what some refer to as a UFO or Ezekiel's Wheel, is passing judgment on the nations of the Earth. After passing judgment He then cedes his power and authority to his Son, His Messiah. Global leadership is now in the hands of His Anointed ones.

Job Description of The Messiahs

If we were to create a fictional Job Description for the Messiahs, the job description would specify the following criteria, based on a compilation of requirements culled from the Scriptures:

1. The Messiahs will come from a community of Black people who have suffered oppression (slavery, sharecropping, Jim Crow apartheid) at the hands of a strange people, in a land not theirs (America) for over 400 years.
2. They must be Black Americans living in the West.
3. The pigmentation of the epidermis would have to be of a dark hue (as detailed in the Books of Revelation, Ezekiel, and Daniel). However, the Black skin of the Messiahs is not unique. The Messiah figures in Buddhism, Hinduism (Krishna, the Black Hindu Christ, for example); Osiris, the Christ of the Ancient Egyptians; as well as Quetzalcoatl, the Mexican Messiah—all have been depicted as Black men imbued with Africoid features. The first physical depiction of Jesus was that of a Black child with a Black mother, the Black Madonna and Child.
4. Pope praying to the Black Madonna.
5. These pictures and statues are still prominently featured in many Eastern European churches today, as well as in the private prayer room of the Pope of Rome. Therefore, the Blackness of Farrakhan and Muhammad is totally in line with the Christ figures throughout history.
6. The Messiah (Son of Man) must be able to drive a UFO, or what the Jewish scholars call a Merkabah, and use the Wheel to destroy the enemies of God.
7. The Messiahs will make their appearance when the Arabs have the Letter of the Law but not the Spirit of the Law.
8. They will be hated by the chief enemies of God (the Jewish leadership/Synagogue of Satan).
9. They will perform miracles, such as the Million Man March, Dope Busters, and Justice Or Else Movement.

10. They will teach the illiterates a knowledge of themselves and the Wisdom of the Scriptures.
11. Must come from a family that is as old as the Earth.
12. Must exhibit sublime moral and ethical characteristics.
13. Must be able to exhibit justice to both Black and White people.
14. Must be a musician, able to be in tune and in rhythm with all of humanity.
15. Must be a Spiritual Genius.

The Messiahs are not to be played with or disrespected. In the paraphrased version of the Living Bible (Ezekiel 33:30) we learn:

Son of dust, your people are whispering behind your back. They talk about you in their houses and whisper about you at the doors, saying, "Come on, let's have some fun! Let's go hear him tell us what the Lord is saying." So, they come as though they are sincere and sit before you listening. But they have no intention of doing what you tell them to; they talk very sweetly about loving the Lord, but with their hearts they are loving their money. You are very entertaining to them, like someone who sings lovely songs with a beautiful voice or plays well on an instrument. They hear what you say but don't pay any attention to it! But when all these terrible things happen to them—as they will—then they will know a prophet has been among them.

If we accept the above as the characteristics of the Messiahs, then the above can only apply to two men— Elijah Muhammad and Louis Farrakhan. No one else need apply.

SAN DIEGO TRIBUNE STORY STINKS, REHASHES ANTI-FARRAKHAN PROPAGANDA

Michael Muhammad
Muhammad Mosque No. 15, Atlanta-Georgia

The San Diego Union-Tribune has published a slanderous and defamatory article that was an inaccurate and deceptive depiction of the "Black Nationalist" movement, in particular the Nation of Islam. The title of the article, "Which Hate Groups are Operating in San Diego?", was published on the San Diego Union-Tribune website on May 26, 2019. The preface of the article is to propagate the "so-called" findings of the, notoriously hateful and bigoted Israeli Lobbyist and Division of AIPAC known as the Southern Poverty Law Center (SPLC) and Anti-Defamation League (ADL). The SPLC and the ADL have "advised" governmental agencies across America as to potential threats based on the bias of Israeli political interests.

The SPLC as well as the ADL have utilized their influence for intimidation and subversive tactics to neutralize the critics of Israel and the Jewish community. Through their dossiers and intelligence reports, they manipulate governmental agencies such as the Department of Homeland Security, the IRS, and even Congressional oversight Committees. And they have also negatively influenced local police to view their enemies as the enemies of the American people. Your source, Matt Wagner (ADL's Associate Director for Law Enforcement Initiatives and Community Security) is a perfect example of the intermingling of these Jewish groups, the American government and law enforcement agencies. Mr. Wagner's bio lists him as:

"Matt comes to ADL from a career in federal law enforcement and diplomacy, having served as a Special Agent with the U.S. State Department's Diplomatic Security Service. He served tours in New York, NY; Algiers, Algeria; Paris, France; and on the FBI's Joint Terrorism Task Force in San Francisco, with shorter missions in over a dozen U.S. states and more than 20 countries..."

Mr. Wagner's prior work for the American government and current work for the ADL highlights the intertwined nexus of persons and groups that go back and forth from governmental jobs to private sector work on behalf of the Israeli special interest groups. The SPLC has been, and continues to be, a force bent on intimidating Black leadership that does not conform to its desires, using the IRS, FBI and governmental other agencies as their own law enforcement.

Shockingly, it was the first president and lifelong Board member of the Southern Poverty Law Center, Julian Bond, who spoke with and had a peaceful relationship with the Leader of the Nation of Islam, the Most Honorable Elijah Muhammad. Below is an excerpt from an exclusive interview with Muhammad Speaks in 1971, commenced by correspondent Bob Dale. This was the same year that Julian Bond became the first president of the Southern Poverty Law Center:

"I have a great deal of respect and have met and have been in Mr. Muhammad's house. I was very fortunate and honored to have had a meal with him in 1968. He, like me, is from Georgia you know. I don't know if that means that we "Georgia boys" like to stick together. (It's okay for us to call ourselves boys.) But I have a great deal of respect for him particularly for the kind of discipline he imposes and the Muslims accept. I think that is what we need. Things like this (cigarettes) you know – drinking and running around at night – are things we need to try to eliminate if we can. It takes more people to do it. But I think over the years the Black people have come to have respect for Mr. Muhammad. Partly because we have had more respect for ourselves as a people and partly I think it is because we have had more exposure to Mr. Muhammad's philosophy. We just found out more about it ourselves than having to be told about it by other people."

These are not the words of the Nation of Islam but the words of the very first president of the Southern Poverty Law Center's founding president and life Long Board member, until his passing in 2015. What happened to the relationship between the Southern Poverty Law Center's founding, which was to defend the voiceless and give aid to those disenfranchised by a racist and xenophobic system? As you can see the SPLC stated that the teachings of the Honorable Elijah Muhammad were respectful and good for Black people to become productive citizens of America and ultimately, productive citizens of the world. What happened to this critical observation by such a prestigious institution in 1971? It is hypocritical of the SPLC to state anything other than the truth about the Nation of Islam as a tool of hope, security and inspiration.

During the 60s, and until the time of this writing, the FBI and the CIA have also done an extensive and thorough analysis of The Nation of Islam and every Black Nationalist Movement in America (FBI SAC letter, # 55-43). The very explanation of our teaching as a "subversive cult" was predicated on the fear of a "Black Overthrow" of the United States Government. This fantasy of paranoia is from a self-analysis of one's own cognitive thinking. It is the United States Government who has fostered the overthrow of every black and indigenous government that does not capitulate to its will. The Nation of Islam does not possess the desire nor the history of such a threat to the United States of America. Including more recently Iran and Venezuela America has subverted Libya, Iraq, Central Congo, and by its own admission, every Black organization ever created in America including the Nation of Islam. There has never been a plan or desire of the Nation of Islam to kill or commit acts of violence against anyone. The Nation of Islam prohibits its membership from carrying weapons on our person or storing them in our homes. The truth is our weapon of choice.

The basis of the teachings of the Nation of Islam is "Self-Improvement", as accurately illustrated by the founding president of the Southern Poverty Law Center, Julian Bond, in 1971. There has never been any terroristic attack against anyone by an active member of the Nation of Islam. Instead, the Nation of Islam continues to the recipient of the financial sanction of the intimidation of such groups as the SPLC, the ADL and B'nai Brith.

Amazingly enough, scholars such as University of Windsor Professor Martha F. Lee, who is white, contributed to a book titled "Violence and New Religious Movements" as edited by James R. Lewis. Her findings about the Nation of Islam are as such:

"In many ways then, the Nation of Islam provides a case study and how a religious movement with a radical belief system did not engage in violence related to its doctrine." -Professor Martha f. Lee, University of Windsor.

There are those who would like to equate criticism and rebuke with hatred. This is a manipulative psychological device. It is called "hate speech" when Minister Farrakhan holds the Jewish community accountable for their wrongdoings to Blacks and the Palestinians. Calling the Minister, a hater and a bigot are just a way to cope with the stinging fact-based rebuke the Minister boldly delivers.

Violence and TRUE hate are raging supreme in America. In 2018 there was a meeting between ethnic groups and various religious organizations in America who have witnessed an urgent need for the FBI to take measures to protect the citizens from a very real an existential threat of White Nationalists. In a letter dated March 18, 2018 to the Director of the FBI Christopher Wray, at that time, by many American ethnic groups requesting a meeting to deal with, this terroristic violence in America. Deputy Director Naheed Qureshi of Muslim Advocate wrote:

"We, the undersigned national civil rights and faith-based leaders, write to express our deep concern regarding recent attacks against our houses of worship and communities. We request an urgent meeting with you to discuss the role of the Federal Bureau of Investigation (FBI) in addressing the threat to public safety and our communities by white nationalist violence.

Attacks against houses of worship in the United States have been far too common in recent years. For example, in 2012, white supremacist Wade Michael Page murdered six and injured four, when he stormed a Sikh gurdwara in Oak Creek, Wisconsin. In 2015, Dylann Roof, who spewed deep racial hatred and espoused white nationalist ideals, entered the Emanuel AME Church in Charleston, South Carolina, killing nine individuals. In 2018, Robert D. Bowers burst into the Tree of Life Synagogue in Pittsburgh, Pennsylvania and shouted anti-Semitic slurs, killing 11 worshippers. This hate manifested itself again last week in New Zealand, when Brenton Harrison Tarrant live streamed his attacks against Masjid al-Noor and the Linwood Mosque in Christchurch where he murdered over 50 people and injured many more. Tarrant too, was a virulent white nationalist, and even cited Roof as an inspiration in his manifesto."

Last year, the FBI reported a 17% increase in hate crimes overall since 2016, marking an increase for the third consecutive year in a row. Given the enormous threat of hate violence to our communities and our nation, we request that you meet with us along with our partners in the civil rights and faith communities to discuss the FBI's role in protecting houses of worship, our communities, and all Americans."

As you can see, the Nation of Islam poses no threat to anyone. The Nation of Islam has been the true defenders of those who have no voice. While I can appreciate the aim of the SPLC and the ADL to protect the Jewish people from any potential existential threat, we will not be silent and allow these nefarious groups to lie and deceive the public as to the true record and intentions of Minister Farrakhan and the Nation of Islam. Minister Farrakhan has directly, and through his representatives like San Diego's Muhammad Mosque No. 8 Student Minister Abdul Waliullah Muhammad, put forth numerous requests for a public debate with all of those who falsely accuse us of hatred and bigotry. And none of these groups have accepted the more than reasonable request to face us in the sphere of public debate. Their refusal to argue the issues in a public forum, where representative s of the Nation of Islam are present to defend our history and rebut their lies, is the clearest sign that these groups aren't interested in the truth, only political propaganda.

This challenge was put forth publicly during the anniversary of the Million Man March in October 2018 by the Honorable Minister Louis Farrakhan. Instead of assassinating the character of Minister Farrakhan, the SPLC needs to be concerned with the white Nationalists who continue to terrorize everyone in America. Today, we are mourning the death of yet another senseless mass shooting on behalf of another citizen in the city of Virginia Beach. None of these attacks have ever been committed by a member of the Nation of Islam. Mr. Wagner or other ADL and SPLC representatives should accept Minister Farrakhan's request for a public debate of the issues.

The article written by Ms. Kristina Davis that continues to characterize the Nation of Islam as a hate group should be retracted and corrected. Investigative journalism into the unsavory and criminal history of the ADL and the SPLC would be of great interest to your readers. That kind of article would demonstrate the San Diego Tribune has some measure of objectivity. If you investigate these groups, you will find that these very groups who castigate and falsely label others as haters and bigots are rife with criminal conduct themselves. As far as the

Nation of Islam goes, either report the truth about us or don't report anything about us. Leave us alone to do the work of redemption and restoration among our people that Allah (God) has called us to do.

RABBI BOTEACH, SENATOR BOOKER & THE FARRAKHAN LITMUS TEST

Nzinga Muhammad
Muhammad Study Group Rochester-New York

While this is the season of presidential campaigning, it is also the season of handing out the Farrakhan Litmus Test to black politicians. The Farrakhan Litmus Test is generally placed upon black leaders or influential black people who try to excel in the world. It is designed to discredit them until they denounce a man who white political leaders see as a threat to their power. We have seen this before in the 2008 Democratic Primary Presidential Debate where Barack Obama was publicly scolded by Hillary Clinton for not "rejecting" the Minister the way she wanted him to.

The Minister is exclusively targeted by those in the white power structure in such a way that his presence in albeit predominantly black spaces is feared and opposed. Leaders and organizations that have a relationship with him are accused of "supporting anti-Semitism." This kind of white gatekeeping of black leadership is constantly intended to dictate who black people can and cannot talk to, listen to, or be around.

Recently in an article by Rabbi Shmuley Boteach, he voiced his disapproval of candidate Senator Cory Booker for his statements about the Minister and the Nation of Islam in Columbia, South Carolina. Senator Booker was responding to a question that asked if he was familiar with the Minister and whether or not he would meet with him. He answered,

"You know, I have met — I live in Newark, so we have famous Mosque 25, we have Nation of Islam there. As mayor, I met with lots of folks. I've heard Minister Farrakhan's speeches for a lot of my life. So, I don't feel like I need to do that. But I'm not one of these people that says I wouldn't sit down with anybody to hear what they have to say. But I live in a neighborhood where I'm getting guys on the streets, offering and selling his works. I'm very familiar with Minister Louis Farrakhan and his beliefs in his opinions."

Like Hilary Clinton in her reaction to Senator Barack Obama,
462-STUDENTS OF FARRAKHAN

Rabbi Boteach felt that Senator Booker did not have a strong enough condemnation. He wanted him to strongly and forcefully denounce Minister Farrakhan. In telling Sen. Booker what he "should" have said when asked about our Minister, Rabbi Shmuley Boteach wanted to remind him of their work together and all of the support he has received from the Jewish community. Rabbi Boteach reminded him that he served as president of the L'Chaim Society at the University of Oxford, and was treated well by members of the Jewish community after speaking at many synagogues throughout the United States. He also mentions that he has "enjoyed wide moral and financial support from the Jewish community" throughout his political career. According to Rabbi Shmuley Boteach, some of what he wanted Sen. Booker to say was,

"I would never insult my Jewish friends and supporters by meeting with a man who demonizes Jews and incites violence against them, especially a time of rising global anti-Semitism."

Minister Farrakhan has never demonized or incited violence against any Jewish person. Those who have researched, studied, or closely listened to the Minister would know that he has taught his audiences to respect people of all faiths and backgrounds. By now, we should expect the Nation of Islam to be wherever black people are found. We are no strangers to the community. It is impossible to work among our people and not run into the Nation of Islam at some point. You cannot work for black people without including the Nation in that conversation because we have been doing the groundwork of salvation for our people for almost a century. As fare as the Black community is concerned, it is to be expected that if you are in a position of power, whether public service or within the private sector, you will eventually cross paths with the work and influence of the Nation of Islam. The work and impact of the Nation of Islam is well respected and universally laudable. Meeting with Minister Farrakhan has been an honor for those who have ever met with him and had a conversation with him.

What is particularly interesting, though, is how Rabbi Shmuley Boteach reminded Senator Booker of what the Jewish community has done for him. In other words, he reminded him that he is indebted to the Jewish community for the success of his political career. It is the view of Rabbi Boteach that payment for the debt involves the repudiation and condemnation of a man that has done so much for our community. Let this remind us of the open letter that Minister Farrakhan penned to black leadership in which he said the following:

"As they call upon you to denounce me as an anti-Semite and, because of the favor you believe you owe them for what they have done to help make life comfortable for you; I am asking you to stand down."

In this political season, we must be wise to the tired and worn out use of the Farrakhan Litmus Test. It is a trap.

The denunciation of Minister Farrakhan is a method to keep black people at the beckoning call of our oppressors. And any political leader to who does so will become alienated from the poor and grassroots community who view Minister Farrakhan as a champion and hero.

The regulation of our leaders and friends and the control of our elected officials is a hindrance to the political progress of the Black community. Minister Farrakhan has become the bogeyman for white people. Influential black leaders and groups are threatened that they should stay away from him. It would be better for these men and women of influence to do as the Minister has asked and stand down. Don't participate in the Farrakhan Litmus Test. Stay out of it.

During this season of political campaigns, we are sure to see this 1980's era political trope rears its ugly head frequently. Called the "Farrakhan Litmus Test", it is ultimately a gauge to measure a political candidate's prioritization of Jewish interests over the interests and needs of the Black community.

And yet as it is, the "Farrakhan Litmus Test" does have some modicum of utility for the Black community; it bears one positive aspect for those of us who are Black community stakeholders. The Farrakhan Litmus Test acts as a filter. It helps to expose those who are not willing to unapologetically speak truth to power. In this way it provides the Black voter with much needed visibility into the core of the political candidate's heart. Because any candidate that 'plays the game' and repudiates Minister Farrakhan is a politician who believes that those who give money are more important than those who give votes. All those who succumb to the pressure and bow in compliance with the demand to denounce Minister Farrakhan are unworthy of the Black community's support. Thusly, in a way, the Farrakhan Litmus Test lets Black voters know who our true leaders really are.

DEFENDING FARRAKHAN MYTH BUSTING: "OUR MINISTER IS NO MISOGYNIST!"

Nzinga Muhammad
Muhammad Study Group Rochester-New York

One of the most inaccurate and recycled lies about the Honorable Minister Louis Farrakhan is that he is misogynistic. The media has convinced many people that he holds attitudes that objectify, demean, and belittle women. Yet, seldom do his critics sit down and have dialogues with those of us who are in the ranks of the Nation of Islam as M.G.T & G.C.C and M.G.T Vanguard. Those who are not a part of the Nation of Islam would like to believe that they know what we are taught more than those of us who are actually in the ranks. No other black leader in America or otherwise delivers a message about women, particularly black women, with such reverence and respect as the Honorable Minister Louis Farrakhan. To charge our Minister with promoting misogyny is to participate in defaming the character of a man who has made the empowerment and liberation of women a top priority for decades.

In a world where men have used scripture to relegate women to a subordinate and inferior status within society, Minister Farrakhan has been consistent in making sure that his ministry includes the elevation and upliftment of women. He is constantly reminding us as women that we are "not the woman of man, but the woman of God." In teaching this, he is liberating us from the idea that we belong to men for their pleasure and motives. Minister Farrakhan is always found condemning a prevailing view and idea that women are objects to be used and abused by men. On June 23, 1994, Minister Farrakhan delivered a lecture to all women entitled: A Nation Can Rise no Higher Than Its Woman. In this lecture he addresses how oppressive men have been to women, thus creating an unbalanced world:

"You have become, in this society, a piece of meat. You're not a woman with spirit or intelligence to think and plan and create and be a balance for the man in government, in politics, in business, in religion. You are kept out of everything and by locking you out, man's own power has made him unbalanced. And his own power has driven him crazy and he has made a world that is so wicked and self-destructive that if you don't rise up as a mother and as a woman to take your place, the world will go down and take you down with it."

Minister Farrakhan has also put to rest misconceptions that men have brought to religion when determining a woman's role. For example, he has explained the symbolism behind women coming from a man's rib, according to the story of Adam and Eve in the Bible. We did not come from the rib of man, we came directly from Allah (God), but this picture of coming from a rib has been used to put women on a level of lesser importance than men. Minister Farrakhan teaches that in the Bible, it is written that Allah (God) created both male and female and called their name Adam (Genesis 5:2). This would have to include the woman as sharing the same essence as the man, which is Allah (God) Himself, thus invalidating the idea that we are from a man's rib. The Minister has also criticized and rebuked a common misconception from the Islamic world where some place an overemphasis on the Quranic reference to men being a "degree above women" (Surah 2:228). He has taught us that "one degree" as in the case of a circle of 360 degrees is a minuscule amount of difference, and should not be used a justification for treating women as inferior. We are the equal of men.

Lastly, one of the issues of women that Minister Farrakhan is passionate about is physical and sexual abuse. He has repeated countless times that if someone were to rape a woman, then the proper punishment is death itself. He condemns any man who does this to a woman. In his 2018 Holy Day of Atonement Address, he responded to the controversy of the nomination of Mr. Brett Kavanaugh to Supreme Court justice. Minister Farrakhan first acknowledged that Mrs. Christine Blasey Ford was definitely a victim of abuse and he defended those who have been victims of sexual assault, especially in the workplace. He told how tears were in his eyes when he saw Ford's testimony against Mr. Kavanaugh. He also briefly explained the trauma that rape victims face. He stated:

"When that woman stood up and went through the horror of what Mr. Kavanaugh is alleged to have done to her, she had to relive it. Because that kind of thing when you experience it, you don't forget that. It's seared into your memory; you may put it behind you and think it's gone somewhere, but when you least expect it, that thing will come out and make a problem for you."

Minister Farrakhan also brought attention to the carelessness that female victims go through when accusing men in power. He said,

"A man can go on with his life and become famous. But when you dog a woman nobody seems to give a damn about how much a woman suffers."

"Misogynistic" is not an accurate description of Minister Farrakhan's attitude towards women. Anyone who has doubts about his commitment to women must not have been keeping up with the work that he has done, and the message that he has spread for six decades. People who have never listened to a full lecture, or had a full conversation with a woman in the Nation of Islam have the audacity to be self-proclaimed experts on the man we follow. What he actually says and teaches about women does not match with the charges of belittling and degrading women. Minister Farrakhan has been and continues to be a man who has truly proven his love, and high respect for us.

YOUTH DEFEND MINISTER FARRAKHAN: A DEMAND TO DENOUNCE THE ADVERSARIES OF THE BLACK COMMUNITY

Rahman A. Muhammad

Muhammad Mosque No. 55, Memphis-Tennessee

Bro. Rahman A. Muhammad is 20 years old. He is a citizen of the Nation of Islam at Muhammad Mosque No. 55 in Memphis, Tenn. He is a Master Barber and graphic artist with a passion for producing and engineering music. He joins the growing chorus of those who reject the demand of the white ruling class that Minister Farrakhan be denounced and repudiated. ResearchMinister is honored to share his thoughts with our readers. Read, Reflect, Act & Share

Black America has thrived for its existence among White supremacy for decades. They have been controlled us; how we conduct themselves; how we think, act, live, and the list goes on.

Why can't Black America see things from their own point of view? Why are we denied the freedom to express ourselves? Why are we forced to accept a false reality of an integrated paradise in spite of all that has happened to us, even up to the present time?

Do we still stand as slaves in mental and spiritual bondage among a mental and spiritual oppressor? If not, then why are Blacks denied the liberty of free human beings to love a man like Louis Farrakhan?

The Honorable Minister Louis Farrakhan, a man who needs no introduction to the world, has been used against Black enthusiasts by media persons to make or break their chances to be accepted into mainstream society. Many refer to this as the Farrakhan Litmus Test. Many Black prolific ones in society have been pressured to take this test on public display. As history has shown us, those persons that side with the Honorable Minister Louis Farrakhan and his immeasurable work are taken under scrutiny and are attacked throughout the world. Media tends to defame those Black persons and leave them in the public eye with an ugly image. Why? Isn't it their free will to accept or reject the Honorable Minister Louis Farrakhan's views and not be attacked by the world?

Here is a man that has fought for the freedom and dignity of the Black man among powerful adversaries throughout the world. He speaks to the needs of us as a people, without rest and we feel that he is more than worthy of gratitude and respect. It is true that the Honorable Minister Louis Farrakhan has been made by Allah (God) to be our Black Hero; a champion of the rise and liberation struggle of us as a people.

He has shown us, for 60 plus years, an example of unconditional love. The love he has for his people is seen in how he is always willing to sacrifice his own life to see us free from sin and evil and the wicked plans of our enemies. He has aroused hatred coming from the powers that rule over America, the United Kingdom, and many others, despite the fact that he hasn't fired a single shot from a carnal weapon. Yet, it's his exercise of Free Speech that bothers so many people? Why can't we love a hero like the Honorable Minister Louis Farrakhan?

Well, it is time now for us to ask for America and the World to reciprocate the same for their heroes. The Honorable Minister Louis Farrakhan and his work around the world is so positive that you can't equate it to the works of those continue to pressure the Black man and woman to denounce him. America and the world have committed a great atrocity against the Black man in America and people of color throughout the Earth. If you want us as a people to denounce Farrakhan, then you have some denouncing to do as well.

Denounce the prolific perpetrators in Europe that funded and participated in the enslavement of the Black man out of Africa. Denounce those that took the land of America from the Indigenous people, robbed, raped, poisoned, and killed them.

Denounce Christopher Columbus. Denounce the Founding Fathers that built America off the backs of slaves. Denounce George Washington, Thomas Jefferson and all of those U.S. Presidents who owned slaves on their presidential plantations. Denounce the enslavement of the Black man in America.

Denounce White America that continued the mistreatment of people of Black people in America long after chattel slavery ended, many who turned their backs on us while their White brothers beat and killed us in the streets across America. Denounce the F.B.I. for spying on Black leaders, hunting them down and even taking it further to kill some of them as they grew in popularity. Denounce J. Edgar Hoover for his ordering a "manhunt" for the Messiah among Black people. Denounce the Government of America for its involvement with bringing crack and cocaine into Black neighborhoods and using it to trap the Black man to satisfy the prison industry.

Denounce America for her involvement in facilitating the spreading of disease among the masses of the people and for poisoning the food to cull the population. Denounce the media controllers and/or beneficiaries, for their promotion of Black destruction through the media's use of the airways to destroy the Black struggle for liberation. Denounce EVERYTHING that made the Black struggle what it has become today-arduous, painful and unending!

America and the world are demanding we denounce what THEY feel is wrong, so we have to demand they denounce everything that WE know is wrong. They have to acknowledge, apologize, and denounce what they have done to us as a people, otherwise, their plea for denouncement of others should not be acknowledged.

In the so-called "Land of the Free," we maintain our right to exercise our freedom to think and express ourselves without censure. Calls to denounce Minister Farrakhan proves that the destruction of the Black man has been designed by those who push for the denouncement of our Hero, our Champion, the Honorable Minister Louis Farrakhan!

ANGELA RYE, NAYSAYERS SLANDER OF FARRAKHAN SHALL NOT STAND

Tracee Muhammad

Muhammad Mosque No. 43, Columbus-Ohio

As everyone around the world with access to social media has learned, The Honorable Minister Louis Farrakhan has been banned from Facebook and Instagram. What does that mean for the Believers, followers, supporters, friends and allies of Minister Farrakhan? Nothing really; we have access to hundreds of lectures still available on YouTube, and webcasts on NOI.org. Not to mention the thousands of people sharing the teachings, quotes and images of Minister Farrakhan among themselves on their Facebook pages with the #WeAreFarrakhan hash tag.

Moreover, what does this mean for the naysayers and enemies of Minister Farrakhan and the Nation of Islam? This is their golden opportunity to slander and libel the Minister and the Nation. We would expect this coming from the familiar adversaries in the white ruling class and leaders of Jewish organizations. However, this ban is exposing certain critics from the Black community who are eager to show their loyalty to the white power structure.

Lenard McKelvey came to my attention a few years ago as a result of Minister Farrakhan making reference to him. He is a host on the very popular program known as The Breakfast Club, which has interviewed the Honorable Minister Farrakhan as a guest on their show. Lenard, aka Charlemagne tha God appeared to be positive, supportive and receptive to the Minister anytime he was on the show. Well apparently, they added a recurring guest named Angela Rye who seemed to be a charming articulate intelligent attorney who worked on Capitol Hill with the Congressional Black Caucus; and now is a political commentator on CNN.

These two collaborated to create a new podcast called Sibling Rivalry. Their inaugural show was 50:57 minutes in duration. And the conversation touched several subjects including daily affirmations, the Christian faith, numerology, hair weaves, genealogy, and political commentary. At approximately 26 minutes into the conversation; Charlemagne asked Angela to discuss her views on the recent social media ban on the Honorable

Minister Louis Farrakhan.

Ms. Rye began to say various things that were factually inaccurate and terribly offensive to anyone who has respect for Minister Farrakhan and his leadership. According to Ms. Rye:

"He [Min. Farrakhan] needs to show up consistent. He needs to live out his authentic truth in ways that empower Black people but does not take away from other communities"

In her comments, she encouraged Minister Farrakhan to censor himself. Saying "Stop, just stop", Ms. Rye joined the adversaries of the Black community who want Minister Farrakhan's voice silenced. Ms. Rye's opinion is obviously that Minister Farrakhan should prioritize the hurt feelings of his critics above the urgent need to speak truth to the masses. Her pleading was for the Minister Farrakhan to stop offending our oppressors.

She further had the audacity to tell Minister Farrakhan:

"Don't trick off your legacy and stop the BS. I can't defend stuff you are saying on these clips"

Charlemagne rebutted several of her statements, stating that Minister Farrakhan doesn't criticize all Jews; only the ones who oppress Black people. However, each time he would correct her, she would argue her point with familiar criticisms of the Minister's message, none of which ever prove that the Minister has spoken other than the truth. Angela Rye claimed that the Minister "says homophobic things". Charlemagne attempted to offer the fact that the holy books: Bible and Qur'an teach against homosexuality, and that Minister Farrakhan comes from an older generation. Ms. Rye replied:

"Just because you're older doesn't mean you can be dumb and a bigot."

She tried to show a bit of a clip of one of Minister Farrakhan's addresses; and acted like she was so disturbed by it, it moved her to tears. She followed up by saying:

"If I could have my way I'd ask him to dial back the rhetoric."

I was in disbelief at the insolent comments of this 39-year-old "girl." She would like people to believe she is a scholar just because she has college degrees. Many of us do, but that does not begin to qualify us to compare or compete with Minister Farrakhan's knowledge, wisdom and guidance. He was taught by The Honorable Elijah Muhammad, who was taught by God: in the person of Master Fard Muhammad. Minister Farrakhan is divinely directed and endorsed by these two; he is backed by divine power.

To be crystal clear and for the benefit of Ms. Rye and those whom share her views, Minister Farrakhan doesn't need you to defend or justify anything he says or does. He is also backed by the most brilliant legal defense team in this country. The Nation of Islam has many scholars; we are taught to be studious. Our primary objective is truth and the presentation of actual facts and evidence. No one, even up to this present day and time, has been able to disprove Minister Farrakhan's message; nor has anyone been able to disprove the root out of which that message springs which is the life-giving teachings of the Most Honorable Elijah Muhammad. He has challenged his critics to listen to his message and identify where he is false in his assertions. Minister Farrakhan has said that he would give his life for the truth that he speaks. And even at 86 years of age, he remains ever vigilant and strong as the bold champion of his people!

Ms. Rye's, in her condemnation of Minister Farrakhan, is working for the oppressor! I noticed how she was willing to defend and give the benefit of the doubt to leading Democratic Presidential candidate Joe Biden, despite his support of the racist 1994 Crime Bill.

Minister Farrakhan-whom she would not defend- has no history of helping to send young Black men and women to prison. In fact, the Minister's message instructs young men and women who to steer clear of the traps that have been set to warehouse the youth into prison settings. The Minister and his representatives also visit prisons to teach and provide moral and spiritual reform to incarcerated men and women.

So, Ms. Rye defended a man who helped to send millions of our people to prison. She condemned a man who has helped millions of our people stay out of prison.

What Ms. Rye asked the Minister to do, she should be asking our oppressors to do. Why doesn't she plea to all the law enforcement officers who shoot and kill Black men, women, and children without provocation or justification? How about making a plea to all the random white people who call 911 on Black people for no other offense than being black? Instead Ms. Rye chooses to make a public plea for the only Black leader who has been standing up, representing our people for 64 years consistently to stop hurting the feelings of our enemies!

I concur with Sister Vicki Dillard and others who have rebutted Ms. Rye's false assertions regarding Minister Farrakhan. Her comments have inspired powerful responses that have deconstructed her arguments and mocked the ignorance that spawned them.

I was disappointed with Charlemagne, who stopped defending Minister Farrakhan towards the end of the podcast, and started agreeing with Ms. Rye.

I repudiate you both for your statements regarding Minister Farrakhan; you owe the Minister and Black America an apology!

If you tried to use this topic to generate interest for your new podcast, you achieved your objective. But the steep price you have paid is that you have drawn the rebuke and criticism of millions of us in the larger community of Black people who want nothing to do with you until you make amends!

"YOU CANNOT MAKE REAL LEADERS DENOUNCE THE HON. MIN. LOUIS FARRAKHAN!"

Willie Muhammad

Student Minister Muhammad Mosque No. 46, New Orleans - Louisiana

There is a mounting chorus of voices rising to fight the onslaught against the freedom of speech in America that has targeted the magnificent message of the Honorable Minister Louis Farrakhan as its most significant adversary. Criticism of the state of Israel; criticism of Jewish organizations regardless to how measured and carefully stated is being falsely labeled as "anti-Semitism". To this, Minister Farrakhan's gallant and courageous students are vehemently defending his noble name and reputation. Today, ResearchMinister.Com is honored to share with its readers the defense of Minister Farrakhan by his New Orleans representative, the Minister of Muhammad Mosque No. 46-Student Minister Willie Muhammad. Please Read, Reflect, Act & Share

The New Testament is one of the fantastic series of religious scriptures that are great to read if we desire to understand the Honorable Minister Louis Farrakhan and the controversy that surrounds him because he has the courage to unapologetically challenge the ruling forces of America and dismantle the ideology that is the fabric of this country. The Honorable Minister Louis Farrakhan, like Jesus has had his words purposely misconstrued. The Honorable Minister Louis Farrakhan's enemies, like the enemies of Jesus, were members of the powerful ruling class, such as religious leaders, political leaders and news agencies of his time. The Honorable Minister Louis Farrakhan, like Jesus also was falsely labeled with titles that were diametrically opposed to who he is and what he represents. The recent failed efforts to get one of the prominent organizers of the Women's March to denounce the Honorable Minister Louis Farrakhan has made me reflect on another similarity between the opposition faced by Jesus and the Honorable Minister Louis Farrakhan.

While Jesus traveled to and from giving life to the dead, helping to heal the sick, and exposing the hypocritical leadership, there were secret meetings being held by those who hated Jesus for the sole purposes of discrediting him, destroying his mission and planning his death.

"Then the leading priests and the older Jewish leaders had a meeting at the palace where the high priest lived. The high priest's name was Caiaphas. 4 In the meeting they tried to find a way to arrest and kill Jesus without anyone knowing what they were doing. They planned to arrest Jesus and kill him. 5 They said, "We cannot arrest Jesus during Passover. We don't want the people to become angry and cause a riot." Matthew 26:3-5

The SAME is unquestionably true when it comes to the Honorable Minister Louis Farrakhan as well. The orchestra of news articles and television coverage aimed at painting the Honorable Minister Louis Farrakhan as a homophobic, an Anti-Semite and many of the other false charges are not by accident. Here four years ago with virtually NO mainstream media coverage, the Honorable Minister Louis Farrakhan was able to draw one million people again (most of them millennials) to the Nation's capital twenty years after the historic Million Man March. The media said nothing before nor afterwards. Yet, he declares that he is anti-termite and nearly every media outlet joined the effort to repeat the lie saying that he called Jews termites! When he actually said the following...

"When they talk about Farrakhan, call me a hater, call me an anti-Semite; stop it I'm anti-termite. I don't know anything about hating anyone because of their religious preference. But just like they called our ancestors in the 1930s "voodoo people," they figure "anti-Semite" would be a good thing to put on us. Farrakhan hates Jews. Stop it. You cannot find one Jew that one who follows me has plucked one hair from his head. You haven't found us defiling a synagogue. Our Qur'an teaches us if we see something like that stop it. They call me anti-Semitic. No, you are anti-Black. Now I'm talking to the anti-Black White folk." Source: Oct. 14, 2018 to mark the 23rd anniversary of the Million Man March and Holy Day of Atonement in Detroit at the newly-named Aretha Franklin Amphitheater.

The enemies of the Honorable Minister Louis Farrakhan, the Nation of Islam and Black people –ADL & the SPLC – seized this moment to execute their planned expressed in its Civil Rights Division Policy Background Report ~ Mainstreaming Anti-Semitism: The Legitimation of Louis Farrakhan. In this memo the

ADL acknowledges that any attempt to make the Honorable Minister Louis Farrakhan bow is an exercise in futility, "ADL is not going to make Farrakhan go away." However, they mention several times that they will instead put pressure on other Black leaders and organizations. "What we can and should do is impose an obligation on those who deal with him, or, as in the case of universities, give him a platform. In each case, the burden should be on those who give Farrakhan some measure of credibility to insist that he act responsibly, and put a lid on his bigotry and anti-Semitism."

This is what we are seeing when demands are placed on people like Dr. Marc Lamont Hill, Tamika Mallory, Congressional Black Caucus, Hip-Hop artists, pastors and others to denounce the Honorable Minister Louis Farrakhan as an Anti-Semitic. It's all part of a strategic plan! Make no mistake about it. The journalists recycle the same lies in all of their stories! Farrakhan Praises Hitler as a Great Man! Farrakhan Calls Judaism a Gutter Religion! LIE, LIE and more LIES! Whenever a public figure speaks favorably about the Honorable Minister Louis Farrakhan WITHOUT fail they usher out some Negro politician or whomever needs their money to come out and describe the Honorable Minister Louis Farrakhan in some unfavorable terms. The most recent example, yet again is the Congressmen from Texas, Al Green! It's no coincidence that as social media has been set ablaze with the POWERFUL example of Tamika Malory standing her ground on MAJOR media outlets about her respect and admiration for the Honorable Minister Louis Farrakhan's track record within the Black community, we hear of a statement by the Congressmen saying the Minister is a bigot. This is all a part of the strategy to counter the Honorable Minister Louis Farrakhan! What we are witnessing is the execution of those secret meetings about the Honorable Minister Louis Farrakhan, like those that were written and held about Jesus!

"ADL's National Executive Committee will be discussing the legitimation of Farrakhan at the upcoming meeting in Palm Beach. Regional boards and national committees are therefore invited to share their thinking on the subject of this backgrounder in advance of the Palm Beach meeting."

"Then the chief priests and the Pharisees called a meeting of the Sanhedrin. "What are we accomplishing?" they asked." ~ John

11:47

The beauty of all of this is that they are failing in their attempt to get Black people to separate from a man that has impacted their lives or the lives of family members directly or indirectly! The enemies of the Honorable Minister Louis Farrakhan and Black people were upset when the Minister set on the stage during Aretha Franklin's funeral. We are witnessing a breaking of their power over the minds of our people ESPECIALLY the new Black millennial leaders! The new leaders do not seek the stamp of approval of those who have no track record remotely close to that of the Honorable Minister Louis Farrakhan! The new crop of leadership sees this effort as the height of hypocrisy and yet another form of the slave master trying to dictate to Black people who we should love and see as our leaders! Check out the words of Bishop Talbert Swan...

"For far too long, white folks have tried to convince us who are the respectable and responsible Blacks that we should embrace and the disreputable and irresponsible ones we should reject. These decisions are always based on what's in the interests of their agendas and not of the Black community. In essence, Black people are fed up with white folks dictating who our leaders should be and who we are allowed to respect or support. Thus, Black people often rally to protect people who they may not necessarily agree with or even like, but because they have been attacked by a historical enemy that has never acted in the interests of our people. The arrogance of white folks to determine who we must reject will always be met with cynicism and rejected by the masses of Black people. For sure, those in fear of losing status, opportunities or livelihood will buckle under the pressure of losing something. However, those with nothing to lose will always reject the demands of their perceived oppressors."

There are masses of Black people who do not care to be your slaves anymore! They do not care to have nearness to you nor the trinkets that you offer them and the Honorable Minister Louis Farrakhan is a MAJOR role for them feelings this way! Any Black person who would denounce a man that has placed his life on the line to fight to free us from the grips and harmful impact of white supremacy should be excommunicated from the Black community! Could you imagine contemporary leaders during time of Moses and Aaron, when the Hebrew people were witnessing

Pharaoh's oppression in the form of social engineering to kill their male and exploit their female children and creating economic policies based upon race, hold press conferences, release statements condemning Moses and Aaron as bigots, racist or Anti-Pharaohites, because they BOLDLY challenged the evil of Pharaoh? Imagine Mary and Martha in the New Testament being asked to condemn Jesus as a hater of the Jewish people, by those religious leaders who did NOTHING to bring their brother Lazarus back from death? When Jesus was the one who traveled from a far distance to free Lazarus from the condition that the enemies of Jesus put him in! This is EXACTLY what is being planned by those who are enemies of the Honorable Minister Louis Farrakhan and Black people! But Allah is the Best of Planners!

Allah says in the Quran how Satan plans, but also how He plans. The plans of Allah always supersede and defeats the plans of the enemies of Allah's servants! If we study the Honorable Minister Louis Farrakhan we will see how he maneuvers around their evil plans to keep Black people and other ethnicities deaf, dumb and blind.

In the memo put out by the ADL they mention how they have worked to pressure and scare university presidents from inviting the Honorable Minister Louis Farrakhan to their campuses. "...the League has also urged university officials to distance themselves from him, to deny him formal university sponsorship..." The Minister decided to cover for his own travel expenses and doesn't accept honorariums and ended up speaking in numerous colleges all over the country over the last few years.

In the memo the ADL speaks about preventing the development of relationships between the Honorable Minister Louis Farrakhan and Black leaders. While the ADL worked hard to be the gatekeeper with the old leadership the Honorable Minister Louis Farrakhan, with the use of social media and a cadre of young leadership in the Nation of Islam, forged relationships with Black Lives Matter activists and many more, young men and women who do not care to follow the path of Civil Rights leaders of the past!

Now, on a daily basis hundreds of thousands of youth are viewing clips of the Honorable Minister Louis Farrakhan on Twitter, on Instagram on YouTube, Facebook etc. This is the real reason behind the effort to have him removed from social media! They seek to prevent people from having a direct connection to the Honorable Minister Louis Farrakhan's words! Those of us who love the Minister can immediately post and share the Honorable Minister Louis Farrakhan's actual words and not the trash that is written in these newspapers and shown on these media outlets so-called news!

Anyone that asks us to denounce the Honorable Minister Louis Farrakhan should go to hell! The Honorable Minister Louis Farrakhan is our champion and super hero against white supremacy! We are not seeking the white stamp of approval for our true Black leaders!

I personally would not be pleased with knowing that many in and outside of the Nation have read this article. What would please me is YOU being moved to action based upon what YOU read. Here are some simple courses of action you can take.

#1 – After reading this article go post a clip of the Honorable Minister Louis Farrakhan on your social media, tag several people, share several clips and go to either of the Honorable Minister Louis Farrakhan's social media pages and let him know you stand with him and that you are not falling for the lies that are being put out by his enemies and the enemies of Black people! We have posted a link to a playlist of videos that would allow you and others to hear the TRUE words of the Honorable Minister Louis Farrakhan about Hitler, members of the Jewish community, women and much more.

Defending Farrakhan Playlist – https://youtu.be/cceQ2T5vWJw

#2 – Use these hashtags when you post about the Honorable Minister Louis Farrakhan on social media. #HandsoffFarrakhan #Farrakhan #DefendingFarrakhan

#3 – Follow the Honorable Minister Louis Farrakhan on his social media pages if you don't already. If you do follow him encourage others to follow him. This will allow you and them to have access to his direct words.

#4 – Read the scholarly articles by Brother Demetric Muhammad on his page. Our brother has great resources that can help all of us in our understanding and defense of the Honorable Minister Louis Farrakhan.

www.researchminister.com

#5 – When we hear or see people online attacking and lying on the Honorable Minister Louis Farrakhan simply post one of the links from the playlist we posted above. Doing so will directly combat their lies.

#6 – Order and READ the books the Secret Relationship Between Blacks and Jews (Vol. 1, 2 &3)

"Un-Smiting The Shepherd" -483

ResearchMinister.Com

ResearchMinister.Com
Wholesale Orders Available

Made in the USA
Middletown, DE
02 February 2023